United Nations Development Programme
Arab Fund for Economic and Social Development

THE ARAB HUMAN DEVELOPMENT REPORT 2003

Building a knowledge society

UN
D P

SPONSORED BY THE REGIONAL BUREAU
FOR ARAB STATES

ARAB FUND FOR ECONOMIC AND
SOCIAL DEVELOPMENT

Copyright © 2003
By the United Nations Development Programme,
Regional Bureau for Arab States (RBAS),
1 UN Plaza, New York, New York, 10017, USA

Image on cover of cast copper statue head from Nineveh, copyright Hirmer Fotoarchiv München

Available through:
United Nations Publications
Room DC2-853
New York, NY 10017
USA

Telephone: 212 963 8302 and 800 253 9646 (From the United States)
Email: Publications@un.org
Web: www.un.org/Publications
Web: www.undp.org/rbas

Cover design: Mamoun Sakkal
Layout and Production: SYNTAX, Amman, Jordan
Printed at: National Press, Amman, Jordan

ISBN: 92-1-126157-0

Printed in the Hashemite Kingdom of Jordan

Foreword by the Administrator, UNDP

Last year's inaugural Arab Human Development Report was by any standard a phenomenon. As the more than one million copies downloaded off the Internet so far testifies, its groundbreaking analysis of the region's development challenges catalysed an unprecedented wave of debate and discussion in both Arab countries and the wider world. Even that understates its true impact: measured by the fierce arguments it continues to provoke from coffee houses to television talkshows to parliaments and beyond it is clear why *Time* magazine cited it as the most important publication of 2002. The reason for this impact is simple but important. As a pioneering and provocative study produced by a team of Arab scholars, policy analysts and practitioners at a time of enormous economic, social and political ferment its central messages -- that reform is necessary and if it is to be successful and sustainable then change has to come from within -- carried unique authority. The United Nations Development Programme is proud to have sponsored it.

In the twelve months since that report came out, several Arab countries have taken significant steps toward grappling with the challenges it set out. At the same time, however, two other events -- the intensification of conflict in the occupied Palestinian territories and the invasion of Iraq by coalition forces – have complicated matters. The first Arab Human Development Report carried broad support across normal political divides by highlighting the three deficits afflicting the Arab world – freedom, women's rights and knowledge – and stressing the importance of democracy as part of the solution to bridging them. However, reaction to both the events in Iraq and the Occupied Territories shows, once again, how divided the international community is on the "how" of such reforms. For much of the Arab world – and, indeed, global public opinion – military action was not the best way to promote democratic change. Hence the strong reassertion in this report of a key tenet of its predecessor: lasting reform in the Arab world must come from within.

This year, the authors go on to consider in detail how such domestically driven reform might take place with regard to one of the three cardinal challenges – the knowledge deficit. Reflecting their sensitivity to recent events, however, the report first opens with a frank –and for a UN document untypically angry – acknowledgment of the additional challenges to sustainable reform in the region they believe have been created. The reasons for this are twofold: first, the frustration of the authors at the sense that their internal path for democratic reform in the region has, to a considerable extent, been derailed by the events they describe; second, because of the very special status of this report -- its power comes from the fact that it is not written by normal, internal UN authors, but is the product of leading Arab intellectuals and policy analysts writing primarily for an Arab audience. Its UN sponsorship gives them a platform and recognition for their work which they would not otherwise have but, at the same time, its integrity rests in the fact that these are their views rather than parsed and cautious opinions of international civil servants. As such, we commend them to you as the authentic cry of both anger and hope of a region grappling with change.

In making the core argument that the Arab world must turn outwards and immerse itself in the global knowledge stream, however, the authors make clear they remain firmly committed to engagement. But, they ask, if the outside world seems to dominate militarily, what does that mean for culture and knowledge?

Immersion, yes, but swamped or drowned, no, is their message in providing a comprehensive assessment of the state of knowledge in Arab societies today, the impediments to its acquisition and diffusion, and the prospects of making learning and research a dynamic driver of social and economic innovation in the future.

The Report argues that the potential for developing the knowledge capabilities of Arab countries is enormous – not only because of their untapped human capital, but also because of their rich cultural, linguistic and intellectual heritage. It acknowledges that overhauling the region's antiquated and under-resourced education systems will not be easy, but insists that it is critical if knowledge and economic output are to feed off each other, creating a virtuous cycle conducive to human development. However, the authors also underline once again that if these objectives are to be met, Arabs need to drive the process themselves: promoting local innovation as a necessary complement to harnessing knowledge and technology from abroad. The

stark choice facing Arab countries is: constructively engage with the new world or be left behind. For those who fear that their culture may be compromised by outside influences, this message of openness may be as controversial as the original report.

AHDR 2003 is merely the second step in a long journey. Over the next two years, further reports will follow on freedom and women's empowerment, the other two main challenges facing the region. I hope and believe this latest issue will attract as much attention and provoke as much debate as its predecessor. Even if many of the views taken in this report do not necessarily reflect UNDP or United Nations policy, we are pleased to be associated with a process that is helping stimulate a dynamic new policy discourse across the Arab region and the wider world. I would also particularly like to thank Rima Khalaf-Hunaidi, my colleague and Assistant Administrator, who as Bureau Director for the Arab States has been the driving inspiration behind this important project.

Mark Malloch Brown.
Administrator, UNDP

UNDP is the UN's global development network. It advocates for change and connects countries to knowledge, experience and resources to help people build a better life.

Foreword by the Regional Director, UNDP Regional Bureau for Arab States

Our first Report in this series, published in July 2002, looked closely at Arab human development at the beginning of the new millennium. It probed its present state, diagnosed its most disabling flaws, and advanced concrete proposals for achieving levels of development commensurate with the potential of the Arab region and the aspirations of new generations of Arabs. The Report concluded that promoting human development in the Arab world rests on three great tasks: building, using and liberating the capabilities of the Arab people by advancing knowledge, freedom and women's empowerment.

Public, media and policy attention to the first Report has been gratifyingly wide and vigorous, prompting a keen debate, both in the region and abroad, on the central dilemmas of Arab human development Such attention was not confined to public discussion circles. Some Arab governments and institutions took up the Report in their proceedings, criticising some findings and assenting to others.

Subsequently, and in line with the recommendations of the first Report, several Arab countries crossed new thresholds, particularly in terms of empowering women and enhancing their political participation. This second Report has recorded such accomplishments. It also documents failures and underscores new challenges. The region has recently encountered grave threats, and the dignity and rights of Arabs, especially the right to self-determination, have been grossly violated. Soon after the first Report was completed, Israel re-occupied the Palestinian Territories. Barely one year later, Iraq fell under Anglo-American invasion and occupation. In these circumstances, the challenge of building Arab human development has undoubtedly become more perilous, certainly more arduous and possibly more tenuous.

At this precarious juncture, some observers questioned the wisdom of issuing further Reports, while others worried that special interest groups might exploit their outspoken approach, to the detriment of Arabs. Indeed, the authors are well aware that their work might be misused or misinterpreted to serve the purposes of parties - outside as well as inside - the Arab world whose interests run counter to an Arab awakening.

The majority, however, argued forcefully that to leave the initiative to others would be the more ominous choice. Self-reform stemming from open, scrupulous and balanced self-criticism is the right, if not the only alternative to plans that are apparently being drawn up outside the Arab world for restructuring the area and for reshaping the Arab identity. Turning a blind eye to the weaknesses and shortfalls of the region, instead of decisively identifying and overcoming them, can only increase its vulnerability and leave it more exposed.

It is in this spirit that the second Report is now issued. Its goal is to activate a dialogue among Arabs on ways to change the course of Arab history and afford the Arab people the decent lives to which they aspire and to which they are entitled. Written into every line is the unwavering conviction that reform efforts, which genuinely serve the region's interests, must be initiated and launched from within.

The theme chosen this year is the building of an Arab knowledge society, not only because knowledge is the first of the three core components of the original strategy, but also because it is the most instrumental. Knowledge increasingly defines the line between wealth and poverty, between capability and powerlessness and between human fulfillment and frustration. A country able to mobilize and diffuse knowledge can rapidly raise its level of development, help all its citizens to grow and flourish and take its proper place on the 21st century global stage.

The Report examines the status of Arab knowledge today in terms of demand, production and dissemination, and concludes that all three are ineffectual notwithstanding the abundance of Arab human capital. It contrasts this state with the origins and outcomes of the region's rich, enquiring and pluralistic cultural and intellectual heritage, confirming that the latter provide robust foundations on which to build a knowledge society. It however observes that the positive models found in Arab culture lack effective economic social, and political equivalents. The missing links are either buried in dust or smothered by ideologies, societal structures and values that inhibit critical thinking, cut Arabs off from their knowledge-rich heritage and block the free flow of ideas and learning.

There is therefore a pressing need for deep-seated reform in the organisational, social and political context of knowledge. The Report identifies several key priorities for change. An important set of findings is that, in creating an Arab knowledge society, the reform of governance would represent a turning point, the renewal of education and the Arabic language a rallying point and the pursuit of cultural interaction an international meeting point.

The Report proposes a strategic vision that could support a creative Arab renaissance buttressed by five essential pillars:
• Providing and guaranteeing the key freedoms of opinion, expression and association through good governance.
• Broadening quality education and making it available to all.

• Embedding science in Arab society, broadening the capacity for research and development and joining the information revolution decisively.
• Shifting rapidly towards knowledge-based and higher value-added production.
• Developing an enlightened Arab knowledge model that encourages cognitive learning, critical thinking, problem solving and creativity while promoting the Arabic language, cultural diversity and openness to other cultures.

Undoubtedly, certain arguments in the Report might seem controversial and may be appreciated only after a conscientious reappraisal. Yet the Report claims neither infallibility nor a monopoly of the truth. Its authors will be satisfied if it prompts open dialogue, constructive criticism, disagreement supported by evidence and consent strengthened by proof. Such responses would expedite the quest for common goals and the Arab journey to knowledge and freedom.

AHDR 2003 represents a substantial intellectual endeavour in the region to which many people have contributed. I am deeply thankful to all who participated in its preparation, review and editing. I am especially grateful to the core team, particularly the lead author, Dr. Nader Fergany, for his resourceful involvement at all stages. My sincere thanks also go to the Advisory Board without whose counsel this Report would not have been possible. Finally, I am indebted to Mark Malloch Brown, Administrator of UNDP, for his continued brave support to this series, and to our co-sponsors, the Arab Fund for Economic and Social Development, for their sustained collaboration.

Rima Khalaf Hunaidi
Assistant Secretary General and Assistant Administrator, Regional Director,
Regional Bureau for Arab States, United Nations Development Programme

Foreword by the Director General and Chairman
The Arab Fund for Economic and Social Development

I have the pleasure to collaborate once again with UNDP in co-sponsoring this second Arab Human Development Report, which is part of an annual series that aims to sustain a discussion of specific development challenges facing Arab countries individually and as a group.

Undoubtedly, the first Arab Human Development Report (2002) was an exceptional effort in all respects. Its distinctive analysis of the current state of human development in the Arab world, the obstacles to its achievement and the opportunities for transcending those challenges attracted great interest and generated an extensive debate and discussion. It was the first Arab report to attempt a comprehensive understanding of the Arabs today, as seen through the eyes of Arab scholars, and to explore what Arab societies themselves can do to promote their advancement. Its significant conclusions received wide media and policy attention in the Arab world and in international circles, prompting a spirited debate among Arab intellectuals and development specialists. The Report brought about a lively and vigorous discussion. Its points of view, whether endorsed or criticised, were seen as bold initiatives for much-needed reform in the Arab sphere, and a manifestation of the Arabs' ability to exercise constructive self-criticism.

The first Report stressed that human development centres on the comprehensive and integrated development of societal institutions and people who are indeed the real wealth of nations. It also emphasised that human development involves enhancing people's options for achieving those human goals that support a dignified life, both in the material and moral sense. It further underlined the importance of freedom in the concept of human development, stressing the instrumental role of political, economic and social freedoms.

The authors of AHDR 2003 have chosen for their theme one of the three main challenges identified by the first Report, the knowledge gap in the Arab world, because of its organic relationship with human development, its pivotal role in promoting it and its significance as one of the essential pursuits of humanity. They underline the large deficiency in knowledge capacity in the Arab countries, both in the acquisition and production of knowledge, and point out that only by overcoming this shortcoming in all societal activities can Arab countries succeed and prosper in the modern age.

The second Report identifies several measures for overcoming the underlying obstructions to knowledge and for employing Arab human capabilities effectively in establishing the knowledge society. The knowledge system is an expansive and complex one. It entails transforming knowledge wealth into knowledge capital in order to generate new knowledge in the physical and social sciences, humanities, arts and popular culture. The Report also monitors developments in human development in Arab countries since 2002 and shows that, at the regional and international levels, the Arab world has been experiencing significant challenges and events which will greatly reflect on the evolution of human development. The Report underlines recent developments in the occupied Palestinian Territories and Iraq in particular, and underscores that building intrinsic Arab capabilities is the only sound course for coping with such momentous challenges.

The Report addresses a large number of

interrelated issues in some depth. Some of these pertain to education, the media, the infrastructure of communication and information networks, the production and measurement of knowledge and the organisational context for its acquisition in Arab countries. The societal and political context impacting on knowledge and the reciprocal links between the knowledge society and economic and societal structures are also discussed.

The Report points out that deficient knowledge capabilities represent a formidable impediment for Arab countries in their attempts to face the challenges of the 21st century. These countries cannot make any tangible progress in the long term without acquiring the knowledge and the technological capacities that are indispensable for prosperity in the new millennium. Indeed, the absence of such prerequisites could well invite unforeseen disasters. Ingraining and embedding knowledge in Arab societies is the crux of any attempt to resolve the human development crisis in the region. Knowledge is one of the key instruments of human development, be it in instituting good governance, guaranteeing health, producing the ingredients of material and moral welfare, or promoting economic growth. As such, knowledge is a vital factor of modern production and an essential determinant of productivity and competitive capacity.

The Report presents a vision for instituting human development and unleashing societal creativity; a vision that aims at reforming the societal context of knowledge acquisition and consolidating the knowledge acquisition system in order to move the region towards a knowledge-based society. It argues that Arab countries have tremendous potential for developing their knowledge capacity in view of their – still unutilised - human capital, and their cultural and linguistic heritage. Its vision for liberating this human capital and instituting a human renaissance across the Arab world rests on five crucial pillars elaborated in its concluding chapter.

In co-sponsoring this Report, the Arab Fund for Economic and Social Development and UNDP seek to promote a debate on key questions of knowledge, to help diagnose some of the major challenges facing the Arab states in this area, and to put forward suggestions on ways to achieve an Arab renaissance and consolidate the acquisition and employment of knowledge across the Arab world. It is hoped that Arab countries will pay close attention to the methods for improving and accelerating the diffusion, production and application of knowledge in all economic, social and political fields; and for raising the level of Arab human development. We are confident that Arab countries have all the means required to achieve this end.

In closing, I wish to extend my sincere thanks to all those who have contributed to, and taken part in the preparation of this Report, and to our partner, UNDP, for commissioning it and overseeing its publication in this distinguished form.

Abdel Latif Youseff El Hamed
Director General / Chairman of the Board of Directors
Arab Fund for Economic and Social Development

Advisory group

Rima Khalaf Hunaidi (Chair), Ahmad Kamal Aboulmagd, Abdul Muniem Abu-Nuwar (United Nations Fund for Population Activities), Farida Al-Allaghi, Sami Al-Banna, Turki Al-Hamad, Mohammed Abed Al-Jabri , Abdalla A. Alnajjar, Nabil Alnawwab (Economic and Social Commission for Western Asia), Mervat Badawi (Arab Fund for Economic and Social Development), Ziad Fariz, Nader Fergany (Ex officio), Burhan Ghalioun, Rafia Obaid Ghubash, Milad M. Hanna, Taher H. Kanaan, Atif Kubursi, Clovis Maksoud, Gamil Mattar, Roshdi Rashed, Abdelouahab Rezig, Adnan Shihab-Eldin, El Sayed Yassin.

Core team

Farida Bennani, Hoda Elsadda, Nader Fergany (Leader), Fahmi Jadaane, Atif Kubursi .

Editorial team

Arabic Version: Fayiz Suyyagh
English Version: Kristin Helmore, Zahir Jamal

Contributing authors

Laila Abdel Majid, Fowziyah Abdullah Abu-Khalid, Muhammad Hassan Al-Amin, Aziz Al-Azmeh, Sami Al-Banna, Tarek Al-Bishry, Hayder Ibrahim Ali, Nabil Ali, Sa'adallah Agha Al Kala'a, Muna Al-Khalidi, Mohamed Al-Mili Baqer Alnajjar, Siham A. Al-Sawaigh, Amr Najeeb Armanazi,

Munir Bashshur, Mohammed Berrada, Hichem Djait, Mohamed Mahmoud El-Imam, Dina El Khawaga, Rukia El Mossadeq, Shawki Galal, Burhan Ghalioun, Abd El Hameed Hawwas, Taoufik Jebali, Taher Hamdi Kanaan, Atif Kubursi, Al-Taher Labib, Clovis Maksoud, Mohammad Malas, Imad Moustapha , Fadle M. Naqib, Khalida Said, Adnan Shihab-Eldin, A. B. Zahlan, Mari Rose Zalzal .

UNDP RBAS team-UNOPS

Dena Assaf, Ali Al-Zatari, Shafiqa Darani, Abdalla Dardari, Moez Doraid, Ghaith Fariz, Jacqueline Ghazal, Randa Jamal, Zahir Jamal, Hussein Kermalli, Mahwish Nasir, Madi Musa, Maen Nsour (Report Coordinator), Win Min Nu, Flavia Pansieri, Gillman Rebello, Oscar Fernandez-Taranco.

Readers group

Ismail Sabry Abdalla, Abdulkhaleq Abdulla, Abdul Karim Al-Eryani, Ali A. Attiga, Chedly Ayari, Mahmoud Amin El-Alem, Nawal Faouri, Ziad Hafez, Hassan Hanafi, Michael C. Hudson, Benjamin Ladner, Manfred Max-Neef, Richard W. Murphy, Omar Noman, John Page, Eric Rouleau .

Translation team

Khalid Abdalla, Rania Al-Hariri, Marie-Helen Avril, Doa'a Imbaby, Mahmud Suqi .

AFTA	Arab Free Trade Area
AHDI	Arab Human Development Index
AHDR	Arab Human Development Report
ASEAN	Association of South East Asian Nations
CNN	Cable News Network
DMC	Dubai Media City
ESCWA	Economic and Social Commission for Western Asia
EU	European Union
FDI	foreign direct investment
GCC	Gulf Cooperation Council
GDP	gross domestic product
GNP	gross national product
HDI	human development index
HDR	Human Development Report
IBHR	International Bill of Human Rights
ICT	information and communication technology
IDF	Israeli Defense Forces
IPRs	intellectual property rights
MBC	Major Broadcasting Cable Network
MEDA	Euro-Mediterranean Partnership (financial instrument)
MNC	multinational corporation
MYS	mean years of schooling
NAFTA	North American Free Trade Agreement
NGO	non-governmental organisation
PPP	purchasing power parity
PRCS	Palestinian Red Crescent Society
QAMYS	quality adjusted mean years of schooling
R&D	research and technological development
RBAS	Regional Bureau for Arab States
TAI	technology achievement index
TIMSS	Trends in International Mathematics and Science Study
TRIPS	Agreement on Trade-related Aspects of Intellectual Property Rights
UNCTAD	United Nations Conference on Trade and Development
UNDP	United Nations Development Programme
UNESCO	United Nations Educational, Scientific and Cultural Organisation
UNICEF	United Nations Children's Fund
USAID	United States Agency for International Development
VAT	value added tax
WHO	World Health Organisation
WIPO	World Intellectual Property Organisation
WTO	World Trade Organisation

Contents

Foreword by the Administrator, UNDP
Foreword by the Regional Director, UNDP/Regional Bureau for Arab States
Foreword by the Director General and Chairman, Board of Directors, Arab Fund for Economic and Social Development

List of Figures

List of tables

In the text

In the Statistical Annex

(Tables 1-13 listed separately in statistical annex)

EXECUTIVE SUMMARY

The first Arab Human Development Report (AHDR 2002) addressed the most important development challenges facing the Arab world at the beginning of the third millennium. This second Report continues the process by examining in depth one of these challenges: the building of a knowledge society in Arab countries.

The AHDR series aims at building human development in the Arab world. As part of a continuing watch on human development in the region, this Report therefore opens by surveying some of the most salient trends and events at the global, regional and national levels that influenced the process of human development in the Arab world in 2002-2003. The remainder of the Report is a close study of one of the three cardinal challenges facing the region: its growing knowledge gap. It starts by outlining the conceptual basis of an Arab knowledge society and moves on to evaluate the status of the demand for, and the diffusion and production of knowledge in Arab countries at the beginning of the 21st century. It next analyses the cultural, economic, societal and political context influencing knowledge acquisition in the region at this critical junction in its history. The last section of this analysis culminates in a strategic vision that delineates the landmarks of a deep social reform process for establishing a knowledge-based society in the Arab countries.

> ### Mohammad Hassanein Heikal
> The bell rung by the AHDR and heard by Arabs and other people the world over carried echoes of all the bells ringing through our lives. It was a call to knowledge and learning, an announcement of the last chance to join the trip to the future, an appeal for cleansing, an injunction to make way for an urgent priority, and finally a forewarning of imminent danger – urging us to hasten to douse the flames of a still-small fire waiting to engulf the region in a formidable blaze

A ONE-YEAR OVERVIEW OF HUMAN DEVELOPMENT:

TWO SETBACKS AND THE START OF REFORM

A review of global and regional developments since the publication of AHDR 2002 underlines that the development challenges represented by the three deficits in knowledge, freedom and women's empowerment remain serious. Those challenges may have become even graver in the area of freedoms, as a result of these developments.

> ### United Nations High Commissioner for Human Rights
> The late UN human rights chief, Sergio Vieira de Mello, emphasised that the 'war on terror' was exacerbating prejudices around the world, increasing discrimination against Arabs and damaging human rights in industrialised and developing countries.

Following the bloody events of September 11 and the loss of innocent lives in violation of all man-made and divine laws, a number of countries have adopted extreme security measures and policies as part of the "war on terrorism". These measures and policies, however, exceeded their original goals and led to the erosion of civil and political liberties in many countries in the world, notably the United States, often diminishing the welfare of Arabs and Muslims living, studying or travelling abroad, interrupting cultural exchanges between the Arab world and the West and cut-

Development challenges represented by the three deficits in knowledge, freedom and women's empowerment remain serious.

> ### A Year of Loss, Re-examining Civil Liberties since September 11
> "..over the last year the US government has taken a series of actions that have gradually eroded basic human rights protections in the United States, fundamental guarantees that have been central to the US constitutional system for more than two hundred years."
>
> (American) Lawyers for Human Rights.

One of the worst
consequences of
freedom-constraining
measures in
developed countries
was that they gave
some Arab authorities
another excuse to
enact new laws
limiting civil and
political freedoms.

In contrast to efforts
to restructure the
region from outside,
the AHDR series aims
to crystallise a
strategic vision that
envisages the
restructuring of the
region from within.

ting off knowledge acquisition opportunities for young Arabs.

Among the first effects of these measures was the significant drop in the number of Arab students studying in the United States. Figures available from a number of Arab missions indicate that Arab student numbers in America dropped between 1999 and 2002 by an average of 30 per cent.

One of the worst consequences of freedom-constraining measures in developed countries is that they gave authorities in some Arab countries another excuse to enact new laws limiting civil and political freedoms. The Arab countries as a group adopted an expanded definition of terrorism, which assumed institutional expression at the regional level in "The Arab Charter against Terrorism". This charter was criticised in Arab and international human rights circles, because its expanded definition opens the door to abuse. It allows censorship, restricts access to the Internet, and restricts printing and publication. Moreover, the Charter neither explicitly prohibits detention or torture, nor provides for questioning the legality of detentions. Furthermore, it does not protect personal freedom, since it does not require a prior judicial order authorising the wire-tapping of individuals or groups (Amnesty International).

Israel reoccupied Palestinian territories, inflicting horrifying human casualties and material destruction, thereby committing what one well-respected human rights organization called "war crimes" (Human Rights Watch, 2002). From September 2000 to April 2003, Israeli occupation forces killed 2,405 Palestinian citizens and injured 41,000 others. Most of those killed (85%) were civilians. A large proportion (20%) of them were children. UNICEF estimates that 7,000 children were injured and that 2,500 persons, of whom 500 were children, suffered permanent handicaps.

> **Report of Human Rights Watch 2002,
> Jenin: IDF Operations**
>
> "There is strong prima facie evidence that in some of the cases documented grave breaches of the Geneva Conventions, or war crimes, were committed."

A coalition led by the United States and Britain invaded and occupied Iraq, introducing a new challenge to the people of Iraq and the region. The only way to meet that challenge is to enable the Iraqi people to exercise their basic rights in accordance with international law, free themselves from occupation, recover their wealth, under a system of good governance representing the Iraqi people and take charge of rebuilding their country from a human development perspective.

In contrast to efforts to restructure the region from outside, the AHDR series aims to crystallise a strategic vision by Arab elites through a societal innovation process that envisages the restructuring of the region from within, and in service to Arab human development. Such reform from within, based on rigorous self-criticism, is a far more proper and sustainable alternative.

On the level of internal development in the Arab countries, progress was achieved in the advancement of women and in some aspects of popular participation. Women's representation in some parliaments and in senior positions in Executive Authorities increased. A number of Arab countries witnessed parliamentary elections, some of them for the first time in decades. Yet these bright spots, accompanied briefly by dawning awareness of the need for reform, were partly eclipsed by new setbacks in the areas of freedom of opinion, expression and association.

Assessing the present state of regional cooperation, the Report finds that Arab integration continues to fall far behind in achieving what the first Arab Human Development Report called "An Arab Free Citizenship Zone".

BUILDING THE KNOWLEDGE SOCIETY IN ARAB COUNTRIES

THE STATUS OF KNOWLEDGE IN THE ARAB WORLD

A knowledge-based society is one where knowledge diffusion, production and application become the organising principle in all aspects of human activity: culture, society, the economy, politics, and private life. Knowledge nowadays can provide the means to expand the scope of human freedoms, enhance the capacity to guarantee those freedoms through good governance and achieve the higher moral human goals of justice and human dignity

Contrasting this type of society with the state of knowledge in Arab countries, the Report looks carefully at the characteristics of the two main components of the knowledge acquisition system: diffusion and production.

KNOWLEDGE DIFFUSION: BLOCKS IN EDUCATION, BRIGHT SPOTS IN THE MEDIA

Key knowledge dissemination processes in Arab countries, (socialisation and upbringing, education, the media and translation), face deep-seated social, institutional, economic and political impediments. Notable among these are the meagre resources available to individuals, families and institutions and the restrictions imposed upon them. As a result, these processes often falter and fall short of preparing the epistemological and societal environment necessary for knowledge production.

Studies indicate that the most widespread style of child rearing in Arab families is the authoritarian mode accompanied by the overprotective. This reduces children's independence, self-confidence and social efficiency, and fosters passive attitudes and hesitant decision-making skills. Most of all, it affects how the child thinks by suppressing questioning, exploration and initiative.

Impressive gains in the quantitative expansion of education in Arab countries in the last half of the 20th century are still modest in comparison with other developing countries or with the requirements of human development. High rates of illiteracy among women persist, particularly in some of the less developed Arab countries. Many children still do not have access to basic education. Higher education is characterized by decreasing enrolment, and public spending on education has actually declined since 1985.

In all cases, nevertheless, the most important challenge facing Arab education is its declining quality.

The mass media are the most important agents for the public diffusion of knowledge yet Arab countries have lower information media to population ratios (number of newspapers, radio and televisions per 1000 people) compared to the world average. There are less than 53 newspapers per 1000 Arab citizens, compared to 285 papers per 1000 people in developed countries.

In most Arab countries, the media operate in an environment that sharply restricts freedom of the press and freedom of expression and opinion. Journalists face illegal harassment, intimidation and even physical threats, censorship is rife and newspapers and television channels are sometimes arbitrarily closed down. Most media institutions are state-owned, particularly radio and television.

The last two years, however, have seen some improvements in the Arab information environment, brought about by dawning competition. More independent-minded newspapers have appeared, challenging the iron grip of the older, state-supported press on political opinion, news and information. With bases abroad, these papers can escape state censorship. Some private satellite channels have started to contest the monopoly of state channels over the broadcast media. The most important characteristic of this new information movement is that it broadcasts in Arabic, thereby addressing the largest segment of the Arab audience.

In terms of infrastructure, the newer information channels benefit from the considerable groundwork that a number of Arab countries have laid. However, the general trend gravitates towards the lowest indicators in world standards. The number of telephone lines in the Arab countries is barely one fifth of that in developed countries. Access to digital media is also among the lowest in the world. There are just 18 computers per 1000 people in the region, compared to the global average of 78.3 percent per 1000 persons and only 1.6 per cent of the population has Internet access. These indicators scarcely reflect a sufficient level of preparedness for applying information technology for knowledge diffusion.

Translation is one of the important channels for the dissemination of information and communication with the rest of the world. The translation movement in the Arab world, however, remains static and chaotic. On average,

The most important challenge facing Arab education is its declining quality.

The last two years have seen improvements in the Arab information environment brought about by dawning competition.

The region's corps of
qualified knowledge
workers is relatively
small.

only 4.4 translated books per million people were published in the first five years of the 1980s (less than one book per million people per year), while the corresponding rate in Hungary was 519 books per one million people and in Spain 920 books.

KNOWLEDGE PRODUCTION: MEAGRE OUTPUT, GLIMMERS OF CREATIVITY

Turning knowledge assets into knowledge capital requires the production of new knowledge in all areas: in the physical and social sciences, arts, humanities and all other forms of social activity.

Data in the Report tell a story of stagnation in certain areas of knowledge production, especially in the field of scientific research. In addition to thin production, scientific research in Arab countries is held back by weak basic research and the almost total absence of advanced research in fields such as information technology and molecular biology. It also suffers from miserly R&D expenditure (currently state spending on R&D does not exceed 0.2 percent of GNP, most of which pays only for salaries), poor institutional support and a political and social context inimical to the development and promotion of science. The region's corps of qualified knowledge workers is relatively small. The number of scientists and engineers working in R&D in Arab countries is not more than 371 per million citizens. This is much lower that the global rate of 979 per million. The number of students enrolling in scientific disciplines in higher education in all Arab countries is also generally low, in comparison to countries that have used knowledge to take off, such as Korea, although among Arab countries, Jordan, followed by Algeria have distinguished themselves in this field.

In contrast to their weak production in science and technology, and beleaguered output in the humanities, Arab societies can boast a wealth of distinguished literary and artistic work that stands up to the highest standards of evaluation. One reason is that while science and technology require substantial social and economic investment, Arab artists can, and usually do, produce high-quality work without

The number of books
published in the Arab
world does not exceed
1.1% of world
production.

significant institutional or material support. Innovation in literature and art works under different conditions from those that foster creativity in research and development An Arab scientist would be highly unlikely to win a Nobel Prize in physics without societal and institutional support whereas an Arab novelist might achieve that distinction in literature in the absence of such support. There does not seem to be a conditional correlation between literary creativity and affluence, although financial independence can strengthen an author's intellectual freedom. Difficult conditions may sometimes provide incentives and intellectual and political stimuli for creative literature. Yet while artistic creativity itself defies societal restrictions, the absence of freedoms blocks public access to books and other forms of artistic expression.

> **The Knowledge Block: Censorship**
>
> The author and the publisher are forced to submit to the moods and instructions of 22 Arab censors and this prevents a book from moving freely and easily between its natural markets.
>
> Fathi Khalil el-Biss,
> Vice President of the Arab Publishers Union

Literary production faces other major challenges. These include the small number of readers owing to high rates of illiteracy in some Arab countries and the weak purchasing power of the Arab reader. This limited readership is clearly reflected in the number of books published in the Arab world, which does not exceed 1.1% of world production, although Arabs constitute 5% of the world population. The production of literary and artistic books in Arab countries is lower than the general level. In 1996 it did not exceed 1,945 books, representing only 0.8% of world production, i.e., less than the production of a country such as Turkey, with a population one quarter of that of Arab countries. An abundance of religious books and a relative paucity of books in other fields characterize the Arab book market. Religious books account for 17% of the total number of books published in Arab countries, compared to 5% of the total number of books produced in other parts of the world.

The Report's analysis of the status of knowledge in Arab countries indicates the presence of significant human capital that finds refuge in creativity from a restrictive societal and political environment and that could, under favourable circumstances, provide a solid structural foundation for a knowledge renaissance.

CUMULATIVE KNOWLEDGE OUTCOMES: ENDS AND MEANS

The Report Team polled a sample of Arab university faculty members about knowledge acquisition in the region. Respondents expressed dissatisfaction in general with the status of knowledge acquisition in their countries (the average degree of satisfaction was 38%). Their satisfaction with the extent to which Arab knowledge serves human development was slightly less (the average rating was 35%). The survey confirmed that incentives for knowledge acquisition in Arab countries need to be much stronger, while freedom to acquire knowledge is subject to many constraints.

Rating the various aspects of the knowledge system, respondents argued that the lack of a reasonable measure of freedom in radio and television (30%) was one of the largest disincentives to knowledge acquisition. The same assessment applied to research and development in the public sector although, in the view of respondents, the latter area enjoys a higher level of freedom, thus suggesting that its problems have more to do with matters of organisation and financing.

In order to compare the knowledge capital of Arab countries with that of other countries, the Report explores a new composite index constructed from 10 indicators relating to different dimensions of knowledge capital. This attempt at measurement faced several limitations in data and methodology yet indicated that the Arab countries are far behind the leading developing countries, let alone the advanced industrialised countries, in the quality and quantity of their knowledge capital.

Struck by inconsistent or counterintuitive results from applying this index, the Report Team also considered seven cumulative knowledge outcomes or end results (such as exports with a high technological content and other outcomes), and their relationship to other knowledge indicators. The analysis showed no correlation between the two groups.

The analysis concludes that the key challenge facing Arab countries does not consist only of catching up with other countries in terms of knowledge indicators; rather, it goes beyond that to include working hard to achieve similar knowledge outcomes by developing solid institutional structures and by crystallising the requisite political will, supported by sufficient resources, especially at the pan-Arab level.

IMPORTED TECHNOLOGY: CONSUMPTION VERSUS ADOPTION

Arab countries' experiments with the transfer and adoption of technology have neither achieved the desired technological advancement nor yielded attractive returns on investments. Importing technology has not led to its adoption and internalisation in the host country, let alone to its diffusion and production.

The two biggest gaps accounting for this failure have been the absence of effective innovation and knowledge production systems in Arab countries, and the lack of rational policies that ingrain those essential values and institutional frameworks that support a knowledge society. These problems have been aggravated by the mistaken belief that a knowledge society can be built through the importation of scientific products without investing in the local production of knowledge, and through depending on cooperation with universities and research centres in advanced countries for training Arab scientific cadres without creating the local scientific traditions conducive to knowledge acquisition in the region.

The lack of national innovation systems in Arab countries represented, in effect, a waste of investment in industrial infrastructure and

Incentives for knowledge acquisition in Arab countries need to be much stronger.

Importing technology has not led to its adoption and internalisation in the host country, let alone to its diffusion and production.

> **Ali Mustafa Musharrifah: On the Importance of the History of Science for the Advancement of Knowledge**
>
> "Civilised nations must have a culture associated with their history of scientific thought. ... Our scientific life in Egypt needs to catch up with our past in order to acquire the necessary strength, life and controls. We in Egypt transfer the knowledge of others then leave it floating without any relationship to our past or any communication with our land. It is a foreign commodity that is strange in its looks, strange in its words and strange in its concepts."

fixed capital (buildings, factories, machinery and equipment). Such investments did not bring the wealth that Arab societies had sought through means other than the depletion of raw materials, nor expected social returns. Investment in the means of production does not lead to the real transfer and ownership of technology but rather to an increase in production capacity. Moreover, this is a time-bound gain, one that starts to erode as the acquired technology becomes obsolete. The products and services generated by imported technology become economically unfeasible and uncompetitive in local markets, while at the same time technology and production in the advanced countries are perpetually renewed by their own renovation and innovation systems. This does not take place in Arab countries which, with their aging technologies, are stuck at the wrong end of the technology ladder. They must keep purchasing new production capabilities as and when the technologies of the capabilities they own become outmoded.

At the same time, Arab countries have not succeeded in becoming important poles of attraction for foreign direct investment (FDI). None of them figures among the top ten FDI-attracting countries in the developing world.

The transfer, embedding and production of knowledge that can generate new technologies require an organisational context that provides incentives for knowledge production. Such a context would consolidate linkages between R&D institutions and the production and service sectors and promote national capabilities for innovation.

Ahmad Kamal Aboulmajd

The eternity of Islam does not mean the "rigidity of its law". It rather means the ability of this law to renew itself and make innovations in response to the movement of life and the changes of its forms. The originality and distinction of Muslims do not mean their isolation from the rest of mankind, inward-looking in a closed circuit, surrounded by a wall without doors. They rather mean communication with people, living with them and – through that – providing them with the loftier values and grand principles, which are based on the Islamic doctrine, law and moral structure.

Milad Hanna: Harmony of Religions and Knowledge in the Arab World

This co-existence between Christianity and Islam in the Arab world presents a model of unity in diversity. It is one of the reasons for progress, which has pushed humanity to advance through knowledge acquisition.

Arab countries, with their aging technologies, are stuck at the wrong end of the technology ladder.

Religion urges people to seek knowledge.

THE SOCIETAL CONTEXT FOR KNOWLEDGE ACQUISITION IN ARAB COUNTRIES

PILLARS OF THE KNOWLEDGE-BASED SOCIETY: CULTURE

The knowledge system is influenced by societal, cultural, economic and political determinants. Among the most important of these determinants is culture in both of its aspects: the scholarly culture and the popular culture. Within Arabic culture, intellectual heritage constitutes an essential component. Language is the instrumental carrier of this culture and religion is the main and comprehensive belief system that guides its life. Moral, social and political values govern and direct action in the Arabic cultural system.

Religion urges people to seek knowledge, despite some anti-development interpretations: Undoubtedly, the relationship between religion and knowledge and its production is organically associated with concepts determined by the nature of religion and its overall position towards worldly life. Islamic religious texts uphold a balance between religion and worldly life, or between temporal life and the hereafter. The predominant tendency in Arab-Islamic civilization is a robust interest in worldly life and its sciences and in encouraging knowledge and sciences of various forms.

Developments in the contemporary Arab world and the national political, social and economic problems that appeared following the years of independence did, however, leave deep impacts on the intellectual, scholarly and cultural life of Arab countries. Religion - and its associated concepts and teleology – were among the basic aspects influenced by these developments. An alliance between some oppressive regimes and certain types of conservative religious scholars led to interpretations of Islam, which serve the government, but are inimical to human development, particularly with respect to freedom of thought, the interpretation of judgements, the accountability of regimes to the people and women's participation in public life. Constraints on political action in many Arab countries pushed some movements with an Islamic mark underground while causing others to don Islamic garb. Without peaceful and effective political channels for dealing with injustices in the Arab world, at the country, regional and global levels, some political movements identifying themselves as Islamic have resorted to restrictive interpretations and violence as means of political activism. They have fanned the embers of animosity towards both opposing political forces in Arab countries and "the others", accusing them of being enemies of Islam itself. This has heightened the tempo of conflict and friction with society, the state and "the others". This state of "opposition" to and "confrontation" with the West, in particular, reached its peak following the events of September 11, 2001. In this context, the Islamic religion itself was exposed to a harsh wave of libel, slander, provocation and criticism, which at times betrayed total ignorance and at other times, explicit fabrication.

Far from being opposed to knowledge, pure religion unquestionably urges people to seek knowledge and to establish knowledge societies. Perhaps the best evidence of that is the era when Arab science flowered and prospered, a time that was characterised by a strong synergy between religion, represented by Islam, on the one hand and science, on the other.

The Arabic language: a heritage, a resource and a crisis: The role of language in a knowledge society is seminal, because language is an essential basis of culture and because culture is the key axis around which the process of development revolves. Language has a central position in the cultural system because of its association with a number of its components: intellect, creativity, education, information, heritage, values and beliefs. Today, at the gates of the knowledge society and the future, the Arabic language is, however, facing severe challenges and a real crisis in theorization, grammar, vocabulary, usage, documentation, creativity and criticism. To these aspects of the crisis, one must add the new challenges raised by information technologies, which relate to the computerised automation of the language.

The relation between the Arabic language and the transfer and absorption of technology involves many issues. Chief among them are two central and closely inter-related matters, namely, the arabicisation of university education and the teaching of the Arabic language. The arabicisation of university education has become vital in order to enable young minds to develop firm critical and creative faculties in their own language and to assimilate the rising volume of scientific knowledge. In addition, failure to arabicise science creates obstacles to communication between different scientific disciplines and slows knowledge exchange. The authors underline that language is one of the cornerstones in the human development system while emphasising that arabicisation efforts should be accompanied by greater efforts to teach foreign languages to all.

The teaching of Arabic is also undergoing a severe crisis in terms of both methodology and curricula. The most apparent aspect of this crisis is the growing neglect of the functional aspects of (Arabic) language use. Arabic language skills in everyday life have deteriorated and Arabic language classes are often restricted to writing at the expense of reading. The situation of Arabic language teaching cannot be separated from that of classical Arabic in general, which has in effect ceased to be a spoken language. It is only the language of reading and writing; the formal language of intellectuals and academics, often used to display knowledge in lectures. Classical Arabic is not the language of cordial, spontaneous expression, emotions, daily encounters and ordinary communication. It is not a vehicle for discovering one's inner self or outer surroundings.

The Report thus underlines that it has become necessary to work determinedly on strengthening the linguistic shields of Arabic and on sharpening its practical attributes, which emphasise its universal character and its ability to assimilate new informational and technological developments. This is in addition to consolidating its relationship with world languages and providing the necessary economic, social and technical conditions for enhancing the language and its creative products.

Popular culture, between conformity and creativity: Communal and oral folk culture is a vast repository of experiences and cre-

Language has a central position in the cultural system.

At the gates of the knowledge society and the future, the Arabic language is facing severe challenges.

ative efforts that have enriched, and continue to enrich, the intellectual, emotional and behavioural life of people in all societies. Folk culture is generally very rich in its constructions, encompassing knowledge, beliefs, arts, morals, law, customs and early industrial knowledge.

Arab folk culture shares all these qualities. Its particular feature is that it expresses two voices: one, a conformist voice, which urges adherence to familiar patterns, the other a creative voice, which questions received wisdom and urges the pursuit of knowledge. Arab popular culture is however not devoid of knowledge. Biographies, a common form of story telling, are often full of historical and geographical knowledge, as well as human insight. Romantic tales depicting imaginary ideal worlds express popular yearnings, dreams and ambitions. These and other forms of oral culture are recurrently recited at group evening gatherings and meetings, and are a means of sharing historical knowledge and rules related to customs. Many popular stories extol the value of information, showing it to be more valuable than wealth. The high respect commonly shown for a written text by folk communities indicates the value they accord to learning and knowledge.

Cultural openness, from imitation to creative interaction: Historically, Arab culture did not constitute a closed system, but rather displayed, at major historical junctures, a profound ability to open up, develop and transcend itself. It welcomed the experiences of other nations and incorporated them in its knowledge systems and way of life, regardless of the differences and variations that distinguished Arab societies from those nations and their experiences.

The first of the two major external influences which this culture embraced dates back to the age of scientific codification and the encounter with Greek civilization and sciences – indeed the demand for and importation of these sciences – in the third and fourth centuries A. H. (on the Islamic calendar) – 9th and 10th centuries A.D.

The second major experience came when the modern Arab world encountered Western civilization and opened up to science, literature and other aspects of Western culture at the beginning of the 19th century. The outcome of this encounter was a renovation and modernization of the Arab cultural heritage, descending from the past, opening wide to the future and drawing abundantly on the sinews of modernization and the rich crop of Western production in all fields of knowledge, science, the arts, literature and technology.

Arabic culture, however, like other cultures, finds itself facing the challenges of an emerging global cultural homogeneity and related questions about cultural multiplicity, cultural personalities, the issue of the "self" and the "other", and its own cultural character. These and similar questions raise apprehensions, fears and risks in the minds of its people. Concerns about the extinction of the language and culture and the diminution and dissipation of identity have become omnipresent in Arab thought and culture.

The truth is that Arab culture has no choice but to engage again in a new global experiment. It cannot enclose itself, contented with living on history, the past and inherited culture alone in a world whose victorious powers reach into all corners of the earth, dominating all forms of knowledge, behaviour, life, manufactured goods and innovation. Undoubtedly, some currents embedded in this culture would prefer a policy of withdrawal, of rejection and hostility to all values, ideas, and practices brought about by this global culture. This may appear justified in some ways, but a negative policy of "non-interaction" can only lead to the weakening and diminution of Arab cultural structures rather than their reinforcement and development.

Moreover, the global culture has its own dimensions of knowledge, science, and technology, which countries neglect at their own risk. Openness, interaction, assimilation, absorption, revision, criticism and examination cannot but stimulate creative knowledge production in Arab societies. This is already noticeable in many sectors of contemporary Arabic culture where various creative developments reveal the beneficial role played by global and human cultural interaction. This process continues to take place despite all local deterrents and external obstacles and notwithstanding the difficulties of national and international politics, where some powers pursue total hegemony or choose the path of collision and conflict, rather than of understanding, dialogue, cooperation and alternation in power.

An analysis of the components of Arabic culture indicates that its essence, extending over three millennia, is capable of supporting the creation of a knowledge society in the third millennium as ably as it did towards the end of the first millennium and in the beginning of the second. Furthermore, the strength and richness of Arabic culture may reinforce the capacity of Arab societies to deal effectively with the torrential currents of globalisation.

ECONOMIC STRUCTURE: FROM DEPLETING RESOURCES TO CREATING KNOWLEDGE

One of the main features of the production pattern prevailing in Arab countries, which influences knowledge acquisition, is a high dependence on the depletion of raw materials, chiefly oil, and reliance on external rents. This rentier economic pattern entices societies to import expertise from outside because this is a quick and easy resort that however ends up weakening local demand for knowledge and forfeiting opportunities to produce it locally and employ it effectively in economic activity. A large part of Arab economic activity is concentrated on primary commodities, as in agriculture, which remains largely traditional, and in industries specializing in the production of consumer goods, which depend heavily on production licences obtained from foreign companies. At the same time, the share of the capital goods industry and of industries embodying higher technology continues to shrink. Demand for industrial products is negatively influenced by the small size of Arab markets, the weak competitiveness of Arab economies and the absence of transparency and accountability, which encourages overlap, and sometimes collusion, between political and business elites. Lack of competition reduces productivity and therefore demand for knowledge in economic activity. Instead, competitive advantage and the ability to maximize profits derive from favouritism in power structures, manifested in money and politics. Resistance to opening up to the outside world

by Arab economies and their lack of exposure to foreign competition, coupled with at times excessive protection for local products through import substitution policies, have also slowed the advancement of productivity and the employment of knowledge to that end.

Demand for knowledge has been weakened not only by faltering economic growth and productivity in Arab countries during the last quarter-century but also by the over-concentration of wealth in a few hands. Although some economies of the world have succeeded in the past in achieving economic growth while their income and wealth distribution patterns were skewed, this occurred in a different global context, characterized by a large number of closed economies throughout the world. The opening up of capital markets promoted by globalisation reduces the chances of local growth through concentration. The vast amount of Arab capital invested in industrialized countries and, therefore, denied to the Arab world, is strong evidence that, in human development terms, it is not the possession of money and wealth that matters but how productively such wealth is invested.

Recovery of economic growth in the Arab world and its main driver – increased productivity – are two prerequisites for the advancement of knowledge, but they are not enough. They will be enough only when decision-makers in Arab societies, the business sector, the civil society and the household sector put the goal of building the knowledge society at the head of their priorities and reflect that in all their decisions to spend and to invest.

SOCIETAL INCENTIVES: POWER AND WEALTH WEAKEN THE ETHICS OF KNOWLEDGE

Political, social and economic conditions play a decisive role in orienting systems of values and societal incentives. After independence, most Arab countries came under national political regimes that represented little advance on the autocratic style of ancient and more recent history. Social and individual freedoms were restricted in some areas and were totally absent in others, thus affecting the morals and practical values of people.

In Arab countries, the distribution of

Lack of competition reduces productivity and therefore demand for knowledge in economic activity.

Demand for knowledge has been weakened not only by faltering economic growth but also by the over-concentration of wealth in a few hands.

Arab citizens are increasingly pushed away from effecting changes in their countries.

power, which sometimes coincided with the distribution of wealth, has had an effect on the morals of societies and individuals. The pursuit of personal gain, the preference for the private over the public good, social and moral corruption, the absence of honesty and accountability and many other illnesses, were all related in one way or another to a skewed distribution of power and the resulting social disparities. Justice, before all else, has been the victim of this state of affairs.

Abdul Rahman al-Kawakibi: The Character of Despotism.

We have become accustomed to regarding abject submission as polite deference; obsequiousness as courtesy; sycophancy as oratory; bombast as substance; the acceptance of humiliation as modesty; the acceptance of injustice as obedience; and the pursuit of human entitlements as arrogance. Our inverted system portrays the pursuit of the simplest knowledge as presumption; aspirations for the future as impossible dreams; courage as overreaching audacity; inspiration as folly; chivalry as aggression; free speech as insolence and free thinking as heresy.

The oil boom also played its role in eroding a number of values and societal incentives that would have been helpful in enhancing creativity and the acquisition and diffusion of knowledge. With the spread of negative values during that period, creative abilities were neglected, and knowledge lost its significance for human development. The social standing of scientists, educated people and intellectuals fell. Social value was measured by the criteria of money and fortune, regardless of how those fortunes were gained. Proprietorship and possession replaced knowledge and intellectualism. Perhaps worst of all, the values of independence, freedom and the importance of a critical mind were also buried.

Repression and marginalisation contributed to blunt the desire for achievement, happiness and commitment. As a result, indifference, political apathy and a sense of futility are becoming dangerously common among broad segments of the populace. Arab citizens are increasingly pushed away from effecting changes in their countries.

The Report calls on the state, civil society, cultural and mass media institutions, enlightened intellectuals and the public at large to plant those values that encourage action and innovation in the political, social and economic spheres. 'Reforming the mind' is indeed a significant requirement for Arab culture, yet 'reforming action' is equally urgent.

The emigration of qualified Arabs constitutes a form of reverse development aid.

A centrifugal economic, social and political environment in the region, coupled with centripetal factors in other countries led to the growing phenomenon of an Arab brain drain. The emigration of qualified Arabs constitutes a form of reverse development aid since receiving countries evidently benefit from Arab investments in training and educating their citizens. More significant, however, is the opportunity cost of high levels of skilled outflows: the lost potential contribution of emigrants to knowledge and development in their countries of origin. This double loss calls for serious action to minimise its dangers: firstly by tapping the expertise and knowledge of the Arab Diaspora abroad, and secondly by providing Arab expatriates with incentives to return, either on temporary assignments or for good, to their countries of origin, carrying a human capital much larger than that they had migrated with. This can be achieved only by launching a serious project for human development that would attract highly qualified migrants back temporarily or permanently on productive and personally fulfilling assignments to serve their countries.

The Arab Brain Drain

Roughly 25% of 300,000 first degree graduates from Arab universities in 1995/96 emigrated. Between 1998 and 2000 more than 15,000 Arab doctors migrated.

Data provided by A.B. Zahlan.

Unlike the case of Arab culture, the analysis of Arab social and economic structures reveals ingrained obstacles to knowledge acquisition in the Arab world. Only by overcoming those obstacles through reform can a knowledge society be developed.

THE POLITICAL CONTEXT:

Oppression, Knowledge and Development

Political obstacles to knowledge acquisition, as the Report argues, are even more severe in Arab countries than those posed by their socio-economic structures, which are in turn seen to be more obstructive than any features of culture.

Political power plays a key role in directing knowledge and influencing its development. It fosters knowledge that is favourable to its goals and suppresses opposing patterns. Political instability and fierce struggles for access to political positions in the absence of an established rule for the peaceful rotation of power – in short, democracy – impede the growth of knowledge in Arab soil. One of the main results of that unstable political situation has been the subjection of scientific institutions to political strategies and power conflicts. In managing these institutions, political loyalties take precedence over efficiency and knowledge. Power shackles active minds, extinguishes the flame of learning and kills the drive for innovation.

The Report calls for the establishment of an independent knowledge sphere that produces and promotes knowledge free from political coercion. This is possible only by democratising political life and knowledge and ensuring that knowledge can be freely acquired and produced.

Laws are needed to guarantee Arab citizens the essential rights of knowledge - the freedom of thought and expression that are a precondition for knowledge to flourish. The international human rights conventions have been signed by most Arab states, but they have neither entered the legal culture nor been incorporated into substantive domestic legislation. Yet the problem of freedom in the Arab world is not related to the implementation of laws as much as to the violation of these laws. Oppression, the arbitrary application of laws, selective censorship and other politically motivated restrictions are widespread. They often take the form of legal constraints on publications, associations, general assemblies and electronic media, which prevent these from carrying out their communication and cultural roles. Such restrictions also obstruct the diffusion of knowledge and the education of public opinion.

Yet the more dangerous restrictions are those imposed by security authorities when they confiscate publications or ban people from entering a country or prevent the sale of certain books during fairs while promoting other kinds of books. In committing these acts, these authorities reach above the constitutional institutions and the law, citing the pretext of 'national security' or public order.

Other forms of restriction come from narrow-minded, self-appointed custodians of public morality, and from the censorship of books, articles and media events. Creativity, innovation and knowledge are the first victims of the suppression or denial of freedoms.

A global context that poses a challenge: Globalisation in its current form and existing institutions is often weighted towards securing the interests of the rich and powerful nations and their dominance over the world economy, knowledge flows and, by extension, opportunities for development. Without changes that tip the balance of global governance more towards the needs and aspirations of developing countries, including Arab countries, globalisation cannot help these nations to achieve human progress.

> "If we are not careful, the intellectual property rights system may introduce distortions that would be detrimental to the interests of developing countries."
>
> Commission on Intellectual Property Rights (London, Sept 2002).

Perhaps the most important example from a knowledge perspective is the insistence by industrialised countries, the main producers of knowledge at the global level, that knowledge should be converted from a public good to a private commodity through the instrument of intellectual property rights, which are largely owned by the industrialised West. This is now happening even in cases where the knowledge originated in developing countries and was later acquired by institutions in the industrialised world. This trend threatens to cut down developing country opportunities to acquire new knowledge and it especially jeopardises productive sectors such as medicine and pharmacology.

In the case of Arab countries in particular, a qualitative jump in the effectiveness of the knowledge acquisition system requires closer and more efficient forms of cooperation at the Pan-Arab level.

> "It is quite clear that the dilemma of Arab development will not be solved without focusing fully on human development – the development of the citizen and his/her role in economic, social and political life."
>
> Mustafa Al-Barghouthi

Power shackles active minds, extinguishes the flame of learning and kills the drive for innovation.

Without changes that tip the balance of global governance more towards the needs and aspirations of developing countries, including Arab countries, globalisation cannot help these nations achieve human progress.

A STRATEGIC VISION FOR ESTABLISHING A KNOWLEDGE SOCIETY IN THE ARAB WORLD

The Report pulls together the various threads of its analysis of the status of Arab knowledge in a concluding strategic vision of the Arab knowledge society, supported by five pillars:

1. *Guaranteeing the key freedoms of opinion, speech and assembly through good governance bounded by the law:* A climate of freedom is an essential prerequisite for the knowledge society. These freedoms are the thresholds to knowledge production, to creativity and innovation, and to invigorating scientific research, technical development and artistic and literary expression. Constitutions, laws and administrative procedures need to be refined to remove all restrictions on essential freedoms, particularly administrative censorship, and regulatory restrictions by security apparatuses on the production and diffusion of knowledge and all kinds of creative expression.

2. *Disseminating high quality education for all:* The detailed proposals for reform in education include: giving priority to early childhood learning; ensuring universal basic education for all and extending it to at least 10th grade; developing an adult education system for lifelong learning; improving the quality of education at all stages; giving particular attention to promoting higher education, and instituting independent periodic evaluations of quality at all stages of education.

3. *Embedding and ingraining science, and building and broadening the capacity for research and development in all societal activities.* This can be achieved through promoting basic research, and establishing a centrally co-ordinated regional creativity and innovation network that permeates the entire fabric of society and enjoys supportive and complementary linkages in the regional and international spheres.

4. *Shifting rapidly towards knowledge-based production in Arab socioeconomic structures:* This calls for a decisive move towards developing renewable resources through knowledge and technological capabilities and towards diversifying economic structures and markets. It also requires upgrading

the Arab presence in the 'new economy' and the consolidation of a societal incentives system that upholds the acquisition and application of knowledge for human development in contrast to the current mode in which values are centred on material possessions and in seeking access and favour from the two sources of power: money and authority.

5. *Developing an authentic, broadminded and enlightened Arab knowledge model.* This would entail:

• Delivering true religion from political exploitation and respecting critical scholarship. The components of this reform include returning to the civilised, moral and humanitarian vision of pure religion; restoring to religious institutions their independence from political authorities, governments, states and radical religious-political movements; recognising intellectual freedom; activating interpretative jurisprudence, preserving the right to differ in doctrines, religious schools and interpretations.

• Advancing the Arabic language by undertaking serious research and linguistic reform for translating scientific terms and coining simple linguistic usages. This also includes compiling specialised, functional dictionaries and other reference works that monitor common classical-colloquial words for use in children's programmes and written and audio publications. This must be matched by other persistent efforts to facilitate the acquisition of Arabic through formal and informal learning channels, and to produce creative and innovative writing for young children.

• Reclaiming some of the myriad bright spots in the Arab cultural heritage. These must be incorporated in the core of the Arab knowledge model in a manner far above and beyond the self-centred singing of one's own praises. This legacy must be assimilated and understood as part of the structure of motivation for developing and nurturing an Arab knowledge system in Arab minds and institutions.

• Enriching, promoting and celebrating cultural diversity within Arab countries. This calls for providing safeguards for the protection of all sub-cultures and for encouraging them to interact, intermingle, grow and flourish.

Constitutions, laws and administrative procedures need to be refined to remove all restrictions on essential freedoms.

- Opening up to other cultures. Such interaction would be strengthened by translation into other languages; promoting an intelligent and generous exchange with non-Arab cultures and civilisations; maximising benefits from regional and international organisations and initiating reform in the world order through stronger inter-Arab cooperation.

Al-Kindy: Welcoming the truth regardless of its source

"We should not shy away from welcoming and acquiring the truth regardless of where it came from, even if it came from distant races and nations that are different from us. Nothing is more important than seeking the truth except the truth itself. We should not belittle the truth, or those who utter it or bring it."

As the Report affirms in closing, knowledge closely approaches a religious obligation that Arabs ought to honour and exercise. It points out the way on the Arab journey to a dignified and prosperous future. The pursuit of knowledge is prompted by religion, culture, history and the human will to succeed. Obstructions on the road are the work of mortals: the defective structures of the past and present – social, economic and, above all, political. Arabs must remove or reform these structures in order to take the place they deserve in the world of knowledge at the beginning of the knowledge millennium.

The pursuit of knowledge is prompted by religion, culture, history and the human will to succeed.

PART I

Changes in human development in Arab countries during 2001-2002

This section looks at the period in review (2002-2003) and traces changes in, and impacts on Arab human development arising from trends and developments at the national, regional and international levels. In doing so it revisits the status of the "three deficits" identified in the first Arab Human Development Report (in freedom, knowledge and women's empowerment) and highlights progress and continuing shortfalls since that report was issued in July 2002.

PART I

 # Changes in human development in Arab countries during 2001-2002

Starting with this second issue, the Arab Human Development Report (AHDR) series initiates a new practice of including an opening section devoted to assessing recent trends and events that have influenced human development in the Arab region. The assessment includes events that took place on both the external (regional and international) and the internal (Arab country) levels, and covers the period since work began on the previous report in the series.

INTRODUCTION: THE STATE OF HUMAN DEVELOPMENT IN ARAB COUNTRIES

THE CONTENT OF HUMAN DEVELOPMENT

The concept of "human development" has gained popularity since 1990 when the United Nations Development Programme (UNDP) adopted the term with a specific connotation, advanced a new index (the HDI) to measure it[1], and started publishing an annual report on the subject.

The human development concept, as it has evolved over the years, is based on an intellectual heritage that places people at the centre of development and which culminated in the first Human Development Report (UNDP, 1990). The concept maintains that "people are the true wealth of nations"[2] and that human development is a "process of expanding people's choices". Since freedom is essential for the exercise of choice, freedom is a fundamental requirement of human development. "Choices" is an expression of the more sophisticated con-

cept of "entitlements" introduced by Amartya Sen[3], as an expression of people's basic right to these "choices". The concept stipulates that human beings, simply by being human, have an inalienable right to a decent living in body and soul.

Two important implications flow from this concept: first, human development rejects outright any form of discrimination among human beings on whatever basis: gender, origin or belief. Second, human well being is not limited to material dimensions but extends to the individual's moral participation in society and to all aspects of a decent life, such as beauty, human dignity and self-fulfillment.

People's entitlements are, in principle, unlimited and grow rapidly with human progress. Yet at any level of development, the three main entitlements, in the opinion of the Human Development Report, are "to live a long and healthy life, to acquire knowledge and to possess resources necessary for a decent life". Human development, however, does not stop at that minimum but goes beyond it to include other entitlements such as "political, economic and social freedoms, opportunities for production and creativity, the enjoyment of liberty, self-fulfillment, and respect for human rights".

Thus, human development is much more than the development of human resources. It is a genuinely humane approach to the comprehensive and integrated development of human beings and societal institutions aimed at achieving the higher goals of human existence: freedom, justice and human dignity. The human development process rests on two essential foundations: the first is the building of human capacities that allow for access to an

Human development is a genuinely humane approach to the comprehensive and integrated development of human beings and societal institutions aimed at achieving the higher goals of human existence: freedom, justice and human dignity.

---

[1] The HDI has undoubtedly been a major improvement over GDP per capita as a measure of development.

[2] The phrase was first used in Frederick Harbison's famous book, Human Resources as the Wealth of Nations (1973)

[3] 1998 Nobel Prize winner in economics in recognition of his work on poverty and famines.

advanced level of human well-being. Foremost among these are the capacity to live a long and healthy life, to acquire knowledge and for all people to enjoy freedom without discrimination of any kind. The second foundation is the efficient utilisation of human capabilities in all areas of human activity as well as in economic production, civil society organisation and political life.

THE CHALLENGE OF HUMAN DEVELOPMENT IN THE ARAB REGION

Arab countries have made significant strides in more than one area of human development in the last three decades. Nevertheless, the predominant characteristic of Arab reality today seems to be the existence of deeply rooted shortcomings that stand as obstacles to building human development. As noted earlier, the first AHDR summarised these shortcomings as the three deficits of freedom, women's empowerment and knowledge. Taking these shortcomings into consideration, as the first AHDR did by exploring an alternative human development index, shows that it may be premature to celebrate the achievements of Arab countries on the traditional

HDI. Indeed, the challenge of building genuine human development remains a very serious one for the vast majority of Arabs. From a positive perspective, the realisation of human development in the Arab world requires transcending these deficits and transforming them into their opposites: advantages enjoyed by all Arabs and assets they can be proud of before the rest of the world.

In order to build human development, Arab countries need to embark on reconstructing their societies along three clear principles:
• Full respect for human rights and freedoms as the cornerstone of good governance leading to human development.
• Full empowerment of Arab women, recognising their right to equal participation in politics, society and the economy as well as to education and other means of building capabilities.
• Active knowledge acquisition and its effective utilisation in building human capabilities. As a key driver of economic progress, knowledge must be brought to bear efficiently and productively in all aspects of society, with the goal of enhancing human well-being across the region.

This, in essence, is what it will take to transcend the crisis of human development in the Arab region. It is, however, by no means the ultimate target for Arabs. Meeting the challenges of the future requires building Arab productive capabilities in the face of the rentier nature of Arab economies and societies. It demands the reform of governance at the national and pan-Arab levels on a solid foundation of freedom. It calls for strengthening Arab co-operation and it entails maximising the benefits and minimising the risks of globalisation.

> *The challenge of building human development remains a very serious one for the vast majority of Arabs.*

BOX 1

The Sheikh of Al-Rabwah, Muhammad ibn Abi Taleb al-Ansari al-Demashqi – The Human Being

"Since MAN (insân in Arabic) is the cream of the world, the essence of the universe, the radiating centre in the oceans and the encirclements, the collector of the dispersed contents of the earth and heavens, the descendent, the outcome, the elite and the fruit of existence and its raison d'etre, it was imperative that we conclude this book by noting his apparent characteristics and the wonders of his creation and his manners. We have given in it (i.e., the book) a description of the three generated ones, the seven regions, the seas and their contents, as well as their characteristics and those of the countries. Nothing remained except man, who is the goal of all this and to whom belongs a collection of characteristics, not a single self. He is the empowered successor on earth and the one charged with carrying out God's prescriptions. He is a created being, charged and empowered. Among his characteristics is that God Almighty combined in him the powers of the two worlds and qualified him to inhabit the two houses (i.e., the world and the hereafter). He is just like an animal in his lust and hunger to develop the earth; and he is like angels in knowledge, worship and guidance. Therefore, in return for man's worship and devotion to developing His earth, God nominated him to be His successor on earth. He prepared him to sojourn next to Him in His Paradise and the House of his Throne. This man is composed of two opposite things and two separate substances far removed from each other: one of them is gentle, a heavenly soul, enlightened, all-encompassing, live and perceiving. The other one is dense, an earthly body, inferior, dark, dead and insensitive. That is why he was called "insan", which is the dual of ins (human)."

Source: "The Choice of Time in the Wonders of the Land and the Sea", quoted in: Ahmad Sedqui ad-Dajani, 1994.

BOX 2

How Do Arabs Feel About the Three Deficits?

A large-scale international study (World Values Survey) presents an opportunity to compare Arab attitudes towards knowledge, good governance and gender equality with those expressed in other regions.

The following results are based on field surveys in a large number of countries throughout the world, including four Arab countries (Algeria, Egypt, Jordan, and Morocco) that comprise about half the Arab people.

In addition to the Arab region, the surveys provide enough data to compare the Arab region to eight other country groupings: other (non-Arab) Islamic countries, sub-Saharan Africa, Eastern Europe, South Asia, USA/ Canada, Australia and New Zealand, Latin America, East Asia, and Western Europe.

According to this survey, Arabs value knowledge and good governance strongly but take an ambivalent stand on gender equality.

Among the nine regions, Arabs expressed the highest preference for the role of science in the service of humanity. Arabs also topped the list of those supporting the statement that "democracy is better than

any other form of government" and expressed the highest level of rejection of authoritarian rule (a strong leader who does not have to bother with parliament and elections).

On the empowerment of women, the Arabs came third in rejecting that "a university education is more important for a boy than for a girl" while expressing the highest approval that "when jobs are scarce, men should have more right to a job than women". In other words, Arabs stood for gender equality in education but not in employment. In human development terms, Arabs expressed support for building the human capabilities of women but not for their utilisation.

Evidently, Arab public opinion strongly supports the focus of AHDR1 on the two deficits of freedom/good governance, and knowledge. But AHDR1 might have been ahead of Arab public opinion in stressing women's full empowerment in both education and employment according to the paradigm of building human capabilities and utilising them effectively.

Figure 1
Democracy is the best form of government

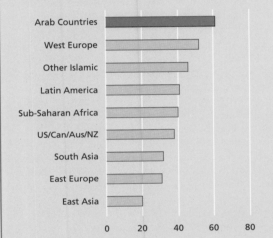

Figure 2
Rejection of authoritarian rule

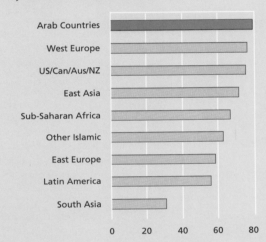

Figure 3
Gender equality in higher education

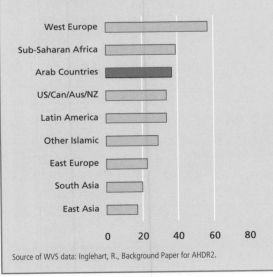

Figure 4
Gender equality in employment

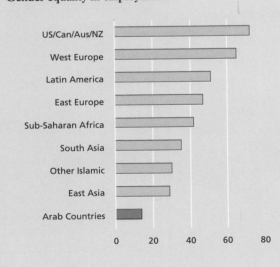

Source of WVS data: Inglehart, R., Background Paper for AHDR2.

BOX 3

Mohammad Hassanein Heikal
The First Arab Human Development Report: For Whom Did the Bell Toll?

In our daily lives, we are accustomed to the sound of the bell as a last call. The first ring to reach our ears was that of the school bell calling us to knowledge and learning. It was followed by other summonses: the train bell announcing our last chance to start a journey; the bells of places of worship beckoning us to prayer; the ambulance or fire engine siren telling us that the usual right of way had changed, and that a new urgency took precedence; the alarms in buildings alerting us to the danger of fire or attempted burglary.

- The bell rung by the AHDR and heard by Arabs and others the world over carried echoes of all the bells ringing through our lives. It was a call to knowledge and learning, an announcement of the last chance to join the trip to the future, an appeal for cleansing, an injunction to make way for an urgent priority, and finally a forewarning of imminent danger – urging us to hasten to douse the flames of a still-small fire waiting to engulf the region in a formidable blaze.

- The truth is that the AHDR was a bell that rang at the last minute of the last hour in the contemporary Arab age – ringing within the framework of a history radically different from anything humankind had experienced before. Indeed, that experience can be fairly summarised (despite the precautions imposed on simplification) by noting that the world has passed a number of milestones:

- The first was the French Revolution, late in the eighteenth century, that arrived after aeons during which human beings lived as subjects of emperors, kings, sultans, and princes. It crystallised the concept of nationhood: a particular people living on territories with set borders. This concept gave rise, among other outcomes, to the idea of one market that guarantees the interest of the group and, as such, the state market appeared.

- The second milestone was the attempt at German Unification, at the end of the nineteenth century, which redefined the concept of the nation as a unifier of a people connected by kinship, neighbourhood, language and culture, and the experience of a continuous history. In this concept, the nation has ties more extensive than the borders of territories belonging to one people and to a national state. The notion of a wider market materialised to fulfill these more extensive interests, one that might be called "the nation's market" and which, by extension, was sometimes called "the region's market".

- The third milestone was the shedding by the United States of its oceanic isolation in the early twentieth century. This was a significant indication that the US, largely self-sufficient though it was, realised that it too needed the world as much as the world needed the US. With this transcontinental meeting – accompanied by great strides in energy generation, aviation and communication – the features of one world appeared, pointing towards a "world market'.

- The fourth and final milestone was passed after World War II and after the revolution in electronics, space and satellite technology emerged and developed. The crisis of political doctrines that climaxed with the end of the Cold War in the last decade of the 20th century led to a profound shift -- in effect, a global transformation. Its thrust has been to convert the "world market" into a "market world" transcending all national, regional and continental borders.

- The danger and the significance of present trends is that the current transcontinental "world market" will indeed turn into a dominant "market world", one that will accommodate, absorb, usurp, and dominate without stopping at any physical or political obstacles. This would ultimately lead to a double impasse:

On the one hand, local and regional identities would be incapable of resistance, and would surrender, leaving the market to govern peoples and nations and manage world affairs.

On the other hand, the power of law would give way to that of the market. As such, international rights symbolised by the United Nations in New York would cede to the authority of the New York Stock Exchange. The strongholds of this authority, the International Monetary Fund, the World Bank and multinational firms, would dominate world affairs. The market would become the plotter of intelligence operations, the order-giver to armies and fleets, and the director of missile payloads.

The AHDR probably came out at the last minute of the last hour to pose a fateful question to the Arab people:

- If we want a world owning "the market", then where are we in that world conceptually and actually, in terms of our capabilities and contributions?

- If we accept a market owning "the world", what will be our position and role in that circumstance? What will be our orientation and what impacts will follow?

In short, where are we?

BOX 4

AHDR1 Web Site Statistics
http://www.undp.org/rbas/ahdr/

Year	No. of downloads	No. of complete downloads
2002	978,000	792,000
2003	346,000	303,000
Total	**1,324,000**	**1,095,000**

CHANGES IN HUMAN DEVELOPMENT SINCE 2001

THE REGIONAL AND INTERNATIONAL ENVIRONMENT

Work on the first AHDR (2002) started at the beginning of 2001; as such its analysis stopped at the end of the twentieth century. On the other hand, since the first draft of this second report was initiated at the beginning of 2003, the timeframe under review in this section is limited to just two calendar years. This is, of course, a very short period in human development terms. Basic human development indicators do not change significantly over short periods. Moreover, updating such indicators requires up-to-date databases, resources that are all-too-scarce in the Arab world, as was sharply underlined in the first report.

In an attempt to maximise information based on weak or incomplete data, this section adopts a qualitative analysis. It focuses on deducing trends inherent in events considered to have an important bearing on various dimensions of human development in the regional and international context of Arab countries. At the time of writing, trends portend momentous alterations that may change not only the status of human development, but the very face and pattern of life in the region for some considerable time.

Certain events may take place over a very short period of time, yet leave a profound impression on human development. Such is the case with changes in human rights and other forms of legislation affecting people's civil liberties. This section records several recent events that have had negative impacts in Arab countries, notably in the two areas of freedom and good governance and the advancement of women.

Furthermore, qualitative analysis also requires sound and comprehensive data. Most of the databases available to support such analysis reflect the viewpoints, if not the prejudices, of the party gathering the data. To minimise this problem, especially in relation to Arab-related events, the authors have resorted to more than one source besides diligently monitoring the mass media during the period under study, including bulletins and reports prepared by the Arab Organisation for Human Rights, and electronic mail lists of human rights violations in Arab countries.

ON THE INTERNATIONAL AND REGIONAL DIMENSIONS OF HUMAN DEVELOPMENT IN ARAB COUNTRIES

The first AHDR (2002) may not have given sufficient attention to the regional and international dimensions of the human development impasse in Arab countries – at least, this is what a majority of the Arab critics of the report have felt. The publication of the report after the tragic events of September 11, 2001, and their extremely serious aftermath, amplified this feeling, although work on the report had started well before those events.

The authors believe that exaggerating the impediments to Arab development imposed by regional and international challenges is futile and self-defeating. This all-too-frequent resort may provide a comforting escape, yet it is still highly counterproductive. Taking refuge in externalities weakens the resolve and undermines the capabilities required for self-reliant development. It also leads to underestimating the task of self-improvement upon which Arab dignity and the national, regional and international prospects of the region must be constructed. Hence, the strategic choice of the first report was to focus on the reform required within the Arab world.

The decisive factor in soundly confronting the regional and international challenges facing the Arab world will be the quality of Arab capabilities in various spheres; knowledge, production and politics. Such capabilities and creative energies, in turn, cannot be unleashed without widening the range of people's freedoms and guaranteeing good governance in practice. History and logic further indicate that a strong system of Arab co-ordination leading to regional integration will be an indispensable source of strength and a condition for success in these endeavours. This system can be seen as "an Arab Free Citizenship Zone", where every Arab would enjoy the full rights of a national in each and every Arab country. Such a system would undoubtedly

The decisive factor in soundly confronting the regional and international challenges facing the Arab world will be the quality of Arab capabilities in knowledge, production and politics.

strengthen the negotiating capacities of Arab countries in highly competitive global arenas, and position Arab countries on firmer and higher ground in the third millennium.

It is now clear that the human impact of September 11 and its political and security consequences have decisively altered international public opinion and sentiment, and thus the parameters of the external challenges to development in the Arab region. A new historical era is rapidly unfolding; not only because of the high human toll, which was a great tragedy, but also because of the political and security consequences of that cataclysm. The fateful events of that horrific day woke the world, especially its rich and powerful countries, from a dream of comprehensive security and invulnerability. The need to rebuild global security has become all the more urgent now, yet the proposed means to reach this end vary. Without question, the killing of innocent human beings violated all human and heavenly laws.

Worldwide anti-terrorism policies have been largely military and security-oriented in nature. The long-term goal of draining the economic and political sources of terrorism has almost faded away.

In the current war against terror, the security policies and restrictive procedures introduced by some advanced countries and adopted in several parts of the developing world, including the Arab region, have created a situation inimical to human development. Governments, stating considerations of security and stability, have found a new justification for their ongoing warnings about the perils of freedom. A flawed yet highly influential rationale has gained ground: if the world's leading democracies find it necessary to backpedal on human rights and civil liberties, other states much further behind on the road to reform may be well advised to pause. After all, in the narrow logic of security, governments with the most to lose by granting freedom are thus most justified in ruling with an iron grip. The expedience of that logic has not been lost on regressive elements in Arab and other developing countries.

Events befalling Arabs abroad and widely broadcast in the media intensified popular disaffection in the region. The US Administration resorted to establishing and enforcing procedures that at times contravened the most basic human rights, according to the (American) Lawyer's Committee for Human Rights (New York, 2002), which found that "over the last year the US government has taken a series of actions that have gradually eroded basic human rights protections in the United States, fundamental guarantees that have been central to the US constitutional system for more than two hundred years...too often, the US government's mode of operations since September 11 has been at odds with core American and international human rights principles."[4] Those procedures, which included ethnic profiling and secret evidence, violated civil and political liberties, particularly those of Arabs and Muslims. They revoked the right to a just trial before civil courts, thus legalising detention without charge and administrative arrests without due process.

The US introduced ethnic profiling of Arabs and Muslims, whether they were naturalised citizens, legal residents, students or visitors. Contrary to a long-established principle under the law, these people became guilty until proven innocent. Many ordinary people were arrested for no reason except their affiliation to Arabs or to Islam. The US required fingerprint records of visiting nationals from 25 Arab states and also instituted registration with security forces, which led to administrative detentions in some cases.

These measures resulted in reducing the number of Arab students in the United States, quite markedly in the cases of some countries (Table 1). Important knowledge acquisition opportunities for young Arabs were thus cur-

Governments, stating considerations of security and stability, have found a new justification for their ongoing warnings about the perils of freedom.

---

[4]The American Lawyer's Committee for Human Rights report (New York, 2002) documents details of the erosion of civil liberties. Among them:
- "The FBI may now be privy to what books an individual checks out at the public library or purchases at the local bookstore.
- The USA Patriot Act could result in long-term detention of non-citizens who have never been charged with a crime.
- The Justice Department's list of the young men targeted for government questioning was compiled strictly on the basis of national origin.
- The Administration has in fact been using the term "unlawful enemy combatant" - a term not found in international law - as a kind of magic wand, waving it to avoid well-established standards of the US and international law.
- Even if suspected terrorists are eventually tried and then acquitted by military commissions the Administration reserves the right to continue to detain them indefinitely.
- In too many cases, opportunistic governments expressed support for the fight against terrorism, while presenting their own domestic insurgencies as conflicts perpetrated by terrorist groups analogous to at least Al-Qaeda."

tailed. The harassment of Arabs living abroad, furthermore, created a climate that undermined the welfare of Arab expatriate communities, damaged the vital process of cultural interaction between them and host societies and interrupted valuable scientific, technical and cultural exchanges between Arab countries and the West.

Perhaps the gravest repercussion of the war on terror is that it gave ruling regimes in some Arab countries spurious justification for curbing freedoms through an expanded definition of terrorism, which found institutional expression on the pan-Arab level in the "Arab Charter for Anti-Terrorism". This document has been widely criticised in Arab and international human rights circles, since an expanded definition opens the door to abuses such as censorship, restricting access to the Internet and suppressing the printing and publication of any material construed as "encouraging terrorism". Moreover, the Charter neither explicitly prohibits detention or torture, nor provides for questioning the legality of detentions. Furthermore, it does not protect personal freedom, since it does not require a prior judicial order authorising the wire-tapping of individuals or groups (Amnesty International).

THE IMPACT OF THE ISRAELI OCCUPATION OF PALESTINE ON HUMAN DEVELOPMENT IN ARAB COUNTRIES

The first AHDR concluded that the Israeli occupation of Palestine constitutes a severe impediment to human development. This occupation distorts policy priorities, retards human development and freezes opportunities for growth, prosperity and freedom across the region, and not in the Occupied Palestinian Territories alone. The harsh indignities arising from occupation extend to all the Arab people, yet the worst repercussions are borne by the Palestinian people themselves.

Occupation denies Palestinians freedom and human dignity and aborts their internationally recognised right to self-determination. Occupation squanders Palestinian resources,

TABLE 1

Number of students from some Arab countries in the United States before and after the September 2001 events

Country	Number of students in the United States		
	1999	2002/2003	% Reduction
Saudi Arabia	5,156	3,581	31%
Qatar	338	250	26%
Oman	459	345	25%
Yemen	188	181	4%

Source: Data collected from Arab Missions by the Permanent Observer Mission of the Arab League to the United Nations.

undermines Palestinian human capabilities and destroys individual and communal security and human lives.

The occupation of Palestinian and other Arab lands exerts a direct and continuous burden on the economies of affected countries and diverts resources from development to military and security objectives. The threat of Israeli domination also creates a pretext for deferring political and economic reforms in Arab countries in the name of national solidarity against a formidably armed external aggressor[5].

Israel's believed possession of a large arsenal of weapons of mass destruction (WMD), which Arabs consider represents a double standard because it is not subjected to an international watch or a regional or international deterrent, drives the Arab region and surrounding countries into an intense arms race that diminishes resources that could otherwise be applied to development.

In 2002, Israel's government, under the guise of the international war on terror, attacked almost all Palestinian territories, de-

Occupation distorts policy priorities, retards human development and freezes opportunities for growth, prosperity and freedom across the region.

[5] Israel's might in the region is not to be underestimated. For example, Israel is among the few countries that very likely own nuclear weapons, even if this is not usually acknowledged (US State Department, from infoplease.com). Israel has refrained from ratifying the Treaty on Non-Proliferation of Nuclear Weapons. The Centre for Non-proliferation Studies affiliated with the "Monterey Centre for International Studies" categorises Israel's ownership of chemical weapons as "probable", and its ownership of biological weapons as "possible", given that Israel has not ratified treaties on banning chemical and biological weapons.

Human Rights Watch Report 2002, Middle East and North Africa: Jenin

"Israeli security forces were responsible for extensive abuses, including indiscriminate and excessive use of lethal force against unarmed Palestinian demonstrators; unlawful killings by Israel Defense Forces (IDF) soldiers; disproportionate IDF gunfire in response to Palestinian attacks; inadequate IDF response to abuses by Israeli settlers against Palestinian civilians; and "closure" measures on Palestinian communities that amounted to collective punishment."

"During its investigation [of IDF operations in Jenin], however, Human Rights Watch documented unlawful and deliber-

ate killings, and the killing or wounding of unprotected individuals as a result of excessive or disproportionate use of force. Such cases are in violation of the international humanitarian law prohibitions against 'wilful killing' of non-combatants. The organisation also found instances of IDF soldiers deliberately impeding the work of medical personnel and preventing medical assistance to the wounded with no apparent or obvious justification of military necessity... There is strong prima facie evidence that in some of the cases documented grave breaches of the Geneva Conventions, or war crimes, were committed."

Source: Human Rights Watch World Report 2002: Middle East & North Africa.

The number of Palestinian deaths resulting from Israeli action in the past two years is, in proportional terms, comparable to the death of about a quarter of a million people in the US.

stroyed farms and homes, disrupted the Palestinian Authority, used unarmed civilians as human shields, and committed, most markedly in Jenin and Nablus, atrocities and what a highly reputed NGO, Human Rights Watch, called 'war crimes'. (Human Rights Watch, 2002).

In April 2003 the UN Commission on Human Rights, with a majority of 33 out of 53 votes, strongly condemned "the violations by the Israeli occupation authorities of human rights in the occupied Palestinian territory, including East Jerusalem", including "the practice of 'liquidation' or 'extrajudicial executions'", and expressed its grave concern "at acts of mass killing perpetrated by the Israeli occupying authorities against the Palestinian people" (Commission on Human Rights, Resolution 2003/6, Geneva). The resolution "reaffirms the legitimate right of the Palestinian people to resist the Israeli occupation." Occupation forces opened fire on ambulances that month.

The human costs of Israeli occupation

Israeli occupation has wrought death and destruction in the West Bank and Gaza. By April 2003, 2,405 Palestinians had been killed, and 41,000 injured as a result of Israeli actions since September 2000. These are not mere statistics but people whose lives have been destroyed, their hopes dashed, their futures

aborted and their families bereaved. Most of those killed were civilians (85%) and a significant proportion were children (20%). UNICEF estimates that 7,000 children have been injured.

The conflict has also claimed Israeli casualties. Over the period (September 2000 – May 2003), the Israeli defense forces reported a total of 781 Israelis dead and 5,468 injured (http://www.idf.il) including soldiers, settlers and civilians. The loss of innocent lives is always an unacceptable human tragedy.[6]

Given that the population of the West Bank and Gaza is about one hundredth the population of the US, the number of Palestinian deaths resulting from Israeli action in the past two years is, in proportional terms, comparable to the death of about a quarter of a million people in the US. The number of injuries is comparable to four million in the US.

In addition to considerable casualties, Palestinian human development has suffered from the loss of freedom, livelihoods, destruction of basic infrastructure and an alarming decline in health conditions. Palestinians were subject to blatant violations of basic human rights, including the right to life, freedom, food, education and employment.

It is very difficult to find a historical equivalent to the division of the occupied territories into clusters. While it shares a few similarities with past segregation policies in the US, it resembles most the Bantustan policies enforced by the former apartheid regime in South Africa.

Collective punishment through closures and curfews affects nearly three million Palestinians in the West Bank and Gaza. Israeli checkpoints and roadblocks divide these territories into 300 separate clusters. Most occupied towns, villages and refugee camps have suffered from extended curfews and closures. Nablus, for example, has been virtually under continuous curfew during the past two years. About 15,000 Palestinians have been denied freedom of movement through detention with 6,000 still in prison, including 350 children.

Closures and curfews have also deprived people of basic services and supplies, creating

---

[6]Other nations also suffered casualties in the conflict: the crushing of the young American peace activist, Rachel Corrie, by an Israeli bulldozer is just one example.

a major humanitarian crisis. They prevent access to medical care and restrict the movement of medical personnel and supplies. Heart, cancer and renal patients cannot obtain treatment or cannot afford it. Pregnant women are cut off from antenatal care and are forced to give birth at home or even at checkpoints. Forty-three women delivered babies at checkpoints, nine of whom were stillborn.[7] Parents cannot have their children immunised just as health risks are multiplying. Children and teachers cannot go to school. Malnutrition is rampant with 30% of children under 5 suffering from chronic malnutrition and 21% from acute malnutrition.[8] Psychological trauma is widespread, particularly among children. Families, friends and communities find themselves physically isolated, unable to meet and support each other.

While Israeli construction of settlements and a separation barrier, "the wall", further tightens Israel's stranglehold on the Palestinian people, Israeli destruction of Palestinian property and infrastructure undermines hope for a viable Palestinian economy. Between October 2000 and April 2002, physical damage amounted to US $ 305 million. In mid-May 2002, after Israeli incursions into several West Bank towns that left almost 260 Palestinians dead, an international donor survey assessed physical damage at more than US $361 million.[9] It was one of these incursions (into Jenin) that Terje Rød Larsen, UN Special Coordinator in the Occupied Territories described as "horrific beyond belief" and "morally repugnant." His outcry and that of the international community did not restrain the destruction. By September 2002 the damage had nearly doubled to US $728 million.

Israeli actions have deprived large segments of the population of job opportunities and income. GNP has been more than halved and total income losses to the Palestinian economy are estimated to be between US $3.2 and US $10 billion (in addition to the cost of destroyed public and private property). About three fourths of Palestinians are now living in poverty (measured at under US $2 a day). The

---

BOX 7

Human Losses in the Occupied Palestinian Territories
(Sept 2001- April 2003)

- 2,405 dead, including 451 children and 265 students:
  - deaths by live ammunition: 1,455
  - by heavy weapons: 496
  - by assassination: 219
- 41,000 wounded, including 7,000 children and 2,981 students.
- 2,500 permanent disabilities, with 500 children affected.
- 9 journalists killed, including 7 Palestinians. 75 journalists wounded 167 journalists assaulted

Sources:
- The Palestine Monitor: 28 September 2002 – 17 April 2003)
- Health, Development, Information, and Policy Institute
- B'Tselem report: Illusions of restraint: Human Rights Violations During the Events in the Occupied Territories 29th September - 2nd December, 2000
- Palestinian Ministry of Health
- UN Special Rapporteur of Commission on Human Rights, March 2002
- Ministry of Education, 17 January 2002
- General Union of Disabled Palestinians
- UN Special Rapperteur of Communication Human Rights, March 2002
- Information from the Palestinian Journalists Syndicate

BOX 8

Material Losses in the Occupied Palestinian
Territories in 19 months
(until April 2003)

- Houses damaged: 11,553
- Houses destroyed: 4,985
- Schools destroyed: 323
- Mosques destroyed: 30
- Churches destroyed: 12
- Wells destroyed: 134
- Trees uprooted: 34,606
- Land sequestrated: 1,162 donums*
- Land Destroyed: 17,162 donums

Source: The Palestine Monitor
- Palestinian Centre for Human Rights, 3rd June, 2002
- Palestinian Humanitarian Disaster, U.S. Agency for International Development, July 10, 2002
- Ministry of Education, 17 Jan 2002, Information for Ministry of Education schools
- Palestinian Council for Justice and Peace
- Al-Mezan 2001
- LAW Society, 29th Nov 2001 (figure from beginning of 2000)

*A donum is 1,000 sq. m. of land.

---

number of poor people has tripled since September 2000. Two thirds of the workforce in Gaza, and half of the workforce in the West Bank, are unemployed. Palestinians are now more dependent on food aid than ever before. The World Bank estimates that if the conflict is resolved and the closure lifted, it will still take at least two years for the Palestinian economy to restore pre-September 2000 per capita income.

Current unemployment rates in the West Bank and Gaza are more than double those

About three fourths of Palestinians are now living in poverty measured at under US $2 a day.

---

[7]The Palestinian Red Crescent Society (PRCS)

[8]Report by the US Agency for International Development (USAID) and Johns Hopkins University, 2002

[9]Physical and Institutional Damage Assessment – West Bank Governorates, March-May, 2002 by the Donor Support Group, Local Aid Coordination Committee, May 2002

that prevailed in the US during the Great Depression. The decline in GNP in the Palestinian territories is also significantly greater than the GNP decline during that period.

Insecurity and desperation are among the unquantifiable, yet profound, human costs of occupation. Through affinity, empathy and intense media coverage, the Arab public identifies with the suffering. Furthermore, it witnesses, daily, the dwindling credibility of Israeli claims to respect for democracy and human rights.

THE OCCUPATION OF IRAQ

At the first draft stage of this report, a coalition led by the USA was preparing to wage war on Iraq ostensibly aimed at ridding the country of weapons of mass destruction that the coalition claimed Iraq possessed, as well as replacing a totalitarian regime by a democratic one. As the report was being completed, Iraq fell under Anglo-American occupation, following a war led by the United States, Great Britain and other partners.

This war against Iraq was waged without a mandate from the Security Council of the United Nations. Answering questions at a press conference in the Hague on March 11, 2003 the UN Secretary-General observed that: "If the US and others were to go outside the Council and take military action, it would not be in conformity with the Charter". In the event, the war was conducted in the face of strong popular opposition not only in Arab countries but also across the world, including in member countries of the coalition.

Although the full impacts of this war were not clear at the time of writing, the initial phase of military operations and the entry of occupation forces into Iraqi cities, including Baghdad, had had severe adverse effects on Iraq and its people.

Undoubtedly, the heaviest losses sustained by Iraq were the killing, injury and displacement of its citizens. Attack strategies and ammunition, including cluster bombs that did not distinguish between civilian and military targets, led to the killing, mutilation and dismemberment of a large number of Iraqis, in-

cluding many children, who will carry disabilities and disfigurements for life. Shrapnel covered large areas; parts of some bombs have not yet exploded and continue to threaten Iraqi civilians, particularly children. On 19 March 2003, Human Rights Watch urged the United States Secretary of State and the British Foreign Secretary to refrain from deploying cluster bombs in civilian areas, because of the unexploded ordnance they leave behind, which continues to threaten civilians well after hostilities cease.[10]

While the physical destruction has been enormous, it is the cultural destruction that has been particularly dismaying. The pillage and plunder of the Iraqi museum, the library and the Centre for Iraqi Arts under the gaze of occupying forces is a violation of the first Geneva protocol which stipulates the responsibility of occupying forces for the protection of cultural objects and religious places in order to preserve the cultural heritage of people who are subjects of occupation. Also the persecution of Iraqi scientists raises fears about its impact on scientific research and technological development in Iraq and more widely in the Arab region. These fears are underlined by the unprecedented restrictions imposed on some Arab scientists and students in Western universities.

This war has overthrown a totalitarian regime that oppressed the Iraqi people and deprived them of a wide spectrum of rights and freedoms. This regime had inflicted on Iraqis all manner of persecution and torture news of which was only whispered about before, while the aftermath of such acts is now revealed daily. The excesses of the previous regime did not stop at Iraq's borders; the attack on Kuwait in 1990 threatened Arab national security and caused harm to Arab collective action. The invasion and occupation of Iraq and the consequent destruction were not restricted to physical structures but also extended to the institutional infrastructure of services and security. Chaos spread and large numbers of Iraqis lost both livelihoods and security. This has, posed to Iraqis a new challenge of a different order, one which they will only be able to meet if they are empowered to determine their own future in accordance with international law; if

Occupation posed to Iraqis a new challenge of a different order, one which they will only be able to meet if they are empowered to determine their own future.

---

[10]Human Rights Watch, A letter to the United States and its allies on compliance with the laws of war, 19 March 2003

they are freed from occupation, and if they are allowed to recover their wealth and helped to build a system of good governance fully representative of the Iraqi people. These are the essential circumstances that would enable the people of Iraq to carry out quickly the reconstruction of their country from a human development perspective.

The repercussions of the occupation of Iraq do not stop at Iraq's borders. Developments in Iraq are bound to have significant consequences on human development throughout the region. For most Arabs, the war has been seen as an attempt at restructuring of the region by outside forces pursuing their own objectives.

In contrast, this series of reports on human development in Arab countries aims at stimulating the formulation of a strategic vision by Arab elites through a process of social innovation aimed at restructuring the region from within, with the ultimate objective of building human development in the Arab world. That vision of self-determined change is at the centre of the current report on building a knowledge society in Arab countries. There can be no doubt that, from a human development perspective, internal societal reforms based on scrupulous self-criticism are the most desirable and sustainable alternative to mapping the region's future from outside.

ARAB INTEGRATION

Six successive decades have witnessed some accomplishments in Arab integration, but the failures were larger, whether in terms of raising the level of integration and bringing it nearer to its final goals or of building Arab human development.

Looking at accomplishments, the 18 Arab states signatories to the Arab Free Trade Area treaty (AFTA) have been active in implementing its provisions. Trade was liberalized in 60% of products traded between states parties by January 2003. It is expected that all trade between states parties will be liberalized by January 2005.

At the level of global integration, eleven Arab states acceded to the World Trade Organization Agreement and five others are in the process of acceding to it. It is not clear, however, whether the current or future Arab member states will be diligent in taking advantage of the GATT provisions, which allow accession to regional trade arrangements. Doing so would mean that the membership of Arab states in WTO and AFTA would complement each other, which would enhance the ability of Arab countries to attract foreign investment from various sources to the whole Arab region.[11]

There is also a rush to adopt integration methods invented to suit the situations of developed societies although these have proved to be a failure in many developing country groupings. AFTA, for instance, is limited to trade in goods, which does not lead to the establishment of an Arab common market for services, capital and labour; nor does it imply the establishment of institutional infrastructures to regulate and control the flow of goods and services and factors of production.

In view of limited popular participation in decision-making processes at the country level, the Arab integration pattern has been marred by the weakness of such participation, namely neglect of the process by which Arab citizens are made aware of the measures and decisions which affect them and of which they are supposed to be the key beneficiaries. Thinking on trade has been limited to discussing the requirements of inter-trade liberalization and the resulting damage to existing interest groups and the struggle over exceptions from the liberalization process. Little thought has been given to the role of integration in enhancing productive efficiency and competitiveness at the pan-Arab and global levels.

In sum, the situation of Arab integration still falls short of the "Arab Free Citizenship Zone" called for by the first Arab Human Development Report.

For most Arabs, the war has been seen as an attempt at restructuring the region by outside forces pursuing their own objectives.

A vision of self-determined change is at the centre of the current report.

---

[11]This cannot be guaranteed in the cases of individual accession to global arrangements or association agreements with the European Union, for instance, without an Arab regional arrangement in the form of a customs union or a common market, because in the case of individual association there will be little incentive for foreign firms to locate their industries in the associated Arab country in view of the abolition of trade restrictions between that country and the associated industrial countries.

DEVELOPMENTS IN FREEDOM AND GOOD GOVERNANCE AS REFLECTED IN INTERNATIONAL DATABASES

This section is based on freedom and good governance indicators as accessed through international databases.[12] The authors recognise the disadvantages of relying on such international sources, yet are obliged to turn to them for lack of better alternatives from the region on this crucial dimension of human development. It is to be hoped that such Arabic alternatives will develop in the future, possibly inspired by this series of Arab Human Development Reports.

LEVEL OF CIVIL AND POLITICAL LIBERTIES (1990-2000)

The first AHDR (2002) measured freedom by using values of the indicator developed by Freedom House, which at that time stopped at 1998. At the time of writing this report, the indicator was available only up to 2000/2001 (Freedom House, 2002). It should be noted that freedom scores, as developed by Freedom House, are far from perfect measures and may reflect certain biases inherent in their source. Yet they constitute the only database currently available for measuring essential freedoms over time.

Figure 5 shows that while the general trend saw freedom rise worldwide, in most Arab countries it fell, with an apparent decline during the early 1990s. Arab countries, on average, continued to evince the lowest levels of freedom among the world regions compared.

In fact, according to this indicator, five Arab countries were among the ten least free countries in the world during 2000/2001.

INDICATORS OF VOICE AND ACCOUNTABILITY

International databases also provide indicators of voice and accountability (Kaufmann et al., 2002), which are among the essential requirements of good governance and which the first AHDR used to illuminate its case. Figure 6 illustrates that, despite a slight improvement in Arab countries between the two years considered, when it comes to voice and accountability, the Arab region still ranks lowest in the world.

PERCEPTIONS OF CORRUPTION IN BUSINESS TRANSACTIONS

Figure 7 presents the latest evaluations of perceptions of corruption in business transactions worldwide according to Transparency International (2002). The lowest values of this indicator are the worst (i.e., the most corrupt).

The figure does not indicate a noticeable improvement in the position of Arab countries in comparison to other world regions evaluated between the years 1998 and 2002. However, the position of one country, Egypt, improved slightly.

EVENTS INFLUENCING HUMAN DEVELOPMENT IN ARAB COUNTRIES

This section documents important events influencing Arab human development on the

Figure 5

**Freedom scores, weighted by population size:
the Arab region and other world regions, 1990-2000 (average values)**

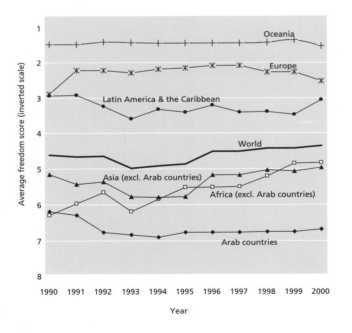

---

[12]Specifically, the 'Freedom Score' published by the US-based "Freedom House". For technical and practical reasons, the first Report made use of this indicator, despite some important reservations. These reasons include a long time series and a detailed database on various political and civil freedoms. In the absence of other comparable sources, the score is maintained here.

national level and examines their effects, both positive and negative. It focuses on two areas: widening freedoms and establishing good governance, and the empowerment of women. (Improvements in the field of knowledge acquisition, while also crucial, require a longer time horizon for assessment).

Probably the most far-reaching change that could have significantly improved prospects for human development in most Arab countries -- had it been adopted and launched effectively -- is the wide-ranging reform initiative declared by Saudi Crown Prince Abdullah at the beginning of 2003. The initiative covers the following dimensions:

"Self-reform and the development of political participation as two basic spring-boards for building Arab capabilities and making available all the conditions conducive to comprehensive Arab revitalisation; the strengthening of Arab co-operation and joint Arab capabilities; attaining the requirements for positive involvement in the arena of world competition; and the achievement of sustainable development." (Documents of the Arab Summit, March 2003, Al-Ahram, Cairo, in Arabic).

This initiative was to be presented to the Arab Summit during its March 2003 ordinary session in Bahrain. However, an urgent summit (held in Sharm El-Sheikh) took place before the Bahrain meeting and its communiqué lacked any reference to this initiative. Evidently the extraordinary circumstances under which the Sharm El-Sheikh summit was held, namely the looming invasion of Iraq, resulted in an agreement to postpone this initiative, at least for the time. As a result, the initiative was deferred to the next ordinary Summit, to be held in Tunisia.

EXPANDING THE SCOPE OF FREEDOM AND ESTABLISHING GOOD GOVERNANCE

While underlining the generally low rating of Arab countries on freedoms and the virtual absence of good governance, the first AHDR (2002) celebrated positive improvements in these key areas in two Arab countries: Morocco and Bahrain.

Encouraging developments in Bahrain

Figure 6

Voice and accountability:
the Arab region and other world regions

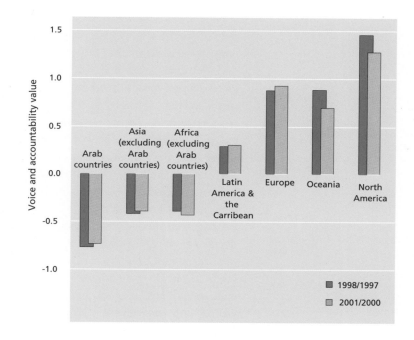

1997/98-2000/2001 (average values)

Figure 7

Perceptions of corruption, Transparency International: position of Arab countries in the sample, 1998 and 2000

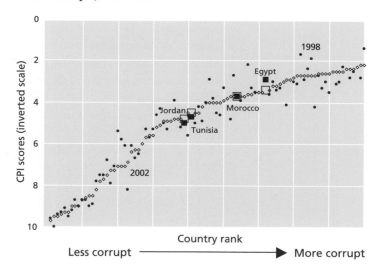

seem to have continued. The State Security Act, a statute and symbol of coercion in the country, was repealed. It was also announced that the country will guarantee the freedom to form non-governmental scientific, cultural and professional societies as well labour unions, and that strikes are a legitimate means of defending the rights of workers. Moreover, the establishment of "political societies" was permitted. The scope of freedom of speech was widened with the assistance of the judiciary. The Prince of Bahrain declared that the country had been transformed into a constitutional monarchy. The first legislative elections in more than 20 years were held, despite boycotts by some political movements. The government resigned after the announcement of the election results, and the legislative council, comprising elected and appointed members, held its first session on 24 December 2002. Less encouraging was the issuance of a decree (47 of 2002) allowing the confiscation or banning of any publication considered to hold the official religion in contempt, or criticising the king or the policies of the government. (Human Rights Watch, 2001).

In Morocco legislative elections, judged to have been honest, were held. They were notable for a quota reserved for women on national lists, which contributed to a large number of women winning seats. The government changed afterwards.

Positive developments in the field of freedom and good governance included the issuance by the Sudanese President of a decree permitting opposition parties to engage in political activity, provided that they keep to peaceful approaches.

In a development that protects the rights of the Berber minorities in Algeria, the "Amazig" language was classified as a national language and will be taught in the educational curriculum.

Djibouti permitted the establishment of opposition parties and political pluralism. A number of opposition newspapers were allowed in Syria and Tunis while Egypt and Syria moved to authorise private (non-governmental) broadcasting stations to operate.

Parliamentary elections were also held in Yemen in April 2003 – the third such elections since unification in 1990. About 1400 candidates competed in 301 electoral constituencies under relatively peaceful conditions and with a 70% voter turn-out. At the

end of the month, results were declared in 280 constituencies. One woman won.

A number of detainees in Syria, Tunisia, Libya, Yemen, and Morocco were released and several Government officials in Libya and Egypt were tried and convicted upon charges of corruption and profiteering.

Qatar held a referendum in April 2003 on a permanent constitution that allows for a consultative council composed of 45 members, two-thirds of whom are elected, with the right to question ministers and expel them with a two-thirds majority. This preliminary constitution did not allow the establishment of political parties. The Prince preserved the authority to appoint the prime minister and cabinet.

Yet in most Arab countries the march of freedom continued to encounter obstacles.

In one Arab country the deaths of detainees as a result of suspected torture persisted; 11 cases in total were recorded during 2001, all of whom had been detained for public law offences (The Arab Organisation for Human Rights, in Arabic, 2002). The extraction of confessions under torture and the trial of opposition members affiliated with Islamic movements before exceptional courts were also documented occurrences (ibid). The harassment of Islamic activists accelerated with the aim of restricting their participation in legislative elections. In addition, demonstrations were suppressed (including those protesting economic decisions made by the government).

In another Arab country, laws and procedures curtailing freedom, notably press freedom and Internet access, were enacted. A law stipulating the addition of further firm restrictions on freedom of assembly was issued; and the arrest of activists against normalisation of relations with Israel continued. Legislative elections were postponed. However, towards the end of 2002 promises were made to conduct elections in the spring of 2003, to allocate a quota for women in the legislative council and to "raise the ceiling" of freedom for the media and unions.

In a third Arab country, the prince made a statement prohibiting the existence of political parties.

In most Arab countries the march of freedom continued to encounter obstacles.

In yet another country, the President of the Republic reduced the mandate of members of parliament, and the level of participation in elections (May 2002) decreased to less than 20%. In two provinces with minority constituents, it fell to just 2%. Freedom of speech and expression remained under severe restriction, while a presidential statement characterised those criticising their country's policies as "traitors" punishable under the law. The persecution of human rights activists persisted and reportedly more than 1,000 political prisoners went on a hunger strike to demand their release (Arab Organisation for Human Rights, in Arabic, 2002). The Constitution was amended to allow the current President to remain in office for a fourth term: (the former Constitution stipulated only three terms).

The Al-Jazeera satellite channel was subjected to a number of injunctions restraining its activities in several Arab countries on a variety of claims.

Emergency laws were extended in a number of Arab countries, in one instance for three consecutive years. Moreover, the trial of civilians before military tribunals and exceptional State Security Courts persisted in six Arab countries (Egypt, Syria, Jordan, Tunisia, Lebanon, and Palestine).

Some Arab countries opted to impose constraints on popular expressions of support for the Palestinian resistance by harassing its activists, and even confronted popular demonstrations with violence. Security forces' suppression of demonstrations against the occupation of Palestine in an Arab country caused the killing of one university student and the serious wounding of ten others.

The issue of freedom in Arab countries has become a casualty of the overspill from the Anglo-American invasion of Iraq. The conflict between popular sentiments and official positions has led to security forces responding with force, tear-gas bombs and rubber bullets to quell popular demonstrations against the war on Iraq in more than one Arab country. Five men were killed in two Arab countries; two members of a people's assembly were arrested in a third country despite their parliamentary immunity.

CIVIL SOCIETY

Civil society organisations in many Arab countries suffered more legal and practical constraints.

In one Arab country, a law on NGOs was passed which was widely regarded as restricting their activities. It came after the Supreme Constitutional Court had ruled the previous law unconstitutional, for formal reasons.

In another country, an association for citizen rights was closed by an order from the Minister of the Interior, after it allegedly committed financial and administrative violations. A number of activists in professional unions were arrested, apparently for being involved in resisting normalisation with Israel.

In a third country, the President of the Association for Human Rights and some human rights activists were tried under the charges of introducing and distributing publications without permission, as well as spreading false news abroad.

THE EMPOWERMENT OF WOMEN

The cause of women's empowerment, and that of freedom in general, was dealt a strong blow when the elected legislative council in an Arab country rejected a government proposal aimed at allowing women to exercise their political rights. Moreover, the constitutional court in this country refused two challenges filed by two women activists demanding political rights for women.

In Bahrain, women won the right to vote and to stand for election to municipal and legislative assemblies. This important constitutional victory, however, was dampened by the failure of women candidates in both elections – seemingly for reasons of a societal nature.

On a more positive note, in a historical precedent resulting from the allocation of quotas for women on national lists, Morocco's recently elected Parliament convened with thirty-three women members, the largest number ever.

Other affirmative action for women included Djibouti's decision to allocate quotas for women in legislative councils (a minimum 10% share for both men and women in party electoral lists was established) and similar

The issue of freedom in Arab countries has become a casualty of the overspill from the Anglo-American invasion of Iraq.

steps in Jordan allocating a minimum of six seats for women.

More broadly, the ruler of the United Arab Emirates affirmed the right of women to engage in political activity. In Qatar, a woman won, for the first time, a seat in a local council and, at the beginning of 2003, a woman was appointed minister of education. The Kuwaiti government adopted a draft law allowing women to join the security forces. In the Sultanate of Oman, women were allowed to drive taxis and to carry passengers of both sexes. In Yemen a woman was appointed as a State Minister for Human Rights and one woman entered Parliament in a 2003 election. And in a sudden development early in 2003, Egypt joined other Arab countries in allowing women to serve on the Judiciary by appointing a female attorney-at-law as the first woman judge on the Supreme Constitutional Court and appointing two women as commissioners before that court.

The political emancipation of Arab women called for in the first AHDR evidently still has a long way to go; yet the new progress made in this period is evidence of a greater receptivity to women's empowerment at the executive levels of governments and state institutions.

Evidently, the core challenges to human development in Arab countries, as epitomised in the "three deficits" identified by the first AHDR, are still critically pertinent. Arguably, those challenges are even graver than before, especially with respect to freedom. World and regional developments unfavourable to Arab human development have exacerbated these negative trends.

The second part of this report aims to make a continuing contribution to Arab human development through a detailed study of one of the three cardinal deficits – knowledge. This study culminates in a strategic vision for building the knowledge society in Arab countries.

PART II

Section one: the concept of an Arab knowledge society

The Report starts, in Chapter 1, with a conceptual discussion of knowledge as it relates to Arab countries. It defines what is meant by knowledge and sets out an analytical framework for examining the current status and cultural, social, economic and political context of knowledge acquisition, the main subjects of this Report. The chapter contrasts the requirements of a knowledge society with the characteristics of Arab societies, historically and at the present time. The discussion identifies the key challenges that later chapters take up in detail.

CHAPTER 1

 Conceptual framework: knowledge, human development and the knowledge society in Arab countries

This series of Arab Human Development Reports (AHDR) was designed so that the first issue, published in June 2002, offered a comprehensive treatment of human development in Arab countries according to the definition adopted by the series and recapitulated in Part I of this issue. Subsequent issues were to examine, in depth, specific challenges that are of essential importance to human development in those countries. This practice starts with this second issue of the series, dedicated to the topic of "knowledge".

This chapter lays out the conceptual basis for exploring issues of knowledge and defines what is meant by the "knowledge society". Subsequently, it discusses briefly some questions raised as a result of contrasting the characteristics of the "knowledge society" with those of present-day Arab societies. These questions, and the challenges they pose, will be further tackled in subsequent chapters of this Report. It ends by highlighting a major challenge to knowledge in Arab countries, namely the need to create strong, effective and increasing societal demand for knowledge supported by adequate purchasing power.

WHY FOCUS ON KNOWLEDGE?

Knowledge is recognised as a cornerstone of human development, a means of expanding people's capabilities and choices and a tool for overcoming human poverty. In the 21st century, knowledge is also increasingly a dynamic factor of production and a powerful driver of productivity and human capital. The first AHDR identified a serious shortfall in knowledge acquisition, absorption and use as one of three cardinal deficits undermining human development in Arab countries. This second Report starts where the first left off and takes an in-depth look at the causes and conse-

quences of the relative backwardness of the Arab region in this vital arena.

The first AHDR highlighted how weak knowledge bases and stagnant knowledge development condemn many Arab countries to fragile productive power and reduced development opportunities. It is now a commonplace that the knowledge gap, rather than the income gap, determines the prospects of countries in today's world economy. In addition, a consensus is emerging that the gap between developing and developed countries in *the capacity to produce knowledge* is wider than the knowledge gap itself. This calls for serious efforts to regenerate knowledge production in the developing world.

The Report assumes that countries with deficient knowledge capabilities have much to gain by moving towards the "knowledge society" since the developmental returns on knowledge acquisition increase in societies suffering a knowledge deficit. Such societies can take advantage of the abundant stock of knowledge, experience and best practice available worldwide. They can learn from the mistakes and profit from the achievements of early knowledge leaders. In a comparative perspective, for Arab countries, the need to invest in knowledge is great and the dividends that can be realized are proportionately large.

For Arab countries, the need to invest in knowledge is great and the dividends that can be realized are proportionately large.

THE ACQUISITION OF KNOWLEDGE AND HUMAN DEVELOPMENT

Knowledge is one of the few human resources that does not perish, but rather proliferates through consumption.

KNOWLEDGE

Knowledge consists of data, information[1], instructions, and ideas, or the sum total of symbolic structures possessed by individual human beings or by society at large. These symbolic structures guide individual and institutional human behaviour in all walks of life and in all spheres of public and private activity.

Knowledge includes, for instance, the symbolic structures which are acquired through formal education and experiences learned from work and life. It also encompasses facts, stories, pictures and any mental construct informing human behaviour, whether documented, oral or implicit. The *institutional* knowledge of a society includes history, culture, strategic orientations and organisational forms.

Consequently, knowledge can be *explicit* (recorded in one form or another) or *implicit* (in the form of spontaneous behavioural prescriptions, for example). Moreover, the production of knowledge is not limited to the standard forms of science and scientific research, it also spans knowledge embodied in the various forms of artistic and literary expression and in both popular and formal cultures[2].

Knowledge transcends the mere acquisition of information. Indeed, information overload in the age of the Internet, media saturation and fast communication can sometimes smother true knowledge. The explosion of readily available data, opinions, articles, documents and other types of content triggered by the digital revolution can be overwhelming and requires a process of selection, extraction and judgment in order to retrieve useful and usable knowledge. Moreover, while knowledge ranks higher than information on the scale of human values, it is one step lower than wisdom, which entails a commitment to high human ideals such as freedom, justice and human dignity.

In all human systems, only a small amount of total organised knowledge is recorded. In human systems where the acquisition of knowledge is weak, the extent of *unrecorded* and implicit knowledge residing in individual and collective knowledge models, in the culture and in spontaneous prescriptions for human conduct, is still often substantial.

One of the quintessential, and seemingly contradictory, characteristics of knowledge is *that it grows with use*. Knowledge is one of the few human resources that does not perish, but rather proliferates through consumption.

It is useful to draw a distinction, on the

BOX 1.2

Collective learning: a means for developing knowledge capital or reinforcing the status quo?

In all societies there is a number, large or small, of people who possess some knowledge. The challenge of building knowledge capital within a human system, however, resides in converting individual knowledge to collective knowledge.

A large amount of knowledge exists in the minds of individuals in the form of answers to the questions: how and why? This constitutes a knowledge model on the individual level. A higher order type of knowledge is acquired through conceptual learning, which can change knowledge frameworks and thus the world-view of individuals. Conceptual learning can be distinguished from lower order procedural learning, which simply leads to changes in actions. A change in the knowledge model occurs when new actions, embedded in new knowledge frameworks, are established. Generally speaking, it can be said that individual knowledge models arise from a world-view (Weltenschaung) of the system embedded in the general knowledge model internalised by system members.

This discussion raises questions as to the content of the dominant knowledge model in the Arab world and whether it reinforces or hinders human development.

Most human systems possess common knowledge models that aim to protect the status quo and to entrench it in the form of conservative societal institutions, knowledge transmission mechanisms, and reward systems. Such models deter members of these societies from challenging the status quo and deprive them of opportunities for learning. From a developmental point of view, such learning is not useful and could be harmful. An example of this type of learning in Arab countries is the widespread culture of myths and the supernatural.

Controversy often springs up around what could be deemed useful versus harmful learning. The controversy, in fact, reflects the differing social interests behind these viewpoints. The only way out of this impasse is to adopt a decisive criterion.

In this case, it is suggested that the criterion be the extent of contribution to building human development, according to the definition adopted by this Report in Part I. This is the measure by which the elements of the Arab knowledge model must be judged, so that those features enhancing human development may be identified and fostered.

---

[1] The conversion of data to information requires processing such as evaluation and analysis.

[2] It is accepted that many technologies embedded in popular knowledge provide brilliant solutions to local problems. Consider, for example, the use of palm-tree stems in reinforcing buildings and roofs in Arab desert environments, which surpasses "modern" technologies in combating the harshness of the tough desert climate. This is also evident in the case of popular medicine in developing countries, especially in Latin America, where indigenous cures can have real commercial value. Several multinationals have rushed to possess this popular 'know-how', and convert it into monopolised knowledge through patents.

[3] The term "capital" is not limited to financial assets. The term in English means "man-made means of production" (Oxford Dictionary of Economic Terms, 1997).

level of society, between knowledge *wealth and knowledge capital*[3]. Knowledge wealth is the sum total of knowledge assets, or symbolic structures in society; knowledge capital is that part of knowledge wealth used in producing new knowledge, which in turn leads to the further growth of knowledge wealth.

The knowledge wealth of a given society extends, at least in principle, to the general, and ever-renewable, stock of human knowledge. However, two types of impediments hamper the free use of this stock. First, aspects of the institutional structure and the societal context of the knowledge system in the society itself can present internal obstacles. Second, features of the international context of knowledge acquisition can interpose barriers, as will be outlined in a later section.

Effective knowledge is knowledge that is widely disseminated, absorbed and used. The most fundamental driver of that process, on the individual or the societal levels, is *learning*. Individual and collective learning are two of the most important capabilities for building knowledge capital.

KNOWLEDGE AND HUMAN DEVELOPMENT

In the broad concept of human development, acquiring knowledge is a fundamental human *entitlement*. People, simply by virtue of being human, have a right to knowledge as a public good. At the same time, knowledge acquisition is also a *means* of achieving human development, since it enables people to enlarge their capabilities and widen their horizon of choice. Moreover, in the present phase of human progress, the acquisition, absorption and production of knowledge drive social and economic *transformation*. Knowledge can liberate individuals and societies from human poverty in a given cultural context and elevate them to higher planes of human existence. Thus, in human development terms, knowledge is multi-dimensional: an inherent human faculty and a basic human right, a human product and that which enhances what it means to be human in the first place.

In the developing world, knowledge acquired and expressed through education and learning, research and technological development, and literary and artistic forms in both popular and formal cultures -- together with the effective use of such knowledge in societal activities - will not only increasingly expand the frontiers of human potential. It will also be the means to enlarge the scope of human freedoms and to guarantee those freedoms through good governance and the promotion of equity and human fulfilment. Knowledge will thus serve the loftier goals of freedom, justice and human dignity.

As noted previously, knowledge has become an essential factor of production, and a basic determinant of productivity. There is a strong connection between knowledge acquisition and the productive capacity of a society. This connection figures prominently in high value-added production activities, which are increasingly based on knowledge intensity, and which lead to the rapid obsolescence of knowledge, technology and skills. Such activities are the mainstay of competitiveness worldwide, they will create the wealth of the future and they therefore constitute a major gateway to development for developing countries.

Yet in most developing countries, the knowledge system faces a dual crisis. On the one hand, the system itself suffers from the

Knowledge is multi-dimensional: an inherent human faculty, a human product and that which enhances what it means to be human.

BOX 1.3

Economic characteristics of knowledge

Knowledge has special features that determine its economic character.

Knowledge is non-spatial. It can traverse distances and borders at high speed, especially when digitised. Knowledge is also durable. It does not perish by being transferred from its owner to whoever demands it. This means that it can exist endlessly without any need for further production.

Some types of demand stimulate the reproduction of knowledge itself, at an additional cost to meet particular needs or preferences. Such preferences include reducing the cost of knowledge, or the time taken for its production, or its closer adaptation to the particular circumstances and resources of a society or its environmental requirements. Developing countries have a particular stake in expressing this latter preference, or taking adaptation into their own hands.

In practice, much knowledge is transferred to developing countries in forms originally developed for rich countries. This can reduce the value of knowledge transfers, and waste scarce resources. Such arrangements often burden poorer countries with additional and sometimes unjustified requirements, as in the case of conditions governing franchises. They can also impose requirements for expertise or capital assets not available locally. This reduces the benefits to developing countries of technology transfers owing to high transaction costs and the absence of domestic systems that would allow such countries to derive the maximum benefits from imported technology.

Hence the value of knowledge does not necessarily lie in its abstract content but rather in how much it can contribute to finding solutions to problems affecting a society at a particular time.

Source: Mohammed Mahmud Al-Imam, background paper for AHDR2.

---

backwardness of the society of which it is an inseparable part, and its efficiency and impact are limited by restrictions emanating from its societal context. In some less developed societies, rooted constructs, concepts and precepts may actively hinder human development. Those symbolic structures need to be challenged by other knowledge structures that stimulate or enhance human development. Moreover, the elements of the knowledge system in developing countries are typically dispersed in various individual and non-formal forms. Dispersion makes it difficult to assess and manage knowledge wealth, let alone amalgamate scattered assets into an effective knowledge system built on firm knowledge capital.

On the other hand, the principal hope for overcoming underdevelopment and achieving competitiveness in developing countries is precisely a mobilised, well-organised and well functioning knowledge system. No other development investment promises greater exponential returns in an era of knowledge intensity and knowledge-driven competition. Cutting this Gordian knot is one of the most formidable challenges facing developing countries today.

SOCIAL DETERMINANTS OF KNOWLEDGE ACQUISITION

The global stock of knowledge is renewable and grows ceaselessly. Yet its human, cultural and economic potential will not blossom in any country where the social climate does not actively encourage knowledge acquisition, dissemination, production and use. A system of knowledge can be sustained or stunted by the social soil in which it grows and by the surrounding regional and global environment. These conditions influence whether education, learning, R&D and literary and artistic expression flourish or fail and therefore whether productivity and human development prosper or not.

Regional issues take on special significance for Arab countries, whose small markets logically point towards greater regional integration. The dominance of the global economy poses different challenges. Experience suggests that attempts by each Arab country to

belong to the world on its own usually result in that country assuming a marginal and dependent position.

A society that does not clearly incentivise knowledge acquisition and use through education, technical research and development and all kinds of literary and artistic expression traps itself on the lowest rungs of learning. A society that does not value knowledge highly does not provide for the knowledge acquisition system the necessary resources and social environment for its effective activity. The outcome is lower productivity and lagging human development.

The four most significant aspects of the societal context affecting Arab knowledge systems are: links with societal activities, especially production; the role of the state; the regional context; and the international environment. The first and second aspects are discussed next; the regional and international contexts are taken up in chapter 8.

Strong links between the knowledge acquisition system and societal activity

In a well functioning knowledge system, the enterprise sector (both public and private) and government and civil society organisations are dynamically connected. Such linkages energise the system and maximise its role in advancing productivity. For example, the modern conception of technological development demands a symbiotic link between societal activity sites and research institutions. This contrasts with the older, one-way view that technology is an *application* to society of scientific discoveries in research institutions. As a second example, the best education, especially in technical fields, cannot play a vigorous societal role without a strong connection to labour markets, firms, factories and enterprises.

A vigorous role for the state and all its institutions

This second aspect is particularly important in developing countries, where the "knowledge market" is traditionally notorious for failure. Knowledge, in the language of economics, is a public good whose producer does not necessarily capture all the returns on the initial investment. It is also non-rivalrous: its use by one party does not prevent others from using it. As such, the returns to knowledge production accrue to society as a whole rather than exclusively to its producer.

Where knowledge is concerned, the relative weakness of the profit motive discourages profit-oriented enterprises from investing in knowledge production, especially in developing countries. Leaving knowledge acquisition entirely to the for-profit sector in less developed countries thereby risks reducing the supply of knowledge and depriving weaker social groups of its benefits. At the global level, this market failure can actively retard knowledge acquisition by developing countries and, as happens at the national level, leave the weaker social categories in those countries facing the greatest knowledge deprivation. The World Bank Report on Knowledge for Development (1998) emphasises these matters in more than one respect and concludes by stressing the decisive role of the state in developing countries in fostering efficient knowledge acquisition.

It is true that the for-profit sector plays a major role in the knowledge acquisition system in developed economies. However, the role played by the state remains pivotal, particularly in fostering basic research and education, areas that do not yield quick, tangible profits in developing countries yet which are indispensable to any vital knowledge acquisition system in the long run. In most developed countries, the role of the state was strongest during periods of nation building, a phase still in progress in most developing, particularly Arab, countries.

The role of the state is especially decisive in developing countries undergoing economic adjustments that excessively curtail the state's societal functions and services. At the same time, newer approaches to economic growth and development recognise that state activism does not stop at merely overcoming "market failure" but extends to taking initiatives in the public interest and becoming actively involved in knowledge acquisition and public innovation.

Ultimately, how dynamically a society participates in knowledge acquisition and how effectively such knowledge serves human development depends on societal structures:

cultural, social, economic, and political. The presence and efficiency of key societal institutions are also key factors, as will be discussed later.

THE KNOWLEDGE SOCIETY

It is now understood that the cognitive assets of society -- knowledge and expertise -- and not its material assets -- raw materials or financial and physical capital -- increasingly determine its productivity and competitiveness.

The term "knowledge society" refers to this current phase in the evolution of human progress, as it is unfolding in advanced societies.

Specifically, the knowledge society is organised around the dissemination and production of knowledge and its efficient utilisation in all societal activities: the economy, civil society, politics, and private life, in a continuous quest to advance human development.

In such a society, knowledge plays a paramount role in shaping social structures; in influencing the performance of the economy, society and polity; and in changing the occupations and life-styles of its citizens as the knowledge content of their daily lives intensifies steadily. In a knowledge society, the number of workers in the knowledge system, as well as their share of the total work force, rises. In addition, the ratio of work time devoted to knowledge-intensive activities increases for all workers.

In economic terms, building the knowledge society in Arab countries means shifting towards a knowledge mode of production in place of the *rentier* mode of production[4] that currently dominates most parts of the region.

In a knowledge society, societal institutions belonging to the knowledge system, either as producers or disseminators, are many, varied and interconnected. The knowledge society guarantees a social context conducive to the vitality of the knowledge system. Eventually, a "knowledge culture" evolves, embodying values motivating the acquisition and use of knowledge. This culture is supported by effective societal incentives for disseminating and producing knowledge. In

State activism does not stop at merely overcoming "market failure" but extends to taking initiatives in the public interest .

The cognitive assets of a society, and not its material assets, increasingly determine its productivity and competitiveness.

[4]This applies to countries where economic value is basically derived from depleting raw materials, either directly in oil-producing countries, or indirectly in others through dependence on aid and expatriate workers' remittances from the former.

short, a virtuous circle develops between the effectiveness of the knowledge system and the extent of support it receives from the societal context.

In other words, the challenge of knowledge acquisition consists of transforming society from a system that comprises some knowledgeable individuals to a societal system *fully* anchored in the production and dissemination of knowledge and its efficient utilisation in advancing human development

As noted earlier, societies possess a huge amount of knowledge scattered in individual reservoirs in institutions, in people's minds and in a variety of media. Less formalised knowledge assets are implicit in the spontaneous activity of individuals and the popular culture of the society. Nevertheless, a rational societal leadership can mobilise uncoordinated institutions and dispersed knowledge through a deliberate societal programme. The potential dividends are handsome and will serve the strategic purpose of building human development.

To put this challenge in one sentence, the knowledge society means instituting knowledge as the organising principle of human life.

The knowledge society means instituting knowledge as the organising principle of human life.

To put it in a regional context, it can be said, without prevarication, that Arab countries are far removed from such a society.

Indeed, the divide between developing countries, including Arab countries, and knowledge societies is large and widening rapidly. Chapter 4, on the measurement of knowledge, reveals this gap clearly as reflected in the different performances of Arab countries and the East Asian "Tigers" in accumulating human capital.

Some analysts (e.g., Az-Zayyat, in Arabic, 2003) go so far as to maintain that if developing countries are to catch up with agile knowledge societies, they will have to pursue a path of *exponential* growth, (Figure 1-1). Adopting such a path is a tall order: it requires accelerating the dissemination, production and utilisation of knowledge in developing countries at rates faster than those which historically prevailed in today's knowledge societies. This steep gradient should be taken to indicate the seriousness of the challenges developing countries face if they seek to build the knowledge society starting from initial conditions today.

KNOWLEDGE ACQUISITION SYSTEMS

The conversion of knowledge wealth to knowledge capital and the efficient use of knowledge capital in producing new forms of knowledge requires two connected societal processes. The first is the dissemination of available knowledge, whereas the second is the production of new forms of knowledge in all fields: natural sciences, social sciences, the humanities, arts, literature, and all other societal activities. The efficiency of both activities rests on vigorous and efficient societal institutions and social processes.

These are complex systems reflecting the specificity of society, history, culture, and institutions. The success of these systems depends on the fluent exchange of knowledge among all units that produce and utilise knowledge such that the productivity of each unit, and of the societal system as a whole, is optimised.

The societal processes and institutions used in building and utilising knowledge capital in the dissemination and production of

Figure 1.1

Bridging the knowledge gap through exponential growth in knowledge acquisition

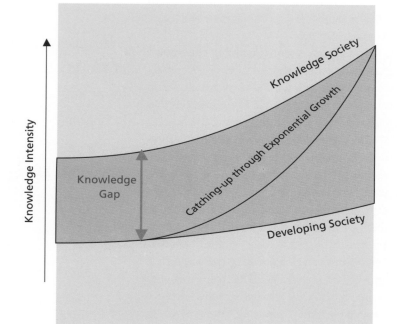

knowledge vary and interact, especially in profit-seeking enterprises, which are expected to contribute effectively to knowledge acquisition, and in particular to technological development in a free market economy.

As a result of this multiplicity, the efficiency of knowledge dissemination and production depends on the organisational context that surrounds such processes and institutions and supports the relationships among them. The coherence of this *organisational context* is an important factor in building the knowledge society.

In less advanced societies, the organisational context surrounding the dissemination and production of knowledge is inefficient. Yet such organisation is the key to knowledge management, transfer, indigenisation and production. Both the state and the enterprise sector have a high stake in the efficiency of these organisational relationships.

Even so, the organisational context is only one component among the complex societal determinants of a successful knowledge system. It is the closest component to the functioning of the system itself. But it depends, in turn, on other important structures, which might seem farther away from the system but which have a stronger impact, positive or negative, on the formation of knowledge capital and knowledge wealth. The crucial structures governing the *societal* context of the knowledge system, particularly from the perspective of the Arab world, include the prevalent *culture, socio-economic structure,* and *political and legal context.* All of these exist in an influential *regional and global environment.*

Culture embraces several components, such as intellectual heritage, religion, and language. The socio-economic structure pertains to modes of production, growth and wealth distribution and to the societal incentive system associated with that structure. The political and legal context governs the processes and institutions of knowledge dissemination and production; especially important in this respect is the status of the key freedoms of speech, opinion and assembly.

All of these components are surrounded by, and subject to the *regional and global* environment of knowledge acquisition. This two-tier environment is especially relevant where

Arab countries are concerned in light of escalating regional challenges and accelerating globalisation.

Figure (1-2) illustrates the elements of the knowledge system and the societal context that affects it as discussed in this Report. The numbered elements correspond to the Report's chapters.

The diagram shows three rings that surround the heart of the knowledge system, knowledge capital, which is discussed in Chapter Four. All elements of the system are subject to two environments – the regional and the international – that influence them. Knowledge capital is circled by the two rings of knowledge acquisition - dissemination (Chapter Two) and production (Chapter Three). This knowledge acquisition subsystem is in turn surrounded by the organisational context for knowledge (Chapter Five). All the foregoing elements are surrounded by the cultural context (Chapter Six) and the socio-economic structure for knowledge (Chapter Seven). The last ring, the political context, and the regional and international environment, are discussed in Chapter Eight.

The establishment of a knowledge society in the Arab world, in the conceptual setting il-

Organisation is the key to knowledge management, transfer, indigenisation and production.

Figure 1.2:

The knowledge system: a schematic representation

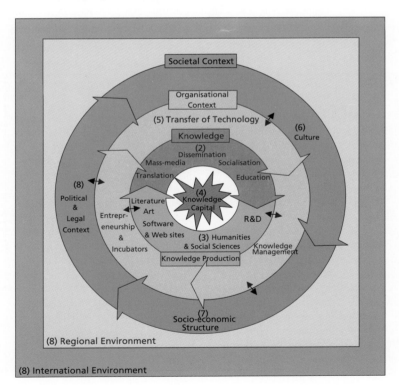

lustrated here, poses considerable challenges, which are taken up in the Report.

ARABS AND KNOWLEDGE

A LONG, MIXED HISTORY LEADING TO CHALLENGES TODAY

The Arab world has a long and mixed history of knowledge acquisition. The first AHDR (2002) concluded that Arab countries have fallen far behind in acquiring knowledge, this now being one of the three main deficits impeding their human development at the beginning of the 21st century. Nevertheless, history tells us that Arabs, in previous epochs, contributed substantially to the production of knowledge and by extension to enriching the global stock of human knowledge. From this perspective, building the knowledge society in Arab countries reclaims one of the brightest treasures of Arab history.

This historical paradox raises an essential question: how can the Arab world truly internalize knowledge acquisition? How can the region move beyond merely importing scientific and technological products in the form of goods and services from companies and institutions abroad?

This question has preoccupied many scholars, intellectuals, politicians and others over the last two centuries. It represents the largest challenge facing the contemporary

Building the knowledge society in Arab countries reclaims one of the brightest treasures of Arab history.

Arab world, which has not succeeded yet in indigenising knowledge as a social institution and an authentic cultural dimension.

The question is actually a cognitive challenge that concerns most developing countries. But in order to avoid over-generalisation it is useful to clarify some distinctive features of the Arab world, both inherited and acquired. Some of these features could help, while others could impede the successful indigenisation of modern knowledge.

THE ARAB KNOWLEDGE CIVILISATION: SOME SIGNIFICANT FEATURES

Islamic culture cannot be properly understood without investigating its scholarly character.

History shows that, with the beginning of the Abbasid state, a scholarly renaissance commenced, one hardly less important than that which transformed Europe during the 17th century. To understand this scholarly renaissance, some factors must be kept in mind.

The first is the role of the political and social authorities of the day in encouraging learning and providing the material requirements and the human capital for knowledge development. The reputations of the Abbasid Caliphs, who established libraries and observatories, were built precisely on this role. This state of affairs continued even after the disintegration of the caliphate and the division of the Islamic world into competing states, each with its own centres of scholarship. These new developments led to the creation of the "scholarly city" with its various and rival colleges. Looking at Baghdad during the mid-third century of the Islamic era reveals a city of thriving scholarship, with scholarly institutions representing various groups.

The second factor stemmed from the material and cultural needs of the new community. The vast new state, teeming with multiple cultures and systems, called out for development and unification. These two challenges prompted the resort to scientific scholarship. The extraction of groundwater, the digging of canals, the establishment of cities, the extension of roads, the organisation of ministries (*diwans*), the levying of taxes, the survey of lands and other activities led to the unification

---

BOX 1.4

A Cauldron of Cultures

"The rich legacy of Islamic civilizations, historians argue, is due in part to its exceptional absorptive quality and relative tolerance for different cultures and ethnic traditions of civilizations from southern Europe to Central Asia."

"Not merely translators, the Abbasids collected, synthesized and advanced knowledge, building their own civilization from intellectual gifts from many cultures, including the Chinese, Indian, Iranian, Egyptian, North African, Greek, Spanish, Sicilian and Byzantine. This Islamic period was indeed a cauldron of cultures, religions, learning and knowledge—one that created great civilizations and influenced others from Africa to China. This

Golden Age has been hailed for its open embrace of a universal science, no matter the source—believing that there was not a "Christian science," "Jewish science," "Muslim science," "Zoroastrian science" or "Hindu science." There was just one science for the Abbasids, who were apparently influenced by numerous Qur'anic references to learning about the wonders of the universe as a way to honor God. Thus, reason and faith, both being God-given, were combined, mutually inclusive and supportive. Islam was anything but isolationist, and Abbasids connected to all cultural traditions, believing as they did that learning was universal, and not confined to their own domain."

Vartan Gregorian, Islam: A Mosaic Not a Monolith
President's Essay, 2001 Annual Report, Carnegie Corporation.

of calculation systems and the utilisation of algebra and geometry. *Sciences were applied to solving practical problems.* Moreover, religious duties, such as fasting, praying, and Hajj (the holy pilgrimage to Mecca) were accompanied by astrological research, which had a great impact on the progress of astronomy. The science of timing and the new social occupation of the "timer" led to the assimilation of scientific research in traditional culture. The development of mathematics and algebra was spurred by the appearance of new ministries and another new social occupation -- that of the scribe. Other examples of applied study can be cited in medicine, chemistry and mechanical engineering. Indeed, *science and its applications became a part of social practice*, through teaching and research. Scholarship was never marginal in the Islamic-Arab city, or in the popular culture. It was one of the main attributes of Arab culture even at the time of decline.

The third factor contributing to the scientific renaissance was that it was preceded by a renaissance in the humanities and the social sciences: specifically, in scholastic theology, linguistics, history, jurisprudence, religious exegesis and other disciplines. The rise of these scholarly fields paved the way for the development of mathematical and other sciences. To cite one example, *Kitab al-'Ain*, by al-Khalil bin-Ahmad, was the *first lexicographic work in history*. This work required scrupulous knowledge of phonetics as well as of the principles of combinatorial mathematics in order to draw up tables of words. In fact, several studies in the humanities raised questions that required drawing on or developing scientific answers. The rise of the humanities provided a large audience to those concerned with science and with language tools and it prepared the Arabic language to receive new forms of knowledge.

This *explosion of learning included all branches of knowledge at the time*; it did not favour some to the exclusion of others. Thus, it included theoretical branches and the applications related to the needs of the new community. *In this way, learning became an essential component of the popular culture*, and was not confined to matters of religion, language and literature. An appetite for

knowledge became one of the hallmarks of Arab culture. It was evidenced by several anthologies exhaustively classifying old and new forms of scholarship, and it permeated popular culture as well.

The establishment of this new scholarly culture began with the transfer of the scholarship of the ancients, especially the Greeks. But on examining the scientific translation movement, particularly in astronomy and mathematics, another profound attribute becomes clear. *Translation is closely connected to scientific research and creativity.* The objective of the translation movement was not to establish a scientific library to enrich the palaces of caliphs and princes, but to *fulfil the needs of scientific research*. Without fully understanding this phenomenon, none of the outcomes of this movement, which undertook the most expansive translation of practical texts in history, can be appreciated.

The translators themselves were leaders of the scholarly movement; indeed, some of them were among its universal authorities, such as al-Hajjaj bin-Mattar, Thabit bin Qurrah, and Qusta bin Luqa. Moreover, the choice of books and the timing of this choice were closely related to what was being researched. To take just one example, when Thabit bin Qurrah translated several books from Apollonius – the finest and most difficult writing in Greek geometry – he needed them in his new mathematical research, especially that related to calculating areas and sizes. The connection between scientific translation and advanced scientific research is not only an historical fact, but also explains why researchers active in astronomy and mathematics undertook so much translation in those fields. It also illustrates some of the attributes of linguistic translation.

A far-reaching result of this meeting between two currents of study -- one in the humanities and languages, the other in scientific research -- was the rise of the scientific Arabic language. This new medium took two simultaneous paths, translation and creativity, reflected in the invention of new sciences unknown to the ancients. Perhaps the most important attributes of the new knowledge produced by Arab culture at this time were: 1) A new mathematical rationality; 2)

Scholarship was never marginal in the Islamic-Arab city, or in the popular culture.

Translation is closely connected to scientific research and creativity.

Experimentation as a pattern of proof.

The new rationality may be described in two words, algebraic and analytic, while the introduction of experimentation, by al-Hassan bin al-Haitham as a criterion of proof in physics research, profoundly influenced both the material and human sciences. Taken together, these historical currents illustrate that the Arab scientific renaissance produced, in its own time, a knowledge society in the full sense of the term.

Oddly, lessons learned from this history of indigenous and acquired knowledge during the early Arab scientific and linguistic renaissance were not enlisted when the modernization of science became a central question in the Arab world. Attempts at scientific modernisation by Muhamad Ali and Gamal Abdel Nasser during the 19th and 20th centuries respectively neither drew nor built upon this legacy. Instead, leaders turned to imitating what the West offered. Neglecting this heritage and settling for the pragmatic importation of science and technology from 19th century Europe – an approach that still dominates the minds of officials and reformist intellectuals today -- was a missed opportunity, historically, and likely created a significant *impediment to establishing a knowledge society in the modern Arab world*

THE ARAB KNOWLEDGE MODEL TODAY

The modern Arab world is the scene of myriad intellectual currents each with its own social, political and ideological direction and sources. As in all other societies, these currents may meet intermittently without being subsumed into a single primordial frame of reference. There are Islamic fundamentalists and Islamic reformists. There are progressive, leftist, nationalist, liberal, technocratic and other intellectual movements. These movements are all variously reflected in writings on politics, history, society, economics, philosophy and science.

Such diversity of thought, though ostensibly a strength, also reflects a continuing crisis of identity and often results in conflict. This is the case despite the fact that Arab writers and intellectuals tackle common core issues --

backwardness and advancement, authenticity and modernity, the self and the other, the Arabs (Muslims) and the West. Such topics have persisted in writings and studies on Arab history, society and politics for more than a century. Indeed, to many, it appears that intellectual life in the Arab world has revolved around itself for several centuries without going beyond the self towards more productive and valuable fields of knowledge. When introspection succumbs to introversion, the wellsprings of creativity begin to run dry. A significant part of Arab intellectual endeavour seems to seek refuge in ideological headlines that either take the form of slogans to glorify and effect a nostalgic revival or that encourage self-pity, blame others for adversity and do not do justice to Arab societies.

These characteristics of intellectual output do not reflect any innate "inadequacy" in the "Arab mentality". Rather, they mirror a socio-political feature that is very common in contemporary Arab history, and which has a profound impact on culture, namely: – the dominance of the polity over intellectual products and their public reception.

The "self", the "other" and related concepts are deep structures requiring a close study of Arab sociology, history, and economics. Their depths are not easily fathomed amid a shifting reality. Yet it is clear that purveying general ideological statements, reducing complex reality and a rich past to a simple procession of glories and disgraces and venerating the heroic acts and struggles against humiliation of a few, do not yield accurate knowledge. One such (and all-too-common) example is simplifying the events of modern Arab history into a gallery of crude opposites: the authentic versus the inauthentic, local versus foreign, continuity versus rupture. Arab history in effect is narrated as though it had been solely one of alienation and corruption at a time when the Arab world had, in fact, witnessed valuable scientific, intellectual and cultural production, had experienced democracy, and had undergone momentous socio-political shifts. Failing to see history and heritage as living, ongoing and self-renewing human processes, where the march of progress is never complete, is misleading and therefore harmful to present and future generations.

The Arab scientific renaissance produced, in its own time, a knowledge society in the full sense.

The modern Arab world is the scene of myriad intellectual currents each with its own social, political and ideological direction and sources.

44

It is worth noting the considerable intellectual contributions to social reform of the pioneers of the contemporary Arab renaissance through three schools in Egypt, Greater Syria and Arab North Africa. The Religious Reform school: Jamal ad-Din al Afghani, Mohammad Abdou, Abdelrahman Al Kawakibi, Abdelhamid Bin Badiss, Chakib Erslan, Allal Al Fasi; the Liberal school: Refa'a al Tahtawi, Ahmad Lutfi Essayed, Qassem Amin, Taha Hussein, Keireddin Al Tunisi, Al Yazigi and Al Bustani; and the Secular school: Shibli Shmayyel, Farah Antoun and Salama Moussa.

At this point in history, Arab countries face societal obstacles to knowledge production arising from ideological conflicts between different political currents. The conflict over the Islamicisation of knowledge is an example. This is because few Arab intellectuals are willing to focus on substantive issues relating to history and reality at the same time. Yet substantial gains would accrue to knowledge production from pursuing serious research on Sharia'a sciences, adopting a reformist scientific view. In fact, none of the characteristics or historical developments of Arab countries should be exempt from rational study.

Undoubtedly, there are certain structural impediments that constrict knowledge production in Arab countries. The cultural conflict between political currents over the Islamicisation of knowledge is one example. This conflict is tied to intellectual reluctance to discuss history and present-day reality together. Yet no essential characteristic or aspect of Arab society should be excluded from a scientific perspective. The question of research into history and heritage and the application of scientific and reformist approaches to that work, hold one of the keys to the production of knowledge and, therefore, to the knowledge society itself. Such questions should be the subject of collaborative thinking and study, not dissension or rancour.

In the final analysis, the Arab knowledge model, or the "Arab mentality", is a project, not a fixed construct. It is a model in the process of formation and, as such, it offers an historic opportunity that should not be missed. Arab countries will do well to indigenise science and knowledge as foundations of the Arab knowledge model in the continu-

ing process of its formation.

THE DEMAND FOR KNOWLEDGE

This chapter has previously considered some of the economic qualities of knowledge; this section analyses in more detail the issue of the demand for knowledge, the low level of which in Arab countries is one of the most serious restrictions on the production and diffusion of knowledge in society.

Undeniably, knowledge supply can be a real constraint in developing countries, especially those where autocratic and absolute regimes restrict freedom of expression and the circulation of knowledge, ideas and information that are critical of authority. Yet there are good reasons to believe that the lack of demand for knowledge also curtails prospects

The "Arab mentality", is a project, not a fixed construct. It is a model in the process of formation.

for building knowledge societies in these countries

It may seem surprising that problems of demand are encountered in disseminating[5] a commodity whose main characteristics are that it is *non-rivalrous*[6] and *infinitely 'expansionable'*[7], as well as *aspatial -- weightless*[8]. A closer examination of the characteristics of knowledge demand in Arab countries reveals why such problems remain widespread.

SOURCES OF THE DEMAND FOR KNOWLEDGE

Sources of demand for knowledge vary in every community. Families demand knowledge as a way to invest in the human capital of their members, and to make social and economic decisions within the family. The state, civil society, and business sectors, public as well as private, demand knowledge in order to perform their respective functions. This demand grows stronger in proportion to the degree of rationalism in decision-making and the value placed on learning. In general, the major drivers of dissemination and demand are the institutional components of the knowledge system.

DETERMINANTS OF THE DEMAND FOR KNOWLEDGE

From a purely economic perspective, purchasing power substantially influences the demand for knowledge on the open market. Low incomes and the high price of knowledge, or the goods and services that embody knowledge, tend to curtail demand. In the Arab world, the majority of people have low incomes, while the cost of knowledge acquisition is high, especially if the commodity is directly imported or is produced locally using imported components. The price of knowledge rises with its transaction costs, which can be heavy. Rents paid to the producers of knowledge, to those who incorporate knowledge into commodities and services and to those who operate local monopolies[9] all bring up its cost.

Figure 1.3 shows the effect of cost on Internet penetration, which is a major means of spreading access to knowledge. It is quite clear that, in the Arab region, as in the world at large, the high cost of accessing the Internet is inversely linked to its diffusion.

The restrictive impact of high Internet access costs on the extent of its availability is illustrated in figure 1.4. High costs and the relatively limited availability of personal computers in the Arab world are reflected in low Internet usage compared to developed countries and South East Asia.

Generally speaking, demand for a commodity is shaped by the extent to which prevailing consumption patterns and their prices generate an appetite for particular goods and services. Some Arab countries are noted for their conspicuous consumption while basic needs often remain unsatisfied and costly to fulfil, because governments reduce the basic

Figure 1.3

Correlation between Internet penetration and Internet costs -- Arab countries and comparators

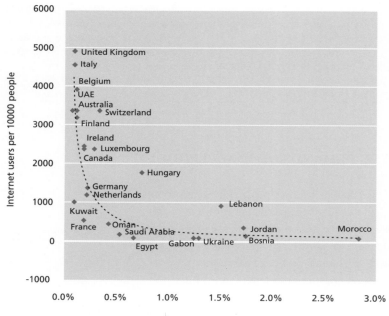

Source: International Telecommunication Union (ITU), 2002.

---

[5]Among the well-known examples is the limited dissemination of open-source software, such as "Linux", despite the fact that this operating system is free, effective and easily available. The impression that the software is difficult or unstable is not necessarily correct.

[6]Non-rivalrous means that the consumption of knowledge by one person does not reduce its availability to others.

[7]Infinitely 'expansionable' means that, no matter how high the cost of initial production, the cost of subsequent use is low.

[8]Aspatial or weightless refers to the ability of knowledge to cross borders, in particular if digitised.

[9] Consider, for example, the high costs of cellular phone services.

services they provide and the competition fails to provide better or more cost-effective alternatives. Not surprisingly, demand for knowledge, as embodied in goods and services, is declining. Imagine, for example, how public demand for Internet access competes with demand for health care.

In the case of knowledge, the characteristics and preferences of its potential users (decision-makers within families, the production sector, state and civil society institutions) largely determine the extent of demand. Arab families have always put great value on educating their children to the highest possible level in an attempt to raise their social status. Families have often been prepared to bear the high costs of education even if this severely strained their resources. This is evident when one considers the rising trend towards private tuition and private schooling in the region. On the other hand, in Arab countries, decision making within community institutions is often in the hands of older, authoritarian generations. In taking decisions, these generations mainly rely on traditional considerations that reflect their narrow affiliations and loyalties more than the broad scientific rationalism that requires decisions based on hard knowledge. In the last three decades, this problem has been compounded by the ascendance of money and power in the structure of societal incentives.

Reference has been made previously to how knowledge system institutions create demand for knowledge simply by playing their natural role. A vicious spiral of deteriorating knowledge supply is set in motion in communities with a poor knowledge system, curbing the direct demand for new knowledge. This is one of the most fundamental factors in the decline of knowledge in developing countries. The inadequacy of the knowledge system indirectly decreases the demand for it. Developing country decision-makers frequently complain, and rightly so, of the feeble support they receive from knowledge institutions when they turn to them for help.

Another shortcoming in the societal context in Arab countries that constrains knowledge demand is the widespread assumption that knowledge is not as effective as power or influence in solving social, economic and po-

Figure 1.4

PC availability and Internet costs and penetration: Arab countries, OECD and East Asia, 2001

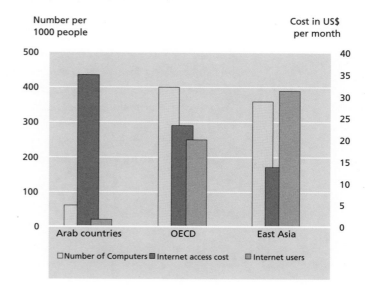

Source: World Economic Forum, 2002.

litical problems -- or that it is simply beyond reach. Hence, decision-makers end up limiting themselves to deploying "traditional" methods and mechanisms. This is a further illustration of the weakness of developing country knowledge systems.

Coercion may succeed in suppressing or containing demand for knowledge more than any economic or social impediment. Certainly, when freedom is curtailed, knowledge is an early casualty and those who seek it apply it sparingly or learn to live without it.

Finally, another constraint is censorship of the Internet. This global media miracle, which originally arose to transcend borders and overcome distances, has fallen under the control of the censor in Arab countries. In Iraq for instance, it was not possible to access the Internet until mid-2000. Even after that, access remained limited. In one rich Arab country, the government closed 400,000 web sites after initially allowing access to the Internet in 1999. The increase in Arab Internet users in 2001 saw both restrictions on access and censorship of the Internet grow stronger once more (World Markets Research Centre, 2002).

The brakes on knowledge demand that have been cited here will be further discussed in Chapter 8, which addresses the political and legal contexts of knowledge.

There is a widespread assumption that knowledge is not as effective as power or influence in solving social, economic or political problems.

Coercion may succeed in suppressing or containing demand for knowledge more than any economic or social impediment.

About the journey towards the knowledge society

The following chapters of the report outline a cognitive journey that follows the contours of the conceptual framework briefly introduced in this chapter, a few of whose most important aspects were highlighted in their relationship to history and the Arab reality. The destination of this journey is a strategic vision for building the knowledge society in the region. This vision identifies the landmarks of societal reform, which precede the establishment of the knowledge society in Arab countries (Chapter Nine). The journey to this destination passes through two waypoints. The first (Chapters Two - Five) is an assessment of the present state of knowledge acquisition, dissemination and production, in Arab countries at the beginning of the 21st century. The second (Chapters Six - Eight) is an analysis of the features of the societal context affecting knowledge acquisition in the region at the present time, which considers culture, socio-economic structures and politics. Emphasis is placed on guaranteeing freedom under the rule of law, and the discussion culminates in a survey of the regional and international environment for knowledge acquisition.

PART II

Section two: the state of knowledge in Arab countries

Chapters 2 – 5 constitute an evaluation of the state of knowledge in the Arab world. Chapter 2 focuses on the dissemination of knowledge in Arab countries while Chapter 3 investigates knowledge production. Chapter 4 represents an attempt to measure the status of Arab knowledge in a comparative perspective and Chapter 5 assesses the organizational setting for knowledge acquisition in the region.

PART II

Section two: Assessment of Knowledge in
Area-studies

Knowledge dissemination in Arab countries

This chapter attempts to describe and analyse the process of knowledge dissemination in Arab countries. It considers the role and state of Arab education, and its most crucial challenge, quality. It reviews the main features of print and broadcast media forms, the extent of public access to them and the impact of their political and societal surroundings on their independence and effectiveness as conductors and sources of knowledge. The chapter further analyses the emergence and early achievements of modern media forms based on ICT, new technology and new patterns of public expression. It concludes with an overview of the state of translation in the region.

KNOWLEDGE DISSEMINATION AND KNOWLEDGE CAPITAL

Knowledge dissemination is about more than the mere transfer of information and data, although such transfer, through multiple channels, should be an integral part of the process. The real challenge is how to turn this information into a strong reserve of knowledge that will impact the production of new knowledge and transform it into knowledge capital that contributes to human development. Knowledge is disseminated chiefly through socialisation, the different stages of education and by the mass media and the translation industry. This chapter looks at the characteristics, achievements and limitations of the main channels for disseminating knowledge in the Arab world. Like other investigations in this field, this attempt is compromised by an acute lack of accurate and reliable data, and thus conclusions regarding the situation in Arab countries are inevitably subject to this limitation.

SOCIALISATION

Socialisation is the process by which the individual acquires knowledge, skills, attitudes and values; and establishes motives, principles and patterns that affect her or his adaptation to the natural, social and cultural environment. Although socialisation is a learning process that extends throughout the different stages of the life of an individual, childhood is the most sensitive and impressionable stage. Despite the fact that children are the core and crux of this process, they are rarely regarded as effective and influential individuals. Nonetheless, this traditional vision has been changing gradually since the early 1980s as a result of social, psychological and anthropological studies that have asserted the importance of the child's experience, and the way (s) he learns and acquires knowledge throughout the socialisation process.

There are three styles of child rearing; authoritarian, permissive and firm. Research shows that children who have been brought up by firm parents demonstrate greater psychological and social adaptation. Also, they achieve better academic results and have higher self-esteem (Buri, 1998).

Studies also indicate that the most common style of child rearing within the Arab family is the authoritarian accompanied by the over-protective. This adversely affects children's independence, self-confidence and social efficiency, and leads to an increase in passive attitudes and the deterioration of decision-making skills, not only with respect to behaviour, but also to how the child thinks. For, starting in early childhood, the child becomes accustomed to suppressing her or his inquisitive and exploratory tendencies and sense of initiative. (al-Sweigh, *in Arabic*, background paper for the report)

Studies indicate that the most common style of child rearing within the Arab family is the authoritarian accompanied by the over-protective.

Starting in early childhood, the child becomes accustomed to suppressing her or his inquisitive and exploratory tendencies.

EDUCATION

The most serious problem facing Arab education is its deteriorating quality.

The quality of education provided in many kindergartens in the region does not fulfil the requirements for advancing and developing children's capabilities.

The first AHDR acknowledged that Arab countries had made great strides in the quantitative expansion of education in the latter half of the 20th century. It however also observed that the general condition of education is still unfavourable compared to the achievements of other countries, both developing and developed. The report concluded that Arab education falls far short of human development needs.

It is a fact that the quantitative expansion of Arab education remains incomplete. High rates of illiteracy, especially among women, persist. Children continue to be denied their basic right to elementary education. Higher education is characterised by decreasing enrolment rates compared to developed countries, and public expenditure on education has declined since 1985.

However, as the previous Report also emphasised, the most serious problem facing Arab education is its deteriorating quality (AHDR, 2002, 47-51). The emphasis here, therefore, will be laid on that crucial aspect of education and its impact on knowledge.

The quality of education

The most important challenge in the educational arena is the decline in quality, which undercuts a basic goal of human development, namely to enhance the quality of people's lives and enrich the capabilities of societies. Allocating insufficient resources to education can certainly reduce its quality. Yet there are other elements that also affect educational quality, chief among which are education policies, teachers' and educators' working condi-

tions, curricula and educational methodologies.

The quality of pre-school education

Early education, centred on the child and the family, is an investment that has long-term economic and social returns. The child's brain in early childhood is known to be flexible and much more sensitive to its surroundings than that of older children. This brain develops according to the experiences it encounters in its external environment. The sensuous parts of the brain reach the peak of their growth when the surrounding environment is rich in stimulants, notably for the senses of touch, sight, hearing, smell and taste. Developing the capabilities and improving the intellectual capacities of the child requires close attention to the pedagogic methods adopted within the family and inside nurseries and kindergartens. Naturally, this should go hand in hand with proper health care and decent livelihoods in a society where the values of freedom and justice prevail.

Despite major efforts to improve pre-school education in some Arab countries, the quality of education provided in many kindergartens in the region does not fulfil the requirements for advancing and developing children's capabilities in order to help socialise a creative and innovative generation. In most cases, these kindergartens focus mainly on teaching children reading and writing, without paying enough attention to their integrated growth. This can be achieved by providing sufficient and effective educational materials and instruments, qualified teachers and educators, as well as an environment conducive to sharpening the child's senses and improving his or her physical, emotional, social and intellectual abilities. A positive pre-school environment is characterised by some essential qualities for children's healthy growth, such as opportunities for play and access to a free space that allows them to move, express themselves, choose, take decisions and enhance their self-respect, which leads to self-confidence. A healthy environment is also characterised by an approach to learning that is interactive, not didactic, i.e., the child should interact with his or her surroundings, and with other children and adults as well.

BOX 2.1

Abdul Aziz Al-Muqaleh – Illiteracy: An Obstacle to Knowledge and Modernisation

Modern Arab history shows that illiteracy has invariably helped to keep traditional anti-development regimes in power. For instance, in Yemen during the 1940s a regressive regime was able to make ignorant parents invite rulers to kill their enlightened children who were accused of sorcery and selling Islam to foreigners. I do not think that the situation has changed a lot in the early 21st century – and not only in Yemen, but in all Arab countries, with one or two exceptions. Any extremist bigot can still set tens of

thousands of illiterate people against any enlightened person, prevent the eradication of illiteracy and make it a strong bulwark against all projects to modernize education and culture.

There is no hope of bringing about a healthy educational and democratic environment conducive to knowledge in countries where illiteracy is allowed to gain near-absolute control and to destroy every serious attempt to escape from the tunnel of alienation in the modern age.

In order to evaluate the level of education, it is necessary to assess teachers' abilities to interact with, motivate, and encourage students to innovate and think critically and creatively. Information published on these qualifications and abilities is scarce and limited to personal observations and general impressions. Undoubtedly, there are a large number of experienced and highly qualified teachers who play a vital role in making the educational process succeed.

However, there are some factors in many Arab countries that adversely affect teachers' capabilities, such as low salaries, which force educators to take on other jobs that consume their energy and cut into the time they can devote to caring for their students. Other constraints are also significant, particularly a lack of facilities; poorly designed curricula; and the indifferent quality of teacher training. Most present-day educators have graduated from institutions that follow an approach to teaching based on rote learning, which is not especially conducive to critical thinking. Finally, many Arab countries face the problem of overcrowded classes. These factors limit the abilities and curtail the desire of teachers to interact creatively with their students.

Curricula and education methodologies

Typically, educational material is contained in the curriculum, which comprises a body of lessons that is ideally a synthesis of the best of what decision-makers and authors agree to be worthwhile and necessary for the learning process. In purely formal terms, curricula in most Arab countries do not appear to be greatly different from what many countries around the world are adopting.

During the last decade several Arab countries have embarked on educational reform programmes that concentrate particularly on revising and making modifications to the content of curricula and syllabi. When it comes to the sciences, content is not usually a controversial matter, save for some themes that are perceived to touch on religious beliefs such as the theory of evolution or on social taboos, such as sex education. But the humanities and social sciences that have a direct relevance to people's ideas and convictions are supervised or protected by the authorities in charge of de-

---

BOX 2.2

Morocco: conflicting signals on knowledge acquisition

Most Moroccan families cannot afford to send their children to kindergarten. Some of these families enroll their children at low-cost mosque schools, where they are taught reading, writing and religion by teachers who are not qualified to educate young children and to take care of them. Families, which cannot afford even this low-cost alternative, entrust their young children to the care of a family member, often an uneducated older brother, or leave them to play in the street if they are over 6 years old.

In 2000, school enrolment of girls was low, reaching an average rate of just 45% in the three educational stages.

Schools need much improvement, particularly in certain rural areas of Morocco. In the northern region of Tangiers-Tatouan, for instance, there are more than 45 students in each classroom on average. In respect of higher education, it is estimated that 40% of graduates remain unemployed. Moreover, 50% of university students drop out of university before completing their studies.

More encouraging statistics can be found in the rapid spread of "cyber-cafes", which increased from 500 in 1999 to 2500 in 2001, a 500% jump. Websites

also recorded a dramatic increase of 700% during the same period. Revenue from the services of communication companies tripled between 1997 and 2001, from 6 to 16 billion dirhams.

In order to deal with the problems of education, the 2000-2009 decade was declared as "The Education and Training Decade in Morocco". The state is called upon to give education at all levels its full support and attention. The plan for the decade requires the government to achieve set targets, e.g.:
- By September 2002, all children aged 6 years or more were to be enrolled in the nearest school.
- By September 2004, all children of age should be enrolled in the first year of kindergarten.
- By 2005, 80% of children enrolled in kindergartens should continue in school until they complete elementary education.

As a result, the rate of enrolment for 6 year olds increased from 37% in 1997-1998 to 91% in 2001-2002. The rate of enrolment of children aged 6-11 increased from 69% to 90 % during the same period.

Source: Country report prepared for the Second Arab Human Development Report (AHDR2).

---

signing curricula and issuing schoolbooks. Consequently, such subjects usually laud past achievements and generally indulge in both self-praise and blame of others, with the aim of instilling loyalty, obedience and support for the regime in power. It is not unusual to find schoolbooks in many Arab countries with a picture of the ruler on the front page, even in the case of textbooks in neutral subjects such as science and mathematics.

Some researchers argue that the curricula taught in Arab countries seem to encourage submission, obedience, subordination and compliance, rather than free critical thinking. In many cases, the contents of these curricula do not stimulate students to criticise political or social axioms. Instead, they smother their independent tendencies and creativity (Munir Bashour, background paper for AHDR 2).

Generally speaking, the assigned curricula, starting from preliminary school or even before, embody a concept that views education as an industrial production process, where curricula and their content serve as

Researchers argue that the curricula taught in Arab countries seem to encourage submission, obedience, subordination and compliance, rather than free critical thinking.

moulds into which fresh minds are supposed to be poured.

There are various means for conveying information: lectures, seminars, workshops, collaborative work, laboratory work and many others. In Arab countries, however, lectures seem to dominate. Students can do little but memorise, recite and perfect rote learning. The most widely used instruments are schoolbooks, notes, sheets or summaries. Communication in education is didactic, supported by set books containing indisputable texts in which knowledge is objectified so as to hold incontestable facts, and by an examination process that only tests memorisation and factual recall.

Education policies

Education policies in many Arab countries lack an integrated vision of the education process and its objectives. Furthermore, these policies are characterised by inconsistency and a lack of direction. Problems, such as those relating to the content of the curricula, forms of examination, evaluation of students, and foreign languages cannot be settled without formulating a well-defined vision of educational goals and necessities.

The policies governing foreign language education in Arab countries illustrate the absence of a well-defined vision for instituting mechanisms that would encourage mastery and dissemination of knowledge and science. Indeed, promoting and enhancing the Arabic language as the medium for acquiring and indigenising modern sciences is the surest way to achieve this goal. Giving importance to Arabic does not however entail neglecting foreign language acquisition: on the contrary it requires the pursuit of both tracks at the same time.

The state of foreign language teaching in Arab countries is an example of the absence of clear-cut education policies and reveals a complicated and confused situation. In reality, only one Arab country (Lebanon) has maintained, since its independence, the teaching of a foreign language starting from the first grade. In 1995, Lebanon permitted the teaching of mathematics and science in foreign languages in government schools. In the government schools of Arab North African countries, the foreign language (French) main-

tained its place despite many attempts at Arabisation. But French is not taught in public schools before the third grade in either Morocco or Tunisia, and not before the fourth in Algeria. Some other countries postponed learning a foreign language to the last two or three grades of primary education, as in the cases of Iraq and some Gulf countries. Recently, other countries, such as Egypt, Syria, Libya and Yemen have realized the importance of providing foreign language teaching as early as possible and are increasingly implementing this trend, where foreign languages are being integrated in the later stages of primary education instead of secondary education. In Jordan government schools have recently started teaching English commencing in the first grade.

Noteworthy in this context is a trend that emerged in Egypt: the establishment of public and private "multi-language schools" that charge relatively high tuition fees. The syllabi implemented incorporate two foreign languages instead of one, together with mathematics and science in a foreign language. The number of these schools has increased during recent years from 195 to 575. In addition, since 1980, a new type of foreign school has emerged, one under foreign supervision that teaches curricula not administered by Arab Ministries of Education. The result has been chaos in terms of the types of certificates received by students in the same country.

Measuring the quality of education

Evaluating the quality of education in the Arab world is extremely difficult owing to insufficient information and data. These difficulties are compounded by the complete absence of any standardised measurements for comparison among Arab countries on the one hand, and with the rest of the world on the other, particularly over time. The following are some features identified from studies conducted in this field of analysis.

Indicators of the quality of achievement in elementary education are available based on specialised studies conducted in some Arab countries including Oman, Egypt and Bahrain. These studies are of limited value as they have been neither designed nor conducted on a comparable basis and do not sup-

Communication in education is didactic, supported by set books containing indisputable texts and by an examination process that only tests memorisation.

The state of foreign language teaching in Arab countries is an example of the absence of clear-cut education policies.

port comparative conclusions. However, their findings offer significant insights into the quality of elementary education in the Arab countries where the studies were conducted.

In Oman, so far, four studies have been conducted to evaluate educational achievement in the fourth, sixth, eighth, and ninth grades in Arabic, mathematics, science and life skills. Two findings about these grades stand out: (Nader Fergany, in Arabic, 2002)

• Grade averages in all subjects are below excellence, or the so-called 90/90 rule (which stipulates that at least 90% of the students should obtain at least 90% in a standard examination that measures how far the skills taught are acquired).

• *Girls* outperform boys in all subjects.

In Egypt, a wide field survey revealed that mastery of the basic skills of reading and writing, and mathematics, which is supposed to be acquired through elementary education, is low, about 40% and 30% respectively.

In Bahrain, an evaluation of educational outcomes at the end of the first stage of primary education (Ministry of Education, Bahrain and Almishkat Centre for Research, *in Arabic*, 2001), showed a low level of student achievement reflected in a lack of mastery of essential skills. The grade average in Arabic hit 43.7%, with a standard deviation of 24.2 on a scale of 0-100. In mathematics, the grade average was 44.9% with a 22.8 standard deviation on the same scale. In neither subject does student performance remotely approach mastery.

Student scores in the two subjects cover the whole range of grades, which indicates that examinations could indeed distinguish the different achievement levels on the one hand. On the other hand, frequency distributions of the scores established the common bell curve of examination grades in a large sample (the further away from the average the grade is, the smaller the percentage of students becomes).

However, grade frequency distribution that deviates from the standard distribution is also important. For example, compared to the distribution of mathematics grades, the distribution in Arabic shows a higher frequency in the lower grades, and less frequency in the middle. These findings demonstrate that the students' grades in Arabic tend to be lower than in mathematics.

When it comes to comparative studies with other countries of the world, only one Arab country, Kuwait, participated in the "Third International Mathematics and Science Study, 1995" (Trends in International Mathematics and Science Study, 1996). It included students who were at the end of elementary education from 41 countries in the world (class 8). Kuwait's participation is highly commendable and a good example for other Arab countries to follow, especially since it took place a few years after the invasion of the country and the consequent physical and emotional impact on its education system.

Yet Kuwait is an exception for other reasons. It has sufficient financial resources as well as a small population. It spends generously on education and has made outstanding progress in its quantitative expansion. Nevertheless, Kuwaiti students came at the bottom of the list and ranked 39th in terms of achievement in mathematics and science, with grade averages of 392 and 430 respectively. This is 121 points in mathematics and 86 in science below the world averages (513 and 516). Compared to Singapore, which was ranked first, with a grade average of 643 and 607 respectively, Kuwaiti students' achievement fell below this average by 251 points in mathematics and 177 in science.

Noticeably, unlike those countries topping the list, Kuwaiti student achievement in mathematics was lower than in science, and more so compared to the world average. It is a well-established fact that mathematics is a crucial basis of knowledge for the sciences of the future. It is worth noting that, in this evaluation, countries such as Bulgaria, Thailand, Spain and Iran ranked above Kuwait. The example points to an important conclusion: ultimately, the quality of education does not depend on the availability of resources or on quantitative factors but rather on other characteristics closely related to the organisation of the educational process and the means of delivery and evaluation.

Three Arab countries (Jordan, Tunisia and Morocco) took part in the Trends in Mathematics, and Science Study (TIMSS, 1999). In mathematics, Tunisia was ranked 29th with 448 points. Jordan was ranked 32nd

Ultimately, the quality of education does not depend on the availability of resources or on quantitative factors, but on characteristics related to the organisation of the educational process and the means of delivery and evaluation.

with 428 points. Morocco came 37th with 337 points. It should be noted that Singapore was ranked first with 604 points while South Africa was last with 275 points. In Science, Jordan was ranked 30th with 450 points, Tunisia 34th with 430 points and Morocco 37th with 323 points. Taiwan topped the science list with 564 points while South Africa was ranked last with 243 points.

The quality of higher education

Although higher education institutions have existed in the Arab world for more than ten centuries (most of which were established in a major mosque such as Al-Azhar, Al-Qairawan and Al-Zaitonah, or with funding from charities or *waqf*), modern Arab colleges and universities are young. Three quarters of Arab universities were established in the last 25 years of the 20th century. Fifty-seven per cent of them are no more than 15 years old. This observation is important: higher education institutions, universities in particular, take a long time to consolidate their institutional structure, and to perfect their role in the dissemination and production of knowledge (Nader Fergany, *in Arabic*, 1998b, 18-19).

The quality of education provided in higher education institutions in Arab countries is affected by many factors, chief among which is the lack of a clear vision, and, as noted earlier, the absence of well-designed policies regulating the educational process. Higher education, particularly in its inception, faced resistance from several quarters. The pi-

oneer modern universities were established through the efforts of civil society and the support of nationalist forces with dreams of progress and prosperity. These endeavours were affected from the very beginning by the colonial presence in most Arab countries at the time. This period witnessed conflicting intentions and competing interests that led to a rupture in the original course taken. The generation of the renaissance strived to institutionalise the basis for academic research in Arab countries. Some of their attempts succeeded, but were not sustained.

One of the main features of many universities in the Arab world is their lack of autonomy, i.e., they fall under the direct control of the ruling regime. Nevertheless, universities are often the arenas for political and ideological conflict, the more so because of restrictions imposed on political participation in general and the promotion of political currents that owe allegiance to the regime. These contextual features have adverse effects on the degree of freedom allowed for education and research.

This lack of autonomy has resulted in a situation where universities are run according to the requirements of the governing political logic, and not a plan or a wise educational policy. Some universities, for example, are overcrowded on account of the uncalculated increase in enrolment rates, simply because the announcement of enrolment numbers in universities has become a political gesture to appease society.

The quality of higher education is also influenced by an ongoing decline in expenditure, reflected in inadequate facilities for students and faculty. Quantitative expansion in higher education came at the expense of quality. University libraries are in a sorry state, laboratories are old and cannot accommodate the increasing numbers of students, and classes are over-crowded, thus creating a wide distance between students and teachers. Moreover, faculty members in many Arab universities earn meagre salaries, and therefore cannot devote themselves fully to teaching or research.

The quality of computer science education in Arab universities

The UNDP Regional Bureau for Arab States is

BOX 2.3

The "Trends in International Mathematics and Science Study (TIMSS)"

In order to address deficiencies in measuring the quality of education, the UNDP Regional Bureau for Arab States is conducting a project for "Evaluating Educational Quality in the Basic and Middle Stages in Mathematics and Science in the Arab World". The project sponsors the participation of five Arab countries in TIMSS 2003, in which 54 other countries are taking part, including five other Arab countries. The International Association for the Evaluation of Educational Achievement conducts this study impartially. The study was previously conducted in 1995 and 1999. The project will collect general data on curricula, classroom instruction, student achievement and teachers' performance in a manner that allows for comparisons of findings with international standards. It will set a standardised scale for ranking countries based on international criteria. The study is expected to give the participating countries the opportunity to measure achievement in mathematics and science through the examination of prevailing trends in primary schools (fourth grade) and middle schools (eighth grade). By the end of the project, participating countries will receive a report benchmarking the performance of their national plans and pedagogical policies, as well as of the schools taking part, against international standards. They will also receive internationally comparable results on students' performance in mathematics and science, and general reference data.

sponsoring a project to improve the quality of university education in Arab countries, which includes a component concerned with evaluating the quality of education in some vitally important scientific disciplines. The project has completed an evaluation of the quality of computer science education in Arab universities Sixteen universities - 12 public and 4 private - in 12 Arab states, namely: Algeria, Bahrain, Egypt, Jordan, Kuwait, Lebanon, Morocco, Palestine, Sudan, Syria, the United Arab Emirates and Yemen participated.

The evaluation of computer science education has been completed for all participating universities except Kuwait University which withdrew just before the external assessment started.

The evaluation (which is conducted in three stages: training, self-evaluation and external evaluation by Arab and international evaluators) is based on 5 major criteria for measuring performance, namely: academic standards; teaching and learning; student progression; learning resources; and quality assurance and enhancement[1], in addition to 11 other detailed criteria.

The project revealed important results concerning the academic standards of programmes. While all participating programmes – except one – achieved "approval", i.e., confidence in the academic level of the programme, that approval was in the category of "approved/satisfactory" and no programme had an academic level high enough to earn "approved with commendation", i.e., the level of distinction by international standards.

Reports pointed to a number of issues that require redress with respect to all the components of academic standards, i.e., curricula and prescribed materials, methods of student evaluation and the students' level of achievement. For instance, a comparison of the content of the curricula evaluated with that of the

---

BOX 2.4
Use of the creative teaching method in Arab medical schools

The creative teaching method (teaching through problem-solving) is one of the most important methods of teaching medicine of the past 25 years. It started at the School of Medicine of McMaster University of Canada in 1976 and has, since then, been adopted by many medical schools throughout the world as a teaching strategy and school curriculum.

The creative method is basically a teaching strategy characterized by the use of medical problems as a framework for teaching students problem-solving skills and proactive learning. In this method, the teaching process revolves around the student, not the teacher, as is the case in the traditional method. The student himself is responsible for his/her learning, which –it is believed- is a preparation for lifelong learning and self-development. Proactive self-learning removes the student from teaching methods based on rote learning and the passive reception of knowledge, thereby increasing his/her ability to understand and absorb in-depth learning. This teaching method also leads to the student's acquisition of important skills, such as the ability to communicate well and to work as a team member in addition to the ability to analyze and use the scientific method in solv-ing health problems in their different organic, social and psychological perspectives. In this method, both student and teacher find the teaching process interesting. The student's role is to analyze, research and derive information and solutions, while the teacher's role differs from the traditional role of merely dispensing information. The teacher's new role is to stimulate the learning process by motivating students and pushing them to think by posing questions and general concepts.

There are three medical schools in the Arab world, which play a pioneering role in using this teaching strategy, namely: Al-Jazeerah University in Wad Madani, Sudan; The Suez Canal University in Ismaeliyah, Egypt; and The Arabian Gulf University in Bahrain. All three started at approximately the same time (1979-1982) and continue to adopt this teaching philosophy with continuous development of curricula. These three schools act as a stimulus to the development of medical education in the Arab region through their Centres for the Development of Medical Education, which have trained many faculty members in various Arab countries.

Source: Arabian Gulf University, Bahrain.

---

international test in computer science, as determined by the American ETS[2], indicated an overall compatibility exceeding 70% in only eight universities. In terms of complete compatibility with each one of the five main parts of the international test, the majority of the universities' curricula reflected over 70% compatibility only in the two traditional subject areas of programming fundamentals and software systems. Just one-third of the participating universities had curricula judged compatible with the other three subject areas (computer organization and architecture, theory of computer science and computational mathematics, and special subjects).

---

[1]**Academic Standards.** This major criterion reflects the confidence of evaluators in three areas: curriculum design and the level of prescribed material; accuracy and effectiveness of student evaluation methods; and actual student achievements.

Methods of teaching and learning. This represents the result of evaluation of the methods used in teaching and learning, in terms of diversity, efficiency and relevance to the programme goals.

Student Progression. This depends on the efficiency of the systems and the arrangements used to guide and support student advancement through the school years.

Learning Resources. This depends on the availability and efficiency of human and financial resources needed for learning, such as the faculty, libraries, laboratories and communications. The latter 3 criteria come under a more comprehensive criterion, namely, "learning opportunities available", although each one is evaluated separately.

Quality assurance and enhancement. This depends on the efficiency and effectiveness of the internal arrangements and systems regularly available to supervise the performance of the programme through the stages of its implementation and the ability of these systems to take the necessary measures for its correction and improvement.

[2]Educational Testing Services.

Private universities, generally, did better than public ones.

The evaluation indicates that private universities, generally, did better than public ones. At the university level, the overall quality indicator value varied from 42% to 91%, an average of nearly 60%. A majority of the participating 15 universities (eight out of 15) were below average (Figure 2-1).

According to the applicable criteria, the evaluation concludes that the overall quality indicator is below the "pass" level for eight universities and close to the "good" level for three. Results indicate that the academic level of faculty members is a strong point in the region, while the sufficiency of available faculty members and the mathematics component in the curriculum represent weak points, which deserve attention, figure 2-2. It is not surprising, therefore, that well-qualified faculty members are nonetheless unable to diffuse and produce knowledge efficiently on account of their small numbers, compared to students, and the meagre resources available to them.

The evaluation concludes by proposing six areas as strategic priorities for the development of computer science programmes in the region, through the concerted efforts of universities and with support from regional initiatives, projects and forums. These areas are: methodologies for the design and development of programmes and curricula; the role of official accreditation organisations; the development of the size and capabilities of faculties; the development of the capabilities of libraries and communication systems, quality assurance and enhancement; and cooperation in the provision of traditional and electronic library sources, both Arabic and Arabicized. (The latter are needed for programmes that are taught in Arabic, which currently represent one-third of all programmes). The evaluation strongly recommends that the latter measure be taken up in parallel with enhancing the English language skills of students. The evaluation also calls for an expanded stage of investment and expenditure on higher education linked directly to goals and indicators of quality.

ARAB MASS MEDIA: CHARACTERISTICS, CONSTRAINTS AND NEW FORMS

Print and broadcast media are a vital means of transferring, and sometimes producing, knowledge. Since their inception, they have played a central role in knowledge dissemination, one that has undergone many changes as a result of scientific and technical development. In early times, printed materials were the most common medium, but had limited influence among communities with high rates of illiteracy. The advent of radio opened new horizons for knowledge dissemination, dispensing as it did with literacy as a requirement. Ultimately, television surpassed all conventional mass media in terms of impact.

What is more important, from the per-

Figure 2.1

Distribution of universities participating in the evaluation according to the overall quality indicator

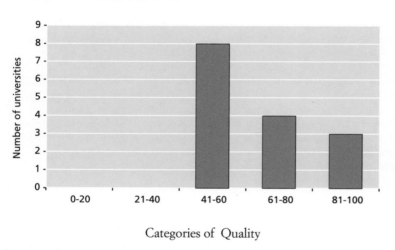

Categories of Quality

Figure 2.2

Detailed evaluation criteria: average values

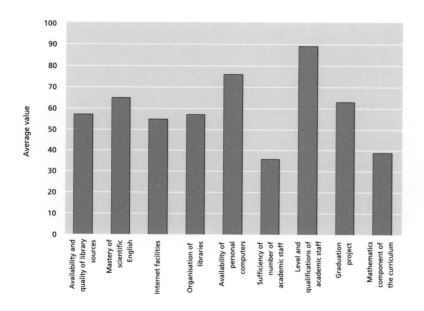

spective of building human development and the knowledge society, is the relationship between the mass media, freedom and progress on the one side and increased demand and supply of knowledge on the other. The more freedom enjoyed by the media and the deeper their involvement in human development issues such as good governance, knowledge and women's empowerment, the stronger the societal incentives for creating a knowledge society become.

The global revolution in communication that is rapidly changing the world into a knowledge-based economy is transforming the means of knowledge dissemination. A contemporary society that does not rely on digital electronic networks to exchange information is unimaginable. For most major corporations, the information and communication industry has become an essential strategic support in ensuring dominance in international markets. In addition, satellite channels, especially in the Arab world, are now a source for the production and creation of values, symbols and taste.

Access to Media

Arab media forms and the means of accessing them, as well as their structure and content, exhibit several shortcomings that reduce their effectiveness in building a knowledge society. Among these, poor public access to information is a serious disability. This can be illustrated by comparing the ratio of the Arab population to the volume of information available to citizens, and the comparable ratio in other regions of the world.

In general, Arab countries have lower information media to population ratios (number of newspapers, radio and television sets per 1000 people) compared to the world average and the average of middle-income countries. Indeed, in this respect, the Arab world is not much better off than low-income countries in some areas.

The low number of newspapers per 1000 people, 53 newspapers in the Arab countries versus 285 in the developed countries, indicates two significant gaps. First, Arab citizens do not generate a large demand for newspapers due to low literacy rates and the high cost of newspapers compared to income. Second, the decline in the quality, independence, and

professionalism of Arab journalism make its products unattractive to broad categories of Arab readers.

In audio and visual media, the availability of radio and television sets in Arab countries as a whole is also below the average in middle-income countries and the world as a whole.

Access to information media varies from one Arab country to another. The number of newspapers per 1,000 people in Arab countries varies from one newspaper in Somalia to

Arab countries have lower information media to population ratios compared to the world average.

Figure 2.3

Number of daily newspapers per 1000 people in Arab countries and other regions in the world, 1998

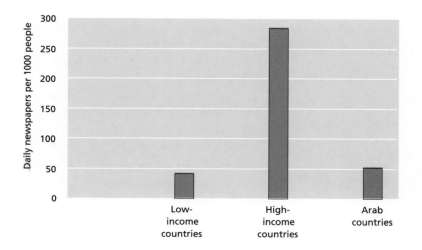

Source: World Bank, 2002.

Figure 2.4

Number of radio receivers per 1000 people in Arab countries and other regions in the world, 2000

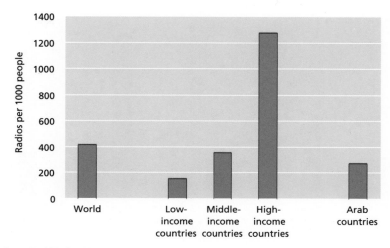

Source: World Bank, 2002.

Official Arab satellite channels dominate the microwaves.

Media in most Arab countries lack multiple, independent sources of information.

374 newspapers in Kuwait, which exceeds the average in high-income countries. In contrast with the ratios of newspapers, Lebanon, which has the highest ratio when it comes to radio receivers (678 radio receivers per 1,000 people), is still well below the average of the high-income countries, which boast 1,280 radio receivers per 1,000 people. However, the ratios of television sets in Arab countries are closer to the ratios of newspapers. Oman, which has the highest ratio among Arab countries (563 television sets per 1,000 people), is close to the average of high-income countries (641 television sets per 1,000 people). But middle-income Arab countries have far fewer televisions than other middle-income countries in the world, where the average number is 275 television sets per 1,000 people. For instance, the number of televisions per 1,000 people does not exceed 67 sets in Syria, 198 in Tunisia, and 189 in Egypt.

The number of Arab satellite channels has also increased. There are now about 120 channels transmitted through Arabsat and Egypt's Nilesat. More than 70% of these channels are state enterprises and broadcast in Arabic. Few are in foreign languages. A handful of private sector satellite channels (about 15% of all channels) broadcast in Arabic from outside the region. A smaller number of private sector channels (10%) broadcast in Arabic from inside the region. In short, official Arab satellite channels dominate the microwaves.

Resources available to the media

In varying degrees, Arab media personnel in most Arab countries encounter serious difficulties in gaining access to information, documents, data and official and unofficial news sources. Authorities often hinder their efforts citing official secrecy or national security. Many countries have a list of prohibited topics, such as the publication of court hearings, decrees or other matters that are said to touch on state security.

The media in most Arab countries lack multiple, independent sources of information. They principally depend on foreign information sources, especially Western news agencies. Although all Arab countries have their own news agencies, these agencies are state-owned and oriented to serve and promote state policies. Most of them also suffer from a lack of human, financial and technological resources and do not have correspondents outside their own countries. However, it may be worth mentioning here the exceptions that stand out among Arab news satellite channels. Some news satellites have succeeded in securing exclusive coverage of major events. The US-based CNN, for example, broadcast bulletins incorporating some of Al-Jazeera's coverage of the events of the war in Afghanistan. Other satellite channels have started building a network of correspondents outside the region, as in the cases of Abu Dhabi, MBC and Al-Arabia.

In general, Arab news channels lack specialised agencies that are able to cover thematic news topics, such as economics, sports, the environment, health, women and science, despite the significance and popularity of these topics amid the current information explosion.

Many Arab media institutions do not have information centres housing libraries or archives. The few archives that exist are old-fashioned and far behind the tremendous boom in information technology. Elsewhere in the world, such centres have become the backbone of in-depth media services, incorporating the flow of events and news within a general context, in order to help the audience understand developments and take an in-

Figure 2.5

Number of television sets per 1000 people in Arab countries and other regions of the world, 2000

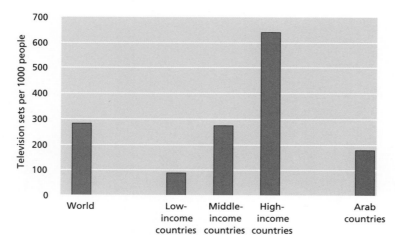

Source: World Bank, 2002.

formed stand on them.

A few capable information centres affiliated to some Arab media institutions continue to lead the field. For example, Egypt's al-Ahram Information Centre and other such centres, namely Annahar, Al Bayan, Al Khaleej, Al Hayat and Al Sharq Al Awsat keep up with successive developments in information technologies.

Typical content

The role played by the media in different Arab countries is very similar, albeit in varying degrees. A review of media programmes and research indicates that light entertainment is the most common offering, and is predominantly superficial, repetitive in content, and promotes values that encourage consumerism and a depreciation of work. This is particularly evident during *Ramadan*, which sees an increase in game shows feeding popular dreams of easy riches.

The Arab world has two cultural satellite channels (*Nileculture* & *Tanweer* -- Egypt) and two religious channels (*Almajd* and *Iqra'* -- Saudi Arabia), in addition to several educational channels in Saudi Arabia and Egypt, as well as a special information channel, the Nile Information Channel. The region also receives information services from some land-based television stations. Nonetheless, Arab television at large is not a vibrant force for knowledge or culture.

Some Arab news satellite channels, notably *Al-Arabia*, *Al-Jazeera*, and *Al Manar* have brought new content and form to the screen by airing free debates. They have thus spurred many Arab ground and satellite channels to provide more space for a diversity of voices and viewpoints and to allow more freedom of expression on political, social and cultural issues usually hidden behind a curtain of silence. These new talk shows, though at times sensational and vociferous, have nevertheless raised audience awareness, and could effect a radical change in the Arab public scene in the long run, opening it up to a culture of pluralism and dialogue.

News coverage

The Arab citizen's trust in media is affected –

to a great extent – by the level of news coverage in different mass media. Despite attempts to improve news services – due to competition between news satellite channels and to the extraordinary developments in communication technology that have turned the world into an electronic global village – a number of trends continue to hamper effective news coverage in Arab countries.

The main focus is still on official news and on senior political officials. Certain news values predominate, notably those favouring celebrities, idiosyncratic behaviour, humour and conflict. These values control the news that makes the front pages of newspapers, and occupy prime time on radio and television. More space and time is allocated to news of this kind than to other content. News of interest to the majority of the population, and which relates to their daily concerns or which could enrich their scientific and cultural knowledge, is scarce. Despite more openness that allows the media to address certain events, some news items are suppressed or dealt with in a manner not equal to their importance. News stories can sometimes be overstated or understated and on occasion present very different accounts of the same event, as the case of Arab media coverage of the fall of Baghdad shows.

News reports themselves tend to be narrative and descriptive, rather than investigative or analytic, with a concentration on immediate and partial events and facts. This is generally true of newspapers, radio bulletins and televised news. The news is often presented as a succession of isolated events, without in-depth explanatory coverage or any effort to place events in the general, social, economic and cultural context.

Needless to say, this type of news coverage does not help the ordinary citizen to comprehend events, increase his or her awareness and knowledge or develop a considered and informed point of view on national, regional and international issues.

Features of media messages

An analysis conducted on samples of content from Arab media in many Arab countries (Ali Al-Qarni, Arab Media Discourse, 1997), and dozens of studies conducted at country levels,

Some Arab news satellite channels, have brought new content and form to the screen by airing free debates.

News reports themselves tend to be narrative and descriptive, rather than investigative or analytic.

characterise the common features of Arab media messages, with some exceptions, as follows:

Authoritarian: Authority heavily controls the media discourse, imposing its own topics, directives, values, details, preferences, and timing.

Unidimensional: The discourse mostly excludes the other point of view, keeping it away from the public mind.

Official: The majority of Arab media institutions are incapable of taking action or reporting on events until they receive official direction, even if this entails ignoring an important event for a certain period of time. This of course discredits the media in the eyes of its audience.

Sacred: In many cases, a sacred aura is bestowed on the discourse, one that might not exist in other regions. This aura is not necessarily religious, but reflects the determination with which the objective of a particular discourse is being pushed.

One of the dilemmas facing Arab media is a continuous conflict between the impulse to "seek more freedoms and independence" and to "preserve the national interest". This deliberately exaggerated conflict should not obscure the fact that the search for more freedoms is an indigenous, national and positive effort that ultimately helps achieve the national interest.

THE ENVIRONMENT SURROUNDING THE MASS MEDIA

Legalised restrictions on freedom of the press and freedom of expression in Arab countries curtail the independence and vitality of the mass media. In practice, the harassment of the press under the law is an all-too-frequent violation of freedom of expression, with newspapers sometimes facing closure, seizure, confiscation and sequestration. Furthermore, journalists are not given sufficient guarantees to perform their job and are liable to arrest, compulsory detention and severe penalties on charges related to publishing and the expression of critical opinions. Some journalists have been threatened with assassination, physical assault and intimidation. Reports issued by the Arab Journalists Federation as well as in-

ternational and national human rights organisations provide plentiful examples of such persecution.

Governments also impose restrictions on issuing newspapers and establishing new television channels. These restrictions sometimes take the form of impractical requirements, such as requiring large capital deposits as a condition for establishing a corporation, or restricting ownership of television channels to satellite (as opposed to terrestrial) stations.

At the same time, it must be acknowledged that some newspapers and journalists pursue irresponsible practices and disregard the ethics of their profession. Tabloid journalism purveying sex, crime and sensation in pursuit of advertising profits and sales has become widespread in some Arab countries. Violations of citizens' right to privacy have increased, and many people are subjected to slander, libel, defamation and abuse.

The momentous events facing the Arab region undoubtedly pose large challenges to the media, particularly since they have now become important tools in conflicts and wars. This was evident in the case of the occupation of Iraq. Some media, including a number of Arab ones, have risen to these new challenges, displaying new levels of objectivity and courage. Others have dropped in public estimation for providing biased or one-sided accounts. Reporting on modern theaters of conflict often, incurs harassment and dangers for journalists, who sometimes suffer casualties, especially when the aggressor has something to hide from the public eye. Eight journalists, seven Palestinean and one British, have been killed under Israeli occupation in less than 2 years. During the invasion of Iraq, Al-Jazeera correspondent, Tareq Ayoub, was killed in an attack on the network's offices in Baghdad.

MODERN MASS MEDIA

The core platform on which a modern information system rests is built around its associated technologies, equipment, computer networks, software, databases and communication systems. In most societies, this infrastructure serves to educate and enlighten the public, improve the management and co-ordi-

The harassment of the press under the law is an all-too-frequent violation of freedom of expression.

nation of research and development, promote the increased effectiveness and efficiency of public and private institutions, and support informed and streamlined decision-making.

The communications infrastructure in any country is the backbone of attempts to benefit from the broad applications of the communication revolution, especially multimedia services. This infrastructure includes telephone lines, television cables, satellite installations, fibre optic lines, computers and peripherals, information networks and media and culture-based industries.

Telephone networks

Telephone networks are access roads leading to the information highway. They are one of the most important indicators of information availability. Some Arab countries have succeeded in improving their infrastructure in this regard, while still lagging behind international levels. The number of lines in Arab countries is about 109/1,000 persons, while it amounts to 561 in developed countries. There is only one telephone for every 10 Arab citizens, while in developed countries the ratio is 1/1.7 persons. (See Figure 2.6 for a world comparison).

The Arab Joint Economic Report indicates that some tangible improvements in communication services have taken place in Arab countries. Phone density increased in the 1990s, and some countries have converted their networks into digital systems.

There are four international and regional projects in communication and information technology of particular importance in the Arab world. Most Arab countries are taking part in these projects with the goal of developing the information and communication sector. They are:

• The Cable Project: 300,000 km long, and connecting more than 100 countries including 14 Arab states;
• The Fibre Optic Cable project: 27,000 km long, in which Saudi Arabia, Egypt, UAE, and Jordan are participating;
• The Simoueh III Project: started operation in 1999 with Egypt, Morocco, and Djibouti participating;
• The Africa Project: This involves all African Arab countries and Saudi Arabia.

Figure 2.6

Number of main phone lines per 1,000 persons(*)

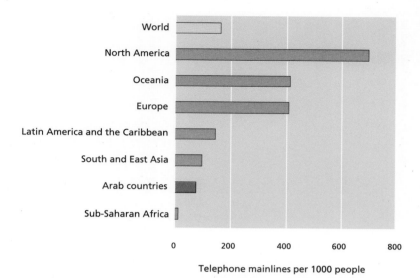

Telephone mainlines per 1000 people

(*) The average is taken as the country-specific likely average (based on population size in 2000) of basic phone data extracted from UNDP HDR 2002. Data on 173 countries (out of a total 179) includes 19 Arab countries.

Yet despite some advances in telephony, overall, public demand for telephone lines in the region outstrips supply, while connections are unreliable and service remains generally poor when compared to developed countries.

Communication technologies

Arab countries have made considerable strides in communication technology, and a number of networks have been digitised. With the creation of Dubai Internet City in 1999, an integrated electronic business, research and development society, UAE demonstrated that it had made rapid progress in ICT. The creation of Dubai Media City (DMC) marks another milestone on the road towards providing a modern infrastructure for an advanced Arab media. DMC has already attracted some major TV channels, including Al-Arabia, MBC, CNN and Reuters TV.

In satellite communication, the modern *Arabsat* network delivers content from various sources across the Arab world. The system delivers a large portfolio of media and information products and services to all Arab countries and parts of Europe as well.

Computer availability is one of the basic standards against which to measure access to information technologies through new technological media. Here, the figures indicate a severe shortage in all Arab countries. There are

There are less than 18 computers per 1,000 persons in the region, compared to the global average of 78.3.

Figure 2.7

Personal computers: Arab world and other regions

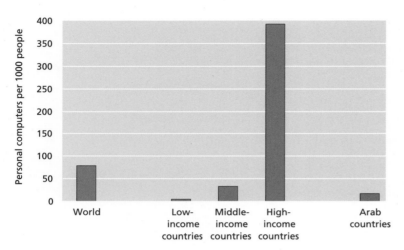

Source: World Bank, 2002.

Cost, political culture and societal context militate against knowledge diffusion through new technologies.

less than 18 computers per 1,000 persons in the region, compared to the global average of 78.3 computers per 1,000 persons. This is hardly an appropriate base for using informatics to spread knowledge and increase demand for it, or for accessing the vast array of scientific research networks, universities and other knowledge sources that throng the Internet.

Figure 2-8

Internet penetration in Arab countries, users as % of population, 2001

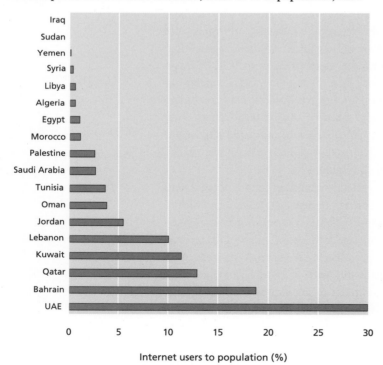

Source: World Markets Research Centre, 2002.

Access to Modern Media

Statistics indicate that the number of Internet users in Arab countries in 2001 reached 4.2 million, i.e., 1.6% of the Arab population compared to just 1% in 2000, a considerable increase even though Internet penetration in the Arab region is still limited in a comparative context.

The low number of Internet users in Arab countries is due to a number of factors, the most important of which are: computer and Internet illiteracy, the high cost of the lines used and high personal computer prices and access fees. Several initiatives have been taken to deal with these problems, including measures to increase competition among service providers, reduce subscription fees and lower telephone line costs. Other initiatives focus on teaching computer skills on a large scale, as is now the case in many schools and universities.

CHALLENGES FACING THE ARAB MEDIA

Evidently, the Arab mass media faces rooted external and internal constraints on its role in transmitting knowledge and encouraging its acquisition. These challenges are intensified by the rapid development in communication and information technologies and the global knowledge explosion that have given the media in other parts of the world a central role in building knowledge societies. To sum up, in Arab countries:

• People do not have sufficient access to the media and information technologies, compared to world rates and to other countries in the region, and in proportion to the population of the Arab world.

• The social and intellectual benefits of mass media and communication are diluted by government restrictions on content and by superficial market preferences.

• The public relates to the media as a passive recipient, rather than an active participant.

In other words, cost, political culture and societal context militate against knowledge diffusion through new technologies.

The information and communication policies of most Arab countries are similar, inasmuch as they place the media under the dominant political authorities and institutions and employ media channels for political propaganda and entertainment, at the expense of other functions and services.

Within the Arab media establishment itself, deficiencies such as lack of planning, lack of information, documents and research and a high degree of centralisation impair the organisation, relevance and flexibility of media services. In-depth awareness of audience habits and preferences with respect to information, especially outside the capital and major cities, is also lacking.

State ownership of the media is the norm, particularly in the case of radio and television. (Lebanon, where these mass media services are run by private organisations, is the exception.) Newspapers in the region can be state-owned or jointly owned. Some countries, such as Egypt, Tunisia, Morocco and Lebanon, allow parties to issue newspapers. Yet these publications are subject to specific controls and limitations, particularly for individuals. For these reasons, many individuals and groups have resorted to issuing newspapers from foreign countries such as the United Kingdom, Cyprus and France.

The revolution in communication technology has made it possible for some individuals and corporations to launch private satellite channels in Arabic from foreign countries. Egypt recently permitted the broadcasting of private Egyptian satellite channels from within the country. The conditions governing media ownership in Arab countries raise many questions about the real opportunities available to Arab citizens for exercising their right to issue newspapers, attain information, express thoughts and opinions and monitor government institutions. Another point of concern is the selective homogeneity of Arab media content, considering that diversity of information is an important prerequisite for the attainment of knowledge.

Globalisation has led to an intense debate about the viability of state-owned media, and the ability of governments to sustain their monopoly in an age of free information. This direction of change could potentially support media freedom and people's right to communicate. Some Arabs fear that reducing the role of the state may, however, favour the expansion of the role of multinational corporations (MNCs). This question goes to the heart of the independence of the Arab media, since one of the main obstacles facing Arab attempts to own communication technologies is the monopoly of major MNCs in the production and marketing of these very technologies.

Arab countries, therefore, need to co-operate closely to raise the performance and independence of the media as a vital conduit of knowledge transfer and as a means of increasing the transparency of government and public services.

The Beginnings of Free Media

The last two years have, however, seen some improvements in the Arab information environment, compared to dominant trends in past decades. While there is still some way to go towards creating an informed, open and knowledgeable public, observers discern a new, more enquiring and therefore more hopeful spirit in the media.

Despite the continuing dominance of monolithic official media channels marked by a single political point of view, the Arabic press has entered a new stage characterised by dawning competition. Newspapers and information media that have enjoyed a monopoly over Arab readers for a long time are encountering new challenges. Arabic newspapers – some published abroad, such as "Al-Hayat", "Asharq Al-Awsat" and "Al-Quds Al-Arabi" – and some published at home, such as "Annahar", "Assafeer", "Al-Khaleej", and "Al-Bayan" are producing highly professional journalism and enjoy a margin of freedom much larger than that of the official press. With their political and intellectual advantages and their greater financial resources, these newspapers attract a large number of the best Arab writers.

The official press can no longer ignore its new competitors. The challengers have managed to cross borders and overcome censorship barriers, using the Internet to reach farther than paper-based media. Newspapers, such as "Tishreen" of Syria and "Al-Ittihad" of the United Arab Emirates, have gone as far as to open public dialogue forums through their web sites.

These changes have not been limited to the press. Television has also undergone re-

The conditions governing media ownership in Arab countries raise many questions about the real opportunities available to Arab citizens for exercising their right to knowledge.

The Arabic press has entered a new stage characterised by dawning competition.

markable changes during the past two years. Private Arabic channels are able to compete for news items and pictures with the strongest international television establishments, as was demonstrated clearly during the Anglo-American war on Iraq. These private channels have instilled a new spirit in Arabic television, helping to change thinking and procedures among some Arabic satellite stations, many of them government-run, such as the "Abu Dhabi Television Station", the "Nile News Channel" and other official channels in North African Arab countries. There is no doubt that independent Arabic channels have managed to break the monopoly of the big channels over images and news. Some analysts have ventured to conclude that although the international coalition won the military battle in Iraq, the Arabs may have won the information battle. Whether this is speculation or fact, there is clearly a larger role for the Arab camera to play in presenting the world through its lens.

Although the political environment surrounding the Arab media is not the most favourable to knowledge development, some actors have succeeded in creating information and documentation centres, such as those established by "Al-Ahram", "Al-Bayan", "Al-Hayat" and "Asharq Al-Awsat". These offer Arab researchers opportunities previously not available to reap the benefits of the information and digital revolutions.

The creation of Arabic Internet newspapers marks an important further step towards a more inclusive and pluralistic media open to young talent. Several of these newspapers play a positive role in publicising Arab issues in the international arena, through their networks with newspapers managed by international non-governmental organisations. Some, however, still lack credibility with the Arab public and need time to mature: their content often suggests an inability to distinguish between chaff and grain.

The hope is that these beginnings will widen the margins of political freedom in the Arab world, raise the quality of its media and strengthen the important relationship between good governance and the knowledge society. The most important characteristic of these recent developments is that the new media use

the Arabic language, and are therefore starting to reach the largest segment of the Arab public. This contrasts with the prevailing situation where Arabic newspapers, which are published in foreign languages, still enjoy a wider readership than those published in Arabic. Some of the former, such as the "Al-Ahram Weekly" in Cairo, "The Daily Star" and "L'Orient Le Jour" in Beirut, and "Gulf News" in UAE have achieved a high degree of excellence.

TRANSLATION

Translation is a means of seeking knowledge. It represents an interaction among civilisations through the transfer from one language into another, by humans or machines, written or oral, with the goal of achieving scientific and cultural objectives. The question facing Arab countries is: how can translation become an asset in building knowledge? How can it be mobilised to enhance the frame of mind of individuals and increase the intellectual and cultural reference of society? How can it contribute new values, new ways of thinking and new forms of empowerment? Certainly, translation creates opportunities for the acquisition and transfer of knowledge within the framework of global communication networks built up by communication culture. It opens up spaces for mutual interaction and influence, and protects societies from becoming passive recipients of imported knowledge, especially when those societies cease to be producers of knowledge themselves.

Developed and developing countries alike are moving fast to acquire the ever-increasing quantity of knowledge in its original language. Today, English represents around 85% of the total world knowledge balance. Thus, more and more knowledge-hungry countries are paying attention to translation from sources other than English. Efforts in this regard are not restricted to recent or contemporary knowledge, but extend to heritage, history, classical literature and other extant knowledge. Countries mastering these sources are becoming encyclopaedic global knowledge banks and authoritative centres of reference on world information and terminology. New corporations specialised in translation have been established and there have been significant initiatives by official institutions, such as the UK WORDBANK, which employs 550 professional translators. According to Newsweek, translation costs in 1989 amounted to $20 billion. There are more than 100,000 translated titles published in the world every year. The total number of publications, authored or translated, exceeds 830,000 titles annually, and the market for translation continues to boom.

Consider the case of Japan: at the outset of its phase of advancement (the Meiji era), Japan set about transferring all scientific and cultural knowledge into Japanese, in addition to sending outstanding students to learn advanced sciences from the West. Japan has also concluded agreements with major international publishing houses to publish a Japanese edition of each scientific publication immediately after its publication in its original language. It is estimated that 1,700 titles are translated annually. Now, Japan translates 30 million pages a year.

The United States has set its sights on being the global reference point and data bank of the world. Despite the fact that almost 85% of the world's scientific production is in English, the US makes it a point to translate all scientific publications, as well as the cultural legacy of world civilizations.

The state of translation in Arab countries

For Arab societies, translation is a formidable challenge and a vital requirement that necessitates the organisation and planning of efforts within the framework of an ambitious and integrated Arab strategy.

The history of translation in the modern period began in both Egypt and Lebanon for different reasons, and thus it followed different courses. In Lebanon, translation started as an attempt to protect the Arabic language from Ottoman "Turkisation". In Egypt it started during the era of Muhamad Ali and took the form of an active social movement. Sheikh *Rifaa Al-Tahtawi* managed to make translation a social institution, which contributed to the achievement of a national project, and which aimed at bringing about an overall revival of science and industry. This ac-

tivity, though, was obstructed and eventually failed.

Most Arab countries have not learned from the lessons of the past and the field of translation remains chaotic. In terms of quantity, and notwithstanding the increase in the number of translated books from 175 per year during 1970-1975 to 330, the number of books translated in the Arab world is one fifth of the number translated in Greece. The aggregate total of translated books from the *Al-Ma'moon* era to the present day amounts to 10,000 books - equivalent to what Spain translates in a single year (Shawki Galal, *in Arabic*, 1999, 87)[3].

This disparity was revealed in the first half of the 1980s when the average number of books translated per 1 million people in the Arab world during the 5-year period was 4.4 (less than one book for every million Arabs), while in Hungary it was 519, and in Spain 920. (Figure 2.9.)

There are no accurate statistical data regarding the academic level of these translations. But a marked shortage of translations of basic books on philosophy, literature, sociology and the natural sciences is quite evident. Meanwhile, translations of some titles of much lesser importance exist. A crucial policy for the future will be to organise the selection of

The aggregate total of translated books from the Al-Ma'moon era to the present day amounts to 10,000 books - equivalent to what Spain translates in a single year.

---

[3]This number was erroneously stated as 100,000 in AHDR1.

books for translation in order to fulfil Arab academic research needs. Such a policy is required to make translation an effective force in advancing research and knowledge in the region.

Figure 2.9
**Number of books translated in Arab countries
(per 1 million people) compared to selected countries, 1981-1985**

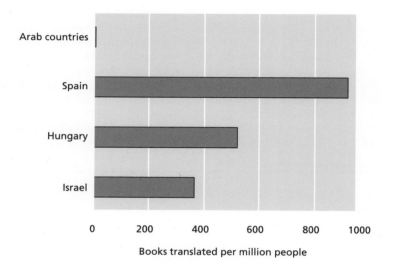

Books translated per million people

Source: Unesco, 1995.

This chapter shows that the dissemination of knowledge in Arab countries is beset by many difficulties. Chief among these is the absence of a strategic vision and societal incentives that provide a solid foundation for knowledge dissemination through education, media, publishing and translation. These channels have the potential to be major shapers of a cultural and scientific climate conducive to knowledge adaptation and production. Yet in all three, quality, excellence and independence, which remain the most important dimensions of a knowledge society, have suffered. This trend has to be reversed through conscious policy-making. The following chapter discusses knowledge acquisition on higher levels of society, focusing on the production of knowledge.

CHAPTER 3

Knowledge production in Arab countries

The production of knowledge, the focus of this chapter, takes place at an advanced stage of knowledge acquisition in any society and is the widest, if not the only, gateway to the world knowledge society. The quantity and quality of knowledge produced by a society is evidence of its ability to add to the world reserve of human knowledge and to renew the wellsprings of its own creativity.

What is the status of Arab scientific, technological, literary and artistic production today? What are the factors that have shaped the current situation? This line of enquiry holds the essential keys to the development of knowledge producing societies in the region.

This chapter seeks to evaluate the amount of knowledge produced in the Arab world. It also analyses how far the conditions required by a knowledge society (qualified research workers, innovative institutions, supportive policies) are present in the region. In doing so, it investigates the quality of scientific research and technological development, and the products of creativity in the humanities, social sciences and the arts. The two central questions that all Arab countries must answer are: what in the past and present points to a brighter future for the advancement of knowledge production in Arab countries, and what are the means that will enable countries to own science, rather than merely importing some of its applications and results?

The history of scientific development shows that science cannot be developed without institutions dedicated to this purpose and without promoting the vocation of scientists and scientific applications. Moreover, scientific culture can only pass from one society to another, whether by means of translation or the transfer of scientists and know-how, if the requisite infrastructure and institutions for embracing science and owning it are in place.

Europe would not have been able to utilise scientific knowledge at the beginning of the industrial revolution had not scientific education, on the one hand, and scientific culture, on the other, permeated society through many channels.

BOX 3.1

Muhamad Ali's Experience in Scientific Modernisation

The first attempt at scientific modernisation in the Arab world was made by Muhamad Ali in the first half of the 19th century. This attempt, as well as others that followed it, encountered several stumbling blocks.

Two illusions thwarted the attempt and they continue to trap many developing countries. The first was the belief that scientific production could be transferred without planning and building a strong infrastructure for research, and without laying the foundation of a scientific and technological culture in society at large. The second, an outcome of the first, was the erroneous belief that basic research is dispensable for financial reasons.

Source: Roshdi Rashed, in Arabic, background paper for AHDR2.

BOX 3.2

Ali Mustafa Mosharrifah* - On the importance of the history of science for a knowledge renaissance

Civilised nations must have a culture associated with the history of their scientific thought... Our scientific life in Egypt needs to be attached to our past in order to acquire the necessary strength, vitality and controls. We in Egypt transfer the knowledge of others and leave it floating without any relationship to our past or any contact with our land. It is a commodity that is foreign in its features, foreign in its words and foreign in its concepts. If we mention theories, we associate them with faceless names that we hardly know. If we talk about concepts, we use intimidating words that drive away thoughts and unsettle the mind.

We have first to publish the scientific books authored by Arabs and translated by Europeans, like the books of al-Khwarizmi and Abu Kamel in algebra and arithmetic, those of Ibn al-Haytham in physics, of al-Buzjani, al-Bayroni, al-Battani and other leaders of scientific thought and talented researchers... We must pay attention to honouring our ancient scientists and researchers. This will prompt us to imitate them and follow in their footsteps.

*The first professor of mathematical physics and the first Arab Dean of the Faculty of Science, Cairo University.

Source: Roshdi Rashed, background paper for AHDR 2.

SCIENTIFIC PRODUCTION: NATURAL SCIENCES AND TECHNOLOGICAL DEVELOPMENT

SCIENTIFIC RESEARCH AND TECHNOLOGICAL DEVELOPMENT – OUTPUTS

Arabic research activity continues to be far from innovative.

Up-to-date and accurate information about the outcomes of research and development (R&D) in the Arab region is hard to come by in the absence of comprehensive statistics on specialised sectors or research topics. Yet certain outputs can be measured through scientific publications, patents and inventions.

Scientific research

Based on the number of scientific publications per million people (26 research papers in 1995), Arab countries fall within the advanced group of developing countries, which include Brazil (42), China (11) and India (19), although they are still far removed from the production levels of developed countries, such as France (840), the Netherlands (1,252) and Switzerland (1,878).

The scientific publication movement in the Arab world experienced a substantial increase in the last three decades of the 20th century. The number of papers published by Arab scholars in specialised global periodicals increased from 465 papers in 1967 to nearly 7,000 in 1995, i.e., by 10% annually. This increase was, however, modest in comparison with some developing countries, such as Brazil, China and East Asian Tigers such as Korea. Calculating the rate of increase in published scientific papers per one million people makes an instructive comparison with these countries. Based on that indicator, the number of scientific papers per one million people in the People's Republic of China in 1995 was 11 times what it was in 1981. In South Korea, it was 24 times greater. In Arab countries, however, it was only 2.4 times greater, increasing from 11 papers per one million people in 1981 to 26 papers in 1995.

At the institutional level, only 26 Arab scientific institutions published more than 50 research papers each in 1995, while only five such institutions published more that 200 pa-

Research in advanced fields, such as information technology and molecular biology, is almost non-existent.

pers.

Most of these publications were in applied fields, such as medicine, health and agriculture. Medicine, health and life sciences accounted for 32% of the total R&D products published by Arab countries in 1995 and chemistry accounted for 19% of total research products for that year. When one adds to these fields the papers published in agriculture, engineering and associated fields the total products of applied research represented 90% of all publications. Publications in basic sciences, astronomy, chemistry, physics and mathematics did not exceed 10% of total research (Amr Armanazi, background paper for this report).

These rates have important implications. Despite the increase in the number of published Arabic research papers in specialised global periodicals, Arabic research activity continues to be far from innovative. Most of it is applied research and only a small portion is related to basic research. Research in advanced fields, such as information technology and molecular biology, is almost non-existent.

Among the indicators for measuring the quality of research in general is the number of references made to it. The higher the level of a research paper and the more it adds to human knowledge the more references it attracts. The first Arab Human Development Report indicated that only one paper each in Egypt, Saudi Arabia, Kuwait and Algeria in 1987 was quoted more than 40 times, while in the United States 10,481 papers were quoted more than 40 times and in Switzerland 523 papers (First Arab Human Development Report, 2002, p. 67).

Patents

Indicators of the number of patents in Arab countries confirm the weakness of R&D activity, which lags far behind that of developed countries and other countries of the developing world. Table 3-1 indicates the number of patents registered in the United States during the period 1980-2000 for some Arab countries, compared to patents registered from selected non-Arab countries. It should be noted that a large number of patents registered in Arab countries are by foreigners. (Amr Armanazi, background paper for the Report).

Scientific publications and patents are useful but insufficient indicators of scientific research and technological development activity. They do not indicate the full spectrum of innovation activity, which is more related to development support products. National innovation, in general, includes the development of new products, production processes and services and the development of modern technologies for sectors where technology plays an important role in performance and increases efficiency. Indicators related to innovation processes, such as the design and engineering of products, production processes and software, are not readily available. Innovative capabilities can, however, be gauged by demonstrating the widespread presence of innovations in national and foreign markets that can be counted and evaluated. On that criterion, there are virtually no Arab innovations on the market, a fact that confirms that Arab scientific research has not yet reached the innovation stage.

TECHNOLOGICAL RESEARCH AND DEVELOPMENT – INPUTS

Producing knowledge workers

Higher education fuels the knowledge society and produces those who will work in it. National scientific research and development activities, as well as industries, need highly qualified graduates and researchers with enquiring and trained minds and flexible skills.

Statistics indicate a sustained increase in the number of students in higher education institutions in Arab countries over successive years, with a noticeable increase in the number of female students. These statistics indicate, however, that only a small number of students and graduates have opted to specialise in basic sciences, engineering, medicine and other scientific subjects. The low rate of graduates, both researchers and technicians, in science and technology disciplines undercuts efforts to build balanced human capacity in the field of science and technology. There is also a need for larger numbers of graduates of intermediate technical institutes to enlarge the pool of workers with technical know-how and skills of a practical nature.

TABLE 3.1
Number of patents registered in the United States from Arab and non-Arab countries during the period 1980-1999/2000

Arab Countries		Other Countries	
Country	**No. of Patents**	**Country**	**No. of Patents**
Bahrain	6	Korea	16,328
Egypt	77	Israel	7,652
Jordan	15	Chile	147
Kuwait	52		
Oman	5		
Saudi Arabia	171		
Syria	10		
UAE	32		
Yemen	2		

Source: Abdulkader Djeflat (March 1999) and Omar Bizri (April 2000).

Training in Arab countries in general is driven by supply rather than demand and the focus is on quantity, not quality. With a few exceptions, higher education systems respond weakly to labour market needs related to science and technology. This situation is not expected to change noticeably, barring a strong push on the demand side from industry, business and national institutions and in the context of coherent and comprehensive science and technology policies, which clearly emphasise these urgent orientations. Upgrading the level and quality of training also depends on an increase in funding. Higher education institutions generally underscore that they lack resources, a complaint borne out by statistics related to per capita expenditure, with some variations between Arab countries. The under-funding of higher education impacts negatively on science and technology in particular, because these fields require the provision and renovation of costly special facilities, equipment and materials. Meagre facilities inevitably lead to a marked decline in the level of graduates in science and technology fields, which in turn limits the ability of research centres and productive firms which employ these graduates to achieve advanced levels of scientific and technological performance and accomplishment.

In general, the ratio of students enrolled in scientific disciplines in higher education in Arab countries is small, compared to advanced countries in the field of knowledge, such as Korea, although Jordan, followed by Algeria, are distinguished among Arab countries in this field. See Figure 3.1.

Training in Arab countries is generally driven by supply rather than demand and the focus is on quantity, not quality.

The under-funding of higher education impacts negatively on science and technology in particular.

Workers in scientific research and development

The data available on the number of R&D and technical workers in the region and by individual countries is scarce and incomplete.

Figure 3.1

Ratio of students enrolled in scientific disciplines in higher education in selected Arab countries and Korea, 1990-1995

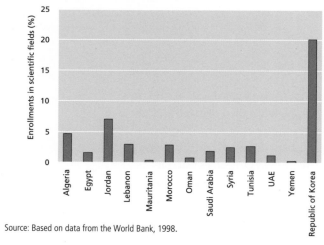

Source: Based on data from the World Bank, 1998.

Figure 3.2

Number of scientists and engineers working in research and development (per one million people)*

Regions of the world, 1990-2000

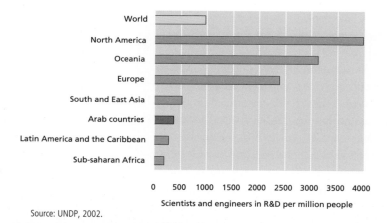

Scientists and engineers in R&D per million people

Source: UNDP, 2002.

There are, however, a number of telling indicators of the present situation:

• The total number of full-time researchers in Arab countries, including those pursuing the equivalent of full-time research among teaching staff, is around 35,000. Half of this number works in Egypt.

• There is an average of 3.3 researchers holding masters and doctoral degrees for every 10,000 persons in the Arab work force (1996 statistics). This is a very low percentage, representing 3% to 10% of the rates of the same indicator in developed countries.

• There are only 50 technicians for every one million citizens, another very low figure when compared to the 1000 technicians per million citizens in developed countries.

• Women and their talents are significantly under-represented in scientific research institutions in Arab countries. In Egypt the percentage is relatively higher than in other Arab countries. Nevertheless, across the region, considerable potential exists for investing much more in women scientists, engineers, and technicians. (Amr Armanazi, in *Arabic*, background paper).

Figure 3.2 indicates the low ratio of scientists and engineers working on research and development in Arab countries compared to other regions of the world.

The number of countries on which data are available was 91 countries (out of 179), of which only 5 were Arab countries.

Expenditure

Stimulating research and development requires the political will to indigenise science and establish the necessary infrastructure. This calls for greater R&D outlays than the fractional sums Arab countries currently invest, which do not exceed 0.2% of GNP, although this ratio varies from one country to another. For comparison purposes, the ratios spent by developed countries vary from 2.5% to 5%. Furthermore, 89% of expenditure on R&D in Arab countries comes from governmental sources, while productive and service sectors spend only 3%, as against more than 50% in developed countries. (See Table 3.2)

The low level of investment in research by

---

* The average number in the region is calculated as a weighted average (population number in 2000) for data on the number of scientists and engineers working in research and development by country.

the productive sector, both public and private, is a clear indication of the poor environment for, and weak level of innovative activity in Arab countries, considering that government spending largely covers only salaries.

As these figures illustrate, societal awareness of the far-reaching importance of supporting scientists and science is extremely weak. The enormous gains in knowledge that accrue from a vital local R&D establishment should not be held hostage to social indifference. Leadership is required to motivate Arab societies to take responsibility for research and innovation. In developed countries, enterprises, wealthy individuals, foundations and non-profit organisations all finance such research.

In the long run, boosting public and private investment in R&D activity will raise the added value of products, processes and services generated from such research, provided that new research is translated through innovation activities into commercially marketable results. Successful commercialisation would make it possible to invest a portion of the resulting profits in financing future innovation activities. This would generate a sustainable financing dynamic, which would continuously replenish R&D. It would transform R&D from a drain on state and private sector budgets to a profitable investment, supporting the gross national product and driving the wheel of economic and social development. Encouraging the private sector to finance R&D does not, however, imply that the state should relinquish its important responsibilities in this field. Scientific research, especially basic research, cannot be a captive of the market. States play a large role in ensuring policy conditions conducive to institutional research, and in incentivising the private sector, through tax and other instruments, to invest in research and innovation.

Institutions

There are essentially three categories of Arab institutions that focus on research and knowledge development. The first are higher education institutes and their affiliated research centres; the second are free-standing specialised centres of scientific research; and the third are R&D units with links to industry.

TABLE 3.2

Rate of expenditure as a percentage of GNP and sources of R&D funding: Arab states compared with selected countries, 1990-1995

Region or group of countries	Average expenditure (% of GNP)	Percentage share of funding sources		
		Government	Industry	Other
United States, Japan and Sweden	3.1	20-30	55-70	4-10
Germany, France, United Kingdom, Italy, Australia and Canada	2.4	38	52	10
Greece, Portugal and Spain	0.7	54	35	11
Turkey and Mexico	0.4	65-73	14-31	5
Arab states	0.2	89	3	8

Source: Subhi Al-Qasim, 1999.

According to some estimates, there are a total of 588 such entities in the region.

There are 184 Arab universities, all with activities associated with higher education and scientific research and promotion. Scientific research in higher educational institutions and some associated centres is often academic in character, although there are visible moves in some Arab countries (Algeria, Iraq, Qatar, Libya, Egypt and Morocco) to link a portion of research projects to societal needs.

The specialised scientific research centres associated with some universities vary in size, means and productivity, but most of them focus on agricultural, health and engineering research. (The total number of centres specialising in industry, energy and petrochemicals does not exceed one-third of the number of centres specialising in agriculture). According to available estimates, there are some 126 of these affiliated centres in all Arab countries. (Taha Tayeh Al-Nu'aimi, Scientific Institutions in the Arab Homeland and their Impact on Scientific Research Activity, 2000.)

In the second category, there are approximately 278 scientific research centres and organisations outside universities, including central research organs (national research centres and institutes) and those connected with ministries or industrial and agricultural firms. Table 3.3 indicates the distribution of these centres in the various Arab countries.

The great majority of these centres specialise in agriculture, water resources, health, nutrition and the environment. Centres specialising in biotechnology or electronics do not

Leadership is required to motivate Arab societies to take responsibility for research and innovation.

Scientific research, especially basic research, cannot be a captive of the market.

TABLE 3.3
Number of scientific research centres (outside of universities) in Arab countries

Country	No. of centres	Country	No. of centres
Algeria	30	Oman	2
Bahrain	1	Palestine	13
Djibouti	1	Qatar	3
Egypt	73	Saudi Arabia	7
Iraq	22	Somalia	3
Jordan	9	Sudan	14
Kuwait	5	Syria	15
Lebanon	9	Tunisia	24
Libya	18	UAE	3
Mauritania	3	Yemen	9
Morocco	16		
	Total		**280**

Source: Al-Nu'aimi, 2000.

Research projects often lack clear objectives, a firm results orientation and a sense of urgency.

exceed 3 percent of the total.

The third category of R&D institutions is the research and development units associated with productive enterprises or established as independent units. These units are small in number and their performance is below expected levels. There are no specific data about their total number, but it is estimated that there are some 16 units belonging to the private sector and concerned with industry. (Amr Armanazi, background paper for this report.)

The amount of R&D activity in the organisations and centres outside universities seems, in general, to be the same level as that carried out in the universities and the centres associated with them. University-based research itself is often either purely academic or narrowly applied in orientation, and is mainly driven by supply. In both arenas, research projects often lack clear objectives, a firm results orientation and a sense of urgency linked to producing high-impact developmental outcomes within a time-bound plan.

TABLE 3.4
Number of scientific and technological research centres (outside universities) in Arab countries, by field of specialisation and number of countries of location

Research field	No. of centres	Percentage	No. of Arab countries of location
Agriculture and water resources	76	27	15
Industrial	34	12	14
Construction and development	8	3	7
Health, nutrition and environment	43	16	11
Space and remote sensing	17	6	10
Energy	22	8	12
Basic and pure sciences	11	4	6
Informatics, computer and communications	5	2	4
Biotechnologies	4	1	4
Electronics	4	1	3
Other	54	20	15

Source: calculated from data by Al-Nu'aimi et al., 1988.

Possibly the most telling sign of weakness in Arab scientific R&D agencies is their inability to transform research results into investment projects. This vital orientation is usually either missing in research plans in the first place, or is simply beyond the knowledge, expertise, and facilities these institutions can muster.

PRODUCTION IN THE HUMANITIES AND SOCIAL SCIENCES

The human sciences have historical traditions dating back to the time before the independence of the Arab countries, as is the case with studies of history and civilization, for instance. Social sciences as full-fledged disciplines, however, did not emerge and take hold in these countries until after independence when universities and research centres were established to teach and research these sciences. In other words, social sciences did not exist in the Arab world before the 1960s, with a few exceptions, mainly Egypt. In some countries, such as the Arabian Gulf countries, they did not emerge until a decade later.

The status of human and social sciences differs from one Arab country to the next in the level of their development, scholarship and social and political returns. There is not enough accurate data to draw an Arab map of their distribution. There are, however, general trends, which can be monitored on the basis of partial indicators. While Iraqis and Syrians, for instance, made excellent contributions to the study of history and civilisation, Egyptians made advanced contributions in the field of economic and political sciences, compared to other Arabs. Research traditions in sociology and anthropology seem stronger in the Arab *Maghreb*, in terms of both theory and methodology (Al-Taher Labib, background paper for this report).

The emergence of specialised research and training in these fields is tied to the rise of the modern nation-state, the national projects it proposed and the difficulties it faced in its early stages. From the outset, social sciences and human sciences dealing with "national history" were subject to political and bureaucratic steering. Directives to "find practical solutions" defined their mission. This pragmatic trend incurred for certain disciplines, particularly sociology, an unjust reputation for being purely empirical, with no theoretical structure. That prejudice continues today. It also led to the emergence of certain "specialisations" with direct practical goals, such as "social service", a trend that spread throughout universities in countries of the Arab East, but which did not affect most of the *Maghreb* countries.

Many Arab scholars in the human and social sciences draw attention to a paradox in their situation. They note that, for Arab academics, students and researchers in particular, higher barriers have, in the course of events, actually accompanied the globalisation of knowledge, despite its promise of freer flows of knowledge, ideas and people. Undeniably, strained relations between some Western countries and Arab countries at different times have had an impact on the development of the human and physical sciences. This obstacle partly accounts for a regression in knowledge of foreign languages among university students and graduates who have remained in their own countries. A new kind of monolingual professor and researcher has started to gradually replace the kind of bilingual academic who in the past dominated most Arab universities and research centres. It has also affected Arab participation at international scientific meetings and, consequently, the Arab presence in international scientific groups and networks. (Al-Taher Labib, background paper for this report.)

A form of Arab self-containment hobbles co-operation with international partners in the humanities and social sciences. The emphasis on the "specificity" of Arab societies, a common preoccupation in Arab countries, has played a negative role in this respect, leading to a neglect of anything that is not "related to our reality" and a narrow focus in research on local or purely Arab subjects. This tendency has sometimes deprived Arab scholars of a comparative perspective and the capacity to link the particularities of their context to general structures and trends in the wider world. There is no accumulated tradition of Arab scholarship on the "Other". Institutions concerned with the study of other societies are almost non-existent. This is a striking incongruity, given the external challenges faced by Arab countries.

Meanwhile, this form of insularity also affects Arab students pursuing research abroad, the majority of whom concentrate on research topics about their own countries or region. Few Arab PhD theses earned outside the region deal with the society in which the researcher temporarily resides. On the other hand, students and researchers who come to the Arab world, often do so to become more closely acquainted with the Arab world and to study it.

As a result, there is no accumulation of an Arab stock of scientific knowledge about "the Other". While Arab scholarship is becoming more inward looking, this tendency is not related to the will of scholars as individuals, but rather to a whole tradition and set of political choices.

Difficulties in the cognitive relationship with the "Other", and those arising from communication in Arabic, have thus limited how far Arab research is integrated into international networks. This, in turn, places restrictions on the universal dimension of research in Arabic. There are only a handful of Arab scholars and researchers who regularly write in foreign languages, whether English or French, and who commonly address issues of global interest.

It must, however, be said that Arab researchers, for all their concentration on Arab issues, have yet to establish a single dynamic Arab network or scientific group. A few scientific societies and professional associations have sprung up in disciplines such as economics, sociology, philosophy and history. But on the whole, Arab production in the social and human sciences remains an essentially individual effort and there are no circles or institutions that consistently work on bringing Arab researchers together and supporting them in an organised manner.

Thus, Arab researchers in the humanities and social sciences frequently work in a vacuum. They are integrated with neither global nor Pan-Arab groups. This isolation has led in several cases to observable frustration that has begun to turn into a general mood, reflected in a withdrawal into individual pursuits and a kind of indifference, not only to public affairs

There is no accumulated tradition of Arab scholarship on the "Other".

While Arab scholarship is becoming more inward looking, this tendency is not related to the will of scholars as individuals, but rather to a whole tradition and set of choices.

but also to questions of knowledge *per se.*

Freedom of intellectual expression may be a more central issue in human and social sciences than in natural science because of the very nature of the study rather than the nature of the intellectual. In the Arab world, the former sciences are subject to many factors that limit freedom of thought. In addition to social and cultural limitations inherited and internalised, there is the intervention of politics and laws associated with politics, which directly or invisibly draw red lines for research in the humanities and social sciences.

Freedom of thought and of expression, and the laws to guarantee them, are primary enabling requirements for quality scholarship and intellectual development. These requirements ought to be seen not only in a political perspective, but also from the standpoint of knowledge. Serious work is needed to persuade Arab governments that restricting intellectual freedom is tantamount to depriving society of its capacity to generate the meaningful, innovative and productive knowledge that is a precondition for survival and success in the 21st century.

LITERARY AND ARTS PRODUCTION

Literary production, as a field of knowledge, transcends material reality, yet a powerful intrinsic relationship remains between the creative imagination and reality. A work of imagination is both mirror and lamp. It reflects reality and illuminates it at the same time. Literary knowledge is intricately tied to social dialectics. It is a form of knowledge inasmuch as it draws on reality and is inspired by it. It then transfigures that reality in a manner that surpasses what is and looks forward to what can be.

It is important to distinguish between the status of literature and the arts and the status of scientific research and technological development. Compared to the extent of knowledge production in the sciences, Arab societies have produced a wealth of distinguished literary and artistic work that stands up to high

standards of evaluation. The main reason for this divergent performance lies in the essential difference between the prerequisites for literary and scientific production. While it is impossible for an Arab scientist to win the Nobel Prize in physics without having access to the basic requirements of scientific research – such as a serious political commitment to supporting R&D and a social context that values science and scientists and offers requisite facilities, including laboratories, qualified work teams and sufficient financing – it is possible for an Arab novelist to win the Nobel Prize for Literature without institutional or material support. There is no causal connection between prosperity and good literary production. In some instances, difficult circumstances and intellectual and political challenges can actually motivate artists and stimulate literary creativity. Yet while censors cannot defeat creativity itself, they can lengthen the gauntlet to be run in putting creative products into the hands of the public.[1]

Nevertheless, Arab authors and artists face great difficulties of their own. While there may be no conditional relationship between literary creativity and prosperity, yet, for this creativity to flourish and grow and benefit the surrounding environment, artistic expression needs a climate of freedom and cultural pluralism. It also benefits from strong financial and institutional support. These circumstances are not available to most Arab creative artists. In general, Arab artists in all fields (literature, plastic arts, music, theatre, and cinema) work without support from institutions. Success or failure, sustained or sporadic production, depend largely on the personal circumstances of each artist.

THE SHORT STORY AND THE NOVEL

The rise of the Arab novel and short story are linked to the beginnings of the modern era. They have come to represent a new creative discourse parallel to the movement of society and expressive of its struggles and crises. In the second half of the 20th century, the Arab

Restricting intellectual freedom is tantamount to depriving society of its capacity to generate the meaningful, innovative and productive knowledge that is a precondition for survival and success in the 21st century.

A work of imagination is both mirror and lamp.

---

[1] A paradox of Arab censorship: the novel which won the prize for creativity in the Arab cultural capital in 2002 was banned from distribution in that same capital by the censor. In another case, the novels of the author who won the first prize in the largest book exhibition in the region in 2002 were subsequentry banned.

novel and short story achieved a qualitative and quantitative presence as accepted art forms. All Arab societies now contribute to producing both forms, with no substantial difference between countries at the centre and those on the periphery.

Poetry, on the other hand, which is the distinctive literary genre of the Arabs, has been touched by the winds of change. The movement of modern Arab poetry testifies to this. Moreover, while poetry once dominated Arab culture the modern Arab literary tradition has widened to accommodate the novel and short story as well.

There are no accurate statistics on the actual amount of literary production in the Arab world; and the conflicting figures that are available call for prudent treatment. For example, sources note that between 1990 and 1995 in Lebanon, approximately 564 works for children were published, compared to 730 in Egypt (Faisal Hajji, in *Arabic*, 1995). However, there are many books for both children and adults without registered numbers, as a visit to Egypt's National Library would confirm, which renders the process of tracking books very difficult. Turning to UNESCO statistics on the volume of world publications shows that, in 1991, Arab countries produced *6,500* books compared to 102,000 books in North America, and 42,000 in Latin America and the Caribbean, (Figure 3-3.) Book production, including literary production, in Arab countries is evidently far from vigorous in comparison to the size of the population and with other countries.

Book production in Arab countries was just 1.1 percent of world production, although Arabs constitute 5% of the world's population. The publication of literary works was lower than the average level of book production. In 1996, Arab countries produced no more than 1945 literary and artistic books, which represents 0.8% of international production. This is less than what a country such as Turkey produces, with a population about one-quarter that of the Arab countries. In general, Arab book production centres mainly on religious topics and less on other fields such as literature, art and the social sciences (see figure 3-4). A look at book distribution or accessibility shows that, despite the existence

The Ambition of Creativity in the Arab World

Our civilisation, with all its deep historical and human roots, is a civilisation of text par excellence. Other deep-rooted civilisations are also civilisations of texts and codes, not only of images. Textual creativity continues to be present in us as one of the inputs of the question of advancement, progress and development in our Arab societies, which are still going through the labours of social liberation, as one of the presumed important outputs of the stages of political liberation, crowned with independence. Since we are in the knowledge era, where knowledge and sciences are boundless and encompass all, we live by the group, as represented by civil society institutions, not by individualism. Our era is one of institutions, not of the noble knight who carries a magic wand, which turns dirt into gold. Amid this huge explosion of knowledge, the Arab world is required to reconsider what human advancement means today and to benefit from humankind's accumulated achievements in knowledge, achievements which demonstrate that the world is a call for existence, not non-existence. How creative are societies that continually recreate their own crises?

Man in our current era cannot live like Albert Camus' "stranger" who leads his own life in cold neutrality and total indifference; or as Heidegger says, "as though human beings were thrown into existence", or like Shakespeare's hero, Hamlet, equivocating without any action on his part; or perhaps like Qais (the mad man in love with Layla), satisfied with mentioning Layla without having her with him. Which half of Kafka's cup do we want, while we look at the status of creativity in the Arab world: the full half or the empty half? Perhaps Ibn Arabi showed us the way, when he said: "You think that you are a small planet, while the whole world is embodied in you."

Obstacles to creativity, or, let us say, the glow of creativity in Arab societies are numerous. They are not isolated or individual but are the outcome of extended and multiple interactions with the various issues and crises of Arab societies. Creativity and knowledge are eclipsed by more urgent issues, such as bread for the poor, literacy, unemployment and the low status and marginalisation of women. Ignorance becomes a tax paid by the poor, and creativity regresses to the backbenches. It is associated only with occasions on which we may need creativity to beautify an ugly face from among life's visages.

Another obstacle to creativity in the Arab world is its collision with the "prohibited", which prevents a free discussion and debate on issues of politics, sex and religion. Yet talking about one of the taboo issues of this "trinity" does not necessarily imply hostility towards society or irreverence. It is not a form of tactlessness or impudence or blasphemy.

When talking about women's creativity, a question to ask is: Are women absent or "absented" from the intellectual and creative scene? Are they a totem standing on the dividing line between what is sacred and what is tainted? Are they viewed in the collective conscience as ceremonial objects or, even worse, as handicapped individuals whose subjective outpourings call for society's help? This often seems to be so, although studies indicate that the first creative text in history was produced by a woman, i.e., the text of Enheduana's Hymns to Inanna in Ur, beseeching her and calling her the resplendent light and the Guardian of Heavenly and Earthly laws.

We, therefore, welcome studies on the feminine intellect that do not make it the monopoly of women but expand the subject in order to unleash society's creative energies and establish human rights, democracy and human justice for both women and men. We seek to be free from oppression in our social structures, which leads to negative attitudes towards life itself that find pleasure in harming the trees, the stones and the roads. Our involvement in creativity and work and our attachment to humanitarian causes are only one expression of our need for protection and safety, which we had found in the mother's womb, an intimate place neither antagonistic nor painful. Our involvement carries the glad tidings of new births into life, bridging the gap between developed societies at the "end of history" in creativity and knowledge acquisition and the globalisation of human development, which remains a challenge for developing societies that are still trying to find their feet as the least advantaged in the world arena. But we always raise hope.

Refqa Muhammad Doudeen

Figure 3.3

Number of publications – original writing and translation – per million people in the Arab world and other regions, 1991

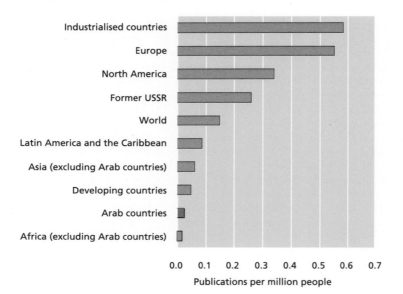

Source: UNESCO Yearbook, 1999.

Figure 3.4

Relative distribution of published books by field, ten Arab countries and the world, 1996

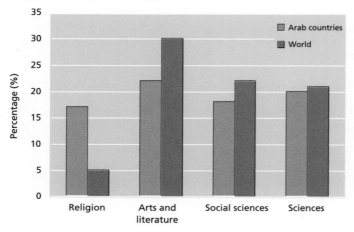

Source: UNESCO Statistics Institute, March 2003.

the educated elite, is one of the most acute challenges facing creative writers in the Arab world. High illiteracy rates in some Arab countries and the declining purchasing power of today's Arab readers are undeniably real factors influencing the size of this readership.

However, would literate Arab citizens who can afford to buy some books for themselves and their families purchase literature to read in their leisure time? There are no accurate statistics on the types of books preferred by Arab readers, but according to many publishers and observers, the bestsellers at the Cairo International Book Fair are religious books, followed by books categorised as educational. This observation reflects on the educational process itself. Issues such as the almost total absence of reading classes in schools, apparently the result of "not having enough time to teach the basic curricula", and neglect of the modern Arab literary heritage should give knowledge advocates food for thought.

Arab writers often feel remote from their assumed audience. Moreover, the absence of a direct relationship with the readers' market undercuts their financial independence, an important guarantee of that degree of freedom in society that most creative writers require. Nonetheless, some Arab authors have been able to reach a wide base of people through films and the mass media (the press, the radio, and television). Many authors are also practising journalists, a profession which helps them to reach readers and to introduce their works to them.

Creating scripts for films is another popular resort for writers. The Egyptian cinema, for example, contributed to introducing Naguib Mahfouz's works to the public during the mid-20th century. The author wrote or collaborated in writing screenplays for many popular films. Radio and television have also contributed to the popularisation of literary works, especially those literary genres, such as colloquial poetry, that do not lend themselves to publishing. While such opportunities are not equally available to all authors, their importance as venues for making literary works accessible to the general public should not be underestimated. (Jacquemond, 2003).

Faced with an anaemic local market, cre-

Arab writers often feel remote from their assumed audience.

of 270 million Arabic speaking Arabs in 22 countries, the usual published number of any given novel or short story collection ranges between 1,000 and 3,000 copies. A book that sells 5,000 copies is considered a bestseller. Once again, there are no accurate statistics on the market reality or on the actual scope of distribution, yet all indicators suggest that the literary book market is modest, even for acclaimed writers such as Naguib Mahfouz or Youssef Idris.

A small readership, generally only among

ative writers cherish the translation of their works into foreign languages. Following the award of the 1988 Nobel Prize for Literature to Mahfouz, a great change occurred in the international status of contemporary Arab literature. Translations of Arabic literature experienced an unprecedented boom in the last decade, and Arabic novels and short stories have started to appear on the comparative literature syllabus in universities around the world. Yet in spite of this widening distribution in new markets, Arabic literature still needs active support to achieve the international renown it deserves.

THE CINEMA

There are film-makers across the Arab world, there are qualified and skilled artists and technicians in the cinema industry and there is adequate equipment for film production. Yet in some Arab countries cinema production does not exist or is very limited. Egypt is the only Arab country that actually has a film industry. Film production started at the beginning of the 20th century, a few years after the invention of the cinema. It had evolved into a full industry by 1919. Important institutions were established, which had a great impact on this new art. Since then, the Egyptian cinema has developed an audience and a market in Egypt and in Arab countries alike.

The first Syrian film came out in 1928, but by 1968 no more than 20 films had been produced. In Lebanon film production started in 1929, but the country did not turn out more than 100 films until 1978. In the 1960s, particulary after the Arab defeat in 1967, a new cultural and critical movement evolved aimed at connecting the cinema with national culture and societal problems. New cinema production appeared in Egypt, Syria, Lebanon, Iraq, Kuwait, Tunisia, Morocco, Algeria and Mauritania: the films of this new wave generally rejected the commercialism of the mainstream industry.

Some Arab countries, such as Egypt, Syria, Algeria and Iraq took important initiatives in the 1960s to support cinematic production. However, they lacked a well-defined cultural policy. As a result, film making receded considerably in the 1980s, and all but disappeared

BOX 3.5

Arab Books- A Threatened Species

Arab book publishing is in crisis. The number of new publications is falling and the number of copies of each issue printed is becoming smaller, reaching only a few hundred readers in many cases. This trend threatens to make the book industry economically unfeasible. Big publishing houses are avoiding the publication of serious scientific and cultural books, which would contribute to in-depth knowledge.

This may seem paradoxical, since the number of Arabic publishing houses springing up in countries previously without book industries is increasing. But most publishing houses actually confine their activities to small production runs of university textbooks, often of poor quality, or to the production of quick-circulating popular books on ephemeral topics.

The book crisis stems from several factors:

Censorship and the recession of democracy and freedom of expression

The distribution of any book in Arab countries requires a prior permit from local censors. The strictness of censorship varies from one country to another. While the book industry flourishes in some countries, such as Lebanon and Egypt, strict laws are often being flouted, depending on the prevailing political situation. These laws are, however, applied randomly and strictly against certain titles and authors classified as violating religion, public morals, the regime or friendly countries. Censorship in Arab countries adopts different standards. What the censor in one country considers banned, another censor in the same or a different country considers acceptable. In most cases the censor exercises his/her role based on state instructions. He/she reads the texts searching for certain words.

Authors and publishers are hard put to accommodate the whims and instructions of 22 Arab censors. As a result, books do not move easily through their natural markets. Censorship in this way adversely affects creativity and production.

Low readership

The Arab Publishers Union notes that readerships in Arab countries are declining, despite the increasing number of educational institutions of all forms. This is attributed to several factors:

• The curtailment of active political life and the failure of major intellectual projects: The state often dictates what readers may read and what authors may write.

• Unimaginative educational systems: many schools and colleges rely on dictation rather than motivating students to search for information in books and other sources.

• Purchasing power: economic stagnation, declining purchasing power and the increasing cost of living, have left the average Arab citizen preoccupied with basic issues of livelihood. Books are becoming luxury items for educated elites and for under-funded scientific institutions, schools and universities. The small number of public libraries, their meagre acquisitions and limited catalogues exacerbate the problem.

• The lack of cultural development plans that encourage reading and instil this habit in individuals from childhood whatever their social background.

• Competition from the mass media: given these other factors, Arab citizens rely more on other, less expensive and less knowledge-based information media to acquire information or entertainment.

The infrastructure for book distribution

A lack of major specialised book distributors with wide distribution networks, (as enjoyed by newspapers and magazines) further hampers book production and circulation. Books are usually only available in a limited number of bookshops in major cities, reflecting weak demand. These bookshops offset their financial losses by selling popular periodicals, stationery, gifts and other items.

Intellectual property rights violations
Plagiarism and violations of copyright also undercut book publication. In most Arab countries, deterrent laws, which protect the rights of the author and the publisher, are either absent or are not enforced.

Fathi Khalil al-Biss, Vice-President, Arab Publishers Union

when economic crises and security challenges paralysed the region's political economy. On the other hand, other Arab countries have left the film market entirely to the private sector, which became the sole player in production, importation, distribution, the construction of cinema theatres, the setting of prices and the levying of taxes. A few other countries do not encourage a film market at all and ban public shows and halls. It may be noted parenthetically that the new cinema in Arab North African countries would not have flourished had it not been technically, artistically and financially supported by producers from the West, particularly France and Belgium, and had some European countries not opened their cinema and television markets to the newcomers.

This trend has appeared recently in the eastern parts of the Arab world as well, and there were at one time some important experiments in Egypt, which relied on funding from Arab institutions.

Arab films have won awards at international festivals, particularly the Cannes Film Festival in France. The Algerian film, "Chronicles of the Years of Fire" won the Golden Palm award at that Festival. A Lebanese film, "Hors la Vie" by Maroun Baghdadi, won the Jury award in 1991. The Egyptian director, Yusuf Shahin, won the Golden Palm award for his work in the film industry when his film, "The Fate", was entered in the 1997 competition. And the Palestinian

film, "A Divine Hand", by director Elijah Suleiman, won the Jury award in 2002.

Although Arab films are earning a distinguished position in the international arena, the situation of the Arab cinema industry remains well below its potential and depends on individual initiatives.

The challenges to Arab cinema are those of the market. The cinema is a popular art form with mass appeal, and the film market is tied to several strata within the audience. In the absence of shrewd cultural policies, standards of taste have been pegged to favour commercial and light films. Distributors have come to control the market for Arab films, with the aim of garnering quick profits. In Egypt, when the state withdrew its support for the cinema industry, film production receded from 60 per year to between 15 and 20. As a result of the general decline of the industry, many cinema theatres were closed down. At a time when the population of Egypt is nearing 70 million, only 165 cinema theatres are still in business, including those situated in "Cultural Palaces". The international rate, by contrast, is one theatre, seating 250 people, per every 100,000 persons. Moreover, the difference in the availability of cinema seats from one Arab country to another is considerable. See figure 3.5.

THEATRE

Conditions surrounding the art and production of theatre in different Arab countries vary enormously. Some countries have no theatrical movement at all. Others have a history of theatre that dates back to the beginnings of the modern state, especially Egypt, Syria and Lebanon. In these countries, theatre has passed through phases of recession and prosperity, depending on political, economic, and social conditions.

During the 1960s in Egypt, for instance, government institutions supported theatrical activities that reflected the state's ideological orientation. With the transformation of political direction in the 1970s, the National Theatre turned into a bureaucratic institution, with few exceptions. Lebanon was the centre of an active theatrical movement during the 1950s, which produced some distinguished

The challenges to Arab cinema are those of the market.

Figure 3.5

Number of cinema seats per 1000 persons in selected Arab countries and Korea in the second half of the 1990s

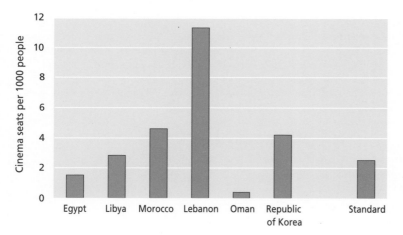

Source: UNESCO Statistics Institute, March 2003.

works, but this movement withered after the outbreak of civil war in the 1970s. The 1980s, on the other hand, witnessed the rise of commercial theatre in several Arab countries. This trend was profit-driven, and favoured audience entertainment and distraction at the expense of serious drama. Tunisia, however, has a distinguished theatrical tradition, with four independent troupes, supported by the state, which have succeeded in establishing a high-quality theatrical movement. Iraq had a very good theatrical movement, which was destroyed at the beginning of the 1990s after the imposition of international sanctions.

MUSIC

Arabic music, as a creative knowledge product, is a branch of oriental music. The Arabic language imparts to Arabic song a special character that makes the Arabic musical phrase distinctive. In Arabic arts, music comes second only to poetry. Its importance derives from its association with poetry and songs. Singing was the rhythmical recitation of poetry, based on the unity of Arabic culture, which depended on shared features of Arabic art in all its forms, including improvisation, musical keys and rhythm.

The 20th century carried the winds of development to Arabic vocal music through contact with the Western world and as a result of the upgrading of the linguistic structure of the song. This in turn brought genuine contemporary music that gave a rhythmical expression to the written Arabic image. Music was also influenced by the development of musical instruments and techniques, as well as by surrounding educational, social and cultural concepts. This changing environment is characterised by new technology for realising various creative products, which mix human and technological instruments of expression. These new forms pave the way for techno-musical products and reflect the impact of global trends on local cultural traditions and behaviour.

In short, while knowledge production in the arts shows signs of real vitality and quality,

it is small and disproportionate to the size of the Arab world with its human and natural resources. Moreover, artistic production is still largely the outcome of individual initiatives, or conditions favourable to particular artists. Arab institutions and societal structures rarely play an effective role in supporting the arts and creative artists.

FREEDOM OF RESEARCH AND EXPRESSION AS A CONDITION FOR KNOWLEDGE PRODUCTION

Freedom is a muscle which, when exercised, grows, and when neglected, atrophies. Non-democratic political systems which do not express the interests of the people, which suppress freedom and which ultimately let individuals lose their ability to act and take initiatives, are weak hosts to creative ideas and knowledge production. [2]

Most laws governing higher education and university scientific research institutes include statutes and regulations that curb the independence of these institutions and place them under the direct control of the ruling regimes. This leads to the curtailment of academic freedoms, and encourages academics and researchers to avoid embarking on creative or innovative endeavours that may lead to controversy or political problems. Such laws effectively kill the spirit of enquiry and creativity in researchers. But distinction still remains, and Arab universities host many excellent researchers; however, their distinction is usually the consequence of individual efforts or personal circumstances, rather than of institutional support and, as such, this does not establish an academic tradition or a research orientation

The visual and performing arts have a direct connection to the public, and therefore have a special status among other forms of art. If freedom of speech is vital to the health of the arts and creativity in general, it is an essential prerequisite for these highly "public" arts, which are about communicating freely with people, activating awareness and developing free critical thinking. The art of the theatre, for

Arab institutions and societal structures rarely play an effective role in supporting the arts and creative artists.

Freedom is a muscle which, when exercised, grows, and when neglected, atrophies. Non-democratic political systems are weak hosts to creative ideas and knowledge production.

[2]Undoubtedly, significant scientific production has been achieved under oppressive regimes, particularly in the natural sciences and technology, most specifically those concerned with armaments, through strong support from national authorities. The benefits of such knowledge production, however, were not universal to all in these societies and production itself was not sustained. The most important example of that is the former Soviet Union.

example, is a collective art practised in a public place. One of its basic requirements is the availability of a space that allows a group of persons to practice this art freely and to communicate with the audience directly. If restrictions are placed on freedom of assembly or communication with people, the theatre loses a primary condition for its vitality. Wise cultural policies can prevent this loss.

The cinema, though not a live medium, also speaks to the soul and mind of the audience. It projects feelings, ideas, and visions that can enrich the audience's life experiences and provide insight into its surrounding reality, history or inner worlds. However, not all Arab countries pay due attention to the cinema as an expression of culture and creativity. At the same time, cinematic production is not only an artistic endeavour, but also an industry, investment and a market. That dimension of the medium is also widely neglected by the state and dominated by private distributors. Since the cinema is a wide-reaching popular art, the societal power structures in Arab countries have formed an ambivalent relationship with the medium: they may prohibit or prevent its production, but have no qualms about its consumption for commercial profit.

Arab film production is subject to commercial rules and regulations that treat the cinema as a consumer commodity. There are no special tax incentives for the cinema that recognise it as an art form and a tool of knowledge. In fact, some Arab countries impose high taxes on the cinema, and treat it as an entertainment commodity on the same level as night-clubs and cabarets. The same logic is applied to theatrical performances: very high taxes are imposed on theatre tickets, a cost that undermines the sustainability of private troupes.

The degree of social freedom also affects the accessibility of literary works, and the extent of their circulation amongst Arab countries. Publishers face severe obstacles to the distribution of books in the Arab world for several reasons, most important among which are the laws and regulations governing the movement of books across Arab countries. The Arab book is often treated as a banned commodity, and is usually subject to censorship and bureaucratic procedures that place exorbitant costs on publishers. These laws inevitably hinder book publishing and circulation. As a result, some Arab scholars resort to shopping in bookstores in France or the United Kingdom to gain access to Arab literary works, an option hardly available to most under-paid researchers.

Censorship substantially hinders the creative process. Though no society in the world is completely free from some form of declared or hidden censorship, the types of official censorship in Arab countries exact a heavy toll on the arts in general. Authorities that impose censorship over the arts vary. Some social groups assume the role of the censor over literary and artistic production by protesting in the press over what they consider infringements of socially appropriate standards. These groups sometimes even resort to the courts to stop a film or confiscate a book. Members of the same profession may also practise a form of censorship over each other. But the main threat to free literature and art in Arab societies is the dead hand of the state censor on ideas that are not compatible with its political direction, or that may stir social unrest, or mobilise people over a political or social issue. Regimes that do not permit political diversity or social plurality create fertile ground for the rise of extremism and regressive thinking that is hostile, not only to the arts and artists, but to social progress as a whole. Ironically, tightening the state's grip on literature and the arts loosens the reins on regressive currents opposed to human development.

Censorship regulations vary from one art form to another: the more popular the art and the greater its ability to communicate directly with the audience, the harsher these restrictions are. In the theatre in Egypt, for instance, a script is subject to revision by the censor as a condition for receiving a permit to perform. Rules of censorship over the theatre are loosely phrased and permit various interpretations according to the leanings of the censor and the ruling regime. Usually, the rejection of a text is justified by claiming that it violates public morality and the supreme interests of the state (Sayyed Ali Isamail, *in Arabic*, 1997). In this way, censorship effectively suppresses criticism or innovation, and thus contributes to deepening the current crisis of Arab theatre.

The main threat to free literature and art in Arab societies is the dead hand of the state censor.

Censorship regulations vary from one art form to another: the more popular the art, the harsher these restrictions are.

Cinema production, in Arab countries, is also subject to censorship laws and regulations that place many obstacles before creativity and the treatment of vital subjects. In addition, because cinema producers cannot cover their expenses exclusively from the local market, many take into account the censorship laws not only of the producing country, but of other Arab countries as well.

Arab censorship bridles Arab artistic creativity and denies Arab artists their native inspiration. A fundamental social function of the artist is to challenge social, political, and ideological orthodoxies and expose the uncontested received wisdom dominating a society. Innovation and critical questioning of the status quo are the very sources of creativity. Arab artists are confronted with unbending social, political and ideological frameworks that are above accountability, and that treat innovation and change as signs of disintegration and unrest. Moreover, some dominant intellectual elements in the Arab world hold nostalgically to the past, and are ambivalent about the present and the future. These elements fear innovation and oppose it fiercely. Thus, the Arab artist is surrounded by ideological and social currents that view and treat art with suspicion and is subject to the control of political regimes that sweep social challenges under the carpet in order to maintain their dominance.

Fear of innovation and change is also one of the driving forces behind policies that stifle the creative capabilities of school and university students. A social culture that encourages and appreciates art, creative writing and music

sees to it that these subjects are widely taught. There are entire generations of Arabs who have not learnt how to play a musical instrument, and who have not read literary works because they were not accustomed to do so in school. Creative pursuits taken for granted in developed country schools have simply been neglected in the Arab world, with damaging results to the creative potential of its people.

Finally, it is important to point out that strained international relations create certain obstacles to knowledge creation. The unease in Arab relations with some Western countries in modern times has negatively affected knowledge production. When an Arab writer criticises his or her society, he or she is often accused of promoting the interests of foreign powers against the interests of the nation, because (so the argument goes) by exposing the weaknesses of society, the writer is supplying those powers with ammunition for attacking Arab countries. At the same time, Arab writings critical of Arab countries have been mobilised to aid self-serving policies towards the Arab world. The hijacking of Arab art, literature or research to serve vested interests presents its own problems for Arab scholars, scientists and creative artists and, ultimately, diminishes the impact of their work for human development at home and abroad.

In short, a new Arab renaissance requires a new policy environment that liberates human capabilities in the sciences and arts by actively promoting freedom, creativity and innovation. Without that prerequisite, the Arab knowledge society will remain an elusive dream.

When an Arab writer criticises his or her society, he or she is often accused of promoting the interests of foreign powers.

This chapter suggests that Arab countries possess significant human capital, which under new circumstances, could serve to lead, support and sustain a knowledge renaissance centred on knowledge production. It observes that an unsupportive policy and institutional environment for scientific research, an archaic environment for developing and encouraging education and a hostile environment for scientific and artistic freedom and creativity could negate such progress.

CHAPTER 4

Measuring knowledge capital in Arab countries

This chapter attempts a quantitative measurement of the state of knowledge in Arab countries, focusing on knowledge capital, the core of the knowledge production process. Ideally, the chapter would provide the most accurate assessment possible of the state of knowledge in Arab countries at the beginning of the 21st century. Yet in practice this attempt faces many serious difficulties. The first is the poor database on knowledge, particularly on the quality of human capital accumulated through education. Another data gap relates to the quantity and quality of knowledge production in Arab countries: the information base on these aspects is woefully short on accurate and up-to-date data comparable across time and space. These gaps underscore that the establishment of such databases is one of the most pressing priorities in building the Arab knowledge society.

INTRODUCTION

Measuring knowledge is not easy - either conceptually, methodologically or practically. Knowledge consists of abstract, symbolic structures in the human mind that are almost impossible to grasp, even on an intellectual level, let alone when it comes to concrete measurement. Measurement becomes even more difficult when considering knowledge capital, the determinants of its growth and its effectiveness on the societal level. So a resort to approximate measurement becomes inevitable in order to arrive at a first approximation of knowledge capital, its growth rate and characteristics and particularly the infrastructure for its formation and development.

Knowledge, whether looked at as a system, wealth or capital, is a multidimensional and complex phenomenon. As a result, the comprehensive measurement of knowledge must involve a relatively large number of indicators that would be difficult for the human mind to deal with simultaneously. To surmount this challenge, known statistical methods for constructing composite indices can be adopted. However, simplicity comes at a cost. Such methods are sometimes criticised for reducing complex phenomena to a single composite index that over-simplifies its subject's manifold dimensions and masks the information content of constituent indicators.

Consequently, this chapter adopts both approaches. It examines some basic indicators of knowledge acquisition in Arab countries that are especially relevant to building a knowledge society, as compared to other countries and regions of the world. But it also explores the construction of composite indices of knowledge acquisition that depend on the availability, and credibility, of various data.

Knowledge capital contains elements that are not readily quantifiable. Its measurement ought, therefore, to combine quantitative with other *qualitative* and *subjective* elements, especially when it comes to literary and artistic production. The Report team aimed to present a pilot opinion poll on those issues conducted among faculty staff members at Arab universities, as a sample of Arab intellectuals. Although the survey was designed to minimize difficulties to the extent possible, it still encountered obstacles typically faced when conducting research in Arab countries. Nevertheless, the attempt yielded useful information summarised later in this chapter.

In principle, it is advisable to take the quality of the elements of knowledge capital into consideration. The Mean Years of Schooling (MYS) indicator, for example, is a useful yet insufficient measure of human capital, the solid nucleus of knowledge capital. The MYS should rather be weighed by a measure of the quality

Measuring knowledge is not easy - either conceptually, methodologically or practically.

of educational attainment (derived, for example, from international studies of educational attainment). This balancing is important since econometric analysis indicates that the quantity of educational attainment is not as strongly associated with economic output as its quality. Indeed, economic output becomes increasingly sensitive to educational attainment when the quality of education is taken into consideration (Fergany, 1998). In the case of scientific output, measured by the number of published articles in peer-reviewed journals, for example, quantity could be weighed by the frequency of citation, assuming multiple citations of a certain article are an indicator of its knowledge value.

The following attempt at measurement also compares Arab countries, individually and collectively, on the different criteria of knowledge capital, to other relevant countries and country groups in the world. The countries and groups taken for comparison include countries considered important from the comparative knowledge perspective. Those countries include, where the data permits, China and India, large nations with ancient civilisations, and the principal 'Asian Tigers' i.e. Korea, Taiwan and Hong Kong. All these countries are known to have adopted a knowledge-based approach to development, with recognised success.

It is necessary to comment once again on the paucity of data on most aspects of knowledge in Arab countries. This deficiency is a major obstacle to the accurate and comprehensive measurement of Arab knowledge in general and Arab knowledge capital in particular. Turning to international databases did not resolve the problem since data on Arab countries is generally scarce. For example, in the most important international database on educational attainment, indicators of MYS in 1990 were available for only 11 Arab countries. The number fell to 9 countries in 2000.

Measures of the *quality* of educational attainment were not available except for a single Arab country in each of the two years, (Jordan and Kuwait, respectively).

Data on expenditure on R&D relative to GDP at the end of the 20th century were available for only two Arab countries; the number of scientists and engineers was available for

only five Arab countries. Except for six Arab countries, the percentage of high-technology exports of total manufactured exports was not available.

THE ADEQUATE MEASUREMENT OF KNOWLEDGE CAPITAL

The adequate measurement of knowledge capital requires considering the following three main aspects of knowledge acquisition with their corresponding basic elements:
a. ***Knowledge Dissemination***: essentially through education, translation of books, mass media (press, radio and TV), cinema houses and theatres.
b. ***Knowledge Production***: in two dimensions: Inputs: knowledge workers, expenditure on R&D (quantity and structure), and R&D institutions. Output: including scientific publishing (quantity/quality), patents, the publication of books, literary (novels, stories and poetry) and artistic expression (drama, cinema and music).
c. ***Infrastructure for Knowledge Capital***: includes ICT infrastructure, R&D support institutions, and professional organisations of knowledge workers.

Adequate measurement, naturally, requires accurate, up-to-date and comparable information on all these fields in Arab countries as well as in the countries of comparison. The Report originally set out to explore how far Arab and international databases would allow for sufficient measurement of all these dimensions of knowledge capital. For reasons already stated, this initial ambition was set aside for more modest goals.

TOWARDS THE BETTER MEASUREMENT OF KNOWLEDGE CAPITAL IN ARAB COUNTRIES

Measuring knowledge capital and its characteristics and following up on their development and limitations are of special importance in Arab countries. The elements of knowledge capital are key in determining the ability to acquire knowledge and thus in building human development itself. Knowledge capital, its characteristics and development, are at the core of knowledge acquisition. For reasons noted, the current attempt to measure Arab knowledge capital is neither complete nor completely adequate. Yet it is important to make a serious start in this direction and to explore approaches and measures that, if taken further, would significantly strengthen the measurement of this crucial phenomenon.

The initial contours of some proposals are evident. To start, all periodic statistical operations (censuses and specialised surveys) should include elements for measuring human capital (i. e., educational attainment and experience[1]). Efforts to quantify human capital should be complemented by good measures of its quality. This is attainable either by expanding the participation of Arab countries in international studies of the quality of educational attainment or – even better – by conducting Arab comparative studies on the quality of human capital. The latter, unlike international studies, would benefit from proficiency in the Arabic language assessed.

Good measurement of human capital is important yet insufficient. To arrive at an adequate measurement of knowledge capital as a building block of human development, consideration should be given to conducting specialised studies, both quantitative and non-quantitative, in various other departments of knowledge.

The prospects for better data on knowledge acquisition in the Arab countries would improve if pan-Arab or international organisations undertook to collect and evaluate such data, ensuring its maintenance, credibility and comparability.

A SURVEY OF ARAB INTELLECTUALS ON THE STATE OF KNOWLEDGE

As noted earlier, the Report team sought to poll a number of faculty members in Arab universities, representing a sample of Arab intellectuals across the region, on knowledge acquisition issues. Annex 2 includes a brief description of the design of the questionnaire and survey. At the time of writing, however, the team was able to ascertain such views in only seven Arab countries (Bahrain, Lebanon, Egypt, Sudan, Tunisia, Algeria and Morocco).

In four countries, the number of intellectuals who responded to the questionnaires was less than the targeted 96, bringing the total number of replies to only 383. This reduced the benefits of the exercise.

Thus, in presenting the results of this survey, it is emphasised that the sample used was not selected by a standard probability method, which would support generalised attributions to the Arab intellectual community at large. This does not, however, negate the usefulness of the responses. Each response is undeniably subjective, but the value of a subjective view on knowledge issues increases with the increase of the knowledge capital of the individual concerned. In the case of university faculty members in particular, their views acquire more importance because of their ability to contribute to the formation of human capital through their higher education functions. From a statistical point of view, subjectivity was restricted by canvassing the views of hundreds of faculty members of Arab universities, thus increasing the objectivity level of the sample[1].

The sample responding to the questionnaire was almost equally divided between men and women (56% men). Most of them were PhD holders (63%), and one-third master's degree holders (33%). The majority of them (58%) were specialised in humanities and social sciences.

The respondents generally expressed dissatisfaction with the status of knowledge acquisition in their countries (the average ratio of satisfaction was 38%). Satisfaction with the extent to which knowledge acquisition serves human development was even lower (35%). These assessments clearly reflect the urgent need to stimulate knowledge acquisition in Arab countries.

In characterising the knowledge acquisition process in their countries, the respondents came up with low rates in their evaluation, as indicated in figure 4.1.
• On a scale from 0-100% respondents rated freedom to pursue knowledge in their various fields at 41%.
• Conditions for knowledge acquisition in their fields of scholarship satisfied the right to knowledge at 33%.

Prospects for better data on knowledge acquisition in Arab countries would improve if pan-Arab or international organisations undertook to collect and evaluate such data.

Respondents generally expressed dissatisfaction with the status of knowledge acquisition in their countries.

---

[1]Research in some Arab countries indicates that experience takes precedence over educational attainment as a determinant of earnings. This implies an indirect recognition of the poor quality of educational attainment in the region.

• Incentives to acquire knowledge were considered just 30% satisfactory.

• The extent to which knowledge acquisition in their disciplines serves human development was rated only 30%.

• The degree to which knowledge acquisition reflects cultural diversity scored 30%.

• The extent to which Arab knowledge acquisition takes into account the global state of the art was judged 30%.

• Improvements in knowledge acquisition in their branches of learning during the past 10 years were rated only 28%.

In short, according to the majority of scholars in this sample, and with the reservations indicated, Arab knowledge systems are neither sufficiently free nor adequately incentivised. Arab knowledge pursuits do not serve human development adequately, nor do they reflect the cultural diversity of Arab society. Local knowledge development and acquisition do not capture or keep up with the global knowledge explosion. Finally, in the Arab world, knowledge acquisition rates compared to those of other regions have improved relatively slowly.

The questionnaire included questions comparing the status of different knowledge areas in the Arab world to their equivalents in certain non-Arab countries, including India, China and the East Asian Tigers. Respondents to the questionnaire clearly had difficulty answering these questions. Many answered with: "don't know". Indeed, only one-third of all respondents addressed questions requiring comparisons with non-Arab countries.

Women respondents were more critical than men, attaching less value to ongoing knowledge activities and evincing more concern over the absence of adequate incentives for knowledge development and acquisition across the spectrum of Arab endeavours.

Holders of a master's and PhD degree, were more critical of the status of current knowledge acquisition than holders of lower degrees. PhD holders rated Arab knowledge performance lowest compared to India and the East Asian tigers, see figure 4.2.

Respondents from scientific disciplines generally took a dimmer view of the state of Arab knowledge than those from the social and human sciences. The latter group's assessment tended to be lower relative to the comparator countries. Many of the respondents lacked knowledge of translated books, reflected in the number of "don't know" responses to this question across all categories of the survey.

Figure 4.3 reflects the respondents' evaluations of the extent of freedom in key areas of knowledge compared to their assessments of incentives for its acquisition. The scale 0% – 50% reflects the low overall estimate of both freedom and incentives.

Respondents evidently judged that the extent of freedom, low as it is, is higher in general than levels of incentives to acquire knowledge, particularly in higher education,

Figure 4.1

Assessment of key features of knowledge acquisition in Arab countries by gender of respondent (%)

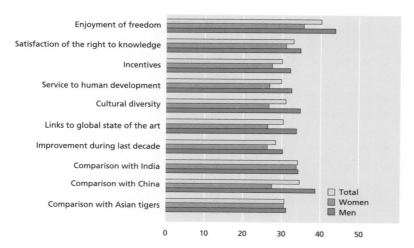

Figure 4.2

Assessment of the knowledge acquisition process in Arab countries by academic level of respondent (%)

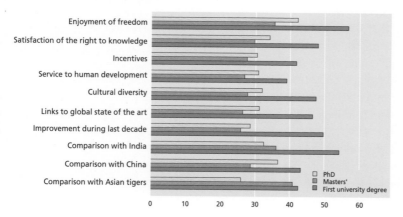

research and development and arts production. This suggests the existence of obstacles to knowledge acquisition in Arab societies beyond questions of freedom. Two areas of knowledge activity, radio and television, were clearly judged to be very circumscribed in terms of freedom. Cinema and theatre production, on the other hand, did not appear as constrained. Thus, relatively low levels of production in the latter two areas could be attributed to organisational and financial problems; the same observation applies to scientific research and technological development in public sector projects.

Most respondents thought that Arab countries are weak in technological research and development, particularly compared to the East Asian tigers, despite their opinion that there is no restriction of freedom in this area: the discrepancy points to other (societal) obstacles. On improvements in knowledge acquisition over the past ten years, the lowest assessment was given to basic and secondary education, the two areas most consistently faulted by Arab university faculties.

Respondents considered that the most important impediment to knowledge acquisition in Arab countries is the deficient knowledge system itself. They focused on a general lack of resources and facilities and weak teaching systems, followed by poor governance and management, stressing restrictions on freedom and on civil society. They also evinced keen interest in seeing society provide better material and moral rewards for contributions to knowledge acquisition.

INITIAL APPROXIMATION OF THE MEASUREMENT OF KNOWLEDGE CAPITAL: HUMAN CAPITAL

The paramount importance of education and learning in the knowledge system has been highlighted in Chapter 1. This pivotal relationship suggests that human capital, which is the sum total of knowledge, capacities and skills acquired by human beings through education and practical experience, represents a relatively solid nucleus of knowledge capital.

Databases on human capital are well stocked since educational statistics are relatively accessible and are regularly available.

Figure 4.3

Freedom to pursue knowledge and incentives for knowledge acquisition

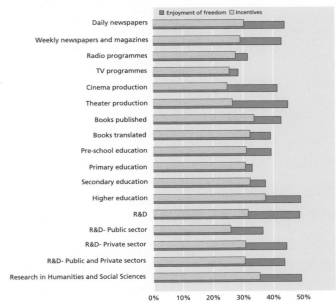

Yet those statistics have their weaknesses: they tend, on the one hand, to exclude knowledge acquisition through practical experience on which acceptable measures are available only through specialised field surveys. On the other hand, readily available educational statistics relate generally to the quantitative aspects of education, such as enrolment. Data related to the quality of education, on the contrary, are much less plentiful and often less credible, since they normally relate to *inputs* to the educational process (spending levels, number of schools, classrooms or teachers), or to *intermediate* indicators (e.g., the proportion of pupils to teachers, classrooms or laboratories).

Capturing the real outcomes of the educational process, reflected in the knowledge, capacities and skills students actually acquire, requires specialised field surveys, preferably of a comparative nature. Such studies would help ascertain the relative position of educational outcomes in one society as compared to other similar or competitive cases.

Efforts to measure the quality of Arab education are still limited – in itself an indication of a crisis in education in the Arab countries – and thus only a few, scattered measures of the quality of educational outcomes are available. They are found in international studies, which are marred in turn by their own shortcomings. For example, they exclude language from their testable fields. Moreover, very few Arab coun-

The most important impediment to knowledge acquisition in Arab countries is the deficient knowledge system itself.

tries have participated in such studies (Jordan and Kuwait were the only Arab countries that took part in one of two international studies conducted at the beginning and in the middle of the 1990s, respectively).

The stock of human capital at the beginning of the 21st century

The MYS (for populations older than a minimum age limit, usually 15 or 25 years[2]) is the most common indicator for measuring the stock of human capital through education. It is not, however, free of drawbacks. Apart from the shortcomings of averages – the most dangerous of which is neglecting the question of distribution within the society concerned – the most significant limitation of this indicator is its confinement to formal education It excludes non-formal education and the acquisition of knowledge through experience. But even in this confined domain, the MYS, as an indicator of human capital, neglects the quality dimension. This at a time when evidence is accumulating to the effect that quality, rather than quantity, is the more important determinant of productivity enhancement and progress through knowledge acquisition and innovation.

Figure 4.4 illustrates the position of Arab countries with available MYS data at the beginning and end of the 1990s, relative to seven comparison countries with available MYS data as well. It also shows averages for all Arab countries and for sub-groups of the countries compared.

From the figure it is clear that:

First: Arab countries fall far below the countries in the comparison, the Asian Tigers in particular.

Second: the MYS of all countries included have improved between 1990 and 2000. The improvement, on average, appears larger in the Arab countries than in the comparator countries as a whole or even in the Asian Tigers. The improvement, however, should be weighed against the fact that the lower the initial position of a country's MYS, the easier it is for it to make gains on the scale. In other words, the countries compared preceded the Arab countries in raising their MYS to a peak level at which point further improvement becomes harder.

HISTORICAL COMPARISON: ARAB COUNTRIES AND THE ASIAN TIGERS IN THE SECOND HALF OF THE 20th CENTURY

This next section traces the development of educational attainment in Arab countries in the last four decades, focusing on a comparison with the Asian Tigers. For a more valid comparison, the criterion used here is the MYS for people 25 years of age or older.

Literature on the "Asian Miracle" has accumulated in recent years. From an Arab perspective, the "miracle" factor is quite intense since in conventional economic development terms Arab countries used to fare better relative to the Asian tigers. But in 1970 Arab GDP per capita was half that in East Asia: by the opening stages of this century it dropped to less than one seventh of GDP per capita in that region. This is due to the significant improvement in economic performance in East Asian countries since the 1970s when there was a decline, albeit slight, in Arab countries (table 4.1).

One of the most important developmental lessons of the Asian experience is the critical role that early and intensive investment in human capital played as the foundation of de-

In 1970 Arab GDP per capita was half that in East Asia: by the opening stages of this century it dropped to less than one seventh of GDP per capita in that region.

Figure 4.4

Mean years of schooling (MYS), population 15 years of age or older, Arab countries compared to selected countries, 1990 and 2000

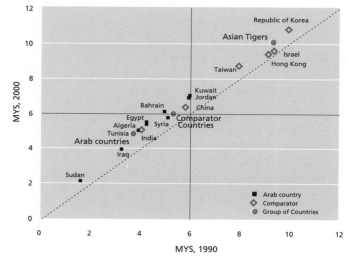

Source: Barro and Lee, 2000.

---

[2]The latter age limit (25 years) takes into consideration educational attainment levels among the older groups of the population. This age range tends to "penalise" Arab countries, since education is widespread among younger Arabs whereas illiteracy is still rife among older age groups.

velopment. Does the disparity in human capital formation between Arab and East Asian countries account for their divergent development fortunes?

To try and answer this question, one of the richest international databases on educational attainment (Barro and Lee, 2000) was used. Through it, the MYS in nine Arab countries on which data was available throughout the comparison period (and comprising about two thirds of the Arab population in the year 2000) was compared to the MYS for three pioneer Asian Tigers.

Figure 4.5 illustrates the large gap in the level of human capital formation between both groups (Arab countries and Asian Tigers) since 1960, disaggregated by gender.

Arab countries, obviously, did not manage to narrow the gap that separates them from East Asia in this respect. Rather, the gap widened, as the difference in educational attainment in general grew larger: from 3.02 years in 1960 to 5.26 in 2000. The gap was relatively wider among females, increasing from 1.87 to 5.42 years over the same period, despite the fact that the distance between the two groups on the individual progress lines, as shown in the figure, is less in the case of females. This is because the Arab countries with high levels of educational attainment among

their female population were among the less populated oil producing countries.

The level of human capital formation in the three Asian Tigers was substantially higher than that in the Arab countries at the beginning of the comparison period (1960). In addition, improvement in educational attainment in the first group was faster, noting that educational expansion becomes increasingly harder to achieve when higher levels of educational attainment are reached.

Moreover, the gap between the two groups would have appeared even wider had the averages included values for the Arab countries on which no data had been available. With the exception of a few low-population countries such as Lebanon, this category comprises the majority of less developed countries in the region and other countries with relatively low educational attainment.[3]

The comparison at hand reveals one of the most important "secrets" accounting for the successful East Asian development experi-

Does the disparity in human capital formation between Arab and East Asian countries account for their divergent development fortunes?

TABLE 4.1
Percentage of real Arab GDP per capita (1970 and 2001), compared to Asian Tigers

Year	Arab countries	East Asian Tigers
1970	9	18
2001	7	52

Source: UNDP, Calculations by the Human Development Report Office.

Figure 4.5

Mean years of schooling (population 25 years of age or older) by gender, Arab countries and three Asian Tigers, 1960-2000

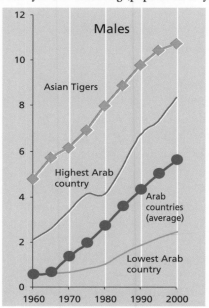
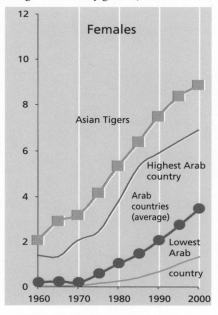
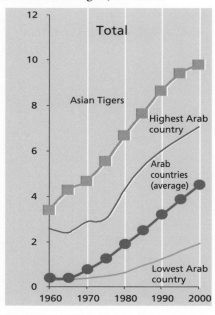

[3]Countries with no available data: Comoros Islands, Djibouti, Somalia, Mauritania, Yemen, Morocco, Libya, Saudi Arabia, United Arab Emirates, Oman, Qatar, Lebanon and Palestine.

ence: *early and intensive investment in education, accompanied by sustained and rapid improvement of its level.*

The quality of education: findings of international studies

As mentioned earlier, the number of Arab countries with comparative measurements of the quality of educational attainment dwindles to only one in each of the two international studies available. To benefit from this scant information, it was assumed that the average relative score for both countries in the two studies applied to all Arab countries at the end of the 20th century.

However, before continuing with the analysis on the basis of this assumption, it is worth noting that this average is attributed to two countries where the quality of education can be expected to be better than the average for all Arab countries. Jordan, for example, is known to have a relatively better educational system and a high societal motivation for education. Kuwait, with its relatively generous spending on education, also stands out among the Arab countries.

Thus, it can be said without exaggeration that the average quality of educational attainment in Jordan and Kuwait is expected to surpass that in the majority of Arab countries, particularly the countries with limited educa-

tion budgets and those with disadvantageous legacies in education. This means that the relative position of the Arab countries, as a result of applying the average quality indicator of Jordan and Kuwait to all Arab countries, is a projection brighter than the present Arab reality.

Figure 4.6 illustrates the relative position of Arab countries between 1990 and 2000 on a human capital composite index. In addition to the MYS, the index takes into consideration the quality of educational attainment (by multiplying the MYS by a coefficient for the quality of educational attainment). Compared to figure 4.4, the figure shows an increasing divergence between Arab countries on the one hand and the comparator countries in general on the other hand. In other words, taking the quality of human capital into account accentuates the relative backwardness of the Arab countries vis-à-vis the other countries in this comparison, notably the Asian Tigers.

It is reiterated that the comparison at hand and the inferences drawn are rather weak owing to the scarcity of data on the components of the composite index, especially on the quality of educational attainment.

TOWARDS A COMPOSITE INDEX OF KNOWLEDGE CAPITAL

This section seeks to characterise knowledge capital in Arab countries within the comparative framework adopted. Although the multiple facets of knowledge enjoin the use of multiple indicators, data availability on any indicator, in Arab countries and the world at large, was a major criterion for including that indicator in the analysis. Taking into account the earlier discussion about measuring knowledge capital adequately, it was decided to consider ten indicators relating to different facets of knowledge capital.

The following are the ten indicators on which data were available worldwide and for Arab countries around the year 2000:
1. The quality-adjusted MYS
2. Daily newspapers (per 1000 people)
3. Radios (per 100 people)
4. TV sets (per 1000 people)
5. Scientists and engineers (per million people)
6. Patent applications filed (per million peo-

Taking the quality of human capital into account accentuates the relative backwardness of the Arab countries.

Figure 4.6

Quality adjusted mean years of schooling (QAMYS), population 15 years of age or older, Arab countries and selected countries, 1990 and 2000

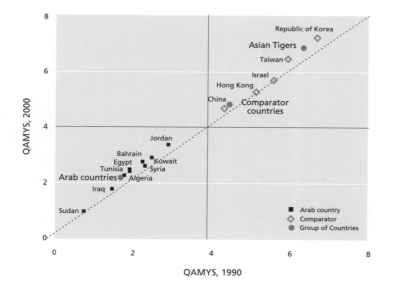

ple)

7. Book titles (per million people)

8. Telephone mainlines (per 1000 people)

9. Cellular mobile subscribers (per 1000 people) and

10. Internet hosts (per 1000 people).

Table A-10 in the statistical annex gives the values of those ten indicators, which were available on 109 countries, including eight Arab countries and five of the countries chosen for comparison. There were, however, no good data available on all indicators for all the countries. The percentage of the countries with non-available data varied from one indicator to the other; all countries had data available on information infrastructure whereas more than a quarter of them had no data available on some basic indicators, e.g., scientists and engineers engaged in R&D, the number of book titles, and even on the core indicator, the quality-adjusted MYS.

To overcome these limitations in the basic data, statistical means for estimating the missing observations, based on the values of those available, were resorted to. The result was a completed array of data; Table A-11 of the statistical annex shows the completed data set, with imputed values for missing observations framed.

The 'Borda' rule was applied to the completed data array. The rule consists of assigning an overall rank to each country through summing its ranks on each of the ten indicators. This overall rank represents a valid "social welfare function". The result of this procedure is given in Figure 4.7, where the lowest rank is the best.

In general, the figure indicates the relatively low position of the Arab countries included in the analysis (the average overall rank for the eight Arab countries included is 69).

Yet a striking disparity is evident in the relative positions of individual Arab countries. Dividing the index into four groups, stagnant, intermediate, aspiring and leading, puts Korea among the leaders while only one Arab country, Kuwait, falls within the aspiring group. Other Arab countries for which data was available occupy intermediate or stagnant positions. (Several Arab countries without data would undoubtedly have fallen into the lower positions on the knowledge capital contin-

uum).

More importantly, the conclusions implied by the figure cast considerable doubt on both the indicators used and the prototype composite index itself. For example, India, with its nuclear capability, space programme and otherwise recognised technological capacity in more than one sphere, occupies the tail of the composite index along with some Arab and other countries notwithstanding the fact that there is a significant gap between these countries in terms of their scientific and technological capabilities.

This prompted an enquiry into the knowledge outcomes which signify the presence of knowledge capabilities and a comparison between them and the composite index just discussed.

The knowledge outcomes considered included the following:

• High technology exports (as a percentage of total commodity exports)

• Nuclear facilities (ownership of a nuclear reactor)

• Existence of a space program

In addition to:

• Technology Achievement Index (TAI) values (UNDP), as well as some standard development indicators:

• Arab Human Development Index (AHDI) rank

• Human Development Index (HDI) value

Dividing the index into four groups, stagnant, intermediate, aspiring and leading, puts Korea among the leaders while only one Arab country, Kuwait, falls within the aspiring group.

Figure 4.7

Ranking of Arab countries compared to other countries and regions on the composite indicator of knowledge capital, 2000

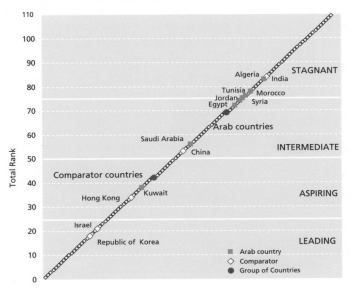

Figure 4.8

Correlation coefficient between knowledge capital indicators, knowledge outcomes and other development indicators around the year 2000

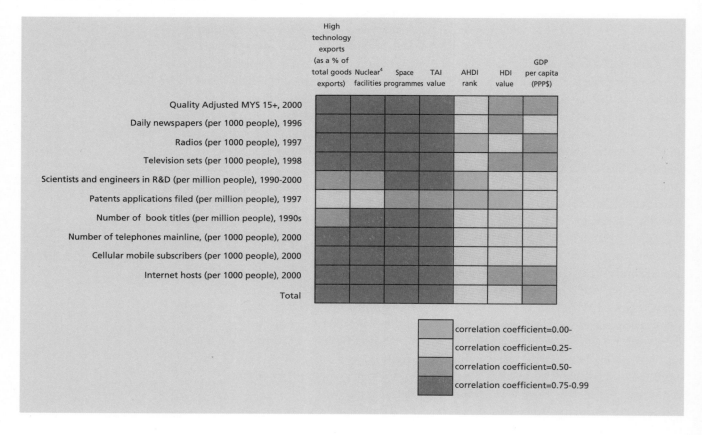

	High technology exports (as a % of total goods exports)	Nuclear[4] facilities	Space programmes	TAI value	AHDI rank	HDI value	GDP per capita (PPP$)
Quality Adjusted MYS 15+, 2000							
Daily newspapers (per 1000 people), 1996							
Radios (per 1000 people), 1997							
Television sets (per 1000 people), 1998							
Scientists and engineers in R&D (per million people), 1990-2000							
Patents applications filed (per million people), 1997							
Number of book titles (per million people), 1990s							
Number of telephones mainline, (per 1000 people), 2000							
Cellular mobile subscribers (per 1000 people), 2000							
Internet hosts (per 1000 people), 2000							
Total							

correlation coefficient=0.00-
correlation coefficient=0.25-
correlation coefficient=0.50-
correlation coefficient=0.75-0.99

• Per capita GDP (in PPP, US dollars).

Data on these indicators are given in Table A-13 of the statistical annex.

Analysing the relationship between the ten knowledge capital indicators utilised in the prototype composite index and these knowledge outcome indicators, (Figure 4.8 and Table A-14 in the statistical annex), demonstrates a relatively weak correlation between both groups of indicators, with the exception of human capital (quality and quantity) where the correlation with knowledge outcomes is relatively strong.

The question now is: what do we eventually conclude from this measurement attempt?

A valid, simple yet perhaps overly simple conclusion is that the indicators used are substantively inadequate and that data scarcity is a major impediment to adequate measurement, aggravating the substantive deficiency of the indicators.

The Report team's preferred conclusion, however, is that cumulative knowledge outcomes offer decisive insights into how knowledge advances are achieved. It is evidently possible for societies to make substantial advances in knowledge even when their standard indicators of knowledge capital are modest – as in the cases of large countries such as India and China. This suggests that valuable knowledge achievements might depend crucially on matters that involve: political will and leadership; the capacity to raise and mobilise material, technical and human resources; and the drive to focus national efforts on attaining an indigenous societal renaissance that is both people-centred and patriotic. *Motivated societies can lift themselves by their bootstraps to achieve large knowledge outcomes ostensibly beyond their means.*

[4]ownership of a reactor

Despite the methodological and other challenges encountered in this attempt at measurement, it is quite evident that Arab countries lag behind the more advanced developing countries in building knowledge capital. The comparison is even more disquieting relative to the performance of the world's front-runners in knowledge capital formation and knowledge production.

Arab countries should, however, not take this as discouragement. Rather, these insights signpost another way forward, one that may lie much less in catching up with others on standard knowledge indicators, and much more through concentrating on knowledge outcomes. With robust and intellectually distinguished institutional structures, and with political determination supported by sufficient resources, particularly on the pan-Arab level, it may well be possible to emulate some of the striking knowledge outcomes of other developing countries whose conventional knowledge indicators do not surpass those found in the Arab world.

CHAPTER 5

The organisational context of knowledge acquisition

This chapter discusses the organisational context in which knowledge is acquired in Arab countries through the transfer and adaptation of technology. The discussion considers issues such as: the importance of national innovation systems; policy and institutional prerequisites for establishing a knowledge economy; and the vital role of entrepreneurs. It reviews the experience of Arab countries in transferring and adapting technology in the past, and assesses the role of foreign direct investment (FDI) and business incubators in contemporary Arab market economies.

INNOVATION SYSTEMS AND TECHNOLOGY[1]

Innovation is the ability to manage knowledge, as embodied in technology, in a creative way in response to market requirements and the needs of society. Dynamic national innovation systems are the key to the efficient management of technology transfer, absorption, adaptation and diffusion in knowledge economies. The basic concept behind such systems is that it takes multiple actors to innovate and produce knowledge. Innovation does not depend solely on how individual enterprises, universities and research institutions perform, but also on how they interact with one another, and with the public sector. Effective innovation systems are flexible networks capable of using existing technologies and knowledge capital to create new forms of technology that raise productivity

and growth, increase competitiveness in world markets and serve human development.

As indicated in figure 5-1, an effective innovation system is a complex whole. Moreover, its success is heavily influenced by social values and culture and by prevailing economic, legal and political systems and structures. The state plays a particularly important role in developing public policies and directions and in establishing institutions and systems capable of diffusing innovation in society. The state is responsible for establishing a favourable economic environment, an effective educational and training system and an advanced communication structure. It provides critical supports to the economy and industry by replenishing factors of production and it encourages the development of markets that can absorb the products of firms and enterprise

Where do Arab countries stand vis-à-vis innovation systems of this kind?

TECHNOLOGY TRANSFER, MANAGEMENT AND ADOPTION IN THE ARAB WORLD

With few exceptions, the experience of individual Arab countries in technology transfer, management and adaptation has not met initial expectations, although technology transfer has always been a top national priority. Arab countries recognised, at an early stage, that their socio-economic development required moving towards industrial (including agricultural in-

It takes multiple actors to innovate and produce knowledge.

With few exceptions, the experience of individual Arab countries in technology transfer, management and adaptation has not met initial expectations.

---

[1]Technology has a life cycle which starts with its birth in research and development laboratories, and continues through its testing and empirical adoption, at which point it is called emerging technology. It eventually reaches the stage of maturity with actual use and, over time with the emergence of more modern technologies, it becomes "old" or obsolete technology.

Technology *management* includes several processes starting with technology testing, followed by acquisition and use. The adaptation of technology is the stage that follows the *import* of technology, when local human resources and institutional structures are able to control and fully understand transferred technology, at which point it becomes possible to employ this technology effectively in realising the purposes of the society. Technology *development* is a more advanced stage that makes it possible to invent new technologies locally, by which new and globally competitive products can be manufactured. This includes the unpacking of bundled technology, reverse engineering, local development and adapting technology to the environment and human development. An even more advanced stage in this chain is the *generation* of technology, which includes the activation of technological research and development, the management of the national innovation system, the adoption of patents and intellectual property rights and the stimulation of human development through the application of new technologies.

Figure 5.1:

Actors and linkages in the innovation system

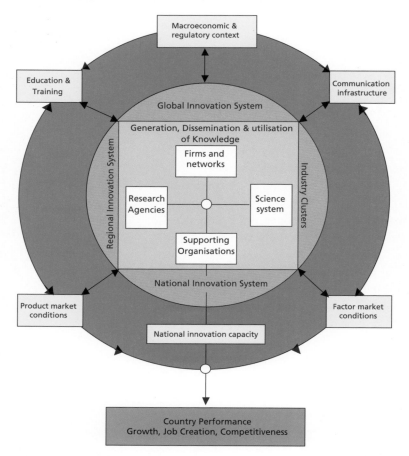

Source: Organisation for Economic Cooperation and Development, Managing
National Innovation System, Paris, 1999, P.23.

For the first time, a dilemma that had long been intractable – the transfer and adoption of technology – seemed to have been resolved.

dustries) and export-based economies. This perception, in principle, was correct, yet it was not translated into effective policies. Industrialisation policies, in particular, centred merely on the acquisition of factories and production technology (purchase contracts), and on the training of local labour to produce goods in acquired factories using acquired means of production. The erroneous belief was that this step in itself would constitute a technology transfer that would be a prelude to the indigenisation of technology.

Initially, such factories used technologies and production processes that kept up with (or lagged only slightly behind) the international state of the art at the time. This allowed factories to meet all or some of the local market's needs for a period of time. But these simple acquisition policies, which did not recognise the importance of managing and adapting these technologies, left the production sector highly vulnerable since the tech-

nologies it depended on became obsolete over a short period of time. Once caught in this trap, most Arab countries responded by passing and enforcing protection laws, which inevitably, and unrealistically, prolonged the life of those early production units. Spread out in the economy, these industrial dinosaurs eventually become a drain on national resources and a major impediment to socio-economic development.

As the crisis of development in Arab countries grew worse, reflected in the severe deterioration of national infrastructure and public services, and as the gap between them and the advanced countries widened, many abandoned their failing industrial policies. They turned instead to liberalising the economy and trade and enacting laws to encourage foreign direct investment (FDI).

Some countries, such as Tunisia and Egypt, espoused wide-ranging FDI-friendly policies. They created a host of legal and financial incentives to entice multinational companies to open subsidiary branches on their soil so that Arab production systems could be part of a vertical integration process reaching up to the international economy and opening up two-way flows of knowledge and technology. For the first time, a dilemma that had long been intractable – the transfer and adoption of technology – seemed to have been resolved.

Arab governments that took this approach bet on the idea that open trade, economic and industrial policies would encourage the advanced world to invest in the growth of the region, strengthen national infrastructures and create an environment conducive to free flows of technology. They believed this new course was superior to the previous acquisition-based approach and part of the logic of globalisation. Indeed, the new laws and investment opportunities did stimulate a financial and economic revival in most of the Arab countries that applied this approach. However, this revival was uneven across the region and within countries its benefits were not equally spread; moreover, it proved to be short-lived.

The windfall that Arab countries experienced from these policy changes was temporary because they were not actively and effectively involved in the global production and export movement. Growth quickly reached a stagnant point and then receded. More significantly, the open door policies that were implemented were not conducive to the real transfer and adaptation of technology.

Reflecting on their experiences with FDI and with vertical integration, Arab countries have come to realise that their expectations may have invited another disappointment. Whether the extended production chain involves the manufacture of spare parts, electronics components or garments, the common experience is that multinational companies reserve the knowledge- and skills-intensive components of the production process for themselves and leave developing country partners to produce at the low end of the technology tree.

In Tunisia, for example, the new policies led to the establishment of companies vertically integrated with the European car industry, on the face of it a sound development. However, a closer look shows that the new companies specialise entirely in the low-technology stages of the car industry, such as the production of seats and electrical systems. Yet this experience can also be judged from a broader perspective: integration on these terms represents only an entry point to technology acquisition and transfer, and to becoming an active part of the global production system, one that avoids protectionist policies that are eventually harmful to the host economy.

TECHNOLOGY POLICIES IN ARAB COUNTRIES

Experts estimate that more than 45% of the increase in per capita income in the West in recent years is attributable to technological advancement. Investment in R&D brought in the highest gross investment returns, compared to investments in other sectors. (Imad Mustapha, background paper)

Some Arab researchers maintain that Arab industrial and technology acquisition policies since the mid-20ᵗʰ century have been largely ineffectual (Antoine Zahlan, *in Arabic*, 1999). Although Arabs invested more than US $2.5 trillion in gross fixed capital formation be-

tween 1980 and 1997, chiefly in factories and infrastructure, the average gross domestic product per capita actually declined during that period.[2] This indicates that those substantial investments did not promote real technology transfers; *what was transferred were the means of production and not the technology*. Agricultural production in the region represents a striking example of a sharp decline in productivity and poor use of modern technologies: more than 50% of the Arab labour force work in this sector, yet value added from it accounts for just 10% of Arab GDP.

Evidently, Arab countries have not attained a level of development that would enable them to adapt the technologies they have imported at different times. In the absence of national science and technology policies geared to the creation of national innovation systems, this is hardly surprising. Practically speaking, the absence of such systems in Arab countries means that past investments in industrial infrastructure and fixed capital have been wasted. Those investments have yielded neither gains in technology, nor increases in productivity or social returns.

Investment in the means of production does not mean a real transfer and ownership of technology; it only means an increase in production capacities – a gain enjoyed for a limited period of time and one which quickly starts to vanish as the acquired technology becomes obsolete. Products and services generated by this technology become economically unfeasible and uncompetitive in local markets, while at the same time technology and production in the advanced countries renew themselves and accelerate forward, thanks to the dynamism of their national innovation systems. The Arab world, which is obliged to purchase new production capabilities whenever the technologies it owns become obsolete, is currently – and expensively – stuck at the wrong end of the technology ladder, a situation which drastically reduces Arab investment returns.

The common experience is that multinational companies reserve the knowledge- and skills-intensive components of the production process for themselves.

The Arab world, which is obliged to purchase new production capabilities whenever the technologies it owns become obsolete, is currently – and expensively – stuck at the wrong end of the technology ladder.

---

[2] It is only fair to point out that a large portion of gross investments in Arab countries went to infrastructure projects which, in most cases, were urgently needed and which do not necessarily bring in quick economic returns.

ORGANISATIONAL ISSUES OF KNOWLEDGE PRODUCTION IN ARAB COUNTRIES

Industrial R&D institutions are weakly linked to production priorities and the knowledge level of basic industrial technologies remains low.

The current state of knowledge institutions and networks in the Arab world is far removed from what is required to establish an effective Arab innovation system. While this state persists, major problems will recur in the transfer and adaptation of technology and in knowledge production. The following paragraphs highlight some salient differences between the current and the ideal situation in innovation and knowledge production.

LINKS BETWEEN RESEARCH INSTITUTIONS AND PRODUCTIVE SECTORS

Promotion of R&D Results

The vigorous promotion of scientific research and the active utilisation of research results in development are among the most important criteria for measuring how far R&D institutions have achieved their goals and succeeded in diffusing new knowledge in society. Yet the promotion of R&D results faces major difficulties and obstacles in most Arab countries. Among the reasons are weak links between R&D institutions and the production and service sectors and the absence of, or marked gaps in, vital innovation "brokers" such as research institutes and think tanks that occupy an intermediary position between R&D and production and marketing.

Industrial R&D institutions are weakly linked to production priorities and the knowledge level of basic industrial technologies remains low. Moreover, many R&D centres lack design and modelling abilities and demonstration and experimentation units. These institutions also suffer from poor planning and organisational capabilities and lack appropriate methods for managing technology, innovation and diffusion. Academicism in research is another significant flaw. There is a trend in many R&D institutes to reward and promote researchers on the basis of academic research and published scientific papers rather than for purposeful applied research and its contribution to solving problems faced by the production sectors. Research projects of interest to industry, firms, enterprises and services that help industry absorb and develop imported technologies and advance their innovation activities are few and far between.

As a result, many accomplishments of Arab R&D institutions remain incomplete, because they do not reach the stage of investment. Some Arab countries have taken initial steps to adopt effective mechanisms for the use or promotion of R&D results. Chief among these is the introduction of "contract research" in universities and research centres, a modality that ties research more closely to market demand. This approach has increased the ratio of completed research projects in universities for the benefit of recipient sectors, helped to identify appropriate local substitutes, penetrated the industrial secrets surrounding some industrial components, enhanced the performance of some production units and overcome obstacles to manufacturing. The size of this experiment, however, is still extremely limited. In Egypt, for instance, the number of research contracts the results of which have been marketed in this way was about 142 during the period 1971-1997. Projects completed on demand from recipient firms did not exceed 43 during the same period (Amr Armanazi, background paper for the Report).

Intermediate Institutions Supporting Technological R&D Production

In addition to the direct links between R&D centres and universities on the one hand (supply side), and production firms on the other (demand side), R&D efforts can gain force and find their way to production firms through various intermediary institutions and structures, both governmental and private, which can offer key technical, professional and support services in one or both directions (supply and demand), according to their specialisation. These structures include industrial R&D centres linked to specific production activities, design bureaux, contract research institutes and business incubators. In Arab countries, industrial R&D centres are almost non-existent, and design bureaux are limited almost entirely to the construction sector.

In the absence of the sophisticated and

Many accomplishments of Arab R&D institutions remain incomplete, because they do not reach the stage of investment.

value-adding services normally associated with intermediary institutions, such as design engineering, project engineering, production engineering, process engineering and quality engineering, R&D remains largely decoupled from the process of technological change. A promising change in this respect is the growth of business incubators, which are starting to play an increasing role in Arab countries.

No knowledge economy can take off without substantial, targeted and risk-tolerant investment. Such investment requires a supportive financial and banking system. This includes the development of venture capital systems of all kinds to help kick-start new industries based on knowledge and modern technology. Investment banks, development capital banks, venture capital funds for innovation and grants for the employment of scientists and researchers in industry and the private sector are much needed intermediary institutions in Arab countries. These financing entities provide critical links between R& D, production and services.

The Role of the Creative Entrepreneur and Technological and Business Incubators

Many Arab countries are moving quickly to establish free market economies. Reaping the rewards and efficiencies of the market, however, requires two basic conditions: competitiveness and the encouragement of a critical mass of creative entrepreneurs ready to accept risks in seeking new areas of technology generation and goods and services production. Neither condition is a common feature of Arab economies. The realisation of both requires changes throughout the entire fabric of society, from systems of upbringing and societal values to the public policy environment and the supporting institutional infrastructure, including educational and financial institutions. The dominant value and educational systems in Arab countries remain largely risk-averse. There is little recognition that entrepreneurs are natural and necessary innovators in the economy. Moreover, financial institutions in Arab countries are still not limber enough to respond quickly to new opportunities, particularly when it comes to providing funds for small and micro-enterprises. In the West, many new and value-adding projects start

small, particularly in the field of information and communication technology. Venture capital plays a substantial role in catalysing technological change by supporting start-up firms and businesses.

Business incubators are relatively new structures for supporting innovation in small and medium-sized enterprises and for encouraging pioneering creative developers who lack the necessary means to develop and market their research and technological innovations. The basic concept behind incubators is that the authors of a new project or innovative idea need sponsorship and a learning environment in which to grow and acquire the means for success. Incubators provide a controlled environment, services, including skills and advice, and materials that fledgling enterprises need to take off. In short, incubators connect talent, technology, capital and know-how to leverage entrepreneurial talent, accelerate the development of new knowledge-based businesses and thus speed up the commercialisation of new technology.

Arab countries have taken more and more interest in business incubators since initial attempts and trials started in Jordan and Egypt in 1989 and 1994 respectively. Recently, Tunisia (1999) and the Emirates (Abu Dhabi in 2000) have started their own projects of this kind. In other Arab countries incubators have appeared in technological capacity-building plans or in various support programmes for small and medium sized enterprises.

The experiments of Jordan and Egypt provide further examples of the development of incubators in Arab countries. The Social Fund for Development in Egypt, originating in a UNDP initiative in 1992, established a major network of incubators as part of its programmes for the development of small enterprises and income generation. The Egyptian Incubators Association, a non-governmental organisation established in 1995 for this purpose, implements the incubator programme. The Association has conducted feasibility studies for 37 business incubators and technology support and services centres in various Egyptian governorates. Nine have already been implemented. In Jordan, the Jordanian Technology Group has established 17 independent companies in various technological

No knowledge economy can take off without substantial, targeted and risk-tolerant investment.

Financial institutions in Arab countries are still not limber enough to respond quickly to new opportunities.

fields.

FOREIGN DIRECT INVESTMENT

It was noted earlier that the traditional industrialisation policies of Arab countries did not lead to the transfer and adaptation of technology, nor did they push the wheel of development forward. New Arab policies for encouraging foreign direct investment (FDI) may not lead to this goal either unless they take into account the basic conditions for the creation of a knowledge-flow environment that would contribute to developing innovation systems in Arab countries. The basic and most important factor in the process of technology transfer and adaptation remains the R&D sector, which drives the process from the initial stage of flawed transfers through adaptation and then on to technology generation and effective participation in the world technological system. Understanding that today R&D is the weakest link in Arab innovation systems is the first step in overcoming present-day impediments to knowledge production.

Until Arab countries develop and seamlessly connect the elements of their innovation systems, technology transfer and development through FDI will remain capped by certain technological limits. Countries will not be able to transform their rentier economies into high value-adding economies, let alone knowledge economies that would allow human development to take root in the Arab world.

FDI and its role in technology transfer and adaptation in Arab countries

Arab experts continue to debate the merits and demerits of FDI as an international technology transfer channel. Some point to the failures of vertical integration with global industrial chains. Others argue that Arab countries have not done enough to take advantage of such chains, and the FDI they funnel, or to create local capacities and environments conducive to the transfer and indigenisation of technology. They note, for example, that, as partners, Arab countries have been incapable of negotiating effective management contracts or responsive technology licensing agreements.

It remains a fact that Arab countries have so far met with little success in attracting FDI. It would be optimistic to expect to see any Arab countries listed among the top ten recipients of FDI worldwide, given that current global patterns favour the wealthier countries and East Asia; certainly none is. But not one Arab country appears in the top ten among developing countries either. Table 5.1 illustrates the anaemic level of FDI in some Arab countries in the period 2000 - 2001.

The table makes it clear that FDI levels in the region are very low. Morocco comes high only as a result of selling 35% of the shares of the Morocco Telecommunication Company to a foreign investor for US$ 2.7 billion, which helped to raise its inflow in 2001. Yet this is obviously neither a recurrent nor sustainable trend.

The investment environment in Arab countries remains an obstacle to FDI inflows. Figure 5-2 shows that in 1999 this environment was well below the optimum level in all the Arab countries in the sample.

Tunisia and Egypt have tried to link FDI flows to technology transfer by adopting policies that promote that connection. For example in Tunisia, all investments geared towards energy preservation, research development and marketing of new capacities are entitled to a 10% discount on import taxes. In addition, value-added tax (VAT) on imported goods and materials that have no local substitute is

Until Arab countries develop and seamlessly connect the elements of their innovation systems, technology transfer through FDI will remain capped by certain technological limits.

TABLE 5.1

Estimated Net FDI flows, by host country 2000-2001 (millions of dollars)*

Country	2000	2001
Algeria	438	1196
Bahrain	358	92
Egypt	1235	510
Jordan	39	169
Kuwait	16	-40
Lebanon	298	249
Libya	-142	-101
Morocco	201	2658
Oman	23	49
Qatar	252	237
Saudi Arabia	-1884	20
Syria	270	205
Sudan	392	574
Tunisia	779	486
United Arab Emirates	260	-156
Yemen	-201	-205

* Net FDI flows in five cases (Kuwait in 2001, Libya in 2000 and 2001, Saudi Arabia in 2000, United Arab Emirates in 2001, and Yemen in 2000 and 2001) were actually negative.

Source: World Investment Report (2002) UNCTAD.

suspended.

Tunisia's philosophy is to invest in human resources. The state's active investment policy is guided at the highest governmental and national levels. Top priority has been given to training Tunisia's human resources and labour force (one quarter of the country's general budget is earmarked for education and training). The focus of training is on technological specialisations, particularly information and communication technologies. As an Arab country which launched a national initiative to upgrade its technological level, and which established a special organisation for FDI promotion, Tunisia is a good example of what an Arab state can accomplish in this field.

FDI actually receded globally in 2001, with the bulk of its flows confined to channels between the US, Western Europe, the NAFTA region and South East Asia. While Arab policy makers and experts continue with their debate on the benefits and risks of FDI, the fact remains that Arab countries are fractional players on the margins of this global economic activity. Whether FDI leads to the transfer and adaptation of technology, or simply stimulates job opportunities, new dynamics in the economy and the movement of technology in the Arab region, any talk about expanding Arab countries' participation in the general trend remains notional at this time.

Arab policymakers often speak about attracting international investments by granting firms tax incentives and promoting their countries' comparative advantages, yet they frequently ignore the fact that FDI flows are also related to a number of other equally vital factors that are part of the national innovation system, as identified in Figure 5.1. That figure illustrates the various factors that positively or adversely affect FDI in the fields of technology and industrialisation, particularly the availability of flexible, trained and highly skilled workforces.

Very likely, economic growth based on R&D, rather than simply on FDI, holds out the principal hope for accelerating development in the region and narrowing the gap between Arab countries and the technologically advanced world. The reason is that growth never occurs merely as a result of the accumulation of resources (the conventional approach

Figure 5.2

The Environment for Investment: 14 Arab countries rated, 1999

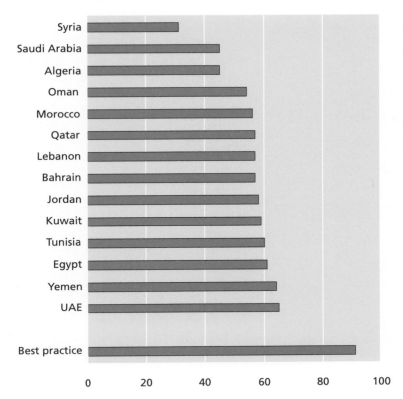

Source: the Economist Intelligence Unit, 1999.

adopted in the past in Arab countries), but as a consequence of the enhancement of productivity and of increasing the value added in production.

In this context it is worth noting that most commercial activities in Arab countries are confined to trade between industries abroad and consumers (import agencies) inside the region. Notwithstanding calls in the WTO for more trade between the North and the South based on mutual benefit, this pattern of trade only benefits one party in the trade formula. The commercial relationships that give momentum to development and that play a major role in technology and knowledge transfer are those that involve inter-industry trade. Since this kind of trade is much stronger amongst industrial countries, and is almost non-existent between them and Arab states, the current trade patterns of Arab countries will not have much effect on technology transfer.

A further reality to be borne in mind is that when multinational companies make direct investments in developing countries, they normally keep their core technology and knowledge within the company itself.

Economic growth based on R&D, rather than simply on FDI, holds out the principal hope for accelerating development in the region.

Knowledge and know-how transfers and technology diffusion are seldom if ever part of their primary strategies. This simply underscores once again why Arab countries need to strengthen their national innovation systems in order to take more advantage of technology-carrying FDI and technology imports.

THE ROLE OF THE STATE AND SCIENCE AND TECHNOLOGY POLICIES

Arab countries need to realise that technology transfer and adaptation entail re-thinking their understanding of the role of their technology-earmarked investments. This requires a shift away from their customary tendency to invest in tangible assets (machinery, facilities and infrastructure) and towards investing in intangible assets (knowledge and human resources). Without significantly increased investment in the latter, Arab countries will not be able to create successful national innovation systems or approach the achievements of other developing countries that have put the ideas, skills and abilities of their people first.

R&D institutions and research activities are subject to many influences originating with governments that can either facilitate or obstruct their healthy development, efficient performance, impact, and objectives. Government policies and legislation that bear on the financial, tax and legal environment for research are one set of important factors. Another set are national policies relating to conditions of employment, general infrastructure, education, health and social security. Policies related to development sectors, such as industry, agriculture, communications, information and energy comprise a third set; while import-export policies and state-sponsored measures to raise public awareness of the importance of science and technology can also be influential.

Add to this the role of the state in building scientific and technological infrastructure, establishing and financing independent and university-affiliated R&D centres and their programmes, and supporting the education, training and skills development of research personnel, and it is clear that governments have large responsibilities for promoting knowledge. Indeed, the role of the state takes on greater significance wherever local scientific, technological and innovation capacities are weak, as is the case in most Arab countries. Cogent and comprehensive national and regional science and technology policies are therefore a top priority in the Arab world.

Concentrated efforts have been made in the past to formulate such science and technology policies, with varying degrees of completeness from one country to another. The prime movers were generally government authorities, research centres and universities, and the resulting plans usually reflected the interests and requirements of the supply side, rather than of those parties on the demand side (the business sector, the state and civil society). Most of these plans have therefore remained vague, unpublicised and under-utilised. Those Arab countries that did succeed in formulating coherent science and technology policies were still held back for lack of strategic and operational plans. Egypt, Jordan, Saudi Arabia and the United Arab Emirates, all of which have taken steps to launch initiatives in science and technology with specific and well-defined goals, have been exceptions to this pattern.

Several Arab countries have established central organs to plan and design scientific research policies. Some of them were charged with the task of coordinating the work of specialised research institutions, while others were associated with their own research centres. In other cases, Ministries of Higher Education and Scientific Research assumed the task of designing scientific policies. However, these institutions rarely settled down to a stable programme of work; some were eventually abolished and others succumbed to structural weaknesses, which compromised their results. Scientific concepts and practices remained rigid, and were not influenced by the new thinking that took place in developed countries during the 1980s and 1990s. Successive waves of change bypassed an inward-looking Arab scientific and technological establishment, leaving it isolated from the dynamic global mainstream.

Governments have large responsibilities for promoting knowledge.

Successive waves of change by-passed an inward-looking Arab scientific and technological establishment, leaving it isolated from the dynamic global mainstream.

MISSING PARTNERS: NATIONAL AND PAN-ARAB FUNDS FOR FINANCING R&D

Governments continue to bear the biggest burden of financing scientific and technological institutions in an environment where absolute spending on R&D is insufficient.

While recent increases in government expenditure on the various levels of education in many Arab countries are laudable, the volume of expenditure on scientific and technological activities also needs to be boosted significantly. Yet governments have difficulty meeting these additional financing requirements themselves. The strongest justification for establishing specialized financial institutions to take up the slack in funding is the importance of stimulating qualitative changes in the scientific and technological policies and activities in Arab countries and promoting demand for the outputs of Arab scientific and technological institutions. These are tasks that dedicated funding agencies can best address.

More than 25 years after the unsuccesful attempt to create an Arab Fund for Science and Technology Development and following several country and national efforts in that vein, the region is still in need of specialized financial institutions for scientific and technological development. There are some exceptions, however, such as the Institute for Scientific Research in Kuwait and King Abdul-Aziz City in Saudi Arabia.

Without underestimating what some institutions (such as the Arab Fund for Economic and Social Development and the Islamic Bank for Development, for example) have been able to provide in this area, their priorities and the structure of their technical organs have not enabled them to play an influential and decisive role in bringing about the required qualitative leap. At the same time, international specialized agencies, such as UNESCO, are not set up as funding agencies and moreover face constraints in staffing that handicap their efforts to play such a role effectively.

While regional and international assistance, both technical and financial, to some Arab countries has grown in recent years, most of this assistance has been directed towards reorienting economic policies, restructuring the

economy and developing infrastructure, in addition to humanitarian assistance and social services. In education, aid to the region has concentrated on reforming and developing basic education, particularly increasing the rate of enrolment at schools and the teaching of girls in rural areas. Only a very small part of regional and international resources has been allocated to scientific and technological development, and most of that has gone towards projects concerned with the preservation of the environment.

Thus, the many justifications for an Arab Fund for Science and Technology Developmen, put forward more than 25 years ago, remain valid. Rapid changes in technology as a driver of economic development have created additional justifications that make the establishment of national and regional funds even more imperative to help Arab countries take advantage of new opportunities and potentials. The Kuwait Institute for Scientific Research for instance, is a promising example of what can be achieved.

Among their purposes and priorities, these proposed funds could help to:

• Formulate policies and create machinery to encourage increased demand for the outputs of Arab science and technology institutions.

• Encourage qualified Arab scientific and technological institutions to become regional centres of excellence and more competitive at the global level.

• Support studies, research and projects, which focus on finding scientific and practical solutions for enhancing the quality of institutions in education, science and technology.

• Enable general and university education institutions to benefit from the enormous pos-

The many justifications for an Arab Fund for Science and Technology Development, put forward more than 25 years ago, remain valid.

BOX 5.1

Pioneering Successful Non-governmental Initiatives - The Kuwait Institute for Scientific Research

The Kuwait Institute for Scientific Research is a pioneering example of an active and successful non-governmental foundation established with support and encouragement from a government. The Foundation was established in 1978 on the initiative of the current Emir of Kuwait, when he was Prime Minister, and the Kuwait Chamber of Commerce and Industry. Under a Bill of the Emir, joint-stock Kuwaiti companies offer 5% (later reduced to 2% then 1%) of their annual net profits to the cumulative resources of the Foundation, whose assets have now reached around one billion dollars. The Foundation spends money on scientific activities in Kuwait and the Arab world from the proceeds of these funds. Perhaps its most famous activities are the five annual Kuwait Scientific Awards given to Arab scientists every year.

Source: Adnan Shihab-Eldin, Background Paper For AHDR2.

sibilities of information and communication technology and connect learning and scientific research activities and outcomes to economic development.

The Arab Fund for Science and Technology Development: The Bold Venture That Almost Succeeded

In 1976, a serious attempt was made to create an Arab Fund for Science and Technology, which almost succeeded. Several positive factors were in place at the time, including the availability of relatively adequate financial resources deriving from lucrative oil export proceeds and the then-prevailing belief in the importance of joint Arab action.

The Conference of Arab State Ministers in charge of the Application of Science and Technology for Development had recommended in its meeting held in Rabat in 1976 the establishment of an Arab Fund to provide assistance in the financing of scientific and technological activities.

The Outstanding Ministerial Follow-up Committee established by the Conference entrusted the Arab Fund for Economic and Social Development, the Kuwait Fund for Economic Development and the Kuwait Institute for Scientific Research with the task of carrying out a technical feasibility study and of preparing a draft agreement to establish an "Arab Fund for Scientific and Technological Development".

The document establishing the proposed fund set the main goal of the Fund as "the creation of an organ to help Arab states in their efforts to overcome the backwardness of their scientific and technological capacities, their dependence and their marginal activity and to promote the dedication of these capacities to the service of economic and social development."

The project set out a plan to translate this goal into a number of objectives, proposing that they include the provision of financial and technical assistance to:
• Develop appropriate policies in the fields of scientific and technological development
• Exploit the scientific and technological capacities, which are already available
• Promote the consolidation and development of these capacities
• Intensify the use of services that science and technology can offer to the various branches of production

• Encourage the appropriate transfer of scientific and technological knowledge from abroad and set the terms and conditions upon which such transfer will be based
• Support private initiatives on inter-Arab cooperation in the field of technology.

The feasibility study indicated then that the range of purposes and functions was very large. It was, therefore, necessary to establish work priorities in light of the priorities of member states. It was also proposed that, with regard to the methods chosen to support scientific and technological projects, the Fund should adopt a flexible policy, including the provision of scholarships and financial subsidies, technical services and loans.

It was also proposed that the Fund should focus its efforts on high-impact projects under specific programmes and not on financing institutional support. It should assume a complementary role in relation to subsidies and loans provided by others. It was also proposed that the minimum capital required as a target for the Fund should be 150 million Kuwaiti dinars. The amount should be regarded as an endowment asset dedicated to the Fund's purposes. The capital would not be touched but instead invested in safe financial assets. The income accruing from this investment would constitute the actual resources placed at the disposal of the Fund to carry out its activities.

Despite the availability of relatively adequate financing in some Arab countries at the end of the 1970s and the declared commitment of these countries to contribute to the Fund's capital, political differences over the management of the Fund's operations and its headquarters prevented its establishment at that time. As the region's development prospects began to change at the beginning of the 1980s, and with diminishing financial resources accruing from oil exports and the fatigue that afflicted joint Arab action, enthusiasm for the Fund diminished and its establishment was abandoned.

Source: Adnan Shihab-Eldin, Background Paper For AHDR2

NETWORKING OF R&D INSTITUTIONS AT THE PAN-ARAB AND INTERNATIONAL LEVELS

Networking is key to the success of scientific and technological work because it enables many actors to contribute to raising the knowledge and value-added content of problem-solving research. Studies reveal that in many cases nearly half the inputs needed to solve a scientific problem come from unexpected sources. Productive scientists usually belong to several networks, which provide them with channels for enhancing their knowledge and experience. Some Arab R&D institutions have made efforts in the past two decades to develop institutional networks to increase performance and support product development, but achievements at the country and pan-Arab levels have been limited, while initiatives at the international level have proved stronger.

At the Arab level

Networking among R&D institutions at the pan-Arab level is generally limited and, where it occurs, is often temporary and not sustainable.

Significant indicators of collaboration include scientific publications. In 1995, for instance, the number of scientific publications by scientists from Morocco, Algeria and Tunisia amounted to 1,205 papers. Of this number, 769 papers included contributions from outside the country, but only seven included contributions from a researcher in another *Maghreb* country. Out of those seven papers, only one publication did not include a contribution from a Western country. It is obvious that scientists from the *Maghreb* countries have been deeply integrated into the international scientific community, but do not seem to be as integrated into their national or regional scientific environment. Scientific cooperation at this level has been infrequent, both through exchanges of experience and information.

The situation in member states of the Gulf Cooperation Council is not materially different. In the same year, the ratio of publications that included contributions from researchers in one or more members of the Gulf

Cooperation Council was 3% of the total number of publications. Those including a joint contribution from an Arabic source were only 15% of the total. This chiefly reflects the fact that universities and research centres in the GCC countries employ large numbers of researchers from other Arab universities, while the larger part of joint contributions comes from outside the Arab countries altogether.

In countries of the Arab East (other than GCC member states) the ratio of joint contributions, including by scientists from developed countries, was 25% of the total. Considering that the volume of R&D activities in any Arab country is limited to begin with, it is only logical to assume that networking with other Arab scientists would partially compensate for a low overall level of activity. Moreover, since Arab countries face a large number of common technological and technical challenges that can be solved through effective cooperation, the importance of collaborative research hardly needs to be underlined. In the vital area of water sciences, for instance, there is a wide spectrum of problems that could be dealt with through joint research. Such activities are still weak, however, and can be substantially strengthened if fragmented efforts in every Arab country are brought together and lubricated by an exchange of experiments and experience.

On the international front, an opportunity currently neglected by Arab R&D institutions is to network with Arab scientists and technicians living abroad and, through them, with the R&D centres and universities in which they work or with which they have ties. There are currently several institutional frameworks supporting this pattern of networking. One of them is "TOKTEN", a programme established by UNDP in the late 1970s and which continues to operate.

At the international level

How far Arab R&D institutions benefit from networking with the scientific and technological community in developed countries ultimately depends on their capacity to plan, organise and manage such networks in ways that meet Arab needs and goals. Failure to energise communication and international cooperation can be attributed in most cases to the

---

BOX 5.3

The Arab Science and Technology Foundation, a non-governmental initiative to support research and development in the Arab world

One recent promising initiative is the creation of the Arab Science and Technology Foundation, established in 2000, in the Emirate of Sharjah, with the aim of building a coalition of Arab scientists living in the Arab world and those residing abroad who occupy leading positions in overseas science and technology institutions and universities. The Foundation aims to become an all-embracing Arab foundation, providing scholarships within the framework of a full scientific review by scientists. The Foundation has secured funding to meet recurrent and programme costs and launched its activities, which included two expanded scientific meetings in 2000 and 2002 that brought together a large number of Arab scientists and researchers from Arab countries and abroad. Foundation priorities include the establishment of sustainable relationships with Western laboratories and the funding of joint research projects by scientists from the Arab world and from abroad, aided by Arab researchers living overseas.

Source: Amr Armanazi, Background Paper For AHDR2.

---

absence of institutions with clear objectives. Other factors are the lack of a critical mass of researchers on national levels in areas of priority for the international R&D community, insufficient research funding and poor

---

BOX 5.4

The Arab Academy for Science & Technology and Maritime Transport

The Academy is a unique institute in the region, one originally established to train people in the field of maritime transport that has now developed into a distinguished university for science and technology.

The Academy was established in 1972 in Alexandria, Egypt as a regional project offering maritime education and training to seamen in three disciplines: navigation, maritime engineering and business studies, in addition to the training of sailors. In its first 12 years, its student body grew from 733 students in 1972 to over 2500 in 1984.

In subsequent years, the Academy diversified its syllabus to cover new fields, such as engineering and management, in order to become self-financing. Its name was changed to the *Arab Academy for Science & Technology and Maritime Transport*, and it adopted a collegiate structure which includes the College of Engineering & Technology, the College of Management, Technology and Maritime Transport and the College of Technology. These colleges grant a bachelor's degree in technology.

The College of Maritime Transport and Technology was provided with an integrated complex of simulators used for various maritime sciences and the protection of the marine environment from oil pollution. It combines in one building the following simulators, laboratories and major equipment: a simulator for the management of oil spills, oil pollution control systems, oil analysis laboratories, a simulator for the management and piloting of ships, and simulators for the transportation of liquefied gas. It also houses a Centre for Geographical Information Systems and a Multi-media Centre.

In addition to its three colleges, the Academy includes other institutes, centres and programmes, which contribute to its accomplishments: the Institute of Advanced Administration, the Institute for Productivity and Quality, the Higher Institute for Professional and Applied Studies, the Institute for Educational Resources, the Institute for International Transport and the Centre for Logistics and Community Service.

The Academy's role transcends the boundaries of the Arab world. In the past 30 years, the Academy provided training opportunities to 257,000 students from 58 Arab, African, Asian and other states. It has thus moved beyond its regional identity to become an interregional university of science & technology and marine transport, with recognized technological capabilities and facilities.

In 1999, the Academy was awarded the ISO 9001 Certificate, having developed and implemented a quality system in all its bachelor's degree programmes.

Source: Arabian Gulf University.

Joint Euro-Arab R&D activities in the modern sciences, such as biotechnology and new materials, are few and far between.

prioritisation of research objectives in terms of national goals.

During the period 1992-1995, several cooperation programmes were instituted between scientific and technological institutions in European countries and collaborating institutions in Arab countries, supported by the European Union. Arab-European scientific and technological cooperation received new momentum following the Barcelona Conference on Euro-Mediterranean Cooperation in 1995, which resulted in the launching and financing of new programmes, most importantly the activities carried out within the MEDA Programme, the financial instrument of the Euro-Mediterranean Partnership. These programmes aimed to support technological research and development, redress problems resulting from the widening of the scientific achievement gap, activate exchanges of experience in scientific sectors and policies (to enable Mediterranean partners to narrow the gap between them and their European neighbours), support technology transfer and help build scientific and technological capacities through increased contributions to joint research projects.

Figure 5.3 indicates the distribution of cooperation projects among participating Arab countries. The data shows that Morocco participates in 28% of these projects, Tunisia in 25% and Egypt in 17%.

Figure 5.4 indicates the distribution of cooperation projects by field. It illustrates that most cooperation projects relate to natural resources (51%), agriculture (21%) and health (14%). Projects related to modern technology are limited in number: information and communication technology (8%), materials and production technology (2%) and biotechnology (0.4%).

Evidently, joint Euro-Arab R&D activities in the modern sciences, such as biotechnology and new materials, are few and far between. Among the most prominent programmes of scientific and technological cooperation between the Arab region and the West are the programmes carried out within the framework of an agreement concluded between Egypt and the United States of America in 1995 for a period of five years. The framework was renewed for another five-year period with effect from 2000. This agreement aims to enhance scientific and technological capacities, promote cooperation between scientific and technological communities in both countries and provide opportunities for scientific contacts.

Research has concentrated on biotechnology, industrial technology, environmental technology, standards and measures, information technology and energy. More than 70 research projects were funded in the latter fields in the period 1995-2000. Research institutions in Egypt and more than 30 US research institutions cooperated in the implementation of these projects, some of which produced results that aroused the interest of the industrial sector, paving the way for negotiations to transform the results of these research projects into products.

Figure 5.3

Distribution of Euro-Arab cooperation projects in research and development among Arab countries

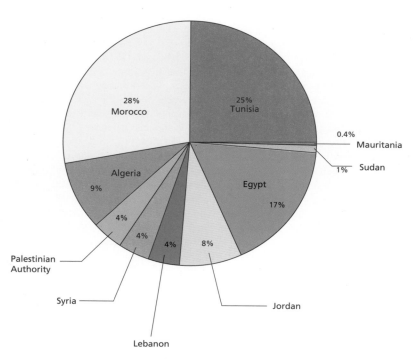

Source: Al-Bizri, 2000.

Figure 5.4
Distribution of Euro-Arab cooperation projects among R&D fields

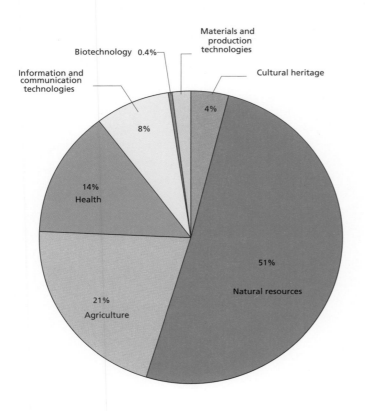

Source: Al-Bizri, 2000.

It is not possible for Arab countries to benefit from the fruits of global knowledge without investing in local production, local knowledge workers and local knowledge traditions.

Chapter five observes that Arab countries' experience with the transfer and adaptation of knowledge through technology, and their efforts to organise and make effective use of their own accumulated human and natural capital, have, on the whole, been disappointing. Weak national innovation systems and institutional frameworks largely account for this outcome and for relatively meagre technology returns on FDI. The general absence of coherent, action-oriented scientific and technological policies is a further constraint. The chapter concludes that it is not possible for Arab countries to benefit from the fruits of global knowledge production and technology without investing in local production, local knowledge workers and local knowledge traditions. Current indicators of research production and economic output tell this story plainly enough.

This chapter completes the assessment of the status of knowledge in Arab countries. Starting with Chapter Six, the Report takes up an analysis of the societal context affecting knowledge acquisition in the Arab world.

PART II

Section three: the cultural, socio-economic and political context

Chapters 6-8 concentrate on impediments to knowledge in the Arab world. This analysis takes in: a) culture, itself subdivided into heritage, religion and language; b) the dominant socio-economic structure, including modes of economic production, growth and income distribution; and class structure, attitudes and values; and c) politics, including political systems, the role of elites, the corruption of knowledge by politics; the importance of codifying knowledge freedoms under the law; the relationship between good governance and freedom of thought and expression; and the regional and global environment for knowledge transfers and development.

CHAPTER 6

Culture

The production of knowledge is driven by strong and increasing societal demand and the political will to secure the resources necessary for stimulating a vital and capable knowledge system. This includes building high calibre human capital as a base, and ensuring an environment of policies and institutional structures conducive to the system's effective functioning. Important as they are, these factors are in turn affected by societal, cultural, economic and political determinants which also have a bearing on the knowledge system – for knowledge does not evolve in a social vacuum but rather in a particular society that has a reality, a history and a regional and global context. It is this last element that has a special significance for the Arab world in this phase of its history.

This next section of the Report, therefore, deals with fundamental elements of the societal context that affect the knowledge system and that are expected to play a significant role in the establishment of the knowledge society in Arab countries. Chapter 6 considers the relationship between culture and knowledge acquisition, and delves into some of the issues that have been briefly touched upon earlier in the Report (in Chapter 1 in particular). The chapter analyses the various components of the Arab intellectual heritage, religion and language, and folk culture.

The term "culture" generally refers to all human contributions to ideas, perceptions, customs, socio-political systems and economic constructs. It also encompasses literary, artistic and technological innovations throughout history. It almost overlaps with the term "civilisation", and has innumerably more specific definitions. The most common and useful definition of culture refers to the status of intellectual progress, of individuals and societies, reflected in intellectual, value-related, innovative and artistic accomplishments that are cor-

related with progress in the thinking patterns and behaviours of a particular civil group. Arab culture can be perceived from two perspectives: formal culture and folk culture. Formal culture is construed to mean the complete array of intellectual tools, comprehensive concepts, systems and values that govern the system of thought and action, and the perceptions and practices of the individual and society. In this definition, and in an Arab cultural context, intellectual heritage represents a basic component of culture, language is said to be the carrier of culture; religion is the major comprehensive belief system that directs the life of this culture; and values (moral, social and political) are the judges of the actions directed within it. Those are the fundamental elements of Arab culture for the purpose of this analysis. Of course, there are other cultural, knowledge-based, scientific or conceptual elements deriving from other sources that could also be added to those three elements. But intellectual heritage, religion and values, and language stand as the most decisive, determining and instructive elements of formal Arab culture. It is those three that ought to be taken into account first when looking at knowledge production as a step towards building a knowledge society in Arab countries.

INTELLECTUAL HERITAGE

Arab "intellectual heritage" is a major component of Arab culture. An Arab knowledge society must connect with the defining sources of knowledge upon which this society is built. Arab intellectual heritage constitutes a living membrane in the cultural body of Arab society, yet it remains a "historical" phenomenon, i.e., the entirety of its facts go back to objective historical conditions. Change, development and transcendence underlie the entire process of

Intellectual heritage, religion and values, and language stand as the most decisive, determining and instructive elements of formal Arab culture.

this heritage's formation, movement and destiny.

If it is assumed that the human being is the starting point and the origin of this heritage, it can also be assumed that the religious text, from the viewpoint of some, remains outside the scope of history, but is nonetheless identified as one of the fundamentals that interacts with historical realities and responds to their needs. As for the elements of the heritage itself, they are embodied in all forms of intellectual, scientific, spiritual, literary, materialistic, man-made and artistic life that the makers of this heritage have.

All those forms of life are manifest in the historical Arab knowledge experience, dating from the pre-Islamic era, (traditionally designated as the period of "Jahiliyya" by the Arab Islamic heritage), up to the age of Western modernity, beginning in the early 16th century. In the middle of the 19th century, with the advent of printing and communication with the West, modern Arabs re-discovered their intellectual heritage in all its components: linguistic, literary, historical, scientific and philosophical.

The issue of Arab intellectual heritage has never been purely a theoretical or scientific question. Rather, it has been, to a great extent, an ideological issue.

HERITAGE: A TUSSLE BETWEEN KNOWLEDGE BUILDING AND IDEOLOGICAL EXPLOITATION

Concurrent with the emergence of Arab "modernity" was the emergence, in reality and in consciousness, of the Arab heritage. The concept of Arab heritage became an important dimension of the modern problematique of culture and civilisation and the Arab past and future. It is with this concept that all of the basic stances and questions concerning the "historical personality" – the "Self", "the civilisational Self", cultural specificity, identity, tradition and modernity, and Islam and modernity – were connected. These issues, in addition to many other binary opposites, occupied shifting positions that were at times conflicting, harmonious or complementary. Indeed, they became related to the modern reality of Arabs, to the challenges of advancement and progress, and to attempts to deal with "crisis", "backwardness", or "defeat" or other situations that call for inspiration from ideas or forces conducive to progress and revival.

The result was that the issue of Arab intellectual heritage has never been purely a theoretical or scientific question in the strict meaning of the word. Rather, it has been, to a great extent, an ideological issue. It relates not only to religion, the sacred and the Arab past but also to new practical causes that require purposeful acts, political or national concessions, and interest-related aims that are distinct from the pure scientific view.

In being connected with and at the same time contradictory to knowledge, Arab intellectual heritage nowadays raises basic knowledge problems. Its link with knowledge comes from its connection with language, religion, sciences and culture. Its contradiction with knowledge arises because heritage is not usually viewed from a scientific standpoint but is rather closely surrounded by emotion, passion, desire, wishes, glorification and sometimes a disregard of reality and discomfiting facts. In other words, ideological leanings often permeate approaches to this heritage.

It is therefore important to distinguish between awareness of cultural heritage on the one hand, and the humanities and history, with all their branches of study, on the other. The reason is that history is based on methodology, on an objective approach and on maintaining an intellectual distance from the past. The goal of any historian of a great civilisation, while sympathising with and understanding the subject of research, should always be the quest for facts. The temptation to fall in love with the heritage must always be resisted.

Nevertheless, the exploitation of Arab intellectual heritage for ideological reasons should not be exaggerated. Modern interest in

---

BOX 6.1

Ibn Khaldoun (1332-1406), On the fact that scientific education is a skill and a profession

Dexterity in science, progress and mastery can only be attained through the faculty of knowing its principles and rules, examining its problems and deducing its branches from its main streams. Until this faculty is owned, no skill can be achieved. The Andalusians have lost interest in science because of the deterioration of their civilization for hundreds of years. Of all sciences they have kept and preserved only the art of the Arabic language and literature. Jurisprudence has completely disappeared and no trace of it is left among them. Intellectual activity is even worse off among them. And that is all a result of the worsening condition of education, a consequence of the deterioration of their civilization; and the fact that their enemies dominate them. They have been more concerned with subsistence than with what is beyond it.

Source: Roshdi Rached , in Arabic, background paper for AHDR 2 .

the Arab heritage has not been motivated by ideology alone; it has also taken the form of an extensive effort that started at the end of the 19th century to revive and publish this heritage. Orientalists first initiated this revival, which was then undertaken by Arabs themselves who expanded it further into scientific and non-scientific spheres. There is also a substantial body of cultural studies, which have examined this heritage in accordance with accepted and rigorous research methodologies. There is a wealth of Arab scholarship in these fields, in addition to scholarship carried out in the West at institutes and universities specialising in oriental, Arab and Islamic studies. Those studies cover all fields of Arab heritage – language, literature, religion, culture, science and art – and they genuinely contribute to the exploration of its intellectual, spiritual and human dimensions. Thanks to such studies, the relationship between Arab culture and Arab heritage has been made accessible to intellectual and human understanding, rather than being left as a passionate ideological relationship or a shallow expedient resorted to under compelling historical circumstances.

Indeed, this objective approach to knowledge deriving from Arab heritage is the most useful approach for Arab countries now and for building the knowledge society in the future. Yet such knowledge also requires a comprehensive historical view of the substance of this heritage. First, it is necessary to address the issue of the "Arab mentality", an obstacle to understanding Arab heritage that has persisted for a long time. *Al-Jahiz*, for example, believed that all Arab thought was gained only through natural disposition, inspiration and intuition and never by affectation and dissimulation.

"The Arab mentality"

Early Orientalists tended to claim that the mentality guiding Arab heritage is characterised by a simplistic analysis of particulars and is incapable of complex constructions and abstraction. Hence, it is the kind of mentality that lacks the competencies necessary for real innovation (for a critique of such viewpoints see Abdul Razek, in Arabic, 1966). A wide debate ensued recently about the nature of the "Arab mentality" and its knowledge mechanisms. An association was also made between this mentality and an Arab "character" that is governed by instinctive desires, emotion, passion and an overwhelming individualism or the destructive absence of rationalism.

Contemporary Arabic literature is replete with accounts of the "Arab self", the "Arab character" or the "Arab identity". Those texts vary in approach and include harsh self-criticism or analysis, in some cases, or appreciation, commendation, glorification, and presumption of superiority, efficacy, perfection and homogeneity in others. Yet the features of any rich human portrait appear accented or diminished depending on the angle of view. Contemporary accounts are full of ostensible Arab cultural characteristics distorted by one interpretation or another. These accounts are generalisations, and selective ones at that. They are erroneously based on abstracting a fixed and formed Arab "mentality" from ever-changing cultural, intellectual, socio-economic and political contexts.

In the course of its actual historical formation and advancement, the "Arab mentality" has never been restricted to what is purely "Arab", but has rather been open to global intellectual, psychological, social and human interactions. Thus, products of this mentality have been varied, rich, and developed; its methodologies have been multiple and diverse. Historical and ideological factors, moreover, have been decisive in directing those methodologies to various ends. The so-called Arab mentality has at different points in history been traditional and imitative, rational and innovative, analogical (in jurisprudence) and figurative, rhetorical, scientific and experimental, intuitive and Sufi, or transcendental and mystical.

The question of the "Arab mentality", then, should be seen in the context of objective reality and within the flow and flux of time. This mentality is not a single construct with a fixed "essence" and unchanging traits outside history. It is not a myth outside objective reality. Rather, it is a dynamically evolving synthesis of the rich diversity of cultural and social influences that, under particular historical conditions and at different times, have gone into forming this "mentality" in the course of a specific civilisation. As Arab his-

Contemporary accounts are full of ostensible Arab cultural characteristics distorted by one interpretation or another.

The question of the "Arab mentality", then, should be seen in the context of objective reality and within the flow and flux of time.

tory advances, changes and varies, so too the "Arab mentality" encompasses and expresses change. (For more on this issue see, Al-Jabri, [in Arabic, 1991]; Al-Aroui, [in Arabic; 1970], and Tarabishi, [in Arabic, 1996])

Renewal, innovation and knowledge production certainly depend on the major elements and values that are rooted and employed in the cultural system. This would make the Arab mentality a system that is developed and open to knowledge, action and creativity; one that has acquired the competencies for production, progress and innovation utilising and expressing this knowledge.

The foundations of Arab intellectual heritage

Arab intellectual heritage, embodied in the Arab historical experience in its golden age, i.e., since the beginning of the Islamic period until just after the era of Ibn Khaldoun (early 1400s AD, early 800s AH), relies upon a set of knowledge, scientific and cultural foundations and formations. It is by those foundations and formations that the Arab intellectual heritage is defined in history. The Islamic "Revelation", undoubtedly, constituted a primary knowledge base, one that guided the intellectual and spiritual proceedings and the worldly life of the Arabs who exemplified Islam and carried it across geographical borders and among humankind. Likewise, the "Revelation" was the starting point of the School that favoured the imitation of the tradition to which early religious scholars, jurists, traditionalists and scholars, in addition to the masses of believers, adhered. Although the "Revelation" was in fact addressed to the human mind for it to comprehend, and therefore to human reason, Muslims in the first and second centuries of *Hijra* (the Prophet's emigration from *Mecca* to *Medina*), with some notable exceptions, did not give reason much attention. Its function, then, was confined to understanding, interpreting and attributing religious texts, or drawing attention to their linguistic connotations.

Yet interaction with other human civilisations and the spread of Islam across other nations and cultures, together with the transfer of the old scientific and philosophical heritage, combined to elevate the position of "rea-

son". Eventually, a new intellectual power emerged and managed to make reason synonymous with, or the twin brother of, the text, if not precedent to it in questions of theory or nature. Soon afterwards, the contradiction between text-thesis and reason-antithesis brought about a third construction, basically a synthesis of both, which became highly renowned and widely disseminated.

The deterioration of political, socio-economic and scientific life, and the decline of the central state and its social institutions after the collapse of the Abbasid Caliphate, produced a tendency towards asceticism, abandonment of the worldly life and immersion in the teachings of Sufism and ecstatic communion. These trends nurtured a tendency that sought to replace communication with the world, society and human beings with communication with God and the Absolute. And once the central state had fallen, in the middle of the 7th century AH (the 13th century AD), the Islamic civilisation retreated and gave way to a new kind of human association, to use Ibn Khaldoun's term. "Arab reason" moved towards mysticism and its supernatural, transcendental sciences. It was released from those pursuits only at the dawn of the 19th century due to a number of historical factors including communication with Western modernity.

Evidently, this liberation was limited because a sub-culture that encourages superstition has remained to the present day and will certainly thrive in popular environments. Such a subculture needs to be uprooted. One of the most effective means of doing so would be to popularise cultural values that respect science and scientific research.

In the Arab historical experience, the Revelation, reason and their synthesis, as well as inner consciousness, ecstatic communion and mysticism, were respectively the epistemological basis of Arab thought until the dawn of the modern age. Each principle has served as the starting point for the development of one or more branch of Arab cultural expression.

The Arab mentality (is) a system that is developed and open to knowledge, action and creativity

The "Revelation" was addressed to the human mind for it to comprehend, and therefore to human reason.

Arab historical knowledge outcomes

Revelation, for example, has been the starting point for the sciences of theology and legislation, such as Qura'nic Sciences and Exegesis, the science of Hadith terminology, Islamic jurisprudence, and also, to some extent, Muslim theology, Monotheism and Scholastic Theology. Each discipline in turn arose in response to historical challenges and needs at different times. Those needs of the time had to do with the understanding of religion and its beliefs, the practice of religious acts of devotion, the enforcement of religious dealings and the application of religious provisions in all fields of life. It is thus not strange to find disparities and discrepancies in the understandings, perceptions and independent juridical judgements that eventually culminated in a number of different schools of jurisprudence based on elements deriving from different principles.

Moreover, the interpretation of the religious text did not stop at one approach; on the contrary it initiated diverse methods of thought: the linguistic method; the rhetorical method; the rational method; the traditionalist method; the school of ecstatic communion or Sufism; and the *Zahirite* school (interpreting the Qura'an according to its literal meaning). These diverse approaches to understanding the religious text testify to its richness, variety and depth. Similarly, the multiplicity of schools of jurisprudence attests to the diversity of principles for arriving at independent judgement. Some schools disclose the wide latitude, others the narrow boundaries laid down before the believers. Most important of all, what the varied nature of this legal heritage confirms is that its contents are not ultimately fixed, but are closely tied to historical subjective conditions and to the living relationship between the "text" and changing reality.

As for Reason, it was the starting point for the sciences of the Arabic language, the science of Scholastic Theology and the body of philosophical sciences that were called "the intellectual sciences". These include logic and philosophy, as well as the natural, medical, engineering and mathematical sciences passed-down to the Arabs from the "predecessors", i.e., the Greeks in particular. Few as they were, the Arab intellectual sciences were not originally entrenched in ancient Arab culture; indeed, they were dubbed "intruding sciences" by the Arabs themselves. Yet they represent a historical manifestation of this culture that has been blurred with the passage of time and with the renewal and advancement of modern knowledge. Their historical value in the advancement of human civilisation is unquestionable.

The synthetic method, which combined the two poles of Arab thought, the imitation of tradition and the exercise of innovative reason, and which characterised the scholastic perspective of the *Ash'arite* school, was the starting point of wide cultural activity. The method produced an eminent group of great religious intellectuals, who were active in the period from the third century AH (the ninth AD) to the current cycle of Arab Islamic civilisation. The impact of this method remained evident in the intellectual thought which accompanied the age of modernity and the modern renaissance.

As noted earlier, with the fall of the central state and the eclipse of scientific rationalism, inner consciousness and ecstatic communion became the principles of a spiritual life that expressed the yearnings of the self towards the Supreme Absolute. This movement was the basis of all subjective and communal Sufi experiences, which filled Arab and Islamic cultural life. Whatever their individual features, the sciences of Ultimate Reality, whether spiritual or philosophical, rational or irrational, reflected a rich intellectual life with a high spiritual value that echoed throughout the East and West, touching upon human spirituality in traditional and in modern times. This is not surprising as those sciences are closely tied to the metaphysical and existential dimensions of humankind. Yet because they are intimate personal experiences, they could not become the founding principles of a collective knowledge system.

On the other hand, the supernatural culture, which was related to astronomy, astrology, the science of Talismans and even to some forms of religiosity, and which held a distinctive position after the great age of Ibn Khaldoun, belongs to the backward stages of Arab intellectual heritage. It is well known that modern enlightened movements have

The interpretation of the religious text did not stop at one approach; on the contrary it initiated diverse methods of thought.

The multiplicity of schools of jurisprudence attests to the diversity of principles for arriving at independent judgement.

Heritage has been a dynamic contributor to thought.

contributed decisively to the withdrawal and elimination of this culture in modern times.

In summary, Arab consciousness arises at the confluence of multiple historical currents flowing through and from its cultural inheritance. That consciousness has displayed itself in diverse forms and in different areas. It has been *traditional*, bound by the limits of the text and the traditional arbiter. It has also been *innovative and intellectual* as in the case of the scholastic theologians, jurists, philosophers and scholars of the "intellectual" and natural sciences. It has been *synthetic*, combining reason and the imitation of tradition; and it has been *mystical*, as in the deep Sufi consciousness open to the Absolute across space and time, yet closed to society with its worldly horizons. Finally, it has been cloaked in the *supernatural*, which in reality signified an absence of consciousness and an abandonment of the scientific and intellectual basis that underpinned the Arab classical cultural experience (Jada'an, *in Arabic*, 1998).

HERITAGE AND THE KNOWLEDGE SOCIETY

There is some kind of consensus among Islamic thinkers to define religion (Islam) as a multidimensional system of beliefs that embraces the spiritual and the material, the divine and the earthly, the heavenly soul and mortal worldly deeds.

What is that part of the Arab intellectual heritage that remains steadfast and alive through history? And what is that part that can, or ought to be upheld, built upon and employed for the sake of active involvement in the knowledge society and in knowledge production? Undoubtedly, Arab intellectual heritage has undergone many changes and developments and quite a number of its components have been superseded by the progress of knowledge and science. Yet some fields of knowledge and sciences have progressed farther than others (Centre for Arab Unity Studies, *in Arabic*, 1985). The conventional religious sciences have remained unchanged and have failed to produce results in the field of religion. Moreover, as these sciences by custom associated the notion of science with "religious science" or only with knowledge "useful" to religion, they also failed to contribute to advancing the fields of natural knowledge. On the other hand, the Arab intellectual sciences, i.e., the philosophical and natural sciences have pioneered a number of valuable and solid methodological approaches at the comprehensive human level. Amongst the most important are:

- Increasing the tone of rationalism in religious thought.
- Fostering objective rationalism in philosophy.
- Founding a new analytical mathematical rationalism.
- Establishing experimentation as a pattern of proof in knowledge.
- Introducing values as principles in thinking.

Heritage, in the sense discussed here, has been a dynamic contributor to thought. The profound and varied cultural influences, methods and values deriving from that heritage and living on in the present, which can be built upon in creating the Arab knowledge society, are subsumed in language, religion and values (moral, social and political).

These building blocks represent what can be termed "formal culture" in contradistinction to "popular culture". What is the status of these building blocks? And how would they contribute to establishing a successful knowledge society in the Arab context?

RELIGION

The approaches of Islamic thinkers and the various intellectual currents underlying Islamic religious experience vary greatly in both their nature and objectives. This is evident when one considers the different approaches of philosophers, theologians, Sufis or fundamentalist thinkers. But there is some kind of consensus among Islamic thinkers to define religion (Islam) as a multidimensional system of beliefs that embraces the spiritual and the material, the divine and the earthly, the heavenly soul and mortal worldly deeds. Therefore the definition advanced by Al-Tahanoui ("Terminology in Arts and Sciences, "1996) exactly reflects this multidimensionality: religion, according to him, is a divine dispensation that inspires rational mortals to focus at one and the same time on bettering their lives on earth while earning their place in the afterlife. This definition confirms the vital relationship between religion as a belief linked to the religious absolute and to reality, in all its flux and flow, as governed by the religious absolute through a cognitive system and its methods of induction, deduction and judgement in relation to the primacy of the Qura'an and Sunna (traditions of the Prophet) and to other judgements as derived from the analogical, adjudicative, public interest and ratiocinative methods.

Yet this section is not aimed at considering the nature of religion, ideas, or subjective and historical facts. Rather, it considers how religion relates to knowledge production in a knowledge society. Its focus on Islam as opposed to other religions is to be expected since Islam is the major religion in most Arab countries. Moreover, Islam was a major inspiration for Arab civilisation. However, this focus implies no detraction at all from the value and importance of Arab communities that embrace a religion other than Islam, especially Christians who have a recognised and dignified position in modern and classical Arab culture. Indeed a multitude of religious groups have played a very significant role in the formation of this culture and in the production of science and knowledge.

RELIGION, THE MATERIAL WORLD AND KNOWLEDGE

The relationship between religion and knowledge is closely linked to the concept of the essence of religion and its comprehensive attitude towards worldly life. Reading religious Islamic texts reveals a balance between both religion and worldly life, and between life on earth and in the afterlife. The recurring focus is on the importance of enquiry, contemplation, science and sound reasoning, and whatever relates to the continuity of humankind on earth. There is emphasis on contemplation of both the heavenly and earthly kingdoms and on subduing the universe for the good of humanity.

Historically, some Muslims drifted from this innate balance by interpreting the principles of science and reason in the light of "Religious Science" and forms of knowledge useful for religion. By limiting and narrowing the concept of science in this way, they did not advance the openness of the intellectual and natural sciences. Other Muslim groups believed that worldly life, being transient, had no

> BOX 6.2
> ### Milad Hanna - Religious Harmony and Knowledge in the Arab World.
>
> All the Abrahamic religions arose and flourished in the Arab region. Judaism emerged with the Prophet Abraham in the city of Or, in Iraq, then moved to Palestine, then Egypt and came back to Syria and Babylon in a long and well-known historical journey. Then Christianity emerged in Palestine and continued in the Arab East up to the present day. There are many Christian communities in the Arab world that represent all three major branches of Christianity: Orthodox, Catholic and the group of Protestant sects. The most famous among them are the Coptic community (most of whose members are Orthodox) in Egypt, the Maronites (Catholic) in Lebanon, the Syriac in Syria and the Assyrians in Iraq. There are also Armenian minorities, who migrated from their original country and found refuge in the Arab region.
>
> Most Arab communities of Christian faith are generally on very good terms with Muslims. They have lived under Islamic rule for centuries and their relations with Arab Muslims are excellent, although there remain some problems that can be easily solved.
>
> The point that is worth emphasising in the context of this report is that these Arab Christian communities have been partners in the shaping of the Arab-Islamic civilisation. It is an established historical fact that they contributed, during the time of the Abbasid Caliphate, to a wide-ranging movement of translation into Arabic of literature that preceded Islamic civilisation, benefiting that movement with their knowledge of the Greek language, in addition to their original Assyrian, Syriac and Coptic languages. Their contributions helped to transfer pre-Arabic heritage and formed a cultural bridge to it, thus maintaining the continuity of knowledge from ancient to modern times.
>
> The knowledge available to humankind today is a cumulative knowledge transferred and enhanced through the translation movement, which flourished at the height of Islamic civilization and was augmented and enriched by the knowledge provided by that civilization itself.
>
> The Christianity that developed in the Arab world co-existed with Islam through successive eras and produced knowledge. Indeed, whatever knowledge humankind achieves, in whatever field, is but an accumulation of knowledge through successive civilizations and a tributary of world human development as a whole.
>
> This Christian-Islamic co-existence in the Arab world represents a model of unity in diversity, which is one of the sources of human progress and advancement through knowledge acquisition.

claim on their attention and so pursued the afterlife on earth. They turned to the life of asceticism and Sufism, abandoning worldly preoccupations. The nature of their choices diminished the influence of worldly sciences and the pursuit of material and intellectual knowledge and science. Nevertheless, the major tendency of early Arab civilisation expressed itself as a keen interest in the world and in acquiring scientific knowledge and in the encouragement of knowledge in all its aspects. Indeed, the production of knowledge was prolific, as witnessed by the Islamic Arab heritage in linguistic, literary, intellectual, physical and other disciplines.

In the modern age, the intellectuals of the Arab Renaissance recognised the diminution of science and knowledge as the main reason for the backwardness of the Arabs and the degradation of their civilisation. Thus, they were anxious to espouse the rational princi-

This Christian-Islamic co-existence in the Arab world represents a model of unity in diversity.

Al Kawakibi (1854-1902) Despots and Knowledge

Knowledge is a firebrand from God's light. God created light for enlightenment and for generating strength. He made knowledge as an example revealing good and uncovering evil, generating warmth in souls and nobility in the mind.

A tyrant never fears religious knowledge or the After World, as he thinks such matters cannot harm him, but rather distract the minds of people interested in them. If any of those thus distracted became knowledgeable and famous among common people, the tyrant would always find a way of using him for his support by shutting up his mouth with scraps.

But the tyrant would shiver in fear of worldly knowledge such as theoretical wisdom, intellectual philosophy, the rights of nations, civil policy, history, literary rhetoric and other knowledge that pierces the veil of ignorance and enlightens people.

Source: The Character of Despotism, pp 50-51.

Islam is a system of religion and worldly life at the same time.

ples behind the surge of global knowledge and science and combine the values of Islamic civilisation with those of modernity (Hourani, 1967).

Religious texts were a significant tool in the process of justifying this new combination and encouraging the advancement of knowledge and science and their applications. The latter, after all, are considered a major factor in the comprehensive development of humanity and a form of worship of God on earth.

However, the course of development in the modern Arab world, and the national, political, social and economic problems that recurred from the years of independence until the end of the twentieth century, had a profound impact on the intellectual, scholarly and cultural life of Arab countries. Religion, and its attendant concepts and objectives, was especially affected by these trends. A major phenomenon that appeared in the religious Islamic sphere in the last decades of the twentieth century gave political aims precedence over any other objectives: social, economic or material. This development resulted in the escalation of conflict and confrontation with the society, the State and "the other".

"Opposition" and "confrontation" with the West reached their climax especially after the tragic events of September 11, 2001. In their aftermath, Islam itself faced an onslaught of defamation, slander and criticism in the media, reflecting ignorance of Islam in most instances and in some cases the tendentiousness of commentators.

It is important to reiterate here that Islam is a system of religion and worldly life at the same time. It is difficult to separate surgically the "political" from other transactions among people in Islamic teaching. Moreover, the prevailing Islamic sect in Arab countries has neither a clergy nor a defined church or religious authority. Hence the separation of church and state is not an issue. What qualifies an individual to have a say in religious affairs is his or her knowledge, and not an affiliation with a religious institution. Authority in worldly affairs is civil, based on people's selection of a ruler from among several candidates.

Nevertheless, the collusion between some repressive regimes and certain types of conservative religious scholars has resulted in certain interpretations of Islam that serve the interests of those regimes. Such interpretations represent serious impediments to human development, particularly when it comes to freedom of thought, accountability of the ruling authorities and women's participation in public life. Furthermore, suppressing political action

Erudition in the Qur'an and the Sunna (prophetic tradition)

The Qur'an [1]

Allah witnesses that there is no deity except Him, and the angels and people of knowledge know that He is the One and maintains justice in all Creation. (Sūrah 3- Āli'Imrān, 18)

Say, "Are those who know equal to those who do not know?" (Sūrah 39- az-Zumar, 9)

Allah will raise those who have believed among you and those who were given knowledge, by degrees.
(Sūrah 58 - al-Mujādalah, 11)

And say, "My Lord, increase me in knowledge." (Sūrah 20- Tā Hā, 114)

Nūn. By the pen and what they inscribe.
(Sūrah 68- al-Qalam,1)

The Sunna

"If anyone travels on a road in search of knowledge, Allah will cause him to travel on one of the roads of Paradise. The angels will lower their wings in their great pleasure with one who seeks knowledge, the inhabitants of the heavens and the Earth and the fish in the deep waters will ask forgiveness for the learned man. The superiority of the learned man over the devout is like that of the moon, on the night when it is full, over the rest of the stars. The learned are the heirs of the Prophets, and the Prophets leave neither dinar nor dirham, leaving only knowledge, and he who takes it takes an abundant portion." (Sunan Abu Dawud, Book 25, Number 3634)

"Spread knowledge and you will congregate so that the un- knowledgeable will know. Knowledge does not vanish save when it is hidden."

Learning and knowledge in the Holy Bible, Old Testament [2]

"And if anyone longs for wide experience, she knows of things of old, and infers the things to come; she understands turns of speech and the solutions of riddles; she has foreknowledge of signs and wonders and of the outcome of seasons and times" (Wisdom of Solomon, 8:8)

"Apply thine heart unto instruction, and thine ears to the words of knowledge." (Proverbs, 23:12)

"And by knowledge shall the chambers be filled with all precious and pleasant riches." (Proverbs, 24:4)

[1]The Qura'an, translated and revised by Saheeh International, Riyadh, 1997.

[2]Electronic Text Centre, University of Virginia Library, http://etext.lib.virginia.edu/etcbin

in many Arab countries has driven some "Islamic" movements underground and pushed others to work under an Islamic cover. In the absence of peaceful and effective political channels for dealing with injustices in the Arab world, at the country, regional and global levels, some political movements identifying themselves as Islamic have adopted extreme interpretations of Islam and violence as means of political activism. They have advocated belligerence towards both other political forces in Arab countries and "the Other", particularly the West as relations have grown more tense, accusing both of being the enemies of Islam itself. Not only are such interpretations inconsistent with pure religion; they also divide societies, taking them further away from the requirements of the knowledge society.

In summary, for religion to regain its role in the development and production of knowledge, the time has come to proclaim those positive religious texts that cope with current realities and the hoped-for future rather than those related to specific historical developments that Islam underwent in one era or another. These positive texts focus on a number of basic values that link the aims of religion with the development and growth of life: the succession and continuity of humankind on earth, the creation of paradise on earth and the enjoyment of the earth's bounties, respect for human beings and their cognitive faculties - curiosity, reason, science, the senses, vision and feelings; and building a good and respectable nation. Certainly, these are all values that motivate the search for knowledge and its production from a religious point of view. Religion urges people to seek knowledge and to work towards the realisation of its founding principles firmly, effectively and with determination. Neither arrogance nor careless disregard of humanity has any place in obeying that call.

Three fundamental conditions need to be fulfilled so that religion can take its proper place in the Arab knowledge model and become an effective force for knowledge. The first is to return to the moral, civilised and humane vision that stands behind the essential objectives of Islam. The second is to free religion from the sway of politics and to free reli-

BOX 6.6

Technology in the Arab Islamic Civilisation

It would seem unnecessary to discuss an obvious factor such as the role played by the Islamic religion in the renaissance of Arabic civilisation, since without Islam probably no such renaissance would have taken place.

The blossoming of science and culture in Islamic civilisations was the result of the increasing quality of material life in Muslim cities. The urban life of these cities, the material prosperity, the varied local industries, the local and international trade, and the flourishing science and culture, were all linked together, while none of the aspects of life in the cities would have flourished without a developing technology. And if Islam was the force behind the rise of cities, as is frequently asserted, then it was also the force behind all aspects of the prosperity of these cities, and hence the technological efforts associated with urban life.

It is estimated that there exist at the present time, in spite of destruction and many losses, nearly a quarter of a million manuscripts, mostly in Arabic, in the various libraries of the world. And this does not include unrecorded collections.

The admirable flexibility of the Arabic language enabled the Muslims to coin and extract scientific and technological vocabularies capable of expressing the most complicated scientific and technical ideas.

The state enabled scientists and engineers to spend all their time on research, inventions and writing.

As is natural in the history of civilisation in general, Muslim scientists and engineers received the heritage of their predecessors, but this grew into their own science and technology through a continuous process of invention, research and development.

There can be no doubt that institutions – academies, libraries, observatories, etc. – played a major role in the continuing vitality of Islamic science. These, together with the readiness of students to travel hundreds of miles to learn from acknowledged scholars, ensured that the whole corpus of knowledge was kept intact and transmitted from one place to another, from one generation to the next, with continual expansion and enrichment.

Source: Ahmad Y. Al-Hassan and Donald R. Hill, 1986, Islamic Technology; an Illustrated History, UNESCO, Paris – Cambridge University Press.

gious institutions from political authorities, governments and radical religious movements. The third is to acknowledge intellectual freedom by reviving scholarship (ijtihad) and the protection of the right to differ.

LANGUAGE

Language is perhaps the most distinctive and defining feature of any human society. The rise of all civilisations was always accompanied by a linguistic renaissance. Some cultural historians also believe that no human conflict exists without an implicit linguistic clash. Language is the living medium that expresses the reality of a society, and the basic tool that determines the relationship between human beings and this reality. Language is the lens through which human beings apprehend the world. It is the decisive attribute that forms their identity and gives society its unique character. Identity is the outcome of meanings created by individuals through language, and the character of a society is the outcome of the interaction of internal linguistic discourses shaped by historical variables, and reflecting the facets of

The time has come to proclaim those positive religious texts that cope with current realities.

agreement and conflict of the societal system.

Such statements on the importance of language in human society are even more applicable to the knowledge society, whether they concern expectations of its promise or challenges to its creation. The Arabic language is undoubtedly the most prominent feature of the Arab culture. If the knowledge society, as delineated in the current report, is the source of hope for Arab human development, the Arabic language system is one of the decisive underpinnings for building that society and shaping its success.

Language is the device by which the individual conceives the surrounding world and expresses his or her individual and social identity. Accordingly language can be defined as the vital player in reviving activity and embodying new genres of creation in the cultural system of knowledge-based communities. Language is pivotal in the realm of information technology, the tool that all modern sectors use, and the foundation on which modern human communication is established. In addition, language articulates the worlds and worldviews of finance, trade, politics and the mass media.

The Arabic language precedes all manifestations of Arab culture and its human artefacts. In the Arab historical experience, Arabic is also connected with two basic matters that are closely associated with both the existence and future of Arabs. The first connection is with "identity"; the second is the question of the "sacred". The Arabic language is the distinctive feature that distinguishes the Arab identity. It is the language of the holy Qura'an. And it was the rallying point for the intellectual, spiritual, literary and social activities incarnated in an entire human civilisation,

namely the Arab Islamic civilisation.

LANGUAGE AND THE KNOWLEDGE SOCIETY

As one of the fundamentals of culture, language plays an essential role in the knowledge society, not least because culture is the seedbed from which the development process springs. Language is instrumental in the cultural system, linking intellect, creation, pedagogy, media, tradition, values and beliefs. Language is instrumental in information technology, instructing the microprocessors that drive that technology and its artificial intelligence. Language is the tool used by all disciplines of knowledge, including philosophy, the human and natural sciences and the arts. The knowledge society, in which education and learning are lifelong endeavours, depends on language, whether natural human language, software and programming languages, or biological genetic language. Language is necessary to build communication skills that are essential to knowledge dissemination. It is the instrument by which the powers of capital, trade, politics and ideology dominate the mass media, the public and the culture industry in general. Language and cognitive discourse occupy a prominent position in all spheres that serve regimes, organisations, institutions, and market interests.

The crisis of the Arabic language

Notwithstanding the seminal importance of language, Arabic today, on the threshold of a new knowledge society, faces severe challenges and a real crisis in terms of theorisation, teaching, grammar, lexicography, usage, documentation, creation, and criticism. The rise of information technology presents another aspect of the challenges to the Arabic language today.

The central aspects and symptoms of this linguistic crisis can be summarised as follows: First, there is a marked absence of linguistic policy at the national level, which diminishes the authority of language centres, limits their resources, and eventually results in poor co-ordination among them. Second, the Arabisation of the sciences and the various disciplines has not proceeded according to expectations.

The Arabic language is the distinctive feature that distinguishes the Arab identity.

BOX 6.7

About Language

Language is that which translates the meaning borne in our minds.
Ibn Khaldun, **Prolegomena**

Most of the blemishes of our life can be traced to linguistic failure that incites disunity, blurs the truth, wastes effort, and impedes sublimity of the soul, body, mind, and heart.
Amin El-Khouly

It seems that there will be no solution to the dilemma of language neither in mathematics nor in logic, but the key to the linguistic secret is in biology.
Noam Chomsky

If language is truly a mirror of the mind, it must reflect not just the algorithms of syntax but the mind as a whole, the complete set of rules by which a human being, in Lakoff's words, "gives form and sense to his universe, where without them there would be none."
Jeremy Campbell, **Grammatical Man**

Third, there is a chronic deficiency in translation efforts in the sciences and the humanities. Fourth, linguistic theory suffers from stagnation, isolation from modern philosophical schools and methodologies, and a lack of awareness of the role language plays in modern society. Fifth, the situation of the Arabic language is further complicated by the duality of standard and colloquial Arabic. Sixth, Arabic electronic publication is weakened by the scarcity of advanced Arabic software. Finally, the Arabic language continues to suffer from the duplication of research and development projects and the absence of co-ordination among them, conflicting diagnoses of the ills afflicting the language, and the conspicuous absence of a clear vision of linguistic reform.

The crisis of the Arabic language is no less central and no less dangerous or complicated than the other crises facing the Arab world, particularly on the verge of a radical shift in the importance given to knowledge. Yet crisis is also opportunity. Moving towards the knowledge society will force countries to address the challenges facing the Arabic language in order to harness its latent powers and address other challenges. The most significant opportunities include:

• The revolution in modern linguistics, which has ushered in several scientific methodologies[3]. These can help address many difficulties besetting the Arabic language.
• Massive technological development in "language engineering", in which the language system, with its extreme complexity, constitutes a rich subject for new approaches to the art of manipulating sophisticated systems.
• The Internet, which has become a resource for teaching and learning the English language and could become a platform for promoting the use of Arabic in multiple formats.
• Increased awareness of the importance of linguistic diversity. World awareness of this problem has reached new levels, so much so that UNESCO has drawn attention to a crisis of linguistic diversity and the risk of extinction that threatens several languages.
• New and viable initiatives in some Arab countries in the theory of literature and lexi-

cography; and recent successes in the digital processing of Arabic, especially in the domains of morphology and grammar, and the use of computers to create a modern Arab thesaurus.

Advancement of the Arabic language

But these options on their own, or together, are not sufficient to resolve the crisis of Arabic and render it responsive to profound contemporary developments in culture, knowledge and education, or to recent global challenges. There is another aspect of the problem; the many-faceted relations between Arabic and the system of knowledge acquisition, notably:
• The relation between the Arabic language and thought.
• Arabic and access to sources of knowledge.
• Arabic and the communication and assimilation of knowledge.
• Arabic and the utilisation of knowledge.
• Arabic and the generation of new knowledge.

Language and thought: understanding the nature of the relationship between systems of language and thought requires exhaustive analysis on the psychological, pedagogical, and social levels. This aspect of language has not received due attention from Arab researchers; certainly, classical linguists did not tackle this problem and did not present anything that substantially contributes to the development of Arabic thought.

A number of reasons account for the gap. First, Arabic thought has refrained from engaging with multidisciplinary issues, which are of great importance within the knowledge society. For example, Arab philosophical thought, especially in theology and philosophy, has been isolated from other disciplines, despite the marked attention paid by traditional scholastic theology, philosophy, and traditional jurisprudence to language, concepts, and terminology. Next, research efforts in psycho-, socio-, and especially neuro-linguistics have been marginal. In reality, strengthening the relation between the Arabic language and thought needs a concerted institutional effort by specialists in psycho-linguistics in order to reveal the relations between the characteristics

The crisis of the Arabic language is no less central and no less dangerous than the other crises facing the Arab world.

---

[3]New methodologies cover statistical, anthropological, reproductive, textual, computerised, bio-neurological, hypothetical, mathematical and logical, functional, lexical, and empirical methodologies).

Arab North Africa – Language Duality

In the 1980s, Algeria intensified its efforts to substitute Arabic for French as the dominant language of the country. Its Arabisation policy, which has been in place for more than two decades, particularly in education, communications and justice and in many public administration institutions, has been effective in several respects. Yet some consider that the conversion from French to Arabic of an entire generation of mainly French-speaking professionals has led to a loss of knowledge and capability. Arabisation has been less effective in economic, technological and administrative fields where French continues to dominate. Books, newspapers, radio and TV programmes are published or broadcast either in French or in Arabic (some also in Berber languages) with relatively few translations. This language segmentation has reduced communication among different spheres of society.

Tensions resulting from this language duality appear to have relaxed in recent years, paving the way towards multilingualism in different areas of education and communications.

Source: Country Report prepared for AHDR 2.

of Arabic, its morphological, grammatical, lexical, and rhetorical resources, and the main functions of the brain. Establishing a research centre specialised in the fields of Arabic language in relation to information technology, neuro-technology, and genetic engineering would significantly advance the frontiers of knowledge in this field.

Language and access to sources of knowledge: The contemporary knowledge explosion, with its at times overwhelming information overload, poses a challenge to Arab thought. It would be easy to succumb to a sense of defeat before the sweeping hurricane of data and information blowing in from the global information society. A bold response requires devising a new software toolkit to process texts and to make access to knowledge more efficient, whether in Arabic or other languages. The most important of these tools are: automatic tools for indexing, extraction and abridgement; and intelligent tools for research into the body of texts in order to understand the depth of their inherent structures and extract their intrinsic contents. The application of artificial intelligence and electronic document management techniques and developing an Arabic inference tool would be key supports in this new research.

Access to sources of knowledge in languages other than Arabic is mainly connected with translation. Translation into Arabic is still extremely scarce and is not keeping pace with the global knowledge explosion. This lag emphasises the importance of developing electronic translation. Of course, there are several levels of translation: rough translation used to convey impressions of a subject, which is currently taking place on the Internet in a very modest way; and faithful translation of texts. The state of electronic translation globally is a long way from the level of faithful and accurate translation.

Language and the assimilation of knowledge: The relationship between Arabic and the communication and assimilation of knowledge involves two major considerations: the Arabisation of university education and the teaching of Arabic.

The Arabisation of university education is no longer simply a matter of nationalism; it has become a prerequisite for developing the tools of thinking and the creative faculties of young minds and for assimilating the rising volume of knowledge. For example, the failure to Arabise the sciences is an obstacle to communication among different scientific disciplines. Despite the evident importance of the issue, efforts at Arabisation are still faltering under opposition from many academic quarters. The principal objection to teaching sciences in Arabic is that it would prevent Arab students from having access to the original sources of scientific knowledge that are mostly in foreign languages. Yet modern students are increasingly accustomed to resorting to different sources of knowledge and research anyway. If Arabisation efforts run parallel to efforts to strengthen the teaching of foreign languages in all scientific disciplines, this objection recedes.

It is relevant to observe here that facility with the English language is waning across the Arab world. With the exception of a few university professors and educated individuals, real proficiency in English has ebbed, preventing many Arab researchers from publishing their research in international scientific journals. This trend also explains the wide reluctance to make presentations at scientific gatherings in English, or to participate in seminars or even Internet user groups. Paradoxically, this decline makes developing the methodologies of teaching Arabic mandatory. For the dominant language acquisition theories now hold, contrary to past thinking, that a good command of one's mother tongue is an essential tool for learning foreign languages.

Translation into Arabic is still extremely scarce and is not keeping pace with the global knowledge explosion.

Arabisation requires a fresh look at word structures and encouraging more production in Arabic in different scientific disciplines as well as supporting current efforts in the development of electronic translation. It also calls for more use of what ICT can provide by way of building databanks of terms and helping in the conceptual decomposition of Arabic words. When translating non-Arabic terms into Arabic, the new term should convey accurately and completely the meaning and concept of the original term.

The teaching of Arabic also suffers from an acute crisis, both in curricula and methodology. The most apparent symptoms of that crisis include: concentration on the superficial aspects of teaching grammar and morphology, rather than on the core concepts of texts and their respective holistic structures; inattention to semantics and meaning; neglecting the functional aspects of language use, such as improving linguistic skills in everyday use; limiting language classes to writing rather than reading; abstaining from using conventional lexicons, (which are admittedly difficult owing to the juxtaposition of new and old entries and explanations without distinctions); and the inadequacy of pedagogical research in language teaching.

Indeed, the problem of teaching the Arabic language is not detached from the state of classical Arabic at large. This language today is no longer the "language of conversation". It is rather the language of reading and writing and their official manifestations (religious sermons and political, administrative or social addresses). Moreover, it is the language of the educated and the intelligentsia, often used to display their knowledge in lectures. In other words, classical Arabic is not the language of cordial, spontaneous expression, emotions, feelings and everyday communication. It is not a vehicle for discovering one's inner self or outer surroundings. It goes without saying that the problems of classical Arabic start when one enters school, where it is taught as a concept or an independent subject. In other words it is taught in the first place as an object of thinking, analysis, classification, evaluation, and inference. All this flows from the traditional school and its principles of reading, reciting, narrating, rote learning,

and the avoidance of creativity and initiative. This is a state of affairs that can only lead to the production of knowledge that is stagnant and lifeless. True, since the modern Arab enlightenment, the Arabic school has been connected with the experimental rational European school, and is thus more open to rich and accelerated knowledge and methodologies. Nevertheless, the prevailing methodology that the Arabic school follows in teaching the language still emphasises memorisation rather than the acquisition of dynamic, renewable knowledge.

Language becomes more vital, vivid, and creative in its renewable, active, civilised and human domains inasmuch as it draws its depth and richness from the heritage it preserves. It is hardly possible to distinguish, except in form, between the language of a society on the one hand and the cultural structures, scientific and practical intellectual concepts, and applied methods of that society on the other. The re-birth of the Arabic language through the measures discussed in this chapter is the core and crux of a new Arab renaissance centred on knowledge and human development.

This is why linguistic research is vital. It requires establishing language centres, new dictionaries incorporating words common to both colloquial and classical Arabic, functional scientific dictionaries (written and audio-based) for basic education, specialised functional dictionaries, the Arabisation of scientific terms, the gradual simplification and rationalisation of grammar leading to a median language that neither lapses into the colloquial nor replicates the rigid old structures that are difficult to use. Again, ICT and the Internet can contribute significantly to modernising the teaching and learning of Arabic in both content and methodology. This entails moving forward with research into computer languages and reading theory in addition to the pedagogical, psychological and social dimensions of languages.

Language and the utilisation of knowledge: the link between language and the use of knowledge can best be seen from the perspective of problem solving. Problem solving encompasses the ability to make an accurate diagnosis and compare available choices to find solutions. In other words, it demands ra-

Facility with the English language is waning across the Arab world.

The prevailing methodology that the Arabic school follows in teaching the language still emphasises memorisation rather than the acquisition of dynamic, renewable knowledge.

The re-birth of the Arabic language is the core and crux of a new Arab renaissance centred on knowledge and human development.

Two distinctive features of the Arabic language are its unique capacity to derive words and terms flexibly from its lexicon and its prodigious vocabulary of synonyms and meanings.

tional analysis. To reinforce the definitional and descriptive power of the Arabic language, it is essential to consolidate and enhance glossaries of terminology, thesauruses and specialised lexicons in social and scientific fields. To improve its capacity to frame logical analysis, Arabic discourse needs to update its basics of proof, methods of persuasion and argumentation and use of logic. Other measures for the renewal of Arabic include initiating a fresh formulation of its grammatical rules, and enhancing its communication capabilities by expanding its functional use in every day life, which would make Arabic a more supple medium for living social dialogue.

Language and the generation of knowledge: The role of language in the generation of modern knowledge, especially in the human sciences, is also critical. These sciences contribute to the identification of new research methodologies distinct from those of the physical sciences. If Arabic develops close relations with modern and informational biochemistry, for example, the language can enhance scientific creation. It can also contribute to literary and artistic creation, and indeed to all of the arts of the Arabic language.

Two distinctive features of the Arabic language are its unique capacity to derive words and terms flexibly from its lexicon and its prodigious vocabulary of synonyms and meanings. This flexibility and wealth play a real and effective role in producing knowledge in dynamic and changing contexts requiring new analysis, description and definition.

Linguistic development and societal context: Yet linguistic development and reform are not only related to the internal elements of the knowledge acquisition system, as in the earlier discussion. They are also related to the social context, where language exercises its public functions and to the linguistic-social interaction becomes significant on both the economic and political levels, regionally and globally.

The state has an important role in supporting linguistic development on a number of key fronts: formulating linguistic policies, providing financial resources by which the language academies can perform their duties, directing the official mass media to confront language issues, or supporting the development of

Arabic educational and linguistic programmes. Such efforts, supplemented by those of non-governmental organisations, would advance the protection and development of the Arabic language. Moreover, the expected role of Arabic within the regional context must be taken into account. The Arabic language – with its organic relation to the Qura'anic text – is a major entry point for the study and revival of heritage. It is also the main pillar of Arab solidarity, national unification and Arab cultural unity. Further still, Arabic is the bulwark against fragmentation emanating from "Information Age Orientalists" who defend the multiplicity of Arabic dialects. Finally, the Arabic language has a significant role in linking Arabic culture to other Islamic countries' cultures. It also has another important role to play in the international context in confronting cultural globalisation and the move towards rejecting linguistic and cultural specificities. In other words, the Arabic language is disposed and able to be an effective party in cultural dialogue. And, although there is no reason to believe that the Arabic language is threatened by extinction, it is necessary to work determinedly on strengthening its linguistic shields and enhancing its practical and subjective characteristics that confirm its international profile and receptivity and its ability to assimilate new informational and technological developments. It is also essential to strengthen its relationship with other languages.

The renewal of Arabic will of course gain strength if the conditions and resources necessary to support Arab culture as a whole – moral, economic and technical - are put in place.

FOLK CULTURE

Until recently, folk culture did not receive much recognition in most contemporary Arab intellectual and cultural accounts. The tendency has been to view it as a blemish on culture, not an achievement, an historical backwater, a synonym of myth, or a defect in formal thought.

This prejudice has receded in recent decades amid the rediscovery that folk culture has a significant role in Arab cultural, social and economic life. The relationship between Arab folk culture and formal culture has been established as a profound reciprocity of influence and effect. Holistic accounts of Arab culture see the two forms as equally authentic components of an integrated pattern.

Folk culture is, in fact, a huge repository of experiences and creative efforts that have enriched the intellectual, emotional, and behavioural life of all Arabs. It is rich in its components, as it consists of knowledge, beliefs, art, ethics, law, conventions, industrial knowledge and the popular creations of Bedouins and rural and urban dwellers. Folk culture is the creation of shepherds, farmers, artisans, and craftsmen who produce that culture outside of formal educational establishments and institutions. This culture, however, has also expanded to reach other social, cultural, and scientific groups. It also permeates old Arab history and has deep roots in the region. Varied as its forms and origins in different Arab societies are, folk culture nonetheless has elements of similarity and unity.

Folk culture is communal and oral and these two attributes account for how knowledge is produced and propagated in traditional societies. Production springs from the demands of the group. Transmission is by way of social interaction and relationship. Surprisingly, such processes often take place efficiently and do not run counter to the acquisition of rational knowledge, as might be imagined.

Folk culture comprises: concrete folk culture, folk knowledge and representations, folk conventions and traditions, and artistic folk expression (music, performing arts, visual arts, drama and linguistic expression).

Each category is blended with an artistic experience that is intrinsically connected to the style and practices of a particular community life. Therefore, some have no relation to the process of acquiring knowledge directly; rather, they are forms of entertainment, such as storytelling and the narration of biographies.

FOLK CULTURE: BETWEEN CREATIVITY AND IMITATION

Yet these forms are not devoid of knowledge.

Biographies, for example, are full of historical, geographical and humanistic knowledge. Imaginary worlds appeal to the creative human instinct for empathy and personal extension. Both forms are popular means of exchanging historical knowledge or rules related to customs. Many folk tales commend the value of knowledge and place it in a position superior to property. The high respect commonly shown for a written script by folk communities indicates the degree of their respect for knowledge, its value and importance.

Commonly, the culture expresses two voices: one, a conformist voice that calls for the imitation of traditional practices; the other, forward looking that advocates creativity, curiosity rationality, and the pursuit of knowledge. Some simple and even thoughtful proverbs originating in the nomadic area of Najd convey this latter outlook: "Ignorance is a lethal malady" and "Need provides the tool", not to mention others such as "Knowledge is illumination", "Be in quest for knowledge even in China". By the same token, the conformist elements of the culture have their own observations and stories. A well-known example concerns the individual who has been allowed to open all the doors in a hall except one; driven by curiosity, he pushes that door open and is punished with exile. English readers are familiar with the popular saw, "Curiosity killed the cat", which expresses a similar caution.

Traditional community celebrations when a young boy graduates from the '*Kuttab*' (the traditional school for memorising and reciting the Holy Qura'an and the basics of arithmetic and other disciplines) indicate the high standing of knowledge in popular culture. The young graduate is treated to a great procession through his village accompanied by eulogies and prayers. A banquet follows and inaugurates a new chapter of social esteem for the latest possessor of knowledge. The community further ensures that, until the age of twelve, the boy continues to be schooled in elementary social disciplines: manners, rules of societal relations and ethics as well as in the fundamental skills for acquiring knowledge in whatever craft he has learned.

The relationship between Arab folk culture and formal culture has been established as a profound reciprocity of influence and effect.

Many folk tales commend the value of knowledge and place it in a position superior to property.

CRAFTS

Traditional occupations and crafts are highly prone to deterioration, decline, and withdrawal from people's everyday lives.

Behind the decline in Arab folk crafts stands a change in modes, tools, and relations of production.

This principle of learning also applies to crafts and jobs, which need physical stamina or an intensive specialised skill. Thus, a boy is motivated to acquire the required learning and techniques through a direct apprenticeship with his master. The "master" or tutor graduates the phases of practical work for the apprentice according to the stages of his learning and actual progress. That is why it is not unusual to find boys in grazing communities herding flocks of cattle or, in agrarian communities, taking part in irrigation, running waterwheels and so on. Of course, they also perform a good part of the routine work required by the crafts or industries they have embraced.

Some crafts and jobs require more time, as well as mental and physical maturity, to master. Other tasks that do not require physical strength, such as scouting human and animals trails, tracking the positions of celestial bodies, and practicing folk medicine, still require dexterity, skill and knowledge to achieve proficiency. Occupations that require physical strength, such as masonry, blacksmithing, carpentry, weaving, and pottery also entail not only practice but skills in using tools and instruments, some of which are mechanically sophisticated. Indeed, craftsmen often devise their own work tools.

Significantly traditional occupations and crafts are highly prone to deterioration, decline, and withdrawal from people's everyday lives. This runs counter to the common assumption that the abstract and speech components of a folk culture disappear before its livelihoods. Field inspections reveal the decline of these crafts and occupations together with their associated knowledge and skills.

Behind the decline in Arab folk crafts stands a change in modes, tools, and relations of production. Demand for the products of those crafts and occupations, which called for experience, dedication, specialised skills and mastery, has withered because inferior mass-produced goods have replaced them at lower cost. With the decline of returns on their products, these craftsmen have given up their tools and their apprentices; and the traditional cycle of learning through the reproduction and communication of skills, expertise, and

knowledge has been broken. What remains are mainly those types of crafts that require no commitment or specialisation, and that are not the main source of a livelihood. The decline of traditional crafts as a source of employment, income and skills development, in both developed and developing societies, is well documented. But it assumes special importance in the Arab region, which suffers the highest rates of unemployment in the world and a growing deficit of knowledge in both new and traditional forms.

THE REVIVAL OF AN AWARENESS OF FOLK CULTURE

Folk culture provides artistic, musical and literary inspiration for several modern Arab art forms. Contemporary artistic solutions, technical methods, and creative forms and images are sometimes found in folk legacies and blended with modern performances and taste. Certain musical composers who take a scholarly approach draw directly from traditional musical compositions following a scientific methodology that results in innovative and creative music. Acknowledgements and evidence of folk influences can also be found among the plastic arts and in painting, sculpture, pottery, the cinema and other modern art forms.

All this points to the fact that folk culture can be a major element in the production of artistic knowledge and a source of cultural creativity. For example, Egypt's experience in mobilising folk culture as a stimulus for contemporary creativity underlines two points:

First: The adoption of a cultural strategy pointing in two directions. In the first direction, folk culture moves out of its confinement and migrates towards the larger cultural structure, taking up new space there. An enriching dialogue and hybrid relationship with other cultural components thus begins. In the second direction, the contemporary cultural structure moves towards the space of folk culture to bring the highest achievements and cultural creations to the broad mass of people.

Second: This cross-fertilisation can pay large dividends in building both cultural diversity and strength. Interaction, amalgamation and new syntheses will inevitably drive new and advanced Arab cultural products, rooted in social pluralism and national identity, and capable of offering a rich alternative to cultural globalisation.

The seeds of this future harvest have already been planted in a number of "festivals" held in Arab countries. Their host cities have become the centres of communication, interaction, synergy and new cultural energy: Salalah in Morocco, Sosa and Kartaj in Tunisia, the Cairo International Book Fair, Ganadriya in Riyadh, Jarash in Jordan, Karien in Kuwait, Baalabak in Lebanon, and others. There are also cultural events and symposia sponsored by civil institutions, such as *Abdelhameed Shoman* in Amman, and the cultural gatherings in Beirut, Abu-Dhabi, and other cities. All these manifestations are vivid evidence of an Arab cultural interaction, which holds folk culture in high esteem and places it in a visible position domestically and internationally. The state, the private sector, and the civil society should make the continuation of this new fusion their first priority in supporting modern Arab cultural development.

CULTURAL INTERACTION

Historically, Arab culture was never a closed system. Through all historical turning points, it exhibited openness and growth. Going beyond the cultural ego, it accepted the experience of other nations and assimilated them in its knowledge systems, customs and daily practices in spite of the differences and dissimilarities among those nations and their experiences.

The first of the two major experiences that touched Arab culture goes back to the age of scientific recording and the encounter with Greek civilisation and its disciplines of knowledge. This was the age of seeking out new disciplines and importing them into the culture, especially in the third and fourth centuries of Hijra, the ninth and tenth centuries AD. Here, an outstanding process of translation of most of the Greek scientific and philosophic heritage took place (Ibn El-Nadeem, in Arabic, 1964; Badawi, in French, 1968; Walzer, 1962). This heritage was profoundly assimilated and

then reproduced in new forms of creation. This interaction with the ancient heritage was the first step towards producing science, knowledge, and culture. The second major experience occurred in the 19th century when the modern Arab world encountered Western civilisation and opened up to its sciences, arts, knowledge and technology. The outcome of this was the renovation and modernisation of the Arab cultural heritage. The Arab world embraced the future and contributed its own prolific production in all branches of knowledge, sciences, arts, literature, and technology.

In both the east and west of the Arab world, cultural production continues to show a profound interaction between Arab intellectuals and creative artists, and the global culture and its different philosophies and intellectual movements. This interaction is revealed in the translation of literary, scientific and philosophical works from their source languages into Arabic. Of course, translation efforts into Arabic are woefully insufficient, compared to those into other languages, since the total body of such translations, as noted in a previous chapter, amounts to about one book per million Arabs according to UNESCO statistics. Arabs continue to translate the works of other cultures, not as exercises in translation, but to study, analyse and criticise those works as knowledge, while seeking out their influence and inspiration.

Regional, geographical and linguistic contexts have to a great extent influenced the interests of Arab intellectuals. Arabic culture in the western part of the Arab world reflects an explicit interaction with French literature and culture owing to the proximity of the sub-region to France and its historical experience with France and the French language. In the eastern part of the Arab world, interaction is greater with the scientific, literary and cultural production of the Anglo-Saxon and American worlds. In addition, similarities and common human and political factors between Arab countries and those of Latin America, as well as other developing regions, have led some Arab writers and intellectuals to welcome the creative works produced by artists and thinkers in those countries.

All prominent names in global culture have found their place in the Arab contempo-

Historically, Arab culture was never a closed system.

Cultural production shows a profound interaction between Arab intellectuals and creative artists, and the global culture and its different philosophies and intellectual movements.

Arab contemporary culture is generally explicit in its openness to human cultures... The single exception is the imitative school of tradition, which is slavishly tied to the past and its legacy.

Arab culture cannot exile itself, feeding only on its past, its history and its intellectual heritage.

rary culture. All global ideologies and methodologies the human and social sciences, including *inter alia* structuralism, functionalism, phenomenology, stylistics, deconstruction – the list is endless – have found both committed adherents and ardent critics in Arab culture. Hence, Arab contemporary culture is generally explicit in its openness to human cultures and the interaction with the contents, concepts and methodologies common in those cultures. The single exception to such openness is the imitative school of tradition, which is slavishly tied to the past and its legacy. However, some representatives of even that school accept, in varying degrees and within certain limits, some of the products of modernity.

Yet despite all these marks of openness, Arab culture today finds itself deeply challenged by aspects of global culture: the unbridled power of mass communication and the gigantic power of the global economy and global finance. It is, like many other cultures, confronting the problems of an emerging monolith while also concerning itself with cultural multiplicity, cultural personalities, the problem of the "self" and the "other", and the problem of its own cultural character. These and similar terms and concepts reveal the obsessions and anxieties of Arabs. Fears about the extinction of their language or their very culture itself, or about the diminution and dispersal of their identity, have become overwhelming obsessions that increasingly haunt the Arabic intellect and Arab society.

The way out will be the way through. The only historical possibility for Arab culture is to go through this new global experience. For it cannot exile itself, feeding only on its past, its history and its intellectual heritage in the new world of overwhelming powers that dominate knowledge, products, technology and global culture.

There is nothing that can justify Arab culture, in light of its rich historical experience and heritage, seeking to escape from the new conditions. Undoubtedly, some currents embedded in this culture would prefer a policy of rejection, indifference, isolation, and hostility to all values, ideas, and practices from outside. This is an understandable response to a global culture that is not impartial in most cases: understandable, but not acceptable. Withdrawal, even if it were feasible, would only lead to the weakening, decline, and fading away of the structures of Arab culture, rather than their flowering and further development. Moreover, as this chapter has argued, the most authentic values and ideas in current Arab culture, especially in the fields of language, religion, and values, are quite capable of holding their own against the challenges of globalisation without retreating from, or rejecting the future.

The global culture has its own dimensions of knowledge, science, and technology, which countries neglect at their own risk. Openness, interaction, assimilation, absorption, revision, criticism and examination cannot but prompt creative knowledge production in Arab culture. It is time to give the most enlightened, the most rational, objective and balanced, the most productive and the most humane impulses and currents of Arab culture their due, perhaps overdue, place in shaping and driving the next Arab encounter with the infinitely expanding world of knowledge.

BOX 6.9

Amin Maalouf: Protecting Diversity

The formidable power lent to Man by modern science and technology may be put to diametrically opposed uses, some beneficial and some destructive. Nature has never been so abused as it is today, yet we are in a much better position than ever before to protect it: not only because of our ability to influence environmental problems but also because our awareness of them is greater than in the past.

This does not mean our power to do good always gets the better of our ability to do harm, as is shown by only too many examples: take the depletion of the ozone layer, for instance, and the many

species still threatened with extinction.

I might have referred to other fields besides that of the environment. I chose that because some of the dangers we encounter are similar to those involved in globalisation.

In both cases there is a threat to diversity. Just as animal and plant species that have lived for millions of years are now dying out before our very eyes, in the same way, if we are not careful, we may witness the disappearance of many cultures that have hitherto managed to survive for hundreds or thousands of years.

Source: Amin Maalouf, In the Name of Identity: Violence and the Need to Belong, 2001, pp 128-129.

This chapter has indicated that there is no contradiction between the defining elements of Arab culture as analysed here and knowledge acquisition.

It concludes that the soul of Arab culture, which has permeated three millennia, has what it takes to build the Arab knowledge society in the third millennium, as effectively as it did at the end of the first millennium and the beginning of the second. Indeed this well-stocked and well-knit culture can be a source of strength in coping with the challenges of globalisation. The next two chapters turn to other key dimensions of building the Arab knowledge society: the Arab socio-economic structure and the political structure on the national, regional and global levels.

CHAPTER 7

Socio-economic structure

The process of knowledge acquisition interacts with, and is influenced by, the social and economic structure of a society. Knowledge is first and foremost a social product, yet in knowledge societies it is also a fundamental economic factor. This chapter considers whether Arab socio-economic structures are geared towards encouraging or inhibiting knowledge acquisition as a means of achieving human development.

It is impossible in practice to separate the social and economic structures of a society from other societal dimensions that affect knowledge acquisition, especially the political context, which is all-encompassing. The analysis in this chapter intersects with the discussion of politics and knowledge in the next chapter and may be seen in the light of that discussion as well.

INTRODUCTION

The economic and social infrastructure of a society, on the one hand, and its knowledge system on the other influence each other through a number of linkages.

The first linkage concerns the pattern of production and the level of technology used by the production sector, including the level of skilled labour, entrepreneurship, equipment and systems. Production patterns, workforce characteristics and technology levels are among the most important determinants of social structures, which, in turn, orient the attitudes and attributes of a social culture. It is no exaggeration to say, as Schumpeter did, that the work in which human beings spend most of their waking lives has a profound impact on their intellectual outlook; and that the place people occupy in the production process heavily influences their worldviews and attitudes towards daily affairs. Work, after all, is what

determines the space within which one can act and influence matters and events (Schumpeter, 1957, Part I).

The second linkage runs in the opposite direction. It concerns how social and economic institutions influence the type and level of knowledge and technology that the production sector develops, which in turn shapes patterns of production, growth rates, living standards and the capacity to sustain growth and progress. The most influential institutions in this respect are those that affect how sources of income are divided and how economic surpluses are allocated. Incomes can be generated by salaries, wages and profits resulting from work in productive activities; or they can come from rent produced by properties and unearned wealth. Depending on the source of income, economic surpluses can be allocated either to "futile investment", exemplified by prestigious properties and other assets which have little or no influence on the building of productive capacities and, thus, on economic growth, or to "productive investment" in the creation of assets and enterprises that increase productivity and economic competitiveness. By definition, the latter are the kinds of assets and enterprises that embody innovative ideas and create new productive assets and knowledge-intensive technologies. Such productive investments are those that most strongly impact economic growth and the building of a knowledge society.

Investment in new productive assets is a prime mover of, and incentive for technological progress, because it is through such investment that the sciences and scientific theory are converted into technological applications. This conversion also tests the extent to which scientific discoveries and inventions are economically useful. The reverse is also true: advances in scientific knowledge open up opportunities

Work is what determines the space within which one can act and influence matters and events.

Investment in new productive assets is a prime mover of, and incentive for technological progress.

for technological innovation, which attracts investment in the production of new goods and services or enhances productivity and efficiency in the production of existing goods and services.

A third factor is that all production systems are characterised by an inner logic, which determines the direction and nature of their development. The system represented by the hand mill, for instance, leads to an economic and social situation where the use of the steam/mechanical mill is a necessity, which neither the individual nor the community can change. The widespread use of the mechanical mill leads, in turn, to the creation of a new economic and social context, which creates new occupations for new groups with new ideas.

How agents of change function in a society is, however, more difficult and complicated than suggested above. Social formations and structures and the intellectual and psychological patterns and orientations that reflect them, which are formed at a certain stage and which reflect a specific production system, do not melt away and disappear as quickly as that stage of production itself. Some of these structures solidify and remain in existence for generations or centuries beyond the stage at which they were formed. It is notable in this regard that the transfer of a production system developed in one society to a different one does not necessarily lead to the rapid change in the social and cultural context associated with that production system in the importing society.

This is why the superstructure of Arab society (including general culture, values and behavioural patterns) is still influenced by the production patterns and relationships that prevailed in the past (Muhammad Jaber al-Ansari, 1998).

ECONOMIC STRUCTURE

MODES OF PRODUCTION

In knowledge societies, economic activities create demand for knowledge and incentives for its dissemination and production. The economy also represents one of the most important sources of investment in knowledge. If

intensive knowledge is *not* an essential determinant of economic output and its distribution among factors of production, societal demand for knowledge will not exist and it will not be possible to build an effective knowledge *system*. In advanced economies, knowledge accounts for a significant part of the value added to production, and the constant generation of new knowledge drives a process of continuous improvement in knowledge-based products and services, which helps to sustain economic growth.

It is possible to distinguish five main features of the dominant mode of production in Arab countries that affect knowledge acquisition.

Dependence on the extraction of raw materials in "rentier" economies

First is the overwhelming dependence on the extraction of raw materials, chiefly oil, in what are often referred to as "rentier" economies: The GCC countries and Libya, Iraq and Algeria are almost completely dependent on oil. Other Arab countries (Egypt, Syria, Sudan and Yemen) depend on crude oil as a primary, though not exclusive, source of gross economic product. In other Arab countries, oil dependence is reflected in aid and workers' remittances from oil-producing countries. In some cases, the *rentier* nature accrues from aid from industrialised countries.

In *rentier* modes of production, economic returns do not necessarily accrue from hard work and high productivity, particularly in political systems that constrain freedoms and do not encourage people to be industrious. Rather, the economy turns on the exploitation of raw materials and the use of foreign expertise in the absence of local knowledge capabilities. This, indeed, has been the historical pattern in many Arab countries.

Rentier economies rely heavily on foreign expertise as this approach provides quick and easy economic returns. By contrast, creating indigenous knowledge requires considerable commitment, effort, time and financial resources. Yet in the long run, such a hands-off approach eventually weakens the demand for localised knowledge, retards the development of local production and postpones the effective utilisation of knowledge in economic activities.

The first consequence of the *rentier* system is that large and easy rents encourage a mindset oriented towards spending and acquisition. Such a mindset is seldom interested in risk-taking or in addressing the difficulties associated with stimulating or managing investment and production in societies whose organisational and economic structures are still fragile and inefficient.

The extraction of raw materials in Arab countries began in the colonial period, and was undertaken by foreign companies with exports to the industrialised West in mind. This pattern of production was associated with reliance on foreign expertise. With a few major exceptions in the oil industry and in water desalination, particularly in Saudi Arabia and Kuwait, almost all Arab countries entrusted most knowledge-intensive aspects of the extraction of oil and other natural wealth – and indeed of other economic activities as well – to foreign corporations, generally on a full contracting, or turn-key basis.

The consequences of this abdication are severe. Foreign experts are costly, their knowledge is seldom transferred and absorbed locally and at times their approaches may conflict with national interests. Worse, over-reliance on foreign expertise in high-skill areas reduces the demand for locally produced knowledge and prevents the growth of skilled Arab knowledge enterprises.

Commodity-based production and franchising

Most production in Arab countries is based on traditional primary commodities in agriculture and other sectors and does not call for advanced skills or technology. Another area of relative concentration is the manufacture of consumer goods under franchising or licensing arrangements with foreign firms. Meanwhile, the share in manufacturing of capital goods with high knowledge content remains small. This industrial pattern limits the local demand for knowledge and perpetuates reliance on knowledge imports under licensing arrangements. It could be said, in fact, that commodity-based production and franchising stimulate knowledge development abroad and stifle it at home. As a result, knowledge sys-

tems in Arab countries remain dysfunctional and Arab economic activities remain knowledge-poor.

Features of this production mode are apparent in the Arab commodity manufacturing structure, dominated by extraction industries (Figure 7.1).

The same production mode is evident in the structure of Arab exports, compared with other regions of the world. (Figure 7.2).

The same Figure shows that the Middle East and North Africa region, as classified by the World Bank, occupies the lowest levels among world regions, even compared to the

Commodity - based production and franchising stimulate knowledge development abroad and stifle it at home.

Figure 7.1

Share of extractive industries in commodity production

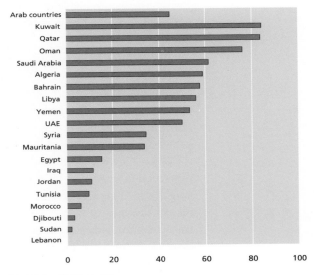

Source: League of Arab States, 2002 (in Arabic).

Figure 7.2

Export structure, selected regions

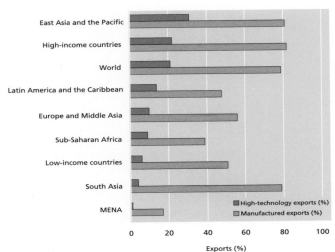

Source: World Bank 2002.

least developed countries, in both the percentage of manufactured exports and the share of high technology exports as an indicator of knowledge intensity in economic output.

Prevalence of low-skill micro-enterprises and informal sector production activities

Many Arab micro- and small enterprises cling to traditional modes of production that are low in knowledge content in the modern sense, and which do not contribute to the generation of new knowledge. In Egypt, for example, the 1996 census showed that practically all such enterprises (98%) employed two or fewer individuals, while the percentage of enterprises employing more than 100 workers was less than 0.1% (Nader Fergany, 1998). In Jordan, the percentage of enterprises employing less than 50 workers was 94% (The World Bank, 2002).

It is important to stress that the absence of knowledge-based production in these enterprises is not related to their size or to the type of economic activity in which they engage. It is rather a consequence of the weakness of the knowledge system itself and of low knowledge utilisation in the surrounding economy. Conventional economic activity, *per se*, is not an obstacle to knowledge acquisition and utilisation. The missing factor is an effective societal system for knowledge acquisition. In fact, there are examples in the region where intensive knowledge production has taken place in conventional economic sectors, such as agriculture, and where such production has not only increased value added but also contributed significantly to the knowledge acquisition system in society at large. Elsewhere in the world, some of the most intensive forms of knowledge utilisation and production are carried out in highly innovative micro- and small enterprises (for instance, Silicon Valley in the United States and its fast-growing equivalent in Bangalore, India).

Scarcity of medium-sized and large companies based in the Arab region

Unlike the case of south-east Asia, where Japanese and global multinational corporations established integrated bases for industrial production in those countries capable of exporting to world markets, the investments of multinational corporations in Arab countries were limited to secondary activities with little effect on the creation of national skills or the adoption of technology. Such foreign investment was characterised by a vertical relationship between Western industrial centres and individual Arab countries, and was encouraged by very weak horizontal relationships between the Arab countries themselves. This so-called hub-and-spoke pattern reflects in part the failure of economic cooperation and integration efforts in the Arab region.

Lack of competition

Healthy competition still eludes Arab economies where entrenched monopolies dominate several sectors. Uncompetitive firms do not seek out knowledge but instead concentrate on maintaining their traditional commercial footholds. In addition, a lack of transparency and accountability has created a certain overlap between political and business elites. This further reduces the competitive pressure to enhance the use of knowledge in economic activities in Arab countries, since profits are mostly derived from access to power rather than through economic efficiency and performance.

Lack of competition marginalises the role of productivity, and consequently the need for knowledge in economic activity. In the recent past, in many Arab countries, the public sector loomed large in the economy with macro policies relating to employment, pricing and management that reduced the efficiency of both public and private economic activity. When some Arab countries moved towards free market economies, the legal frameworks and institutions necessary to prevent monopolies and protect competition were seldom in place, with the result that private monopolies sometimes replaced public ones.

At the same time, limited inter-Arab cooperation has led to the narrowing of markets and to inward-looking economies vulnerable to monopolies. Vigorous inter-country economic cooperation, which could create incentives for innovation and excellence and a demand for knowledge to support production capacity, has not taken off in the region.

The lack of foreign competition in general, coupled with import substitution policies, has

Many Arab micro- and small enterprises cling to traditional modes of production that are low in knowledge content.

Healthy competition still eludes Arab economies where entrenched monopolies dominate several sectors.

also narrowed markets. Yet it is worth noting that in a few cases openness, through international trade – in the heartlands of *rentier* economies such as Dubai, Bahrain and Kuwait – has helped to stimulate the growth of economic capacities capable of competing beyond national borders.

GROWTH, PRODUCTIVITY AND DISTRIBUTION

Economic growth

When societal conditions favour knowledge acquisition, a virtuous cycle develops between levels of economic output and rates of growth and productivity on the one side, and knowledge acquisition on the other. High output and fast growth rates allow resources to be invested in knowledge acquisition. At the same time, intensive investment in knowledge acquisition leads to the production of new knowledge, which then accelerates economic growth. Conversely, weak output and slow growth lead to under-investment in the knowledge system and in its application in society. Ultimately, whether a society allocates resources to knowledge acquisition in the amounts needed to bridge the knowledge gap (Chapter 1, Figure 1.1) depends crucially on its decision-makers. Currently, in Arab countries, both economic growth and production are stumbling, as demonstrated by World Bank figures on the Middle East and North Africa region.

Despite the popular perception that Arab countries are rich[1], the volume of economic product in the region is rather small. Overall GDP at the end of the 20th century (US $604 billion) was little more than that of a single European country such as Spain (US $559 billion) and much less than that of another European country, Italy (US $1,074 billion) (UNDP 2002).

Compared to the relatively high rates of economic growth during the oil boom of the 1970s, growth in combined Arab gross domestic product in the last quarter of the 20th century was extremely modest. (See Figure 7.3.)

The figure indicates that the growth rate in gross domestic product in the Middle East and North Africa region was modest during the last two decades of the past century, falling to less than half its levels in the 1970s (during the first oil boom). Indeed, in the 1980s it was negative. Moreover, the gross product growth rate in the region in the 1970s was well below that achieved in the East Asia and Pacific region; and less than that of low- and middle-income countries worldwide.

Figure 7.3

Annual growth rate of gross domestic product (GDP) per capita (%)
Middle East and North Africa and other selected regions, 1970-2000

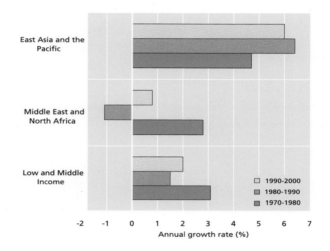

Source: World Bank, 1993, 2000 and 2002.

Productivity in Arab countries

Declining productivity is one of the major challenges facing Arab countries. According to World Bank data (World Bank, 1998)[2], rates of productivity (the average production of one worker) in Arab countries were negative to a large and increasing extent in oil-producing countries during the 1980s and '90s (see Figure 7.4). The gross national product per worker[3] in all Arab countries is less than half that in two advanced developing countries: South Korea in Asia and Argentina in Latin America. (See Figure 7.5).

Dividing Arab countries into three groups

Despite the popular perception that Arab countries are rich, the volume of economic product in the region is rather small.

Declining productivity is one of the major challenges facing Arab countries.

---

[1]This illusion has been accentuated by the concentration of Arab wealth in a limited number of lightly populated Arab oil-producing countries, and the adoption of those countries as representative of all Arab states.

[2]From tables 1, 3 and 1a in the source, with the work force in Bahrain, Djibouti, Iraq, Kuwait, Libya, Qatar, Somalia and the Sudan estimated as a percentage of the population (from the Arab Joint Economic Report, 1998), and on the assumption that the production per worker in Libya, Iraq, Djibouti and Somalia was $5000, $3000, $100, and $700 respectively.

[3]As a preliminary indicator of productivity dictated by the more up-to-date data from one major source, and where the estimate of the labour force in developing countries is reduced to exclude women and children, particularly in informal economic activity, the estimate of productivity in this manner is expected to be higher than actual productivity.

Figure 7.4

Annual growth rate of GDP per worker (%)
Middle East and North Africa Region, 1965-1993

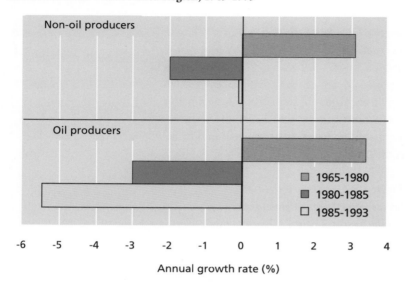

Source: (based on World Bank, 1995).

Figure 7.5

Gross national product (per worker) in Arab countries
compared to South Korea and Argentina, 1997

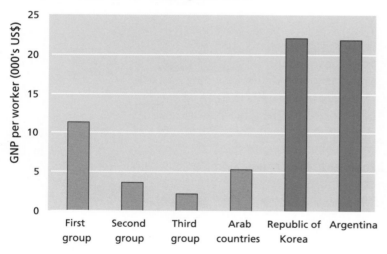

Source: Calculated from World Bank data, 1998.

Excluding oil rents from the picture would reduce apparent levels of productivity in Arab economies.

countries (Tunisia, Syria and Egypt) is about one-sixth that of the comparator countries, while in the oil-poor countries (Jordan, Sudan, Somalia, Morocco, Yemen, Djibouti, Lebanon and Mauritania) it is less than one-tenth.

This means that excluding oil rents from the picture would reduce apparent levels of productivity in Arab economies much more than a simple overall comparison indicates.

More important than the *level* of productivity is the *change* in productivity over time. Based on the data in the World Development Report for 1998/99, it is possible to compare the GDP indicator[4] per worker in ten Arab countries with that of some faster growing countries[5] over a relatively long period of time (1980-1997).

This comparison shows that productivity increased annually by 15% in China, 8% in Korea and 6% in India. By contrast, the growth rate of productivity in the best performing Arab country did not exceed 4% (respectively, according to value: it was 3-4% in Oman and Egypt, 2-3% in Tunisia, Mauritania and Morocco, 1-2% in Jordan and Algeria and less than 1% in the United Arab Emirates and Saudi Arabia).

Revitalising economic growth in the Arab region is a necessary condition for initiating a knowledge renaissance. Yet growth alone is not sufficient. A national consensus is required among public, private and civil society decision makers on the overriding importance of building the knowledge society. This consensus would amount to a new social contract reflected in all Arab spending and investment decisions.

Income disribution

In any society, the distribution of income and wealth – and hence power – has an impact on economic growth and on the allocation of resources for knowledge acquisition. Though global experience shows that some economies were able to achieve economic growth under conditions where wealth was accumulated by a few, this occurred in an economic environment that was relatively closed. Globalisation and its open economies make growth in situations of economic polarisation more difficult.

according to the contribution of oil to their GNP, with each group representing about one-third of the Arab labour force, yields clearer indicators of the low productivity of these countries.

Productivity in the nine richest Arab countries in terms of oil resources – the first group – barely exceeds half the productivity of a worker in two comparator countries. The productivity indicator in the medium oil-rich

---

[4] which reflects productivity better than GNP.

[5] The indicator used here is the total of productivity rates in the two periods, calculated from the data provided in tables 3 and 11 in the source, which give the growth rates of the labour force and the GDP in both periods (1980-1990 and 1990-1997).

The volume of Arab capital invested in industrialised countries and not at home demonstrates this. Wide economic divides result in instability, low productivity, extensive unemployment and further deterioration in the distribution of income, wealth and power. Grossly unequal distributions of income, wealth and power adversely impact opportunities for knowledge acquisition by undercutting sustainable economic growth.

In turn, the skewed distribution of income, wealth and power undermines human development by fettering human capabilities and thwarting popular participation, itself one of the main elements of human welfare. These circumstances deny the poor opportunities to enlarge their capabilities or to influence decisions affecting their lives and thus lift themselves out of poverty. Under these conditions, a society cannot accumulate high-quality human capital, one of the most important requirements for a dynamic knowledge system.

Unfortunately, the data base on the extent and features of poverty and income distribution in Arab countries is extremely weak. There is almost no data at all on the distribution of wealth, and information on income distribution and the extent and characteristics of poverty is minimal, which diminishes the clarity of the picture of poverty and income distribution in the region.

Some researchers estimate that poverty is even more widespread and income distribution is more unequal than indicated by international datasets, due to technical difficulties in poverty assessments as well as data scarcity. In light of different indicators, there is concern that both determinants of welfare are growing worse: it is estimated that poverty is increasing and income distribution is becoming more unequal. Estimates of poverty in Egypt in the 1990s, for instance, vary between 30% and 40%, which means that Egypt alone contributes nearly 10% to the overall poverty rate in the region. And this does not take into account Iraq or Morocco, let alone Sudan, Somalia and Djibouti. Based on country surveys in the 1990s, estimates of poverty vary from 21% in Jordan to 30% in Yemen, 45% in

Djibouti and 85% in the Sudan (UNDP, 1997). Figure 7.6 provides indicators of the extent of poverty in the 1990s, based on a number of criteria. It indicates that poverty in Arab countries is more widespread than is usually reported in international data bases, particularly those compiled by the World Bank and the International Monetary Fund.

Even when field surveys of income and expenditure (which constitute the basic source for estimates of income distribution) exist, such surveys suffer from defects that diminish their credibility, particularly with regard to the parameters of income distribution, as a result of bias in the collected data.[6] In Egypt, for instance, relying on the results of income and expenditure surveys in the first part of the 1990s leads to an improvement of the Gini coefficient[7] – i.e., income distribution becomes more equal. But this does not correspond to the overall economic situation, particularly unemployment and poverty criteria and the observations made of wealth distribution during the same period. The Gini coefficient was estimated in 1997 at about 37% (Datte et al., 1998), compared to 28% in 1995 (World Bank, 2000). This is a huge increase in a short period of time, which indicates an accelerated worsening of income distribution. Labour's share of the value added declined from nearly 40% in 1975 to nearly 25% in 1994 (see Figure

Grossly unequal distributions of income, wealth and power adversely impact opportunities for knowledge acquisition by undercutting sustainable economic growth.

Poverty in Arab countries is more widespread than is usually reported in international data bases.

Figure 7.6

Estimates of poverty in Arab countries in the 1990s

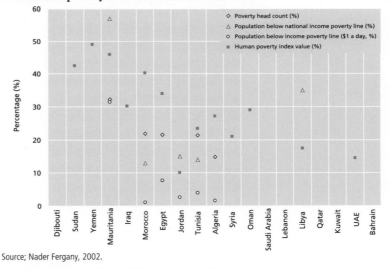

Source; Nader Fergany, 2002.

---

[6] Like the problem of "cutting the right tail" of income or expenditure distribution, which occurs in societies where surveys do not record the extremely high values of expenditure or income. It prevails in societies or historical eras in which high incomes are derived primarily from activities that are socially unacceptable or legally prohibited. "Cutting the right tail" produces values for the characteristics of income distribution that are more equal than the real values.

[7] A numerical measure related to a graphic device that depicts the degree of income or wealth inequality. (Journal of Economic Education)

7.7), which indicates a deterioration of GNP distribution in favour of wealth returns.

The question of distribution has, however, a composite effect on knowledge acquisition. In some societies, the accumulation of wealth in select circles that are willing to make philanthropic contributions to support knowledge activities and endow knowledge-producing institutions has had a salutary effect on knowledge acquisition in the society as a whole. In other societies, however, (perhaps closer to the Arab situation) the very wealthy – with a few exceptions – seek only to accumulate wealth quickly through easy profits, particularly from speculation and property holdings, and to indulge in ostentatious consumption. In such societies, the skewed distribution of income and wealth reduces the society's opportunities for advancement in knowledge acquisition.

It is only fair, however, to recognise that before the rise of autocratic regimes, Arab societies were noted for their substantial philanthropic activities, through non-governmental organisations and Islamic endowment funds, particularly in health and education, including higher education. Autocratic regimes, however, with their restrictions on non-governmental organisations and their control of Muslim endowment funds, have long disrupted such effective non-governmental work.

The middle class in Arab countries is on the wane, contracting under pressure from rising poverty.

The oil welfare state, on the other hand, spent generously on people and on public services, yet did not promote strong non-governmental movements in support of knowledge acquisition.

Creating a knowledge society requires wealthy Arabs, states, institutions and individuals, to provide substantial and sustained support for the diffusion and production of knowledge. This entails creating a societal environment and developing tax and financial policies that facilitate the establishment and activation of civil society organisations that support knowledge acquisition and respond to the call of national duty.

CLASS STRUCTURE

Class structure strongly influences the knowledge system. Wealth can play a positive role in supporting knowledge development and dissemination if a portion is invested in the knowledge system. Another favourable societal condition is the existence of a large educated middle class, able to appreciate and cultivate various forms of knowledge and blessed with the financial security that allows it to participate in sharing knowledge and in producing it (Galal Amin, 2002).

Yet the middle class in Arab countries is on the wane, contracting under pressure from rising poverty and the uneven distribution of income and wealth. This contraction has been aggravated by a gradual decay in knowledge pursuits, particularly in Arabic. The enervating influence of mass media entertainment and mass artistic production, the homogenising impact of global culture, the declining quality of education and the general erosion of societal incentives for knowledge acquisition are all contributing factors.

SOCIETAL INCENTIVES

In their studies of current Arab knowledge systems and intellectual movements, a large and varied group of Arab thinkers across the region has consistently attached great importance to both reason and knowledge. Many of them have sought to justify the adoption of these two values, arguing that classical Arab civilisation exalted reason, experiment, hu-

Figure 7.7
Development of workers' share of GDP (%), Egypt 1974-1993

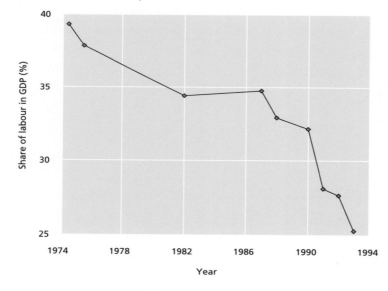

Source: Nader Fergany, 1977 and 1998.

mankind's development on earth and the wise husbanding of nature in its conceptual value system.

Yet other researchers studying modern Arab culture have inferred that it is beset with irrational tendencies and that it underestimates the value of work, manual crafts and applied sciences. A number of these thinkers have gone on to assert that most of the social, political and economic problems in the contemporary Arab world spring from the misuse of reason and a consequent incapacity to handle the process of creative knowledge production.

Attempting to look objectively at the Arab value system, it becomes apparent that political, social, and economic conditions have played a decisive role in shaping values and societal incentives. After independence, most Arab countries came under political regimes that represented little advance on the autocratic style of the past. Social and individual freedoms were restricted in some areas, and were totally absent in others. One need only note the characteristics of autocracy as sharply delineated by Al-Kawakibi and his successors, and how such autocracies corrupt people's morals and values and inhibit creativity and development (Box 7.2).

Traditional Arab social structures, whether represented in patriarchal societies or in tribes and clans, were not less harmful to modern human values. The values of citizenship, law and normal human rights – in addition to religious rights – all gave way to the mentality of the tribe.

In Arab countries, the distribution of power, which sometimes coincides with the distribution of wealth, has had an effect on the morals of societies and individuals. The pursuit of personal gain, the preference for the private over the public good, social and moral corruption, the absence of honesty and accountability and many other illnesses, are all related in one way or another to a skewed distribution of power and the resulting social disparities. Justice, before all else, has been the victim of this state of affairs.

Compared to the 1960s, Arab communities today are witnessing a deterioration in societal incentives, which has a bearing on creative work and the development of knowl-

---

BOX 7.1

Patriarchal Society in Arab Countries

In a valuable analysis of Arab society, Hisham Sharabi diagnosed the characteristics of those relationships that hinder and distort progress in Arab countries. He concludes that Arab society is caught up in a vicious circle, where the "patriarchal collective self" reproduces itself in order to perpetuate the patriarchal pattern of authority and social relations.

Arab society is not a traditional society in the true sense of the word, neither is it a modern society. It is, rather, a confusing mixture of both. One of its aspects is manifest in a set of traditional social relations, values and structures emanating from a patriarchal society allied with ancient tribal, family, religious and sectarian relations. The other aspect reflects a set of modern social relations and structures. The confusion is increased in Arab society because it suffers to a large extent from reliance on foreign political, economic and cultural influences. Sharabi tries to explain Arab patriarchy through its approaches to modernism. He suggests the following comparison between patriarchy and modernism on the basis of six major components:

COMPONENT	Modernism	Patriarchy
KNOWLEDGE	IDEA – MIND	SUPERSTITION – BELIEF
FACT	SCIENTIFIC – REVOLUTIONARY	RELIGIOUS – NARRATIVE
LANGUAGE	ANALYSIS	RHETORIC
GOVERNMENT	DEMOCRATIC – SOCIALIST	NEW PATRIARCHAL AUTHORITY
SOCIAL RELATIONS	HORIZONTAL	VERTICAL
SOCIAL STRUCTURE	CLASS	FAMILY – TRIBE – COMMUNITY

The essence of the new patriarchy in Arab society is the patriarchal family, the importance of which can be grasped by understanding new patriarchal structures and their basic internal relations, particularly those relating to authority, hegemony and dependence, which reflect and are reflected in the structure of social relations.

The father, the ideal new patriarchal personality, constitutes the central instrument of oppression. His power and influence are based on punishment. Oppression in the mind of the family is also associated with widespread irrational attitudes among the general public. This association facilitates the perpetuation of the status quo and leads people to subconsciously oppose change. The scientific mind, which explains phenomena with reference to causes that are subject to testing and proof, has not taken root in the collective personality. Metaphysics and magic continue to dominate the psychological environment of the individual. Therefore, rationality is not the principle that governs individual behaviour or social work in general. Two sectors in the society coexist side by side, one of them is sorcerous and the other is scientific. Traditional structures coexist with modern structures, and a dependent, primitive economy exists next to a modern, rational economy.

Arab societies are managed by many despots of varying degrees of patriarchy: the head of the household, the elders in the family, tribal chieftains, school principals, council chairmen, heads of state and other father figures. In such societies there can be only small scope to develop initiative and innovation in individuals who are under the control of these petty despots. Hopes that Arab educational systems would overturn the influence of patriarchal upbringing on individuals have been frustrated. On the contrary, the traditional patriarchal culture has penetrated the educational system in most schools, reinforcing students' submission to various forms of authority and stifling individual and creative initiatives. Even in schools unburdened by the weight of traditional society, such as foreign private schools, the encouragement of individual initiative and creativity are the exception rather than the rule.

Source: Hisham Sharabi, Neopatriarchy, The Distorted Change in Arab Society, Oxford University Press, 1988. Chapter 2, pp. 17-18.

---

edge. Art, thought and knowledge are evaluated by whether they are "sinful or permissible by religion". The criteria for judgment are fidelity or heresy rather than beauty and ugliness, or right and wrong. Moreover, among the impoverished mass of people, the values of

BOX 7.2

Al Kawakibi (1854-1902): The Inversion of Values Under Despotism

"We became accustomed to regarding abject submission as polite deference; obsequiousness as courtesy; sycophancy as oratory; bombast as substance; the surrender of basic rights as nobility; the acceptance of humiliation as modesty; the acceptance of injustice as obedience; and the pursuit of human entitlements as arrogance. Our inverted system portrayed the pursuit of simple knowledge as presumption; aspirations for the future as impossible dreams; courage as overreaching audacity; inspiration as folly; chivalry as aggression; free expression as impertinence; free thinking as heresy; and patriotism as madness. "

"In your helplessness you accept a miserable life, and you call it contentment; you abdicate responsibility for your daily existence, saying 'God will provide' and you believe yours is not to reason why because what befalls you is God's will. But, in God's name, this passivity is not the proper status of humankind. "

Source: The Character of Despotism, p.126, p.118.

Arab citizens are increasingly pushed away from effecting changes or taking decisions in the interest of their countries.

Status inherited remains a more powerful value than status acquired.

asceticism and other-worldliness prevail. Deprivation has caused them to transpose the lives they desire, but cannot lead, to the afterlife. Yet their non-material values have not prevented the appearance of an ostentatiously luxurious lifestyle among the affluent, drawing on the authority of scripture where it says: "Remember your share in life".

The oil boom also played its role in eroding a number of values and societal incentives that would have been helpful in enhancing creativity and the acquisition and dissemination of knowledge. With the spread of negative values during that period, creative abilities were neglected, and knowledge lost its significance for human development. The social standing of scientists, educated people and intellectuals fell. Education became incapable of providing the poor with the tools and abilities they need for social mobility. Social value was measured by money and fortune, regardless of how those fortunes were gained. Proprietorship and possession replaced knowledge and intellectualism. Perhaps worst of all, the values of independence, freedom and the importance of a critical mind – values by which people can actively exercise choice and lead conscious lives – were also buried. The aftershock of this collapse continues to weaken and undermine Arab societal incentives today. As a result, indifference, political apathy and a sense of futility are becoming dangerously common among broad segments of the populace. Arab citizens are increasingly pushed away from effecting changes or taking decisions in the interest of their countries.

The modern productive person is no longer the model citizen. Instead, Arab societies now offer choices that people should refuse to make. The question as to who is better: the productive or the religious citizen is one such false antithesis. The question should instead be: can the Arab citizen be both productive and religious? And what will it take to combine those two traits? Such soul-searching is, however, far from the norm. Work has ceased to be a precious value, and many still talk about 'rizq', or a livelihood, as a blessing from God. Popular proverbs and sayings denote a return to the view that production, incentives and rewards are subject to fate and destiny. Thus, current values are shrinking the boundaries of the human will. Status inherited remains a more powerful value than status acquired.

Fine speeches about ancestral glory are much in evidence. This narrow homage to the past is held in higher esteem than attempts to rebuild institutions or reinvent the social contract. Meanwhile, personal relations and favouritism outweigh merit and efficiency in both the public and private spheres. This suffocating social climate stifles creativity, innovation and the acquisition of knowledge. It weakens the sense of community and incites a destructive form of individualism driven by envy and hostility, rather than by the healthy entrepreneurial spirit found in industrialised countries. It dismantles corporate teamwork and production, and undercuts collegial exchanges of experiences. The rise and prevalence of ideologies in the Arab world in the second half of the 20th century also led to the dominance of dogmatic tendencies and radicalism and to increased repression by authorities. This has given rise to introverted ideologies and ideas of cultural specificity, difference and the rejection of the "other" on both the local and global levels.

Severe restrictions on independent thinkers who could have contributed substantially to Arab creative knowledge cut societies off from legitimate intellectual dissent. At the same time, a form of historical analysis and writing serving the vested interests of some political and social systems is resurfacing. In the meantime, freedom of thought has been restricted and outstanding and free thinkers have been oppressed. This is taking place amid the contraction of domestic economies and the psycho-political constriction of national development induced by regional crises, the most prominent of which centre on governance, Arab unity and the Palestinian problem. Together, these trends portend a culture of near-despair and rejection.

These value-related issues in Arab society form a vicious circle that stands in the way of cognitive development, open-mindedness and a positive approach to life and knowledge. They militate against human development and an Arab cultural and economic renaissance.

A society that does not value knowledge and innovation highly does not give the knowledge system the required elements or the environment it needs to flourish. Hope is now attached to the emergence of a strong and vibrant middle class, with well-educated members who have distinguished expertise and possess a vision that looks forward to a better and more humane life. The state, civil society, cultural and mass media institutions, enlightened intellectuals and the public at large are all called upon to plant those values that encourage action and innovation in the political, social and economic spheres. Each one of these spheres needs to be the base and instrument of production and innovation in culture and knowledge. Each needs to build a system of values that encourages respect for hard work and productivity and stimulates the capacity to innovate using what is created by the local society or by humanity as a whole.

Promoting an Arab renaissance through democratic values

The acquisition of knowledge is a different matter from the acquisition of material wealth. Quantitative economic advancement is associated with the accumulation of wealth that already exists through the process of capital formation. Such wealth may be concentrated in a few hands, whether in the state or the private sector, depending on the prevailing economic model. Qualitative advancement, however, is associated with the development of a society's knowledge base, with the continuous replenishment of that base through new knowledge and with the free flow of knowledge to all members of society, such that every citizen, regardless of social position, economic level or age group, has an opportunity to contribute to knowledge development and to benefit from its outcome.

Such free flows of knowledge within society require a democratic value system and the elimination of corruption, which diverts knowledge, ideas and information in order to serve the personal interests of a few and hinders their movement for the good of society. Free flows of knowledge also call for the free movement of people who are the vessels of that knowledge. This, in practice, requires respecting the human rights of Arab workers moving from one country of the region to another to enable them to interact positively with all groups in their host societies.

Arab citizens must be accorded the full dignity due to them as human beings. Their initiative, innovation and public participation must be encouraged and rewarded. Their right to different opinions and beliefs has to be recognised. Freedom from discrimination of all kinds must be upheld for all citizens, especially women and children, the groups that suffer the most iniquitous restrictions today. Modern Arab society has not given sufficient attention to women's empowerment. The interpretation of laws and the production of knowledge have not advanced sufficiently to guarantee Arab women their economic, social and cultural rights, consistent with international conventions and without encroachment on Islamic law.

Effective measures must also be taken to eliminate traditions, laws and customs, which entrench narrow traditional loyalties to the tribe and the clan in Arab societies and to replace them with the concept and practice of citizenship, without which there can be no innovation.

In economic life – which is closely associated with political and social philosophy – the value of *justice* must be introduced, because the values of freedom, democracy and equality will not bear fruit without justice. It is justice that makes the values of integrity, accountability and peoples' welfare – which are the basis of a sound ethical community life – possible, viable and effective.

In short, the reform of the Arab knowledge model has to move in lockstep with the reform of Arab social values. The restoration

Free flows of knowledge within society require a democratic value system and the elimination of corruption.

Modern Arab society has not given sufficient attention to women's empowerment.

The restoration of rationality... cannot proceed without the renovation of political, social and economic values.

Between 1998 and 2000 more than 15,000 Arab doctors migrated.

of rationality, scientific methods and open-mindedness cannot proceed without the renovation of political, social and economic values and their wide diffusion as creative principles. The new core values that will drive the Arab renaissance are freedom, justice, respect for human dignity and basic human rights, integrity, the pursuit of public welfare, accountability, pluralism and the ethics of dialogue and political alternation.

MIGRATION

Arab countries have witnessed two great outflows of international emigration that have significantly affected local knowledge acquisition. The first was directed to oil-rich Arab countries and took the form of temporary labour migration. Nevertheless, restrictive policies and circumstances in both the countries of destination and origin, and recurrent political upheavals and armed conflicts, often impeded real human exchanges among Arab countries except in some cases where Iraq is concerned. The level of education and skills among these temporary migrants varied from one country of origin or destination to another. Many "oil" migrants, however, ended up working in the education sector and service industries.

The second outflow went to Western countries and was characterised by a higher frequency of settlement in the countries of destination. Within that second flow two currents can be distinguished: the first originated in North Africa and set out for European countries, especially the former colonial powers. It encompassed all levels of education and skill, but was dominated by unskilled labour. The second current is more significant from the knowledge perspective, as it entailed the emigration of highly qualified Arabs to dozens of Western countries. Settlement in the countries of destination dominated that current.

Emigration to other societies endows migrants with new knowledge and experience. Under favourable conditions, those with whom they mix also acquire knowledge. Arab migration to Arab countries, especially when centred on education, has certainly made valuable contributions to knowledge, most of all in the countries of destination. Migration be-

tween Arab countries, despite serious difficulties at times, has also contributed to strengthening Arab ties.

However, in general, institutional arrangements for intra-regional migration and the general policies of both countries of origin and destination did not foster the best possible returns to migrants or to their home and host societies. Most Arab conventions designed to regulate emigration, protect migrants' rights and ensure optimal developmental outcomes remain little more than ink on paper, even though such conventions do not rise to the level of protection embodied in international treaties.

THE BRAIN DRAIN

Arguably, emigration of highly qualified Arabs to the West has been one of the most serious factors undermining knowledge acquisition in Arab countries. It is no exaggeration to characterise this outflow as a haemorrhage. The trend is large-scale and is steadily accelerating. Data to adequately document the extent of the phenomenon is not readily available, but some indications that point to the extent and gravity of the brain drain are given below (Zahlan, background paper for the Report).

It is estimated that by the year 1976, 23% of Arab engineers, 50% of Arab doctors, and 15% of Arab BSc holders had emigrated. Roughly 25% of 300,000 first degree graduates from Arab universities in 1995/96 emigrated. Between 1998 and 2000 more than 15,000 Arab doctors migrated.

Apart from the sheer scale of emigration and its growth over time, looking into the motives of emigrants reveals obstacles to building Arab knowledge societies that are perhaps more serious than the brain drain itself. Surveys of highly qualified Arabs living abroad indicate that their principal reasons for leaving relate to the absence of a positive societal environment and facilities that would allow them to play their role in the knowledge system and in the development of their countries. Ideally this role should be performed under conditions that permit individual fulfilment and a decent standard of living. The denial of livable conditions to a host of highly qualified Arabs drastically undermines any attempt to create knowledge societies in Arab countries. Their emigration perpetuates weaknesses in both the production of knowledge and the demand for it, since the activities and pursuits of such highly qualified personnel would have significantly increased both supply and demand had they remained in their countries.

Ironically, the Arab brain drain constitutes a form of reverse development aid since receiving countries evidently benefit from Arab investments in training and educating their citizens. More significant, however, is the opportunity cost of high levels of skilled outflows: the lost potential contribution of emigrants to knowledge and development in their countries of origin.

The extent of that loss calls for serious action: firstly to tap the expertise and knowledge of the Arab *Diaspora* abroad and secondly to provide Arab expatriates with incentives to return to their countries of origin either on temporary assignments or for good. If they do come back, they will do so with a larger stock of knowledge capital than that with which they left. Yet this will not happen unless enabling conditions at home are in place – conditions that are conducive to fulfilment in their personal, professional and public lives and that allow them to contribute to national development. Creating such conditions is not an easy task. It requires a serious project in human development in Arab countries, serious enough to attract emigrants back to participate in the task of creating a knowledge society and to share in the honour of seeing it materialise.

Ironically, the Arab brain drain constitutes a form of reverse development aid.

Contrary to the assessment regarding the state of Arab culture, the analysis in this chapter shows that Arab social and economic structures are obstacles to knowledge acquisition. This requires a longer-term approach than that prescribed in the case of Arab culture, a challenge that has to be taken on if a knowledge society is to emerge in the region.

CHAPTER 8

 The political context

Politics is the final, and perhaps the most influential, frame of reference in analysing how knowledge is acquired in Arab countries. As emphasised earlier, the vitality of a knowledge system depends on the political environment in which it grows. Among the most important conditions are intellectual freedom and diversity protected by the rule of law, other institutional foundations of good governance and a political context that supports the efficient dissemination and production of knowledge. Where do Arab countries stand in relation to this model?

The global explosion of knowledge has not only accelerated global economic integration. It has given rise to regional blocs around the world that challenge the new international order for the purpose of extracting maximum gains for individual groupings of countries seeking to join the global economy on advantageous terms. New ties within the European Union (EU), the North American Free Trade Agreement (NAFTA) and the Association of Southeast Asian Nations (ASEAN) are just three examples of a changing world map. How is knowledge acquisition in Arab countries affected by regional and global politics? What regional and global policies would help Arab countries create knowledge societies in the Arab world under these conditions?

GOVERNANCE AND LAW

THE POLITICAL CONTEXT FOR KNOWLEDGE ACQUISITION

Knowledge is the totality of symbolic structures held by individuals or owned by society and it guides human behaviour at all levels of society and in all fields. Politics, on the other hand, is the science of managing the public affairs of a society through material and non-material means, including knowledge as just defined.

The ruling power plays a key role in directing knowledge and in influencing its development or retardation. Since a ruling power works to foster knowledge patterns compatible with its orientation and goals, it inevitably resists or even suppresses other patterns that contradict its general direction. Knowledge conflicts in the Arab world are often versions of political conflicts in societies where both the sanctioned knowledge paradigm and that contesting it are motivated and sustained by the deep and opposing ideological objectives of ruling powers and their opponents.

Glancing through the many strategic reports of political parties, associations or blocs across the region provides abundant evidence of this polarised split. Some documents adopt the official knowledge paradigm and are seen as supporting the prevailing political power, whether or not their authors are actively associated with it; other publications take a challenging stance in flat opposition to that power and its version of knowledge and values.

Political systems and the cultural elite

Cultural elites across the Arab region are either allied with, or stand in opposition to the political authorities in power, adopting a worldview of knowledge that may coincide with one political trend or another. In most cases, however, their knowledge pursuits take an academic path. These groups opt to produce and develop knowledge irrespective of its use in one political field or another. They have set themselves up as stewards of knowledge, attempting to secure its growth through the positions many occupy in universities and scientific research centres. Their academic isolation poignantly reflects the knowledge crisis created by the crisis of political power in the Arab world.

The ruling power plays a key role in directing knowledge and in influencing its development or retardation.

Knowledge conflicts in the Arab world are often versions of political conflicts.

Political authorities have failed to accommodate them. Instead, authorities have focused on assimilating those intellectuals, academics and scientists who are prepared to shore up a knowledge system consistent with their dominant goal of controlling society's socio-economic, political and cultural capabilities.

The isolation of Arab cultural elites has, of course, allowed political systems to marginalise them while polarising society and rewarding sycophants. Thanks to the latter, cultural disputes and debates are often overshadowed by attempts to legitimise the prevailing political system. The result is that Arab regimes tend to underestimate the positive power of knowledge, having grown accustomed to having their fears about its transformative effects calmed. Their view of knowledge is strictly expedient: knowledge is simply another means to consolidate their power and plans.

Neutral academics have either spoken out against their alienation at home, or have been compelled to emigrate abroad to pursue knowledge without political pressure or containment. Although the Arab brain drain appears to be financially motivated, it reflects a deep crisis in the role of knowledge in present-day Arab countries. The stark choices facing independent intellectuals and scholars are quite painful: to commit "treason of the clerks"[1] by declaring allegiance to political regimes, or to seek exile outside their countries of birth.

Yet a few Arab intellectuals do reach and influence the holders of political power. Observers of the Arab intellectual scene note that the Arab scholar-activist influences power, not so much by the weight of scholarship or independent thinking, but to the extent that he or she infiltrates power circles. It has been pointed out that the dilemma of the Arab public intellectuals is that in order to be influential they must somehow connect with the patronage networks of rulers and high officials. In the absence of a public sphere bounded and protected by the rule of law, the Arab intellectual walks a fine line between principle and expediency. More often than not, when authoritative advice on policy choices is required, for a variety of historical, economic and political reasons, Arab rulers and think tanks often continue to prefer knowledgeable outsiders to local intellectuals (Hudson, 2002)[2]

On the other hand, a group of neutral Arab academics resorts to "intellectual migration" at home or is actually forced to emigrate in search of new and broader horizons to develop their knowledge, without political pressures or containment. While the Arab brain drain is commonly understood to be motivated by financial considerations, it in practice reflects a deeper crisis among knowledge workers in the Arab region. These workers are, in effect, resisters of an unacceptable accommodation with ruling authorities.

In between these two groups stands a committed corps of intellectuals that seeks to apply knowledge to serve their communities, guided by their strategic thinking and their affiliation with different civil society organisations. This group has recently started to expand amongst the Arab intellectual elite, along with the increasing vitality of Arab communities and civil society organisations.

BOX 8.1

Jamal ad-Din al-Afghani (1838-1897)
The Nation and the Authority of a Tyrant

It is not Allah that hath wronged them, but they wrong themselves.
(Qur'an: Ch. 3, Al Imran, verse 117)

A nation that has no say in its own affairs is never consulted on its interests and its will has no effect on its public welfare. Rather, is subjected to one ruler whose will is the law and whose desire is the order, who rules as he pleases and does what he wants. Such a nation is one that has no stability and cannot go along a straight path. It vacillates between happiness and misery and between knowledge and ignorance. It alternates between wealth and poverty and between glory and humiliation.

If its ruler is ignorant, uncouth, of vile intentions, greedy, lustful, cowardly, uncertain, stupid, villainous and unprincipled, he will plunge the nation into the abyss, place a veil of ignorance in front of its eyes and reduce it to poverty and destitution. He will rule people despotically, deviating from the road of justice and opening the way to aggression, causing the powerful to usurp the rights of the weak. The system will then be destroyed. Values and manners will also be corrupted, the nation's esteem will be lowered and desperation will prevail. As a result, acquisitive eyes will be focused on the nation and invading nations will strike at its belly with their claws.

Source: Complete Works, Part II, Political Writings,
Study and Examination by Dr. Muhammad Amarah, Arab Foundation for Studies and Publications, Beirut 1981, p.329.

---

[1] In 1927, the French essayist Julien Benda published his famous attack on the intellectual corruption of the age, La Trahison des Clercs. The treason in question was the betrayal by thinkers and intellectuals of their vocation to pursue the truth.

[2] "On the Influence of the Intellectual in Arab Politics and Policymaking", Michael C. Hudson, paper presented to the conference on the Role of the Intellectual in Contemporary Political Life, Georgetown University, April 26-27, 2002.

PATTERNS OF KNOWLEDGE PRODUCTION AND DISSEMINATION IN THE ARAB WORLD

The production of academic knowledge in the Arab world takes place along the following pattern:

• Official institutions sponsored by political authorities produce "party" or institutional knowledge and employ cultural workers and frameworks that legitimise their power.

• Knowledge networks are connected to the Arab world's political parties or blocs, such as the *Al-Ahram* Political Studies Centre or the Centre for Arab Unity Studies.

• Research centres connected to civil society, such as the Cairo Human Rights Centre, are rooted in specific issue campaigns. Various types of associations and federations fall into this cluster, such as the associations for channelling youth requests for employment in Morocco, or environmental preservation associations.

• "Professional" research centres are set up either by researchers with former links to political regimes who seek to establish a strategic vision of international or Arab issues, or by academics under the banner of "providing customer services". These centres have become popular venues for the production of knowledge and depend largely on external financing.

• Foreign research centres include the French Institute for the Near East, formerly the Centre for Studies and Research in Jordan, Lebanon and Syria and the Centre for Studies and Research on the Contemporary Middle East (CERMOC) in Egypt. These establishments produce publications similar to those of national institutions and often serve as sanctuaries for national knowledge producers seeking academic outlets free from censorship.

Open discussion in the Arab press on the distinction between the academic researcher and the political activist, and on the nature and objectives of externally financed scientific research at many of these centres, has helped to create more social space for knowledge producers.

BOX 8.2

Knowledge and Governance in the Arab World

A major reason for the halting, if not arrested progress of learning and cultural advancement in the Arab world may have been the failure of most Arab regimes, or so-called Arab systems, to relate to knowledge, in its multiple dimensions.

Obviously, contemporary rulers and those of yesteryear neither are, nor were, the "philosopher-kings" of Plato's Republic. And they were not expected to be in the first place. Yet in more simple and practical terms, from this governance gap there flowed a number of consequences:

• the rise of rulers from closed, semi illiterate backgrounds inclined to reject any participant in government who advocated the advancement of learning, or the enhancement of the quality of education and culture as objectives of statecraft, or who were committed to the exercise of academic freedom.

• disbelief among regimes in the need to seek cultural change based on those enlightened human values embodied in the Arab Renaissance of the 19th and early 20th century – values that have been rejected and crushed since the 1920's by a resurgence of religious extremism and arbitrary and self-serving interpretation.

• the negation of freedom of thought and expression in public education, including higher university levels, which accounts for the near absence of investment in research, particularly scientific research. The prevalence of state ideologies and autocratic approaches that have led to obscurantism and lack of innovation and of adequate standards for proper education. This in turn has reduced openness to modern technological advances and forward-looking intellectual discourse and debates.

• the absence, generally, as a corollary of absolutist governance, of critical thought. The obvious consequence of intolerant religious interpretations of values and ideals was the freezing of thinking into dépassé ideologies that permeated the minds and souls of a significant majority of so-called intellectuals. To such systems of values, any challenging ideas were considered punishable heresies. Many revolutionary philosophies were denigrated as "self-proclaimed" concepts that did not stand the test of history and time. This attitude contributed to defeats in almost every field - political, diplomatic and military - whereby dependence on foreign assistance and science became nearly total. The glorification of leaders and their systems led to rulers being equated with the nation, which rendered abject submission compulsory, and thus the persecution of free thinking admissible. Witness the endless numbers of jailed dissenters. Leadership was not questioned and the authority of the day, no matter how corrupt or despotic, was above accountability.

• hostility to creative literature, not to mention creative philosophic writing, which was unwelcome and often censored. Intellectual openness to new horizons of modern culture was next to nil, new ideas were held to be unwelcome and destructive and only entered Arab societies through limited windows of opportunity.

The above might be considered a harsh caricature were its consequences not reflected in two major measurable facts:

• regression in literacy and reading, as evident in the decline of Arab writing and publishing.

• The emigration of creative artists that reject conformity. Introversion in the arts became reflected in strange forms of unintelligible surrealism, when not imprisoned in naturalistic landscapes.

A strange polity was born where excessive consumerism sometimes combined with an utter lack of imagination and inventiveness.

Thus, the distressful spectacle of an Arab world where immense wealth was illicitly managed by despotic systems accumulating obscene fortunes while production, except of oil, sank, as did the Arab share of international trade. The people continued to live in a state of ignorance and indescribable poverty, hardly benefiting from this accumulated wealth and unaware of even their most elementary rights to rebel or revolt, rights denied them by an oppressive force, the objective ally of neo-colonial exploitation. See Iraq!

In conclusion, the political outcome of this situation, in the present context, is at one and the same time a sense of tremendous frustration, and a search for "purity" through invitations - at this stage merely invitations - to soul-searching and self-criticism.

Ghassan Twainy

The diversion of knowledge production: separating politics from knowledge

The goal should be to institutionalize knowledge in a domain separate from politics, thereby ensuring its independence.

Power curtails the intellectual and political scope of scholars and the public alike – which in turn shackles good minds, extinguishes the flame of learning and kills the drive for innovation.

The vigorous analyses, varied interrelationships and often contradictory nature that typify such patterns underline the multiple loyalties criss-crossing Arab knowledge production. This is in addition to the tendency of states and political parties to manipulate knowledge selectively for political ends. Add to this the fact that the knowledge efforts of the intellectual vanguard are scattered and it becomes clear that there are some fundamental obstacles to the creation of a well-knit Arab knowledge society. The most serious obstacle is the exploitation of knowledge to serve political ends, internal or external. Overcoming this calls for a fresh look at the knowledge map and those who interfere in it. The goal should be to institutionalize knowledge in a domain separate from politics, thereby ensuring its independence.

Political instability and fierce struggles for access to political positions in the absence of an established rule for the peaceful rotation of power – in short, democracy – obstruct the growth and maturation of knowledge in Arab soil. A major consequence of the unstable political situation is that questions of security dominate the agenda of ruling regimes. This inevitably leads regimes to allocate substantial investments to sectors that guarantee the system's security. Spheres of social activity that do not yield direct and rapid returns are the first casualties when government budgets are skewed towards security measures. In the Arab region, culture, knowledge and scientific research are exceptionally vulnerable to both political and financial neglect. Comparing scientific research allocations in Arab countries with equivalent spending in the industrial world, or even in other developing countries, underlines this distortion.

Another far-reaching and more profound consequence of this state of affairs is that knowledge activities are deprived of human talents. Educated citizens migrate towards bureaucratic, military, security and administrative occupations that provide significantly higher social and material rewards than scientific research and education can offer.

A further grave consequence of the dominant model is that branches of political au-
thority come to control all spheres of social activity, and to intervene in the affairs of scientific, technical, technological and literary institutions. Very often, such authorities direct knowledge workers to serve their own limited goals and impose work programmes, ideological constructs and slogans in exchange for resource allocations. Direct intervention by security or political agencies in appointments to scientific, intellectual and literary positions is the most blatant form of such interference, which of course disrupts knowledge development. It means that for the sake of securing political dominance over knowledge institutions, efficiency criteria are sacrificed. Appointments driven by political allegiance, nepotism or private interest sooner or later lead to the corruption of scientific research and technical institutions, and eventually to the destruction of knowledge itself.

In summary, Arab scientific research institutions are largely at the mercy of political strategies and power conflicts. Political loyalties take precedence in the management of these institutions and both efficiency and knowledge suffer. Power curtails the intellectual and political scope of scholars and the public alike – which in turn shackles good minds, extinguishes the flame of learning and kills the drive for innovation. These factors have impoverished Arab scientific and technical systems and left them at their weakest when the need to liberate and leverage knowledge has never been stronger.

New foundations are needed to create a robust and coherent knowledge society. Far-sighted sociological and legal analyses have emphasised the importance of taking the politics out of knowledge by founding an independent political economy in the Arab world. Co-existence would be the first rule of the polity under this reformation. Politicians would hold public office in a balanced concord with other spheres, without seeking to oppose or stifle them. Studies further suggest that an independent knowledge sphere must also be established in parallel to the political sphere. It would focus on producing and developing knowledge free from political coercion, with the goal of embedding knowledge in society. Neither act of separation, which would truly liberate both spheres of influence, is possible except by democratising politics and knowledge production.

In other words, democratic transformation in the Arab world is a fundamental condition for the independence of knowledge, taking into account that such a transformation requires synergy among economic, political and cultural actors. Whatever level of importance is accorded to individual actors, political power ranks high in comparison to other elements. This fact implies two challenges for society: the first is to establish an independent and self-limiting political sphere, while the second has to do with codifying and harmonising democracy so that both politics and knowledge are independent, yet complementary realms.

Founding an independent polity in the Arab world is supremely important for the establishment of the knowledge society. Yet in the absence of institutional rule, little progress can be made towards that goal.

The role of institutional independence in stimulating the knowledge society

Institutional independence is another facet of the rule of law. It is the normal outcome of establishing political power legally through codification, and politically by democratisation. The fact is that the spirit of the rule of law is not confined to the arrangement of laws within the state but is also embodied in the state's protection of rights and duties, and the maintenance of the dignity of human beings. Political authority requires a certain level of accumulated legal and institutional strength to lead society into democratic transformation.

The absence of sustained institutional independence is a common feature across the Arab nation. Arab polities cannot be characterised reliably by degrees of progress in institutional governance. For example, it is not feasible to set up comparisons on the basis of the type of regime (monarchy/republican), or the extent of community participation (referendums/elections), or the degree of active involvement in the international human rights system. This is because each element has to be measured against the practical progress of Arab regimes in establishing political power on the basis of a constitution and public respect for its legitimacy. Such legitimacy is

often in question, and Arab regimes continue to be driven by the imperatives of survival and security, to the detriment of the balance required in their relations with the governed.

CODIFYING POLITICAL POWER AND DEMOCRACY: A FUNDAMENTAL STAGE IN THE ESTABLISHMENT OF THE KNOWLEDGE SOCIETY

Fate has not decreed that political power in the Arab world should permanently exclude participation by citizens. Whether participation is encouraged or not depends on the will and policies of regimes. Amid conflicts and disputes over state legitimacy the power of democratisation and codification has been under-appreciated. Progress on those fronts would make all people, governors and governed alike, subject to the rule of law and help the institutional state to evolve. That, in turn, would secure the coexistence of all spheres of societal activity in the Arab world under the umbrella of equality. Moving in this direction will entail strengthening some key, yet still fragile, constitutional provisions and tightening lax laws that favour power structures.

Towards political systems that serve the knowledge society

Overcoming the fragility of the constitutional structure has certainly become essential. This requires creating a legal and political culture that is capable of directing and guiding political practice. The effectiveness of this culture, which has to be built on both democratic participation and opposition, will flow from its capacity to produce methodological concepts and tools sharp enough to understand Arab political reality and analyse the structures of power in Arab societies. Attaining this balance requires that Arab intellectuals drop ideology, resist compromises with the status quo and reject nostalgic indulgence in heritage.

Arab intellectuals must be actively involved in building the conditions for democratic societies and especially in defending the importance of their legal dimensions and the limits of political power. The intelligentsia should campaign for institutional rule, the absence of which will impede the rise of the

Amid conflicts and disputes over state legitimacy the power of democratisation and codification has been under-appreciated.

Imam Muhammad Abduh (1849-1905): Justice and Science

These two glorious, fundamental elements, justice and science, are inseparable in human existence. Should one of them reach a country, the other would follow suit immediately; and when one leaves the country, the other will follow on its heels. One can hardly lift a foot or put it down without the other accompanying it. This is what history tells us. The chronicles of states in which the beacon of justice burned bright and where the light of science shone tell us how their people enjoyed both lights at the same time and flew to the heights of happiness with these two wings. Once the times turned around, destroying one of the two foundations, the other one quickly followed, falling to the ground. The afflicted state would fall into the abyss. The atmosphere would become pitch-dark, with thick black clouds and veils of ignorance blocking mortal sight.

The secret of this is now clear. If science spreads in a nation, it will enlighten the ways for its people. Their roads will become brightly lit and they will clearly distinguish between good and evil, between what is harmful and what is useful. It will be firmly established in their minds that equality and justice are the primary cause of lasting happiness. They will then seek them, feeling that no price is too high. They will also know that injustice and oppression are synonymous with destruction and misery. Were justice to have a firm foothold in a nation, it would pave for it the roads to peace of mind and soul. Every person would then know his or her rights and duties. Their thoughts would then become sharp and their senses gentle. Their hearts would be strong in bringing what is useful to them and warding off what is harmful. They would immediately realise that what they have achieved is not eternal and that what they have acquired is not lasting unless they support one another in building true knowledge, and unless education becomes universal, embracing all members of society. They would all rush to acquire the sources of knowledge and spread it to all parts of the nation.

Source: Muhammad Abduh, 1990, p.25.

knowledge society. Intellectuals and academics have a clear stake in seeing due independence established in the respective spheres of knowledge and politics, which would lead to knowledge becoming at last a free entity.

THE LEGAL CONTEXT FOR KNOWLEDGE ACQUISITION, PRODUCTION AND DISSEMINATION

Freedom of thought and expression are among the fundamental principles for shaping free, innovative societies, businesses and individuals. They are the essence of independent public opinion. For example, the protection of innovation though intellectual property rights stimulates intellectual production and investment. The protection of people's rights of free speech and opinion stimulates creative thinking. Yet are Arab legal systems and institutions qualified to protect such basic rights?

Irregularity of the legal structure

While the law is, in principle, the very basis of citizens' rights to knowledge and to freedom

The majority of Arab states have signed the international human rights conventions– yet those conventions have neither entered the legal culture nor been incorporated in substantive legislation .

of thought and opinion, Arab laws suffer from several structural defects that severely limit their effectiveness and credibility.

Firstly, Arab laws do not always capture reality, but rather remain theoretical, which weakens their usefulness. Secondly, the gap between nominal or *de jure* acceptance of laws and actual enforcement or implementation is extremely wide. This gap is quite marked in public legislation, especially that related to issues of freedom and knowledge.

This large gap creates a duality that impedes progress. On the one hand, there is a positivist legal system that fails to interact with society - not surprisingly in a society that implements laws only when forced to. And on the other hand, there is a society that reproduces its values and systems in line with its own notions, democratically legalising and converting those notions to a state of respectability

That people often cannot exercise their rights through participation and are further prevented from exercising them by "legal" oppression certainly contributes to freezing both reality and the laws. Thus, the most hopeful course for legal development lies in a dynamic interaction between the realms of "law" and "reality".

Inactive and nominal laws

The majority of the Arab states have signed the international human rights conventions[3]– all of them refer to respect for fundamental freedoms – yet those conventions have neither entered the legal culture nor have they been incorporated into the substantive legislation of those states. The conventions have remained nominal, as is apparent from the fact that they are rarely raised before the judiciary for implementation, even though they are all binding and enjoy priority relative to local laws. It is presumed that a judge would implement these conventions if a lawsuit were presented before him or her[4], which in practice rarely happens.

Furthermore, these conventions have never been used, at the level of legislation, as a lever; they could be used as tools to urge Arab legislative authorities to enact new laws or to amend unfair ones. This has not happened.

---

[3]Most Gulf States have not yet signed the International Covenant on Civil and Political Rights or the International Covenant on Economic, Social and Cultural Rights.

[4]Some Arab legal systems have introduced in their procedural laws an explicit stipulation that judges are under obligation to apply the international conventions whenever such are brought up before them.

Declining efficiency of the judiciary

The judiciary is one of the fundamental guarantors of the protection of people's rights and freedoms. In turn, its independence and transparency are the primary guarantee of its good performance. While most Arab states have underlined the principle of power separation, reality often exposes a relationship between judicial powers and political powers, at least with respect to appointments and promotions. When judges who collaborate with the executive branch are rewarded with high executive positions the independence and credibility of the judiciary decrease. Moreover, suspension of laws by judges – at the behest of political authorities – and the spread of corruption have caused the judiciary, as an institution and as individuals, to lose the moral immunity they once enjoyed.

At the same time, it must be stressed that judges in Arab countries face an exceptionally difficult task under circumstances that reduce their efficiency. The high number of cases to be heard and inadequately equipped courtrooms with poorly trained support staff lengthen the time needed for outcomes and hamper efforts to serve the public interest. While public faith in the judiciary is not as high as it once was, the institution, especially at its higher levels, remains vital for the people and stands between them and the excesses of political power.

Yet respect for the judiciary did not increase when some Arab countries created exceptional courts that denied people the right to regular civil hearings, due process and the right of appeal to higher courts. The latter right is important because the higher the court the more independent and respectful of due procedure it is likely to be.

Consequently, seeking the judgement of the law and the judiciary has become a marginal resort for resolving disputes in some Arab societies. The public's growing lack of confidence in a judiciary that seems to be becoming more dependent, together with a lack of popular awareness about what the law provides for, may explain why so few cases concerned with the denial of freedoms - economic, political, cultural and social – are being brought before Arab courts.

Restoring the judiciary's credibility and rebuilding its independence are urgent priorities for guaranteeing the freedom of thought and expression inherent in the knowledge society.

FREEDOM OF THOUGHT, OPINION AND EXPRESSION IN THE STRUCTURE OF THE LEGAL SYSTEM

The legal protection of freedom

Freedoms are not confined to political and civil freedoms; they embrace economic, social and cultural freedoms as well. Without freedom of thought, opinion and expression – which head the list of fundamental rights indispensable to the knowledge society – the exercise of other freedoms would remain a mere abstraction.

International conventions and Arab constitutions and laws sanction freedom as a natural human right. Most Arab states have signed the international conventions[5] that protect freedom, and have unanimously agreed to endorse freedom in the substance of their constitutions[6]. They have further introduced in their laws clauses that bear on the protection[7] of freedom as part of legal controls that tighten or relax according to the type of regime: controls may vary between censorship and declaring a state of emergency.

The problem with freedom in Arab countries is not related to the implementation of laws[8], but to their violation. It has to do with the spread of oppression and the erratic nature of the measures used. It also has to do with the hegemony of censorship and its use by political powers to tighten their grip on those very freedoms that they have ostensibly recognised.

General rules for the exercise of freedom

The exercise of freedom, in societies that respect it, is subject to well-defined general rules, wherein a balance is struck between the

Restoring the judiciary's credibility and rebuilding its independence are urgent priorities.

The problem with freedom in Arab countries is not related to the implementation of laws, but to their violation.

---

[5]Such as the Universal Declaration of Human Rights, the International Covenant on Civil and Political Rights and others.

[6]Except for Saudi Arabia, which has not drafted a constitution per se, and the single-party states.

[7]For example, the press and publishing laws in the Arab states provide that the freedom of issuing newspapers, printing and publishing is guaranteed according to those laws and that it is exercised within the framework of the constitution's principles, the provisions of law and the profession's code of ethics. The same applies to the freedom of founding associations and organising general assemblies.

[8]Those laws must be completed and adapted to the needs of Arab societies.

requirements of justice and law on the one hand and those of the public good as agreed upon by all social groups on the other. Thus those rules are perceived positively. Moreover, the legal system in those societies places laws in the hands of a fair judiciary that refers to those laws in the settlement of disputes. In this framework the law has a double role: to provide the basis for resolutions in disputes and to inculcate the values it protects, penalising offenders against those values. People's appeals to the rule of law and the judiciary attest to their confidence in the proper performance of the legal system.

What determines how well freedom of thought, opinion and expression are protected in practice are the general rules for enforcing laws and ensuring public compliance and the degree to which such compliance serves the public interest. If the legal restrictions that enforce compliance with the law are stated clearly in the text of the law, are compatible with the constitution and conventions and the spirit of the legislation, and are implemented by the relevant legal authorities, then these restrictions are effective and useful. Otherwise, they become harmful and oppressive.

In the Arab world, restrictions imposed on freedom take the form of legal constraints on publications, associations, general assemblies and electronic media, which prevent these from carrying out their communicative and cultural roles. Such restrictions also obstruct the dissemination of knowledge and the education of public opinion, notwithstanding citizen's rights as secured by the law and the international charters.

Restrictions on freedom vary in degree from one state to another. They range from prohibiting the publication of new political newspapers to banning the circulation of one or more issues of existing journals, administrative seizure of newspapers and publications and advance censorship of periodicals. Penalties meted out to journalists, publishing houses and news agencies used to be a small fine; they now range from provisional suspen-

sions to outright closure.

Regulations governing the freedom to form associations that were laid down in the colonial period endorsed the rule of free assembly, provided that the founding organisers informed the competent authorities of the association's creation. The situation today is that, except for those older laws, all other amendments governing freedom of association made in the post independence and national liberation era are restriction-oriented.[9]

Yet the more dangerous restrictions are those imposed by the security authorities when they confiscate publications or ban people from entering the country or prevent the sale of certain books during fairs while promoting other kinds of books. In committing these acts, these authorities reach above the constitutional institutions and the law, using the pretext of national security – a criterion seldom clarified by them. Other forms of restriction come from classes of citizens themselves, who, as noted in chapter three, appoint themselves the custodians of public morality, and press for the censorship of books, articles and media events.

To escape this censorship-freedom contradiction, the rule of law should be enforced, as it guarantees freedom and shrinks the role of censorship. Yet, as noted earlier, Arab laws and legal institutions suffer from several structural problems and many have lost their effectiveness and credibility. The restoration and effective application of the law in the interest of public and individual freedoms depend critically on addressing these problems through significant reforms.

Violation of political and legal guarantees for the protection of freedom

Most constitutions have political and legal guarantees for the protection of freedom. Such political guarantees are reflected in the rule of law and exemplified in the principles of people's sovereignty, equality and right to scrutinise the government's policies and work and express their views on them. The legal

---

[9]Originally, the formation of associations did not require a license from the administrative authorities; it only required that the association be proclaimed before those authorities. Now, laws governing associations require, upon proclamation or declaration of an association, that a temporary acknowledgement of recognition be delivered by the administrative authorities. Once the proclamation or the declaration text fulfils all the measures provided for in the same associations law, a final acknowledgement is delivered to the association, within a specified period. This acknowledgement represents a "license" that legitimises the work of the association. Should the authorities fail to deliver this acknowledgement within the specified period the association may operate in accordance with the objectives outlined in the relevant laws. However, by delivering the temporary and not the final acknowledgement, the administrative authority becomes able to revoke it whenever it likes, which is the core of the problem.

Examples of this are the 1909 associations law of Lebanon and the statement of the minister of the interior issued on 17 January 1996; the associations law of Morocco of 23 July 2002 amending and complementing the 15 November 1958 law on the right to form associations. The same provisions apply to the association of general assemblies.

guarantees are embodied in respect for the principle of the separation of authorities, the precedence of the law and in subjecting statesmen and public officials to a common judiciary. Legal guarantees are also embodied in clauses regulating interior affairs. These guarantees, however, are violated and become inactive during times of war and emergency in the Arab world. Their suspension results in intensifying repressive measures – the sole co-ordination framework found between Arab ministers of the interior in their successive summits.

Repression of freedoms in emergencies

The relative expansion in the sanctioning of laws providing greater freedom in Arab countries is a positive sign, yet its value is diminished when contrasted with practices in enacting such laws. This often reveals a failure to reconcile the interests of the government with the rights of the people and the exigencies of state security with the principles of freedom. The positive trend is further undermined when the pressures of security lead political authorities to curb freedoms that they believe threaten the status quo.

Arab countries live in a state of maximum security under the Arab-Israeli conflict. However, internal security procedures cannot always be justified in that context. In fact, those procedures often eliminate all components of civil liberty, opposition and criticism in the name of mobilisation.

Some Arab countries have declared a state of emergency[10]. This act suppresses freedom, and shelves the political guarantees invested in the rule of law and the institutions that safeguard public and individual freedoms. A state of emergency releases the State from constitutional accountability under the rule of law and legal accountability through the judiciary. It curtails respect for the rule of the separation of authorities by sanctioning direct intervention in the affairs of the judiciary and it freezes the legal guarantees that protect individuals from state aggression.

Freedoms that are hostage to matters of security, to censorship and to self-appointed watchdogs of public morality are freedoms denied. The first victims of this denial are creativity, innovation and knowledge.

The stifling legal context that has developed from the crisis of law in the region will cramp Arab minds, inhibit local knowledge production and drive good Arab scholars and thinkers abroad, intensifying the region's knowledge deficit. Overcoming that crisis is a central part of the challenge of building the knowledge society.

Protecting creativity and intellectual freedom: copyright laws

Authors are the fountainhead of literary and artistic creativity. With the ascent of knowledge as a major factor of production and the arrival of digital publishing, the issue of authorship and copyrights has extended beyond its closed world and has become relevant to all fields: cultural, social, economic, political, commercial and others. The growing value attached to individual intellectual, artistic and creative production and the high returns on intellectual investments in development, coupled with the growing vulnerability of intellectual works to blatant or concealed piracy and plagiarism, make copyright protection an important tool of public policy in the new knowledge societies. Copyright has become the concern of administrative, legislative, judicial and executive authorities.

In the international context, copyright issues have assumed great importance for developing countries acceding to the WTO with its articles relating to intellectual property rights (IPRs) and trade. Thus, developing countries, including some Arab countries, have moved to promulgate laws conforming to international conventions on intellectual property rights and to ensure their full implementation. While a few Arab countries, Morocco (1916, 1970)[11], Egypt (1954)[12] and Lebanon (1999)[13] have specific IPR laws, most other Arab states still lack such specialised legislation. Their laws reflect only some articles in this respect; civil codes, for example, cover certain aspects under property, while publication laws embody some others.

Freedoms that are hostage to matters of security, to censorship and to self-appointed watchdogs of public morality are freedoms denied.

The crisis of law in the region will cramp Arab minds, inhibit local knowledge production and drive good Arab scholars and thinkers abroad.

[10] Egypt, Syria, Lebanon and Sudan.

[11] Law promulgated on 23 June 1916. Another law was promulgated on 24 January 1943. Pursuant to said law, the African Office for Copyrights and the African Office for Men of Letters and Authors were founded. A decree was issued on 7 March 1965 concerning the formation of the Moroccan Office for Copyright. The IPR law was promulgated on 29 July 1970.

[12] Law No 354 on Intellectual Property Rights. It comprises 51 articles.

[13] Law No 75, the second law, after the 1924 Law on Copyright.

The Bern Convention on the Protection of Literary and Artistic Works[14] and the International Copyright Convention[15] constitute the international legal framework[16] of copyright. The regional Arab Convention for Copyrights and national copyright legislation (in Egypt and Morocco) are derived from both. There are only six Arab countries in the Bern Convention (by ratification, accession or acceptance) – Tunisia, Morocco, Lebanon, Mauritania, Libya and Egypt. As regards the International Convention on Copyright, five Arab countries have acceded, namely, Lebanon, Tunisia, Morocco, Algeria, and Saudi Arabia[17].

Disregard for intellectual property protection comes at a price for individual authors, published scientists and creative artists who have a right to recognition for their original work. It affects the national economy because value adding knowledge ceases to be produced when it is easily stolen. And it undercuts international cooperation and understanding in the global information age when national laws do not meet international standards of protection.

Arab countries have taken some steps to protect copyright as regards literary, scientific and artistic works in a unified manner[18]. Arab Ministers of Culture ratified in their conference held on 5 November 1981 the Arab Agreement on Copyright Protection[19].

The Agreement had been subject to some criticism. It is claimed that it does not rise to the level of advanced countries' legislation and does not embody the realities of Arab (and Islamic) countries in particular, and developing countries in general. To ensure its applicability, the Agreement had to employ flexibility as a first step. Nevertheless, further steps have not been adopted since, which renders the Agreement imperfect and in need of review.

All Arab countries, except the occupied Palestinian territories and Comoros, participate in one international intellectual property rights organisation or another; 19 Arab countries (exceptions: Syria, Palestine and Comoros Islands) are members of WIPO; 15 Arab countries (exceptions: Saudi Arabia, Somalia, Qatar and Yemen) are members of the Paris Union; ten Arab countries (exceptions: Jordan, UAE, Saudi Arabia, Sudan, Syria, Iraq, Oman, Qatar, Kuwait and Yemen) are members of the Bern Union.

Yet the development of IPR laws in the Arab world is subject to the same variability as other laws. In only a few Arab countries do such laws explicitly stipulate the moral rights of the author[20]. Moreover, numerous literary, scientific and artistic works in Arab countries

---

[14]Dated 9 September 1886. At the beginning, only one Islamic country, Tunisia, signed, on 5 December 1887. Several needs generated reviews of this Convention and reconsideration of new developments as follows: the Convention was complemented in Paris on 4 May 1889; amended in Berlin on 13 November 1908. It was further complemented in Bern on 20 March 1914; re-amended in Rome on 2 June 1928 and Brussels on 26 June 1948. The Convention was then signed by 35 countries, inter-alia, five Arab and Islamic countries. Amidst the economic, social and political developments and transformations in the last half of the 20th century, the Convention was amended at Stockholm on 14 July 1967, in Paris on 24 July 1971 and changed in 1979 (the Convention is managed by the WIPO which replaced in 1971 the World Intellectual Property Offices). The number of countries, up until the 1 January 1994, that acceded, ratified or accepted the Convention amounted to 105, including six Arab countries and seven Islamic countries, inter-alia, Malaysia.

Article 2 of the Convention stipulates: "Literary and Artistic Works" shall include any production in the literary, scientific and artistic work regardless of the mode of expression, such as books ... etc." for more information, see (Ash-Sharqawi, in Arabic, 1995, 31-35, 49-52, 141).

[15]Ratified by the International Governmental Conference on Copyright, Geneva, 18 August - 6 September 1952 (the International Governmental Committee reviewed it for the benefit of developing countries, at UNESCO, Paris, 5-24 July 1971. The Convention was enforced as of 10 July 1974). The number of Islamic countries that acceded to the 1952 Convention up until the beginning of March 1993 had been limited, with only five Arab Islamic countries acceding.

[16]Other international agreements and conventions include: The Hague Convention for International Deposit of Industrial Drawings and Designs issued on 6 November 1925; The London Document (1934); The Hague Document (1960); The Additional Monaco Document (1961); The Supplementary Stockholm Document (1967) amended on 28 September 1979; the law on the implementation of the Convention (1 April 1994); The Lucarno Agreement on International Classification of Industrial Drawings and Designs. In the commercial field, TRIPS tackles intellectual property rights and trade. Furthermore, "industrial rights" have been examined in the Madrid Accord that highlights strict measures against forged or fake data about products. There are other agreements, such as the International Agreement on the Protection of Performers, Sound Record Producers and Broadcast Corporations; the International Agreement on the Protection of Sound Records Producers against illegitimate production of their records. For more details, see Ibid., 15 ...).

[17]Up until 1997; it is likely that other countries have recently acceded to one of the two conventions or both.

[18]According to Article 21 of the Arab Cultural Unity Charter (1964), Arab countries are asked to adopt legislation to protect intellectual property (literary, scientific and artistic) within the sovereignty of each country separately.

[19]The Agreement is a blend of some of the legislative provisions set forth in the Bern Convention and the International Convention on Copyright.

[20]Example: Copyright or the right to notice; the right to "parenthood" (authorship), the right to work, the right to title determination, the right to amendment, the right to regret or withdrawal.

Copyright is an exclusive right. Most legislations name this right "copyright, the right to transmission or publicity". This right is vested in the author who alone can authorise others to use his work in any form. The legislations of some Arab and Islamic countries expressly stipulate this right, I.e., Egypt, Iraq, Libya, Morocco, Senegal, and Turkey.

Concerning the right to parenthood (authorship), i.e. the affiliation of the creative work to its creator, the legislations of some Arab and Islamic countries stipulate this right: Algeria, Egypt, Iraq, Lebanon, Libya, Morocco, Arab Republic of Syria, Tunisia, Turkey, the Sudan, Senegal, Pakistan, Iran and Bangladesh.

As regards the right to work or to complete the work, i.e., the author's right to oppose any manipulation, omission or attempt to deform his work, some laws in Arab and Islamic countries enshrine this right, i.e., Algeria, Egypt, Jordan, Iraq, Lebanon, Libya, Morocco, Syria, Tunisia, Turkey, Senegal, Pakistan, Iran and Bangladesh.

The right to title entails the author's right to the original title specified. As regards the right to amendment, it entails the author's right to introduce amendments to the work after publication. Only Egypt, Libya and the Sudan recognised this right.

The right to regret or withdrawal entails the author's right to recall the published work. Only Egypt, Libya and the Sudan recognise this right. (Ibid., 168-173).

still swing between protection, application and codification[21].

Copyright concerns all segments of society and includes all creators, innovators and thinkers in literary, scientific and artistic fields at all social, economic, commercial, legal, political and cultural levels.

If Arab countries are to realise an economic, cultural and social renaissance, those that have not drafted national legislation on copyright – the most fundamental instrument for protecting and stimulating knowledge production – must do so. Moreover, laws need enforcement: they must be implemented by practical, preventive procedures and intensive public education. Two basic common values need to be respected before freedom and knowledge can be converted into rights protected by law. First the sanctity of human beings as the essential and protected centres of society must be accepted. This is a fundamental value that should not be undermined. Second, society must value knowledge, scholarship and intellectual effort by elevating them to their rightful position. The absence of these two values is a systemic problem: coercion and disregard for people are dominating values in present-day Arab society. Moreover, some segments of the intellectual elite lack an effective political platform while others are seduced by the glamour of power and money, with the result that ordinary people neither trust in nor recognise the importance of knowledge production.

THE REGIONAL AND GLOBAL ENVIRONMENT

Arab regional co-operation can be an important asset in managing closer global integration, enabling Arab countries as a group to pool their capabilities and experience in order to maximise the rewards and mitigate the risks of globalisation. Globalisation offers important opportunities to acquire knowledge from world stocks and to stimulate the performance of the domestic knowledge system, particularly in the fields of education, research and technological development.

But the global context also poses potential challenges to knowledge acquisition in Arab countries. These challenges include exposure to fluctuations in global economic relations through world trade and foreign direct investment; the limited impact of both trade and investment in Arab knowledge acquisition; unfairly restrictive IPR agreements; and the risk that weak production capacity in developing countries, including Arab countries, will condemn them to an inferior role in the global production system, with negative consequences for knowledge acquisition. Stronger regional cooperation can help Arab countries negotiate such issues, whether involving technology transfer and indigenisation, IPRs or pharmaceutical and drug prices, from positions of greater advantage. Moreover, the field is open to Arab co-operation with other developing countries in research, knowledge development and know-how exchanges.

Knowledge is increasingly becoming a private commodity at the international as well as at the national level. This growing link between knowledge production and profit, coupled with greater selectivity in knowledge flows to points outside the rich world, may actually inhibit knowledge production, especially the forms of knowledge required by developing countries and societies. A clear example is the production of affordable drugs to combat diseases that devastate poor countries (tropical diseases, HIV-AIDS). Between 1975 and 1996, 1,223 new drugs were marketed worldwide, only 13 for tropical diseases. In 1998, global spending on health-related research amounted to US $70 billion: of this total, just US $300 million was for HIV-AIDS and only US $100 million for malaria (UNDP, HDR, 2001, 109-110).

Such issues could negatively impact the prices and production of drugs, especially in Egypt and Jordan, and underline why developing countries need to acquire the requisite knowledge and negotiating skills to better leverage their intellectual property rights in international forums. Stronger Arab cooperation would increase the region's bargaining power.

Globalisation, in its present form, risks entrenching the dominance of the powerful over the weak in terms of knowledge and wealth. It is often pointed out that the distribution of

Laws need enforcement: they must be implemented by practical, preventive procedures and intensive public education.

Society must value knowledge, scholarship and intellectual effort by elevating them to their rightful position.

---

[21]Lectures, speeches, sermons; articles on political, economic or religious items; industrial drawings and designs; carpet-related works; architectural work, etc. (Ibid, 286).

Concerns that the world economic system will inflict severe penalties on developing countries that fall behind in the race for knowledge are justified.

Negotiations on the mechanisms and agreements that underpin globalisation are tending to bolster the interests of the stronger parties.

world income and wealth has worsened since the mid 1970s. The goal must rather be to make globalisation a force that helps developing countries achieve human progress. Structurally, globalisation, as it is unfolding today, allows for the free movement of people, goods and services selectively in a manner that often secures the interests of the stronger party. In terms of labour markets, for example, this leads to the migration of skilled developing country personnel to the industrialised countries, which causes a double loss for the countries of origin. Arab countries are especially vulnerable to such outflows, as Chapter Seven noted.

Concerns that the world economic system will inflict severe penalties on developing countries that fall behind in the race for knowledge are justified. In 1998, the World Bank President noted in his introduction to the Bank's report on "Knowledge for Development" that "the globalisation of trade, finance and information flows increases competition in a manner that raises the danger of retarding the poorest countries and societies at an accelerating pace" (The World Bank, 1998).

Negotiations on the mechanisms and agreements that underpin globalisation are tending to bolster the interests of the stronger parties, the industrialised countries. An obvious example is the insistence of these countries, notably the United States, on maintaining agricultural subsidies to their own farmers while pressing developing countries to do away with such measures. The use of environmental and social policy conditionalities can also become a way to debar developing countries from industrial country markets. The misuse of intellectual property rights can transform knowledge from a public good into a private commodity when products originating in developing countries are usurped by large firms and producers, as has happened in the case of pharmaceuticals and some other industries.

The introduction of market principles and mechanisms to govern the supply of services, especially educational services, affects the development of knowledge in developing countries and could lead to unfair competition between local and foreign suppliers, thereby weakening the diffusion of knowledge.

Lastly, current global governance arrangements do not compensate developing countries for losses they incur through adverse terms of trade and exchange. Despite the large literature that exists on the harmful impacts for developing countries of the migration of their most highly educated and skilled people to the West, none of the proposals made for helping these countries to recoup their losses has found a receptive audience in the industrialised world.

In this context of increasing global inequality, the acquisition of knowledge has become one of the key fields where "economies of scale" and "economies of scope" have assumed great importance. Evidence of this can be found in mounting co-operation between European countries in higher studies programmes, in technological agreements within and with other regional blocs and in synergy and mergers among giant multinationals in research and technological development. Certainly, so-called "big science"[22] exceeds

---

BOX 8.4

Integrating intellectual property rights and development policy

Intellectual property systems may, if we are not careful, introduce distortions that are detrimental to the interests of developing countries. Developed countries should pay more attention to reconciling their commercial self-interest with the need to reduce poverty in developing countries, which is in everyone's interest. Higher IP standards should not be pressed on developing countries without a serious and objective assessment of their impact on development and poor people. We need to ensure that the global IP system evolves so that the needs of developing countries are incorporated and, most importantly, so that it contributes to the reduction of poverty in developing countries by stimulating innovation and technology transfer relevant to them, while also making available the products of technology at the most competitive prices possible.

TRIPS has strengthened the global protection offered to suppliers of technology, but without any counterbalancing strengthening of competition policies globally. Therefore, it may be unwise to focus on TRIPS as a principal means of facilitating technology transfer. A wider agenda needs to be pursued...

Because the IP system does little to stimulate research on diseases that particularly affect poor people, public funding for research on health problems in developing countries should be increased. This additional funding should seek to exploit and develop existing capacities in developing countries for this kind of research, and promote new capacity, both in the public and private sectors.

Report of the Commission on Intellectual Property Rights
London, September 2002.

---

[22]Some fields of research and sophisticated technological development require vast institutional and funding capacity that far exceeds the potentialities of any country separately, even advanced countries. These fields include nuclear physics, space, and new energy development. Some advanced countries have pooled all their potentialities in these fields in specialised centres. An early effort of this kind was CERN in Geneva, one of the world's largest research centres in molecular physics. The latest is the International Space Station. Arab countries can follow similar models in the fields of research and development that exceed the potentialities of one single country.

The effects of globalisation on growth and distribution throughout the world - UNCTAD

The difference in the positions of developing countries and advanced countries in the world economy, as a result of globalisation, raises questions about the ascendance of the unfettered market growth model after the collapse of the Soviet Union.

The "Trade and Development" report issued by UNCTAD in 1997 referred to several observable and disturbing trends in this respect, which are paraphrased below:

Titled "Globalisation, Growth and Distribution," the report stresses that the essential characteristic of the world economy since the early 1980s has been the free play of market powers by dismantling restrictions on local markets and opening them to world competition. This has become the new "invisible hand" at work in an environment where state regulation has been weaker than in decades. The notion that world competition would bring about faster growth and eliminate huge disparities in incomes and living standards has proved to be rather optimistic.

In fact, the world economy slowed down during the same period in comparison with the golden era of growth from the end of World War II to the mid 1970s. World growth settled at a rate of about 3% from the mid 1980s, followed by a further drop as a result of the Asian crisis, particularly in Japan, and the end of the boom enjoyed by the United States and Europe in the late 1990s.

Income distribution worsened from the early 1980s. In 1965, the ratio of individual income in the seven wealthiest countries to individual income in the seven poorest countries was 1/20. In 1995 it rose to 1/39. The increasing disparity between countries was accompanied by a similar polarizsation within them. The share of the wealthiest increased at the expense of the poorest, and the pauperisation of the middle classes became a characteristic of income distribution in many countries.

The report attributes these negative trends to the rapid liberalisation of economies in a manner that favoured certain social classes, in the advanced and developing countries alike. Capital was strengthened at the expense of labour: the share of profits rose while the share of labour dropped. Among wage earners, the share of highly qualified groups and traders increased at the expense of producers. And as a result of speedy financial liberalisation, public and private debt increased in the developing and developed countries, which led to higher real interest rates than before. This is clearer in the developing countries in particular where the distribution of wealth is more concentrated and the tax burden on the poorer classes is greater. The increase in public debt meant the redistribution of wealth in favour of the wealthy. There is growing evidence that slower growth and increasingly skewed distribution are becoming permanent features of the world.

According to the report, a more worrying observation, from the perspective of future growth, is that the concentration of income and wealth in the hands of the few was not accompanied by a rise in investment, which normally stimulates faster growth. Hence, in this pattern, the chances of combating unemployment worldwide and alleviating poverty in developing countries - let alone eradicating it - are slim.

The report attributes this discrepancy between the high incomes of the wealthy and low investment rates mainly to the hasty liberalisation of finance worldwide and the absence of well-sequenced national policies for regulating capital accounts. This trend encouraged speculation and volatility in financial markets as unfettered capital flows chased quick profits around the world, imposing high interest rates and breaking the relationship between finance and productive investment.

The report presents a policy package for transforming rising profits for the few into higher rates of investment in a manner sufficient to support a "social contract that could justify the present increasing discrepancy, and reduce it in the end through raising people's income and living standards."

These policies include, at the level of states, providing more incentives for investing profits in improving job-creating production capacity, increasing real wages, closing non-productive channels of wealth accumulation, restricting luxury spending, forging integration between local growth factors - through capital accumulation and increased local technology capacity - on the one hand, and gradual and calculated integration into the world economy, on the other. In individual countries, these policies need to be tailored to the level of development and the capacities of industries and institutional structures. They should be accompanied by new and serious standards of equitable employment and income and access of the poor to capital, services and other assets, which in many countries requires agrarian reform.

At the global level, complementary policy action is required from the stronger powers in the world economy. These policies should aim to introduce checks and balances in globalisation to minimise its harmful side effects on developing country growth. Areas for attention include trade liberalisation, which has been slower in the case of goods where developing countries enjoy a comparative advantage. Rich countries still protect their agricultural products and impose restrictions on imports of textiles from poorer countries. Another priority is to remove selectivity in global labour markets: while most restrictions on the movement of capital and highly qualified individuals are diminishing, restrictions on the movement of unskilled workers are becoming stricter.

Source: UNCTAD, Trade and Development Report, 1997

the potentiality of any Arab country separately.

In the case of Arab countries, a major leap in knowledge acquisition requires more profound and highly efficient forms of co-operation at the Arab level. There are several reasons for this proposition:

Naturally, co-operation among countries to acquire knowledge contributes to the increase of their capacity collectively. This advantage increases if some of the countries have common characteristics, a common language and common challenges, as in the Arab world.

Among Arab countries, there are wide variations in R&D components, especially human and financial resources. Integration will help to ensure that research and development flourishes on a regional scale and will lift the weaker Arab countries up as full partners.

Current literature on knowledge emphasises that a strong synergy among the elements of the knowledge system is a key prerequisite. However, as the first AHDR pointed out, components of the knowledge system at the regional and national levels in the Arab world are not optimised in relation to one other. A

Trade and Development: Prebisch's demands still stand

It is a sign of troubled times when, in the search for solutions to the most pressing policy challenges of the day, it is considered necessary to look to earlier generations for guidance: a Marshall Plan - this time to fight global poverty; a Tobin tax to check financial volatility; and a Keynesian spending package to combat deflationary dangers spring readily to mind. The source of the trouble is the gap between the rhetoric and the reality of a liberal international economic order. Nowhere is this gap more evident than in the international trading system. Even as Governments extol the virtues of free trade, they are only too willing to intervene to protect their domestic constituencies that feel threatened by the cold winds of international competition. Such remnants of neo-mercantilist thinking have done much to unbalance the bargain struck during the Uruguay Round.

Since the third session of the WTO Ministerial Conference, held in Seattle, a renewed effort has been made to address the concern of developing countries, culminating in a different kind of bargain being struck at Doha. Developing countries, by agreeing to a comprehensive programme of work and negotiations, demonstrated their commitment to tackling global political and economic threats; in return, they expect that development concerns will be central to the negotiations. The challenge is now to translate an expanded negotiating agenda into a genuine development agenda.

One voice from the past stands out in the search for a more balanced trading system. In his statement to the first United Nations Conference on Trade and Development in March 1964, Raul Prebisch, then its Secretary-General, called on the industrial countries not to underestimate the basic challenge facing developing countries in the existing system:

"We believe that developing countries must not be forced to develop inwardly—which will happen if they are not helped to develop outwardly through an appropriate international policy. We also deem it undesirable to accept recommendations which tend to lower mass consumption in order to increase capitalization, either because of the lack of adequate foreign resources or because such resources are lost owing to adverse terms of trade."

Prebisch understood that recommending "the free play of market forces" between unequal trading partners would only punish poorer commodity exporters at the same time as it brought advantages to the rich industrial core. His agenda to attack the persistent trade imbalance and create the essential external conditions for accelerating the rate of growth included new modalities of participation for developing countries in the trading system which would guarantee price stabilization and improved market access for primary exports, allow greater policy space to develop local industries and reduce barriers to their exports, establish more appropriate terms of accession to the multilateral system and reduce the burden of debt servicing. Although the participation of developing countries in the trading system has since gone through important changes, the minimum agenda put forward by Prebisch remains the basis for rebalancing that system in support of development.

Source: United Nations Conference on Trade and Development, Trade and Development Report, 2002.

collaborative Arab knowledge system at the regional and national levels would create new and more efficient synergies.

Another factor is that political conditions in the Arab region, notably the Israeli occupation of Palestinian territories and the situation in Iraq, necessitate a more profound degree of Arab co-operation, not only from the perspective of progress but also for the purpose of national security.

Political obstacles to knowledge acquisition by Arab countries may well be more severe than those raised by their socio-economic structures. Those structures were themselves judged more of a hindrance to knowledge acquisition than any supposedly innate cultural traits. Thus, the factors to be reckoned with in creating the Arab knowledge society become more significant as one moves from one societal context to the next. Bold thinking about the separation of politics from knowledge has become crucial.

Unquestionably, freedom requires substantial reinforcement. And good governance needs to be established in order to ensure the sustained expansion and promotion of freedom. Arab co-operation has to be renewed and scaled up in order for Arab countries to meet the world on more equal ground and to knit the sinews of the region. Finally, this chapter emphasises that Arabs need to take a positive, yet vigilant, approach to globalisation as both a source of, and a constraint on knowledge acquisition.

PART II

Section four: a strategic vision- the five pillars of the knowledge society

The last chapter in this Report outlines a strategic vision built on five pillars of the future Arab knowledge society. Its chief goal is to frame a forward-looking and action-oriented discussion on knowledge in Arab countries that takes into account their particular features and circumstances and that leads to specific operational proposals for the advancement of Arab human development.

CHAPTER 9

A strategic vision: the five pillars of the knowledge society

This final chapter continues the practice adopted in the first AHDR (2002) of charting major milestones towards a better future for Arab countries built on human development.

The chapter does not purport to offer ready recipes for building human development in each and every Arab society. Rather, it draws from the preceding chapters a number of common directions that Arab societies could consider to achieve that goal. The term "society" is used deliberately, rather than "country" or "state", in order to emphasise that the "society" concerned could be part of an Arab state or a group of states or the entire Arab world.

Building human development calls for social innovation, a process that can only be led and undertaken by the people of each Arab society themselves, for themselves. The Report therefore stops at delineating the main features of what could be considered a strategic vision[1] for the task of building human development. This vision needs to be taken up, nurtured and debated by human development advocates within Arab society, recognising and paying attention to dissenting views. Where the vision is adopted, a consensus on priorities needs to be accompanied by decisions for implementing the strategic vision under the specific conditions of that society. Indeed, this process constitutes the first stage of social innovation. It can stimulate the emergence of a societal movement for unleashing innovative human potential and utilising this potential in building human development.

The future map of the Arab world must be drawn from within the region. No externally derived construct can elicit the conviction and guarantee the support of the Arab peoples in the long run. The present attempt by Arab intellectuals to articulate a strategic vision of the Arab knowledge society is a contribution to such internal efforts to reshape the underpinnings of Arab human development.

THE STATE OF KNOWLEDGE IN ARAB COUNTRIES AND THE CONSEQUENCES OF PERPETUATING THE STATUS QUO

Knowledge in Arab countries today appears to be on the retreat. Ingrained structural impediments stand in the way of building the knowledge society in the region. Current political and social orientations diminish the role played by knowledge in Arab societies, as previous sections of this Report have indicated. While knowledge in the region stumbles, the developed world is racing towards knowledge-intensive societies. This trend will further accentuate the asymmetry of world knowledge development and endow a few countries with near-supremacy in knowledge production and consumption. Based on their present performance, Arabs would remain in a marginal position in this next phase of human history. This position would be the logical consequence of a decline that has lasted for seven centuries, while much of the world made enormous progress in developing knowledge and human welfare. Continuing with this historic slide is an untenable course if the Arab people are to have a dignified, purposeful and productive existence in the third millennium.

Without a strong and growing contemporary knowledge base of their own, Arab countries will be absorbed into the international knowledge society as passive consumers of other countries' proprietary knowledge, technology and services. Without mastery of the capabilities that knowledge brings, they will re-

Knowledge in Arab countries today appears to be on the retreat.

Without a strong and growing knowledge base of their own, Arab countries will be drawn into the international knowledge society as passive consumers.

---

[1] Which, by definition, does not rise to the level of a "strategy".

main incapable of establishing their own space and growth under the often one-sided and restrictive trade, investment and intellectual property rights regimes of a world that is old and new: old in terms of human struggle and new in terms of its rules of engagement. On the other hand, Arab countries can avert this passive fate by indigenising knowledge and technology and developing the necessary absorptive, adaptive and innovative capacities and structures, which offer them the opportunity to participate proactively in the vigorously growing global knowledge society from a position of dignity and strength.

Yet individual Arab countries are unlikely to go far in that direction on their own. Strong Arab co-operation that approaches regional

unity through "a Free Arab Citizenship Zone" will not only bolster the negotiating powers of Arabs in the world arena and help reduce monopolistic pressures; it will help Arabs to benefit from opportunities created by globalisation and to manage its risks.

THE FIVE PILLARS OF THE KNOWLEDGE SOCIETY

The strategic vision outlined below rests on *five pillars*, the building blocks of which were laid down in the preceding chapters and in sections of the first AHDR.

BOX 9.1

Mustafa Al-Barghouthi – The Road to the Future

The Arab peoples and states are facing fateful challenges at a time of accelerating changes which do not wait for those who are slow or lax in defending their interests.

It is quite clear that the dilemma of Arab development will not be solved without focusing fully on human development – the development of the citizen and his/her role in economic, social and political life.

This calls for the achievement of four goals, which are interdependent and indispensable.

First, the formation of the political citizen and his/her participation through the diffusion and deepening of democratic values and political participation, beginning with the rule of law, independent judiciary, equality before the law, freedom of political action and thought, freedom of the press, political plurality and free democratic elections. Add to that the freedom of civil society institutions from governmental control and the freedom to organize, innovate and develop in society at large. Political participation, from a developmental point of view, means the freedom of citizens to take part in policy-making and contribute to the determination of economic and social decisions affecting them.

The second goal is the comprehensive development of education, beginning with pre-school education and going through higher education. This will not be achieved without opening opportunities for learning to all segments and classes of society, whether through compulsory education or through the establishment of national funds to provide loans for university education in which students enjoy equal rights regardless of their economic, social and political backgrounds. This goal cannot be fully achieved without the de-

velopment of a plan to develop scientific research centres and encourage research.

The third goal is quality health care for all. This does not mean flooding countries with private commercial hospitals and specialized centres for the elite, but developing a comprehensive system of high-quality primary health care, health insurance and social security, mother-and-child care, care for the poor and people with special needs and full concentration on the principles of prevention and healthy life styles instead of wasting resources on medical-biological approaches, which have proven their failure. This entails believing in the simple rule that health is not simply the treatment of illness, but the removal of its causes.

The fourth goal consists in taking the initiative and moving from being reactive to proactive in all walks of life. Democracy, participation and freedom are rarely given. They are most often wrested in the struggle of those who believe in them. This requires that citizens take on the challenges of demanding their rights and calling for sound policies. The same applies to Arab countries in their international relations. Nobody is going to secure their interests for them unless they take the initiative and work for these interests.

Perhaps human development in the Arab world will not be realized without solving the dilemma of effective participation by youth and women. Youth constitutes two-thirds of the Arab world's population. They are mostly denied opportunities to participate and the freedom to innovate and take the initiative. Most women are still marginalized. These two segments of the society constitute a huge human reservoir.

The Palestinian people are perhaps facing the most vicious challenge in their struggle to end aggressive occupation and settlement and to win what all other peoples already have – freedom, genuine independence, sovereignty and the right to their own territory, borders, destiny and future.

A just peace and effective development in our region will not be realized unless the Palestinian people establish a real state with full sovereignty and until the Palestine refugee problem is solved in accordance with United Nations resolutions. The idea of an independent state cannot be transformed into another transitional stage in the form of autonomy without borders or sovereignty. We have learned from experience that avoiding real issues, such as ending the occupation and settlement and the issues of Jerusalem and refugees is only a prescription for more suffering in the future.

While the Palestinian people are struggling to build a national home, citizenship, and real democracy, they have succeeded - in the midst of a ferocious struggle against occupation, and despite huge human sacrifices - in building pioneering human development models, which are copied in many countries. This is due to their positive creative spirit and their rejection of frustration and despair.

The Palestinian struggle is not a conflict between two parties negotiating a difference over percentages. It is the crucial issue of people who seek to achieve what has been achieved by all peoples on the face of the earth: freedom, independence, self-determination and a dignified life in peace and security. This is the natural basis for human development anywhere in the world.

1. UNLEASHING AND GUARANTEEING THE KEY FREEDOMS OF OPINION, SPEECH AND ASSEMBLY THROUGH GOOD GOVERNANCE

Recent history shows that it is undoubtedly possible to achieve significant scientific and technological advances under oppressive regimes, particularly in natural and micro-sciences, and more particularly in the design and manufacture of armaments through strong support and substantial funding by national authorities. Enlightened dictatorships have also hosted knowledge breakthroughs in technical areas, such as economic production, as in the case of South Korea in an earlier period.

But in such cases knowledge gains rarely, if ever, extend into the human and social sciences, the arts or literature. Moreover, gains from targeted knowledge production do not reach all segments of the societies concerned. In other words, knowledge does not permeate the entire society and does not improve people's welfare. An example of this in the Arab world is Iraq; in the wider world, North Korea suggests itself as another case.

Moreover, such knowledge production is not sustainable because society does not have the capacity to continue to provide the necessary resources so long as other elements of the social structure remain weak. The most instructive example in this regard is the former Soviet Union, which collapsed because, among other reasons, it was unable to meet people's basic requirements or to continue to fund its military industries.

From the perspective of human development, scientific advances under oppression are related to the curtailment of social freedoms and choices, which runs counter to the very concept of human development itself.

If Arabs aspire for advanced knowledge in all spheres of creativity and innovation, freedom is a must. If Arabs seek human development through knowledge, freedom is the first and all-defining step.

Thus, freedom and knowledge are central equations of human development. Freedom of opinion, speech and assembly are the *key* freedoms that guarantee other forms of human liberty. A climate of freedom is an essential prerequisite of the knowledge society. These freedoms ensure the vitality of scientific research, technological development, and artistic and literary expression, all of which are means of producing knowledge. They cannot be restricted or curtailed except under very limited circumstances provided for by law, *(that is, after the law is reformed to take into account the provisions discussed below)*, and by the International Bill of Human Rights (IBHR).

The true protection of key freedoms will involve *ridding constitutions, laws and administrative procedures* of every restraint on freedoms of opinion, speech and assembly; it will also require a guarantee that legal provisions and procedures *comply with the IBHR*. In pressing these changes through, lawmakers, jurists and peoples' representatives in Arab countries should not hesitate to model their legislation on that of countries with august traditions in the protection of freedoms[2].

There can be no guarantee of freedoms without the stable rule of law as the only basis for governing all human conduct. Moreover, the execution of the provisions of the law protecting freedoms must be in the hands of an *upright, efficient and genuinely independent judiciary*. It is also imperative to end the era of *administrative control and the grip of security agencies* over the production and dissemination of knowledge[3] and the various forms of creative activity that are the foundations for the knowledge society in Arab countries.

The legislative, executive and judiciary powers of the Arab world have a weighty responsibility to guarantee freedom. But that responsibility does not stop with them. Official and unofficial religious circles have also sought to muzzle freedom of opinion and speech through censorship, banning and libel. It is necessary to recall here a host of Qura'anic injunctions that condemn these practices: "Let there be no compulsion in religion." (*Al-Baqarah*, 256), and "wilt thou then compel mankind, against their will, to be-

A climate of freedom is an essential prerequisite of the knowledge society.

There can be no guarantee of freedoms without the stable rule of law.

---

[2]This may help them atone somewhat for the preoccupation of some with inventing laws and procedures limiting freedoms in previous eras.

[3]Among the crudest forms of this restriction is the limitation of the freedom of researchers in collecting data through fieldwork, which stifles serious scientific research and hobbles solid scholarship in the social sciences and humanities. Not less crude, though, is the banning of views and information opposing the ruling regimes in the official mass media.

The hijacking of
science by politics is
one of the reasons for
the decline of the
knowledge system in
Arab countries.

The battlefield for
freedom is large. . It is
the theatre of
courageous,
groundbreaking and
sometimes fierce
societal engagement
by intellectuals.

lieve?" (*Yunus*, 99). Indeed, if creed is based on free choice, it is only logical that freedom of opinion and speech should not be forced. In that regard, it is helpful to remember "..."Invite [all] to the Way of thy Lord with wisdom and beautiful preaching; and argue with them in ways that are best and most gracious." (*An-Nahl*, 125) and "Wert thou severe or harsh-hearted, they would have broken away from about thee..." (*Al 'Imran*, 159).

These texts provide the authority for a more tolerant and less narrow-minded view of the role of key human freedoms, as sanctioned by Revelation itself.

Knowledge in itself is neutral. It can be used by those in power to serve the interests of authority or it can liberate the weak, the uneducated and the deprived. Science, like art, needs enlightened patrons and champions to assure its independence. Those who carry out scientific research cannot afford its costs, yet science cannot be left solely under state authority. For too long, political regimes have sought to control research and educational institutions, particularly those of higher education, and to manipulate scientists either by reward or intimidation. The hijacking of science by politics is indeed one of the reasons for the decline of the knowledge system in Arab countries. It has opened the sector, its programme and priorities to domestic and foreign interference.

This does not mean, however, that the Arab knowledge system should turn in on itself, a move that would set back knowledge acquisition. It rather points to intensifying Arab and international co-operation in knowledge acquisition along disinterested scientific and intellectual principles. It also underlines the essential roles of non-governmental R&D organisations at the national, regional and international levels and the importance of public-private partnerships for the advance-

ment of research and education.

This Report has exposed the harsh, and severely polarised, societal environment surrounding science and scientists in the Arab world. The difficult choice facing many scientists and scholars in these countries is whether to be "intellectuals", i.e., thinkers, adopting science and knowledge as a means of liberating the weak and advancing the nation; or to be affiliated with the status quo, the ruling regime or even foreign interests in one degree or another. Scientists and scholars who enlist in current power structures, in the region or abroad, enjoy significant financial and political benefits. "Intellectuals" on the other hand, often lack recognition and remuneration and are frequently marginalised by the authorities[4].

It is natural that those who opt to be dedicated intellectuals and socially responsible scientists are few, and that those who persevere on this path are even fewer. Yet the results of this quandary have cost Arab societies dearly. They have, in effect, caused these societies to forfeit the noble mission of science and knowledge as a means of liberation and progress, and have thus brought about the decline of human development in the region.

In other words, society has a massive stake in guaranteeing intellectual freedom. The expansion of freedom in Arab countries begins, first and foremost, with a dedicated effort by its first beneficiaries, i.e., the intellectuals and the producers of knowledge. So long as these groups are silent, complacent or indifferent about their own scope, the cause of intellectual freedom will lack credible advocates. The battlefield for freedom is large. It is the theatre of courageous, groundbreaking and sometimes fierce societal engagement by intellectuals and producers of knowledge. Individual actions matter, but an organised campaign centred on avant-garde knowledge organisations is likely to be more successful.

Freedom, as a human entitlement, requires societal structures and processes that create it and protect it at the same time, while nurturing its growth and advancement. Those structures and processes are epitomised in systems of good governance and embodied in the *con-*

BOX 9.2

Judge Al-Djorjani (290-366 A.H.): The Dues of Science

I would not have given scholarship its due, if, whenever a temptation presented itself, I used scholarship for my own ends. If scholars preserve scholarship, scholarship will protect them. If they glorify scholarship, it will become august. But they have abused scholarship and in so doing they have debased themselves. They have smeared its face with greed until it frowned.

---

[4] The choice is perhaps most difficult in the social sciences and the humanities, with their potential for manipulating minds and masking reality. Yet serious social science is a difficult profession and one that is unrewarded in backward societies. The true scholar in this field seeks to spread his/her ideas for which there are no outlets save the mass media, which are often muted under heavy authoritarian control.

certed efforts of the state, civil society and the private sector. Good governance is based on the following tenets (First AHDR):

• It protects freedom in a manner that ensures the expansion of people's choices.

• It is built on full representation of all the people.

• It is fully institutional.

• Its institutions function with efficiency and complete transparency.

• Its institutions are subject to effective accountability, under the division and balance of power, directly by the people at large through periodic, free and upright elections to parliamentary representation.

• Just law, protecting freedom and rights, prevails equally over all.

• A just, efficient, and totally independent judiciary implements the law.

When all of these elements of good governance are in place, freedom cannot perish, but if even one is absent, it remains at risk. Noticeably, the peaceful rotation of power is both safeguarded and guaranteed by these underpinning tenets.

Good governance guarantees the rationality of decision-making, which in the first instance serves human development. It also increases the demand on knowledge by all social sectors, which pushes the knowledge system forward.

Since Arab governance is quite far removed from the prescribed model, its character as a prerequisite for freedom would seem to make the latter unfeasible, if not impossible. But a more appropriate reading of this link is that neither good governance nor freedom will be achieved without a long, hard and dedicated struggle. Yet history, demography and the majority of Arab people are on the right side of that struggle, and the opponents of this growing movement would do well to weigh the consequences of further delaying the march towards greater freedom in the region.

2. DISSEMINATING HIGH QUALITY EDUCATION TARGETED ON EDUCATIONAL OUTCOMES AND LIFE-LONG LEARNING

A Greek saying (Protagoras) underscores that man is the measure in all things. Human de-velopment embodies this principle from beginning to end. Human beings are the creators and carriers of human development and knowledge is the capability that empowers them to be both. Yet if knowledge is to be acquired for this purpose, Arab countries will have to undertake deep and serious reform of the educational system. The following guidelines point to the chief priorities:

Improving learning in early childhood

Seeds planted in early childhood will influence the quality of knowledge that a society harvests more radically than any comparable investment, while encouraging the blossoming of new generations of intellectually open, active and talented citizens.

This objective can be achieved by extending education to the early stages of childhood and *into* Arab households. This entails broadening educational systems to focus on the cultivation of talents during the early years of life. It is crucial, however, to ensure that educational systems are not heavy-handed and do not place additional fetters on the growth of human talent at this critical stage, since child development depends on rich mental and emotional stimulation (first AHDR). Recourse should be made to the best international practices and experiences in early childhood learning, in parental education and in sound principles and techniques of pedagogic nurturing. Another thrust is to provide fresh and stimulating educational materials for infants and young children *inside the family*, using ICT, audio-visual media and other modern learning tools.

Universal basic education for all, extended to grade ten at least

This step begins with eliminating all forms of deprivation from basic education, notably those suffered by weaker social categories: girls and the poor.

Extending this approach will require creative solutions leading to the development of an alternative educational system that can produce more efficient and higher quality education, and at an appropriate cost. This is an area open to more research, as well as to more social and financial investment, including the scrutiny and reallocation of public budgets.

If knowledge is to be acquired for this purpose, Arab countries will have to undertake deep and serious reform of the educational system.

Seeds planted in early childhood will influence the quality of knowledge that a society harvests more than any comparable investment.

Creating an efficient system for life-long learning

An institutional system for adult education (continuous education) that is highly flexible and ever developing is required to achieve two goals: to combat effectively all forms of illiteracy; and to furnish graduates of the educational system with opportunities to enlarge their knowledge, sharpen their skills and develop the new capabilities demanded by a competitive and constantly changing employment market.

Women merit priority in adult learning, not least because among those many who suffer from illiteracy in the Arab world women are the most affected. To speak of creating the knowledge society in the Arab world is to understand that high illiteracy rates among adult Arabs, especially women, are intolerable. A serious campaign to stamp out illiteracy in the region within the next decade is a task for all Arab countries and joint Arab organisations. This task will require solid planning, qualified and sufficient personnel and the necessary resources to establish effective adult education schemes in every Arab country. With literacy standards falling in the regular educational system, those graduating from that system should also be eligible for remedial coaching. Such an important project is a natural and proper sphere for joint Arab cooperation.

Raising the quality of education at all levels

The quality of education, a long neglected priority in Arab societies, is as important as the availability of education in building the foundations of knowledge. Improving quality will involve inculcating basic capacities for self-teaching and developing people's cognitive, analytic and critical faculties, all of which spur creativity and innovation. It implies a profound reform of Arab educational systems, particularly education methods, which need to become more student-centred, through teams and projects, and more self-evaluating in all dimensions of learning.

Quality assurance also requires adopting *independent* and periodical evaluation of quality at all levels of education, particularly through comparisons among Arab countries and with reference to developed countries as well.

Special attention to improving higher education

Higher education acquires special importance in building advanced knowledge and skills, especially in connection with R&D.

Higher education institutions produce the knowledge workers in a society, notably its R&D scientists, technologists and researchers. They can, if suitably endowed, also become centres of state-of-the-art research and knowledge production themselves. Yet the present state of Arab higher education prevents it from contributing effectively to the creation of a knowledge society.

Four main complementary policies are urgently needed for a serious reform of higher education:

1. **Governance**: The continued responsibility of the state should be affirmed and recast such that higher education is liberated from the domination of both government and the unregulated profit motive. The government's responsibility for higher education does not require higher education institutions to be government owned. In several cases, independent boards with quadripartite representation (the state, business, civil society and academia) could govern higher education through public-private partnerships. The profit motive should be regulated to ensure that the public interest is served, and the creation of non-governmental, non-profit educational organisations ought to be encouraged vigorously.

An independent Arab organisation for the accreditation of higher education programmes would be a major step in this direction. The UNDP/RBAS project on quality assurance in Arab higher education institutions, whose initial results were summarised in Chapter 2, could serve as the nucleus of such an organisation.

2. **Restructuring**: A versatile and flexible system consistent with rapid and ceaseless change in the market for knowledge and jobs should be established in higher education. Such a system should turn out graduates who are capable of continuous self-teaching and of taking their full part in societal progress. Versatility and flexibility are two characteristics that will enable the higher education system to respond to fast changing local and global needs.

In order to achieve versatility, the basic

High illiteracy rates among adult Arabs, especially women, are intolerable.

The government's responsibility for higher education does not require higher education institutions to be government owned.

programmes of higher education institutions should not be replicas of old courses. More attention should be paid to scientific fields and organisational structures that promote knowledge. Such fields include natural sciences and technology development, which receive little attention in the existing educational system. *Higher education should provide individuals with learning opportunities for life.*

In view of the accelerated obsolescence of technical skills in the modern world, *higher education should provide recurrent education to individuals. Collaboration with the state, private business and civil society holds the key.*

Versatility also means an emphasis on the productive function of higher education institutions. This function can boost both the financial and research resources of the institution. Autonomous, multidisciplinary research-and-development centres should be created, in active partnership with the state, business and civil society.

Flexibility, on the *individual* level, means the freedom to drop out and return to various higher education institutions. On the institutional level, flexibility means that the structure of institutions and the content of the programmes they offer are continually revised by review boards to guarantee a quick response to local and international developments. As noted, quadripartite representation in the governance of higher education institutions would be of great value in supporting this type of flexibility.

3. **Expansion**: A great gap still exists between Arab countries and advanced nations in the spread of higher education. This means that, for developing countries, there is no real trade-off between spending on higher or basic education. Both are sorely needed. Building the knowledge society in the Arab world requires the expansion and reform of higher education.

Two important considerations should govern the expansion of higher education: first, it is necessary to end discrimination against weaker social groups, especially young women. Next, account must be taken of the failures of uncalculated expansion in existing institutions, which have led to a tremendous drop in quality. Higher education institutions, old and new, should enjoy high quality, diver-

sity, and flexibility, and should focus on the fields and institutional forms required for scientific and technological progress.

4. **Quality**: A powerful shake-up to improve quality in Arab higher education is long overdue. Quality should be improved in present institutions and no new institutions, public or private, should be created unless they can provide better standards of quality. Independent accreditation organisations should be enlisted to help ensure the quality of higher education programmes.

Rapid and committed implementation of the above would substantially raise the quality and outcomes of Arab higher education. Other priorities that are central to such change are: sufficient and sustained funding for quality education and quality research; improved access to knowledge for students through ICT; and enhanced remuneration for teaching and research staff. None of these measures will however succeed without the overhaul and development of curricula at all educational levels, coupled with appropriate teaching methods that develop critical thinking and creativity.

3. INDIGENISING SCIENCE, UNIVERSALISING RESEARCH AND DEVELOPMENT (R&D) IN SOCIETAL ACTIVITIES AND KEEPING UP WITH THE INFORMATION AGE

The limited achievement of Arab countries in the fields of science and technology is an outcome of several factors: the illusion that importing technology as embodied in products and services is equivalent to aquiring knowledge; policy neglect of basic research in the region, reflected in its under-estimation and under-funding; *rentier* science and technology importation; the weakness of national knowledge systems, and, on the regional level, insufficient Arab co-operation. A serious programme to confront the current crisis must follow a dual strategy: internal reform in every Arab country, on the one hand, and deepening co-operation among Arab countries in R&D on the other.

The process of adapting and localising technology starts with leadership reflected in a

For developing countries, there is no real trade-off between spending on higher or basic education.

A powerful shake-up to improve quality in Arab higher education is long overdue.

cogent national science and technology policy to attract private investors and a supportive fiscal and regulatory regime to encourage enterprise development. It requires the expansion and sustained financing of local R&D in target technology sectors and substantial public and private investment in human resources and professional skills development, especially in mathematics, the sciences, ICT and management. It calls for technology management policies for selecting, adapting, creating and commercialising technologies in response to market signals and opportunities for competitiveness. It entails organisational changes within industries and firms to internalise innovations, raise value added and instill flexibility. Above all, local technology development requires a closely networked national innovation system to tie key public, private and international actors together.

Successful adaptation and localisation takes place over a long period of maturation. Nevertheless, late-starters can benefit from global technology by participating in global production chains on the basis of competitive edge. At the same time, they should focus on building agile workforces and sustaining economic, social and technical innovation in order to convert acquired products and processes into new, useful and marketable technologies that serve national and regional human development. Vision, creativity and risk-taking are indispensable to that process.

As part of this process, Arab governments must support Arab R&D centres and technical consultancy firms so that they can grow and offer services comparable to those sought by Arab countries from firms abroad.

Most of what is produced in the Arab world is not competitive with what international markets offer, due to quality and cost considerations. It is essential to accelerate the standardisation of specifications and quality control in the region and to subject all Arab products to those standards.

At the same time, the link between human power and educational institutions on the one hand, and human power and professional associations in Arab countries on the other, is much weaker than the minimum required for the efficiency of the R&D system. This requires establishing and strengthening all forms of pan-Arab connectivity in all fields of R&D development, utilising ICT formats and channels for fast communication.

At the national level, the goal should be to pull together scientific and research systems as a prerequisite for coming together at the regional level in order to benefit from collaboration and economies of integration and scale. To that end, countries need to develop long-term policies on scientific research, reprioritising their budgets to increase funding for R&D and creating triangular cooperation between R&D institutes, universities and industry. Central to such policies is the realisation that various components feeding into R&D must be developed simultaneously. These components include educational systems and standards, basic and applied research institutions, ICT infrastructure, services and information systems, funding institutions, professional societies, consulting services, technical support systems and science education for students and the public at large.

Policies to strengthen the weak articulation between these components of the knowledge system would help Arab countries to consolidate their national knowledge bases and to sustain higher rates of growth and higher rates of technology acquisition.

Technological development in Arab countries should centre on technologies needed in the region, and those where Arabs enjoy a degree of competitive advantage. Technologies related to oil and natural gas, their by-products and to improving their environmental impact are one such group. ICT, renewable energy technologies, such as solar energy and wind, and water desalination are others. The establishment of regional "centres of excellence" in R&D, with research focus areas selected according to country-specific needs or competitive advantages, is a high priority. The benefits that could accrue from these orientations would, of course, be maximised through close and effective Arab co-operation.

The efficient implementation of these policy directions requires essential contributions by the *state* in building the knowledge society. The basic functions of the state include priority setting, designing policies, enacting laws and procedures, providing tax incentives, allocating resources and facilities. The state can also initiate innovation: it could make a major contribution by instituting R&D as a fundamental activity in public, private, state and civil society organisations and enterprises.

Civil society and actors at the household level can play an influential role in establishing and supporting an effective non-governmental institutional structure to stimulate knowledge efforts throughout society as a whole. A step forward would be to modernise and energise the traditions of *zakat* (alms giving) and *wakfs* (religious endowments) to build human development.

Some specific suggestions for public and private action, already tried with some success, include: creating national business councils to provide a common interface with multinational firms and investors; financing R&D, either through grants to non-profit organisations or through soft loans to profit-seeking enterprises, payable only when the R&D activity increases business revenues; allocating a percentage of business profits, whether public or private, to finance R&D activities within the enterprise and/or in society at large; outsourcing non-core processes in firms to reduce fixed costs that cannot be recovered over short production cycles; and promoting the start-up and operations of venture capital firms and business incubators.

Keeping abreast of the Information Age

The Arab world needs to join the ICT revolution much more decisively. Yet certain special Arab features call for a special model for ICT development. Perhaps the most important of these is the dimension of language, particularly after the spread of the Internet. Indeed, *the Arabic language can become one of the constitutive elements of an Arab information bloc* that could effectively meet the information challenge faced by Arab countries.

The Arab world is facing the challenge of ICT at a time when it is also confronting an acute economic crisis, a situation requiring maximum care in allocating and rationalising the use of resources. Required as well is a strong commitment to sharing information resources on both the national and regional levels. At the national level, action to popularise ICT as a tool for knowledge acquisition should focus on (a) boosting literacy, especially

BOX 9.3

Lebanon: A Bright Future for Information and Communication Technology?

Lebanon is moving to make ICT a force for development. The Government has made steady efforts to improve local information and communication technology services. Out of many programmes being carried out, two notable programmes became operational in 2001: the student information system of the Lebanese University and the wide area network (WAN). Both programmes aim at improving services offered to students and faculty by providing easy access to information and the ability to perform administrative work electronically from anywhere. Other projects include a UNESCO-supported programme to improve scientific and engineering education through ICT and government initiatives to apply ICT to e-government and the management of state activities.

Considerable attention has been given to promoting the wider use of information and communication technology at national level, including rural areas and connecting them to international organizations. Lebanon signed, for instance, an agreement in February 1999 to benefit from the Euro-Mediterranean Information Society (EUMEDIS), which is a regional programme financed by the European Union. The programme seeks to narrow the information and technological gap in the region through the establishment of pioneering regional projects and networks. The areas of interest cover five main sectors: education; electronic trade and economic cooperation; health; cultural heritage and tourism; and industry and innovation.

A new Lebanese national and regional technological centre commenced its operations in October 2001. It acts as a facilitating network for projects and an open space for high technology companies. On the financing front, the Investment Development Foundation has completed a feasibility study to evaluate the best way to offer necessary facilities and incentives to direct foreign and local investments in the information and communication technology sector.

Source: Country report prepared for AHDR 2.

among women; (b) lowering monopolistic barriers for Internet providers and telecommunications developers; (c) lowering other costs affecting access to the Internet; (d) overcoming restrictions on ICT access by gender, economic capability, geographic location or social conditions; (e) using ICT as a tool for life-long learning.

At the regional level, *a strong pan-Arab information policy* could be founded on the following strategic principles:

• Adopting a supra-sectoral approach, i.e., policies that respond to the growing integration of the information, media and telecommunications sectors.

• Adopting a cultural approach to the information industry while recognising the computerisation of the Arabic language is a basic springboard for Arab ICT development and applications.

• Emphasising Arab information integration, especially the principle of sharing resources and data.

• Giving priority to the utilisation of ICT in the fields of education, training, and public health and building an infrastructure for the Arab cultural industry.

The Arab world needs to join the ICT revolution much more decisively.

• Developing concrete regional action plans for ICT development, with visible, high-level government, donor and private sector support.

4. SHIFTING RAPIDLY TOWARDS KNOWLEDGE-BASED PRODUCTION

In Arab countries, even in non-oil countries, the socio-economic structure is dominated by a *rentier* mode of production and behaviour. In this mode, economic value depends on depleting exhaustible natural resources. Moreover, contrary to popular impressions, most Arab countries and most Arabs are not rich. The first AHDR noted that all Arab GDP combined does not exceed that of a single medium-sized European country such as the Netherlands or Spain.

Furthermore, the distribution of economic returns, whether from income or wealth, is not by any means motivated by merit or need; rather, it is often based on narrow loyalties and favouritism. Such a value system does not encourage productive work, let alone knowledge production. Add to this the restrictions on freedoms and the penalties for expressing independent opinion discussed previously, and the formidable gauntlet that Arab knowledge production must run becomes quite apparent.

Arab countries, therefore, have little choice but to pursue deep reforms in their social and economic structures in order to lay better foundations for the knowledge society. The central goal will be to shift to a higher value added structure of production.

In economic terms, that shift would begin with:
• Moving quickly to the upstream or downstream ends of processing in the oil and natural gas industry, which require higher skills and generate more value-adding activities than present turnkey operations.
• Recognising that total reliance on non-renewable oil rents is a rapidly diminishing prospect, and thus investing state resources in diversifying economic structures and markets and developing renewable resources through knowledge and technological capabilities.

This shift will require a stronger Arab presence in the *new* economy where value added is higher and grows faster. As economic activities grow, they create new knowledge as a basis for economic value, thus establishing a dynamic virtuous cycle between knowledge and growth.

Such a transformation, in turn, calls for the intensification of R&D efforts and a sharp focus on technology. Higher education institutions can spearhead this technological shift, as was the case with universities in Brazil and Malaysia, for instance. The state, the business sector and higher education institutions should unite to build consultancy and technology-launching centres and to create an atmosphere conducive to knowledge production through innovation. This large task ought to become a major 'societal project' in every Arab country.

A successful transition to new patterns of knowledge production is contingent on establishing all pillars of the knowledge society set out in this chapter.

5. ESTABLISHING AN AUTHENTIC, BROADMINDED AND ENLIGHTENED ARAB GENERAL KNOWLEDGE MODEL

Effective contribution to human knowledge is not foreign to Arabs or to Arab civilisation, as several aspects of this Report have, hopefully, demonstrated. Nevertheless, regaining this eroded capacity will mean consciously overcoming legacies from the era of decline that still cling on stubbornly today. The establishment of an authentic, broadminded, and enlightened Arab general knowledge model requires essential reforms in the societal context in Arab countries. These reforms are summed up in the following five actions:

Delivering pure religion from political exploitation and honouring ijtihad (scholarship)

Pure religion is innocent of any negative disposition towards knowledge acquisition. The Arab scientific renaissance in the past is clear testimony to that; in fact, at that time a strong synergy developed between religion (Islam) and science as pointed out in Chapter 1.

Nonetheless, what applies to pure religion does not necessarily apply to religious institutions and religious interpretations. There has been enlightened and regressive religious interpretation, the latter increasing after the doors closed on true scholarship.

Over the 20th century, religion, as an Arab institution, lost its institutional distinction and relative independence. This happened with the rise of modern, centralised states that grew and expanded at the expense of relatively independent civil society institutions – a process that ran from the mid-19th century until the mid-20th century. These states then took large leaps towards domination during the second half of the 20th century.

With these last leaps, the modern central state became, and remains, virtually the only societal organisation, pushing non-governmental institutions into the margins of society. The state's approach to these institutions has varied: some were simply abolished, as in the case of the endowments, others were subjected to control and close monitoring, as in the case of NGOs. A third group was annexed, as in the case of universities.

Thus, religious institutions became either state-affiliated, as mosques managed by the state over the past 20 years in particular, or annexed to the state, as was the case with Al-Azhar, religious institutes and Sufi groups. The state and its other agencies evolved as the source "guiding" the outlook of religious institutions on social and political reality. In effect, that outlook then defined the standpoint from which religious jurisprudence proceeded and according to which religious interpretations are issued.

This resulted in the ousting of religious thought incompatible with, or actively opposed to state influence over pulpits. Yet it is precisely such ousted religious thinking that has had the greatest appeal to people, that has come closest to their hearts and influenced their religious consciousness on the spiritual, intellectual and sometimes the political levels.

Emphatically, the restoration of the independence of religious institutions would reinstate their genuine role and strongly empower religion as the protector of the people's interests.

As stressed in the Report, pure religion (Islam) provides great incentives for knowledge acquisition. It is the political, and even commercial, exploitation of religion that have contributed to weakening the quest for knowl-

---

> **BOX 9.4**
> ### Imams (religious leaders) advocate ijtihad (scholarship)
>
> *Abu Hanifa*: "This is the best I have seen; nonetheless, he who provides better would be accepted by me."
>
> *Malik*: "I am but a human being who both errs and says correct things, so look into my opinions."
>
> *Ibn Hazm*: "It is not permissible for anyone to imitate a live or a dead person; everyone has the right to practise scholarship as much as he can."
>
> *Jalal Ed-Din As-Syouti*: "A Response to Those Who Became Idle and Did Not Realise that Scholarship is, in Every Age, a Duty." (Title of work)

> **BOX 9.5**
> ### Al Kawakibi, (1884-1902), on the need for religious reform
>
> All Orientals, be they Buddhists, Muslims, Christians, Jews or otherwise, urgently need sages who are not swayed by the foolishness of the stupid and the careless, nor by cruel, ignorant rulers. We need sages who revive the investigative study of religion, thus restoring the lost aspects thereof, and refining it from any false impurities – which normally attach to any old religion. Thus, each religion needs innovators who restore it to its pure, uncon-taminated origins that can reinstate human will and human happiness; those origins that mitigate the misery of despotism and slavery; those origins that provide insight into correct methods of education and learning, and that prepare its followers for the basics of good upbringing and stable morality – all of which makes people human, and with which people become brothers and sisters.
>
> Source: The Character of Despotism, pp 97-98.

---

edge in Arab countries.

This conclusion is not directed solely, as some may imagine, at certain fanatical political Islamic movements. It applies as well to some Arab governments, societal forces and even certain traditional religious institutions, which have used religious exegesis to secure their dominion or reproduce their hold on the Arab people. The essential point is that the exploitation of religion, for objectives far removed from its sublime purpose and soul, can no longer be tolerated if Arab society is to free itself to build a living knowledge society.

In Arab countries where the political exploitation of religion has intensified, tough punishment for original thinking, especially when it opposes the prevailing powers, intimidates and crushes scholars. Penalties can amount to accusations of heresy, a license to kill offenders or the separation of spouses. Small wonder, then, that scholarship shrinks in the repressive grip of religion perverted from its true course.

Another aspect of the dominant climate of belief that calls out for action is the culture of myths, widespread in Arab countries. It often leads to the publication of worthless books and tabloid journalism, cloaked in religion yet

The exploitation of religion, for objectives far removed from its sublime purpose and soul, can no longer be tolerated.

In Arab countries ... tough punishment for original thinking, especially when it opposes the prevailing powers, intimidates and crushes scholars.

far removed from it. Texts that prey on superstition close the minds and spirits of men and women who have been denied education – and even of some educated classes – to genuine understanding and knowledge.

Advancing the Arabic language

Language is the reservoir of knowledge in general, and a people's mother tongue is the main medium for their creativity and knowledge production. Historically, the Arabic language has proved itself capable of expressing and addressing the deepest, finest, most complex and most nuanced aspects of knowledge. As this Report has emphasised, the major movement of translation into Arabic was closely linked to, and motivated by, an eminent scientific school fully capable of producing knowledge.

Such a language has the structures, flexibility and potential to propel Arabs into the age of information and knowledge-intensity and to sustain their position there. Yet grave dangers beset the Arabic language today and threaten to extinguish the great opportunity it represents for Arabs to build their own knowledge societies.

Advancing the Arabic language entails moving on several fronts. The present discourse on the Arabic language has become sterile. It should be succeeded by a more comprehensive, profound and discriminating perception of the Arabic language system, whether concerning its interdependent internal elements, or their strong relationship with other systems in society. Moving towards the knowledge society is an opportunity to speed up linguistic reform, taking advantage of new developments in linguistic science.

The *Arabisation of university education* is a further priority, not for reasons of nationalism per se, but as a prerequisite for developing native tools of thought, analysis and creativity. Arabisation of higher studies will also accelerate the social assimilation of rapidly changing and advancing knowledge, a marked feature of the knowledge society. Moreover, so long as the sciences are not taught in Arabic, it will be difficult to build bridges between the various disciplines. But it is absolutely critical that efforts to Arabise knowledge proceed in tandem with the improvement of foreign language teaching in all fields of knowledge. Both avenues of knowledge acquisition must be kept open.

Promoting Arabisation also requires a new outlook on the mechanisms of word-construction; encouraging writing in Arabic in various scientific fields; supporting machine translation and using information technologies to build terminology banks and to analyse the conceptual structure of Arabic words so that foreign terms pass into Arabic with maximum fidelity to the concepts they contain.

Perhaps the best way to advance the Arabic language in general is through working to construct a simplified Arabic standard. Some specific suggestions follow:
• One proposal in this regard is to initiate a creative composition movement for young children: a movement conducted by renowned, capable writers able to tame, simplify and modernise the language without sacrificing its inherent values. Success would give new generations of Arab writers and readers a vibrant medium for producing Arab works with new vistas and inspiration.
• Related to this, the inauguration of serious research in Arabic language studies, preferably on the pan-Arab level, is a key priority. Arabic linguists should participate with specialists in other disciplines to:
  • Compile specialised, functional dictionaries and thesauruses. These could be espe-

The best way to advance the Arabic language in general is through working to construct a simplified Arabic standard.

BOX 9.6

Teaching medicine in Arabic is possible!

Medicine is, perhaps, as many see it, the most difficult discipline to teach in Arabic. Yet in 1919 the Arab Medical Institute was reopened in Damascus after a committee passed a draft law comprising 12 Articles, one of which provided that teaching be conducted in Arabic.

The Faculty of Medicine then produced a thesaurus of medical terms in Arabic, consisting of 14,534 terms. This dictionary was critically reviewed by the President of the Arabic Academy, and professor of endocrinology at the Faculty of Medicine at the time. Recommended amendments and additions were then compiled in a large volume containing 1,102 pages and published in 1983. Eventually, the Unified (Arabic) Medical Dictionary was compiled in co-operation with the WHO regional office.

During the period 1970-1991 the Faculty of Medicine, Damascus University, graduated 1,442 specialists, all of whom had studied medicine, and pursued graduate studies, in Arabic.

More than one Arab conference has been held to consider teaching medicine in Arabic:
• The Regional Convention for the Arabisation of Medical Teaching in Arab Countries (Cairo, 17-20 June 1990). Out of this convention emerged The Standing Committee for the Follow-up on Arabisation in medicine.
• The Conference on the Arabisation of Medicine and Medical Sciences in the Arab World (Bahrain, February 1993).

The proceedings of these conferences were strongly in favour of teaching medicine in Arabic, without neglecting foreign languages, and recommended Arab co-operation in this regard.

Source: The Conference on the Arabisation of Medicine and Medical Sciences in the Arab World (Bahrain, February 1993).

---

cially useful in the production of materials for children and educational curricula, in addition to specialised scientific materials.

• Cast scientific terminology in Arabic and coin derived terms free from obscurities.

• Conduct research to facilitate Arabic grammatical rules and simplify their terminology.

• Write general books on Arabic grammar transcending national curricula to present models that show how to teach correct language without excessive reliance on rules.

• Facilitate the acquisition of correct Arabic via various formal and non-formal learning channels.

• Encourage the computerisation of the Arabic language.

• Enrich the Arabic content of information networks and websites.

Renovating the Arab general knowledge model: the past as inspiration for the future

Among the ironies of the present Arab reality and the reasons for its knowledge deficits today is the fact that the creativity and thirst for knowledge that produced ancient renaissances has not been allowed to live on in present-day society. Current tendencies do not spur Arabs to assume their place in the global knowledge society or reclaim their best historical influences. On the contrary, those influences only surface briefly in ceremonies and celebrations, reflecting empty pageantry, and are either quickly forgotten or relegated to museums and the pantheon of memory.

A resolute and concerted effort is required to revive, in a forward-looking manner, sources of illumination in the Arab knowledge heritage, and to encourage those sources to irradiate the Arab general knowledge model, particularly through the mass media and institutions of modern education. This effort has nothing to do with nostalgia. Rather, it is about stimulating the genuine comprehension and re-assimilation of those cultural values, mind-sets and intellectual currents that can nurture a modern Arab knowledge renaissance.

BOX 9.7

Paul Alvarus[5]: Mother Tongues

Christians love to read the poems and romances of the Arabs; they study Arab theologians and philosophers, not to refute them but to form a correct and elegant Arabic. Where is the layman who now reads the Latin commentaries on the Holy Scriptures, or who studies the Gospels, prophets or apostles?

Alas! All talented young Christians read and study with enthusiasm the Arab books; they gather immense libraries at great expense; they despise Christian literature as unworthy of attention. They have forgotten their own language. For every one who can write a letter in Latin to a friend, there are a thousand who can express themselves in Arabic with elegance.

Source: (Menocal, 2002, 66).

Enriching, supporting and celebrating cultural diversity in the region

From the perspective of the International Bill of Human Rights (IBHR), a respected perspective in itself, minorities enjoy inalienable rights that protect their cultural and religious specificity. In addition, the IBHR had become inseparable from the legal structure of the many Arab states that have ratified the international conventions and charters concerned, which makes its provisions binding.

However, above and beyond safeguarding rights – a supreme human end –cultural diversity offers any society incomparable advantages when it comes to building knowledge. "A single flower does not a garden make, nor does a single bird bring spring." Beauty and bounty are the result of diversity. Cross-fertilisation gives birth to strong offspring, whether in nature or in knowledge.

Each Arab country represents an extraordinary cultural and knowledge mix that, through cross-fertilisation among ethnic, religious and social groups, could contribute to the enrichment of Arab societies across the region. An Arab Free Citizenship Area encouraging the interaction of all symbolic structures, ideas and their human carriers in the Arab world would realise dividends even larger than those ensuing from the integration of commodities and capital. Entrance to the world knowledge society from this strengthened base would substantially enhance both what Arabs can contribute to, and what they can acquire from the new age.

A resolute and concerted effort is required to revive, in a forward-looking manner, sources of illumination in the Arab knowledge heritage.

---

[5]Respected Christian luminary of Cordoba in the mid-9th century. Quote is from his famous polemical work, The Unmistakable Sign (Menocal. 2002, 66-67).

Opening up to other cultures

No civilisation in history has ever flourished without interacting creatively with other centres of human advancement, past or contemporary.

The Arab-Islamic culture at its zenith was a role model for borrowing and assimilation, followed by generous giving when it established its distinguished knowledge edifice. What is known nowadays as "Western" knowledge is itself an accumulation of human contributions throughout history, to which the Arab world contributed when the Arab-Islamic civilisation flourished, and afterwards through the Library of Alexandria. As world citizens, as contributors to the global stock of knowledge and as seekers of new knowledge, the Arab peoples can, and should, embrace all opportunities to understand and relate to other cultures in the West and in the developing world.

Translation into Arabic and other languages

Translation is a wide bridge for transferring and localising knowledge. As argued elsewhere, the Arabisation of learning and a return to a vigorous movement centred on translating works from other languages hold the keys to rapid knowledge acquisition and assimilation. This movement is also linked to indigenising science and technology and rebuilding Arab R&D. The Arab world needs to regain its historical prowess in translation as part of opening itself to new cultures and as a prerequisite for building the knowledge society.

Translation from Arabic is a different issue; it is currently limited to a few literary works and essentially depends on personal connections and chance. Important transla-

tions from Arabic await a critical mass of quality knowledge production by Arabs, as was the case historically in Andalusia.

In advancing cultural interaction, Arabs living abroad and the citizens of other countries of Arab origin – many of whom are highly qualified – can be indispensable connectors between the Arab world and other societies. Expatriate Arabs often benefit from relatively free societies and enjoy better access to knowledge and ideas than their counterparts in the region. They can be among the outriders of a networked Arab knowledge renaissance. But Arab countries must undertake to support the Arab Diaspora consciously through explicit channels. This can take various forms: establishing up-to-date, computerised rosters of expatriate Arabs; creating attractive, regular means of communication through the use of ICT; and providing facilities for Arab expatriates to visit and work in *all* Arab countries, as well as supporting Arab culture in countries that host Arab emigrants.

Arab countries can also establish know-how transfer programmes that allow expatriate Arabs to undertake short, intensive consultancies and business advisory services. Models for such programmes exist in the work of UNDP and other international organisations. Arab countries can also sponsor ICT virtual networks among expatriate Arabs and those desiring to benefit from their knowledge and expertise in Arab countries. The fostering of organisations specifically designed to bring expatriate Arabs together will institutionalise two-way ties between emigrants and their countries of origin.

An intelligent way to benefit from non-Arab civilisations

This Report has adopted a wide definition of knowledge as the arterial system that connects all human actions and symbolic structures in human cultures. It has therefore not limited knowledge to scientific production alone but taken a broader view encompassing all the sciences, arts, literature and even values, habits and customs in both formal and folk culture.

Civilisational cross-fertilisation is a sure way to enrich knowledge on both sides of the exchange. Yet Arabs today seem content to accept a passive, one-way relationship with

> No civilisation in history has ever flourished without interacting creatively with other centres of human advancement, past or contemporary.

> The Arab world needs to regain its historical prowess in translation.

BOX 9.8

Ibn Rushd (Averroes), (1126-1198 AD): The Need to Learn from the Efforts of Previous Nations

If we find that the nations which preceded us had a vision and consideration for existing things, depending on the requirements of proof, we must look into what they said on that and what they wrote in their books. Anything of what they said, which complied with the truth, we would take, feel happy with and thank them for. What did not comply with the truth, we should point to, warn against and give previous nations an excuse for (learned people are legally excused if they make mistakes)... Thus, we find that we are legally bound to look into the books of previous nations.

Source: (Ibn Rushd, 1999, P.93.).

---

just one external point of reference and to remain on the receiving end of cultural flows from the West. This is the very antithesis of healthy cross-fertilisation because it leads to the adoption of a poor copy of the other culture.

Relations between Arabs and the West, especially after September 11, have come under intense strain. As noted in this Report, Arabs, Muslims and Islam have since been subjected to defamation and misrepresentation, a reflection in many instances of ignorance and in some cases an expression of unjustified abuse.

While this appears to be growing into more than a difference of opinion, Arabs should not close up to the outside world. From the standpoint of cross-fertilisation and knowledge, American society represents a more enduring source of ideas, cultural resources and values than any single political administration, which is bound to change through democratic processes. Differences at the political level, no matter how intense, should not be allowed to eclipse this all-important fact and to shut the door on cultural dialogue.

The West includes, but is more than the US. Europe represents a pole of values, knowledge and culture that has geographic (the Mediterranean) and historical and cultural ties (especially through Spain) with the Arabs, which need to be invested in for the good of both parties. Cultural, and especially scientific and technological transfers and exchanges, as part of these relations, will further the establishment of the knowledge society in Arab countries.

Arabs need to open up to all cultures, not solely the West. The experiences of the Asian circle and other non-Arab neighbours offer important opportunities for interaction based on a deep common understanding and mutual respect.

Taking full advantage of what regional and international organisations offer and participating in global governance

Regional and international organisations can play an important role in cultural cross-fertilisation between Arabs and other civilisations. Yet Arab countries, as a group and individually, do not benefit from such organisations ef-

fectively, or make optimal use of their services or play a significant role in their governanc. Moreover, the structure of such organisations, where performance has deteriorated in a unipolar world, has reduced the benefits to developing countries of the noble goals of these institutions. To the extent that developing countries, including Arab countries, let disunity and division undermine their representation in international organisations, including the UN, their structures and services will continue to be dominated by other blocs and power interests. Arab countries need to energise their financial, political and technical contributions to regional and international activities, and thus develop a stronger international image while reaping the benefits of closer co-operation and unity through such bodies. This is especially important with respect to those organisations that can contribute to building the knowledge society in the Arab world.

The international architecture of global governance is often weighted preponderantly in favour of the interests of the rich and powerful nations. Without changes that tip the balance of these structures more towards the needs and aspirations of developing countries, including Arab countries, globalisation cannot become a locomotive of human development or a force for the spread of knowledge in the world.

So long as Arabs remain divided among themselves and in disarray, they will not be able to contribute effectively to the rebalanc-

Arabs need to open up to all cultures, not solely the West.

Arab countries need to energise their financial, political and technical contributions to regional and international activities.

ing of systems of global governance and thus nudge these systems into playing their role in facilitating the creation of knowledge societies. Indeed, the present situation can only leave Arabs on the receiving end of an international order that is frequently inequitable and unresponsive to their own objectives in freedom and knowledge.

Building a knowledge society across the Arab world is the only way to lead the region into a renaissance that can change its present course and help all Arab countries to position themselves on a new and much more hopeful curve of development in the region and contribute to a new world for humanity at large. This will require the reengineering of Arab cooperation, and wide restructuring in Arab countries, basing both on full public participation, a key element that has been missing so far. Lack of voice and representation in regional initiatives has greatly reduced the effectiveness and sustainability of joint Arab action.

Bold restructuring by Arab leaders and institutions needs to be supported by sustained, well-designed and efficiently implemented programmes of action for establishing the knowledge society, following the guidelines suggested in this chapter. Committed Arab cooperation can create a Free Arab Citizenship Zone open to all people of the region and a real opportunity for Arabs to participate in globalisation from a position of dignity and strength.

Knowledge lights the lamps that point out the way on the Arab journey to the future. Nothing in religion, culture and history blocks those beacons. On the contrary, Arab heritage declares that knowledge must shine through all the endeavours of humankind. What has blotted out that light is the work of mortals: the defective structures – political, social and economic - that have hidden knowledge from the Arab people and eclipsed its full possibilities. Yet what human beings have wrought human beings can remove, and must, so that the flame of Arab learning can once again burn bright and long in this new Millennium of Knowledge.

References

English References

Amnesty International, 2002. "Israel and the Occupied Territories, Away from the Eyes of the World: The Israeli Defence Force in Jenin and Nablus". International Secretariat, London, November 2002.

Arabic References

'Abduh, M., 1980. "The Complete Works of Imam Muhammad 'Abduh", Part III, Intellectual and Educational Reform and Theology. The Arab Foundation for Studies and Publication, Beirut.

ad-Dajani, S.A., 1994. "Construction, not Oppression: The Renewal of our Civilisation and the Reconstruction of the World – On my Mind". Dar al-Mustaqbal al-'Arabi, Cairo.

al-Afghani, J., 1981. Complete Works, Part II, Political Writings, Study and Examination by Dr. Muhammad 'Amarah, Arab Foundation for Studies and Publication, Beirut.

al-Hajji, F.A., 1995. Bibliography of Arabic Books for Children, second series. Department of Culture and Information, Sharja.

'Ali, N., 2002. "Arabic Informatics: Current Reality and Desired Goals". Second symposium on the Possibilities of Scientific Research and Technological Development in the Arab World. The Arab Foundation for Modern Science and Technology, Sharja, March 2002.

al-Jahez, A.I.B., 1985. "Eloquence and Elucidation", third volume, fifth edition. Maktabat ul-Khanji lit-Tiba'ah.

al-Kawakibi, A.R., 1984. "The Character of Despotism and the Downfall of Slavery", Dar un-Nafa-es, Beirut, 1984 and 1993.

al-Kholi, O., 1986. "Technology and Self-Reliance in the Arab World". Lecture delivered at the 9th Symposium of the Arab Planning Institute: Towards an Arab Development Based on Self-Reliance; Kuwait, April 1986.

al-Nu'aimi, T.T., 2000. "Scientific Institutions in the Arab World and their Role in Scientific Research Activity", paper presented to the Scientific Research Symposium on the Arab World and possibilities for the Third Millennium: Science and Technology, Sharja United Arab Emirates, April 2000.

al-'Orwi, A., 1996. "Arab Contemporary Ideology". The Arab Cultural Centre, Beirut.

al-Qasim, S., 2002. "The Strategy of Science-and-Culture Development in the Arab World: an Analytical Study for Modernisation and Application". Paper presented to the Arab Meeting on the Application of a Science-and-Culture Development Strategy in the Arab World. Sharja, March, 2002.

-------, 1999. "Research and Development Systems in Arab Countries: their Current Situation and New Commitments to Correct Them". Arab League Cultural, Educational and Scientific Organisation (ALECSO) and the UNESCO Office, Cairo.

al-Zayyat, F.M., 2003. "Knowledge Machinery between Acquisition and Activation". Arab Human Development Forum, Arab Gulf University, Bahrain, February 2003.

Amin, G., 2002. "What Happened to Egyptian Culture in Half a Century: 1952-2002?" Points of View, Cairo.

an-Nadeem, I., 1348 A.H. "Al-Fahrast" (Index). The Great Commercial Library, Egypt.

The Arab Organisation for Human Rights, 2002. "Human Rights in the Arab World: Report of the Arab Organisation for Human Rights on the Status of Human Rights in the Arab World), Cairo.

ash-Sharqawi, A.S., 1995. "Intellectual Property Rights: The Basis of Civilisation and Development, Honouring Right and Humanity". Matba'at un-Najah el-Jadeedah, first edition, Casablanca.

at-Tahanawi, M.A., 1995. Index of Arts and Sciences Terminology, Part I, Religion. Librairie du Liban, Beirut.

at-Tahtawi, R.R., 1973. (Complete Works), Part II, "Politics, Nationalism and Education", Study and Examination by Dr. Muhammad 'Amarah, Arab Foundation for Studies and Publication, Beirut.

Badawi, A.R., 1946. "Greek Heritage in Islamic Civilisation", second edition, Maktabat un-Nahdhat el-Misriyyah.

Bahraini Medical Association and the Arab Gulf University, 1993. Conference on the Arabicisation of the Teaching of Medicine and the Medical Sciences in the Arab World: Application Steps. Bahrain, February 1993.

Centre for Arab Unity Studies, 2001. Symposium on an Arab Civilisation: Advancement Enterprise. Beirut.

-------, 1985. Symposium on Heritage and the Challenges of the Age in the Arab World. Beirut.

The Donors' Group, Committee for the Coordination of Local Assistance, 2002.

"Assessment of Material and Institutional Damages – West Bank Governorates". March-May 2002.

el-Ansari, M.J., 1998. "Arabs and Politics: Who is to Blame?"). Dar us-Saqi, Beirut.

Fergany, N., 2002. "A Plan Ensuring Education for All: 2003-2015", Sultanate of Oman: General Perspective and Analysis of the Sector at the Beginning of the Plan: Setting Goals and General Orientations. Al-Mishkat, Cairo, October 2002.

-------, 2000. "The Arabs v. Israel: Human and Technological Capacities" Al-Mustaqbal ul-'Arabi (magazine), issue No. 252. Centre for Arab Unity Studies, Beirut, February 2000.

-------, 1998 a. "The Human Impact of Restructuring in Arab Countries". Development and Economic Policies (magazine), Volume I, Issue No. 1, Arab Institute of Planning, Kuwait, December 1988.

-------, 1998 b. "A Future Vision of Education in the Arab World". Al-Mishkat Centre, Cairo, June, 1998.

-------, 1998 c. "The Contribution of Higher Education to Development in Arab Countries". Al-Mishkat Centre, Cairo, May, 1998.

-------, 1994. "Enrolment in Elementary Education and the Acquisition of Basic Skills in Reading, Writing and Mathematics: a Field Survey in Three Governorates in Egypt". Al-Mishkat, Cairo, October 1994.

Galal, S., 1999. "Translation in the Arab World: Reality and Challenge", The Higher Council for Culture, Cairo.

Ghalyoun, B., 2002. "Assassination of the Mind", third edition, Madboouli Library, Cairo.

Hijazi, I., 1994. "Institutions and Organs of Social Research: Training and Consultation in

Egyptian Sociology". National Centre for Social and Criminal Research, Cairo, May 1994.

Hijazi, M., 2003. "The Machinery of Psychiatric Health: Building Human Capacities and Employing them in Humanitarian Development". Arab Gulf University, Bahrain.

Hitti, P., Georgy, E., and Jabbour, G., 1990. "History of the Arabs". Dar Ghandour lit-Tiba'ah wan-Nashr, Beirut.

Hourani, A., 1997. "Arab Thought in the Age of Renaissance". Dar Noufal, Beirut.

Isma'el, S.A., 1997. "Censorship and the Rejected Theatre": 1923-1988, The General Book Authority, Cairo.

Jad'an, F., 1997. "The Past in the Present". Arab Foundation for Studies and Publication, Beirut.

League of Arab States, 2002. The Unified Arab Economic Report.

Masseeh, M.T.A., 2002. "Cultural Representation between Television and Written Material". The Higher Council for Culture, Cairo.

Ministry of Education, State of Bahrain, and the Al-Mishkat Research Centre, Cairo, 2001.

"Evaluation of Mastering Basic Efficiencies in the Arabic Language and Mathematics at the End of the First Cycle (Third Grade) of Basic Education". Educational Research and Development Centre, the State of Bahrain, May 2001.

Raziq, M.A., 1966. "An Introduction to the History of Islamic Philosophy", Maktabat un-Nahdhat el-Misriyyah edition.

Rushd, I. (Averroes), 1999. "The Final Say on the Determination of the Relationship between Islamic Law and Wisdom", preface and analytical introduction by Dr. Muhammad bed al-Jaberi, Centre for Arab Unity Studies, Beirut, second edition, September 1999.

Shihab ud-Deen, A., 2002. "The Scientific and Technological Dimension of the Arab Advancement Enterprise: Advancement and Knowledge Acquisition in the Arab World". A study in memoriam of Osamah Amin al-Kholy.

Tarabishi, G., 1996. "Critique of the Arab Mind" , First edition, Dar As-Saqi, Beirut.

ul-Jaberi, M.A., 1984. "Critique of the Arab Mind: Formation of the Arab Mind". Dar ut-Talee'ah.

BIBLIOGRAPHY

In English & French

Al-Hassan, Ahmad Y. and Donald R. Hill, 1986.
Islamic Technology, An illustrated history. Cambridge university Press, Cambridge and UNESCO, Paris.

Ali, A. A. G. 1998.
"The Challenge of Poverty Reduction in Africa". UNU/AERC Conference on Institutions and Development in Africa, Tokyo, 14-15 October 1998.

Badawi, Abdel Rahman, 1968.
Transmission de la Philosophie Grecque au Monde Arabe. Vrin.

Barro R. J. & J. W. Lee, 2000.
"International Data on educational Attainment: Updates and Implications". CID Working Paper no. 42, April 200

Bizri, Omar, 2000
"Science and technology and socio-economic development in the ESCWA member countries". presented at the Scientific Research Outlook in the Arab World and the New Millennium; Science and Technology, Sharjah, UAE, 24-26 April 2000, paper AV01.

Buri, J. 1988.
"The Nature of Humankind, Authoritarianism and Self-esteem". Journal of Psychology and Christianity, 29:7.

Campbell, Jeremy, 1982.
Grammatical Man, Information, Entropy, Language and Life. A Touchstone Book, Simon & Schuster, New York.

Commission on Intellectual Property Rights, 2002.
"Integrating Intellectual Property Rights and Development Policy: Executive Summary". London, September 2002.

Datt, G., D. Jolliffe and M. Sharma, 1998.
"A Profile of Poverty in Egypt: 1997". FCND discussion paper no. 49, IFPRI, Washington D.C.

ESCWA, 1997.
"Assessment of Research and Development in Selected ESCWA Member Countries: Local Technological Inputs". United Nations, New York, August.

Fergany, N., 2002.
"Poverty in Arab Countries, An Assessment". Almishkat, Cairo, May 2002.
--------------, 1999.
"Science and Research for Development in the Arab Region". Almishkat, Cairo, February 1999.
-------------, 1998.
"Human capital and economic performance in Egypt". Almishkat, Cairo, August 1998

Freedom House, 2002.
"Freedom in the World Country Ratings, 1972-73 to 2000-01". Freedom House Web site.

Harbison, F., 1973.
Human Resources as the Wealth of Nations. Oxford University Press, New York.

Gregorian, V., 2001
Islam: A Mosaic Not a Monolith, President's Essay, 2001 Annual Report, Carnegie Corporation.

Health, Development, Information and Policy Institute (HDIP), 2003.
"Palestine Fact Sheets: Statistics for the Palestinian Intifada, 28 September 2000 - 17 April, 2003".

Hourani, Albert, 1962.
Arabic Thought in the Liberal Age, 1798-1939. Oxford University Press, London.

Hudson, M. C., 2002.
"On the Influence of the Intellectual in Arab Politics and Policymaking". Presented to the Conference in Honor of Professor Hisham Sharabi on the Role of the Intellectual in Contemporary Political Life, Georgetown University, April 26-27, 2002.

Human Rights Watch, 2003.
"Letter to US and Allies Regarding Adherence to Laws of War". Human Rights Watch Web Site (www.hrw.org/press/2003/03/us0319031tr.htm), 19 March 2003 (visited on 7 May 2003).
--------------------------, 2002.
"Human Rights Watch World Report 2002", ME & North Africa.

Inglehart, R. (Ed.), 2003
"Human values and social change, findings from the values surveys". International studies in Sociology and social anthropology, Brill, Leiden. Boston

International Association for the Evaluation of Educational Achievement, 1996.
Science Achievement in the Middle School Years: IEA's Third International Mathematics and Science Study (TIMSS), TIMSS International Study Centre, Boston College, Chestnut Hill, MA, USA, November 1996.
--, 1996.
Mathematics Achievement in the Middle School Years: IEA's Third International Mathematics and Science Study (TIMSS), TIMSS International Study Centre, Boston College, Chestnut Hill, MA, USA, November 1996.

Jacquemond, R., 2003. "Entre Scribe et Ecrivains. Le Champ Litteraire dans L'Egypte Contemporaine". Arles, Actes Sud Sindbad, 2003.

Kauffman, D., A. Kraay and P. Zoido-Lobaton, 2002.
"Governance Matters II: Updated Indicators for 2000-01". World Bank Policy Research Department Working Paper, Washington D.C.

Klein, D. A. (Editor), 1998.
The Strategic Management of Intellectual Capital, Resources for the Knowledge-based Economy Series. Butterworth-Heinemann, Boston.

Lawyers Committee for Human Rights, 2002.
"A Year of Loss; Reexamining Civil Liberties Since September 11", New York.

Maalouf, Amin, 2001.
In the Name of Identity, Violence and the Need to Belong. Translated from the French by Barbara Bray, First North American Edition, Arcade Publishing, New York.

Menocal, Maria Rosa, 2002.
The Ornament of the World, How Muslims, Jews and Christians created a Culture of Tolerance in Medieval Spain. Little Brown and Company, Boston.

Monterey Institute for International Studies, 2002.
"Chemical and Biological Weapons: Possession and programs Past and Present". Center for Nonproliferation Studies web site (http://cns.miis.edu).

Palestinian Initiative for the Promotion of Global Dialogue & Democracy, 2003.
"MIFTAH's Intifada Report: Statistics and numbers documented, 28 September 2000 – 10 May 2003".

OECD, 1999
"Managing National Innovation Systems". Paris

Qasem, Sobhi, 1998.
The Higher Education Systems in the Arab States: Development of Science and Technology Indicators. UNESCO and ESCWA, Cairo, January 1998.

Reid, D., 1990.
Cairo University and the Making of Modern Egypt. The American University Press, Cairo.

Sharabi, H., 1988
Neopatriarchy: A theory of distorted change in Arab Society, Oxford University Press, Oxford.

Schumpeter, Joseph, 1957.
Capitalism, Socialism and Democracy. London.

Sen, A. K., 1999.
Development as Freedom. Anchor Books, London.

Transparency International, 2002.
"Transparency International Corruption Perceptions Index 2002". Transparency International Web site (www.transparency.org)

UNCTAD, 2002.
"Trade and Development Report 2002: Developing Countries in World Trade". United Nations Conference on Trade and Development, New York and Geneva.
-------------, 1997.
"Trade and Development Report 1997". United Nations Conference on Trade and Development, New York and Geneva.

UNDP, 2002.
"2002 Human Development Report". Oxford University Press, New York.
--------, 2001.
"2001 Human Development Report". Oxford University Press, New York.
--------, 1998.
"1998 Human Development Report". Oxford University Press, New York.
--------, 1997.
"1997 Human Development Report". Oxford University Press, New York.
--------, 1994.
"1994 Human Development Report". Oxford University Press, New York.
--------, 1990.
"1990 Human Development Report". Oxford University Press, New York.

UNESCO, 2000.
"Regional report on Education for All". Arab Regional Conference on Education for All, the year 2000 assessment, Cairo, 24-27 January 2000.
----------, 1999.
"UNESCO Statistical Yearbook 1999". Paris.

----------, 1995.
"UNESCO Statistical Yearbook 1995". Paris.

UNESCO Institute for Statistics, 2003.
"Culture and Communication Sector Data available for 1995-1999". UNESCO web site, March 2003.

USAID and John Hopkins University, 2002.
"Report by the US Agency for International Development (USAID) and John Hopkins University, 2002".

Walzer, R., 1962.
Greek into Arabic. Oxford University Press.

World Bank, 2002.
World Development Indicators, 2002. Washington, DC.
----------------, 2001.
"World Development Report 2002: Building Institutions for Markets". Oxford University Press, New York, September 2001.
---------------, 2000.
"World Development Report 2000/2001: Attacking Poverty". Oxford University Press, New York, September 2000.
--------------, 1998.
"World Development Report 1998/1999: Knowledge for Development". Oxford University Press, New York, September 1998.
--------------, 1995.
"Will Arab Workers Prosper or be Left Out in the Twenty-First Century? Regional perspectives on World Development Report 1995". August 1995.
-------------, 1993.
"World Development Report 1993: Investing in Health". Oxford University Press, New York, June 1993.

World Economic Forum, 2002
"The Arab World Competitiveness Report, 2002/2003". Oxford University Press, New York.

World Markets Research Centre, 2002
"The Expanding Universe: Internet adoption in the Arab region, In Focus 2002-Telecoms, Middle East". WMRC web site, 5/8/2003.

In Arabic

Abdu, Mohammad, 1980.
Al-'Amal Al-Kamela l-el Imam Mohammad Abdu [The complete works of Imam Mohammad Abdu]. Part Three, Al-Islah Al-Fekri w-al Tarbawi w-al Ilahyat, [Intellectual and educational reform, and the Divine], Al-Mo'ssasa Al-'Arabia l-el Derasat w-al Nashr, Beirut.

Abdul Massih, Mari Therese, 2002.
At-Tamtheel Ath-Thaqafi Bain AL-Mar'i wa-l-Maktoob [Cultural Representation Between the Visual and the Written]. Supreme Council of Culture, Cairo.

Abdul Razek, Mustafa, 1966.
Tamhid l-tarikh al-falsafa al-eslamia [An introduction to the History of the Islamic Philosophy]. Al-Nahda Al-Masriya Bookshop, Cairo.

Al-Ansari, Mohammad Jaber, 1998.
Al-'Arab w-al Seyasa: Ain Al-Khall? [Arabs and Politics: Where is the defect?]. Dar Al-Saqi, Beirut.

Al-Aroui, Abdullah, 1996.
Al-Ideolojiya Al-'Arabia Al-Moa'serah [Contemporary Arab Ideology]. Arab Cultural Centre, Beirut.

Al-Dajani, A. S., 1994.
'Omran la Toghyan: Tagadodna Al-Hadari wa T'ameer Al-'Alam-Shawaghel Fekria [Prosperity not despotism, Our cultural renaissance and the reconstruction of the world, intellectual concerns]. Dar Al-Mostakbal Al-A'arabi, Cairo.

Al-Jahez, 'Amr Ibn Bahr, 1985.
Al-Bayan w-al Tabyeen. Fifth Edition, Al-Khanji Bookshop.

Al-Hijji, Feisal Abdallah, 1995.
Ad-Daleel Al-Bibliography Li-Kitab At-Tifil Al-'Arabi [The Bibliographic Guide to Arab Children's Books]. The Second group,

Publications of the Department of Culture and Media, Sharjah.

Ali, Nabil, 2002.
"Al-Ma'loomatiyah Al-'Arabiyah Bain Ar-Rahin Wa-l-Marjoo."
["Arab Informatics: Between the Status quo and the Hoped For."]
The Second Seminar on the Horizons of Scientific Research and
Technological Development in the Arab World, held by The Arab
Institute for Sciences and Modern Technologies, Sharjah, 24-27
March 2002.

Al-Afghani, Jamal al-Din, 1981.
Al-'Amal Al-Kamela [The complete works]. Part Two, Al-Ketabat
Al-Seyaseya[Political writings] edited by Mohammad 'Emara, Al-
Mo'ssasa Al-'Arabia l-el Derasat w-al Nashr, Beirut.

Al-Jabri, Mohammad 'Abed, 1991.
Naqd Al-'Aql AL-'Arabi-Taqween Al-'Aql Al-'Arabi [A Critique of
the Arab Mind- Forming the Arab Mind]. Dar Al-Tali'ah, Beirut.

Al-Khouly, Osama, 1986.
"At-Taqana wa-l-'I'timad 'Ala Dhat fi-l-Wattan Al-'Arabi"
["Technology and Self-Reliance in the Arab World."] A lecture given
at the Ninth Workshop held by the Arab Institute for Planning, entitled: Towards Arab Self-Reliant Development, Kuwait, 12 April
1986.

Al-Kwakibi, Abdul Rahman, 1984.
Tabai' al-Istibdad wa Masari' al-Isti'bad, [The Character of
Despotism and the Downfall of Slavery]. Dar An-Nafa'es, Beirut,
1984 and 1993.

Al-Tahtawi, Refa'a Rafe', 1973.
Al-'Amal Al-Kamela [The complete works]. Part Two, Al-Seyasa w-
al Wattaneya w-al Tarbeyya [Politics, patriotism and education],
edited by Mohammad 'Emara, Al-Mo'ssasa Al-'Arabia l-el Derasat w-
al Nashr, Beirut.

Al-Tahanawi, Mohammad 'Ali, 1995.
Kashaf Estelahat al-Fonoun w-al-'Oloum [Glossary of terms in
Sciences and Arts]. Part One, Lebanon Bookshop.

Amin, Galal, 2002.
Maza Hadas l-el- Thaqafa Al-Masriya fi Nesf Karn, 1952-2002 [What
happened to Egyptian Culture in half a century, 1952-2002]. Weghat
Nazar, Cairo, March 2002.

Amnesty International, 2002.
Isra'il wa-l-Aradi Al-Mohtalla, Ba'aidan A'an Anzar Al-'Alam:
Entehakat Geish Al-Defa'a Al-Isra'ili fi Jenin wa Nablus [Israel and
the Occupied Territories, Away from the World's View: Violations of
the Israeli Defence Army in Jenin and Nablus]. International
Secretariat, London, November 2002.

An-Nu'aimi, T., T., 2000.
"Al-Mo'ssasat Al-'Elmeya fi Al-Wattan Al-'Arabi wa Dawreha fe
Nashat Al-Bahs Al-'Elmi" ["Scientific Organisations in the Arab
World and their role in the scientific research"]. A paper presented in
a seminar on: Al-bahs Al-'Elmy fi-l-'Alam Al-'Arabi wa Afak Al-
Alfeyya Al-Thalitha: 'Oloum wa Technologia [Scientific Research in
the Arab World and horizons of the third Millennium: Science and
Technology] Sharjah, UAE, 24-26 April 2000.

Arab Organisation for Human Rights, 2002.
"Hoqooq Al-Insan fi-l-Wattan Al-'Arabi: Taqrir Al-Monthamah Al-
'Arabia 'an Halat Hoqooq Al-Insan fi-l-Wattan Al-'Arabi." ["Human
Rights in the Arab World: The Report of the Arab Organisation for
Human Rights on the States of Human Rights in the Arab World."
Cairo.

Ash-Sharqawi, Abdul Sai'd, 1995.
Hoqooq Al-Milkiya Al-Fikriya: Os Al-Hadara wa-l-'Omran wa
Takreem Lil-Haqq wa-l-Khalq [Intellectual Property Rights: The
Basis of Civilisation and an Honoring of Rights and People.]
Matba'at an-Najah al-Jadeedah, First edition, Casablanca.

Az-Zayyat, Fathi Mustafa, 2003.
"Alyaat Al-Ma'rifa Bain Al-Iktisab wa-t-Tafe'el" ["The Mechanisms
of Knowledge"]. The Seminar on Arab Human Development, Arab
Gulf University, Bahrain, February 2003.

Badawi, Abdul Rahman, 1946.
Al-Torath Al-Younani fi-l-Hadara Al-Islamia [The Greek Heritage in
Islamic Civilisation]. Second Edition, Al-Nahda Al-Masriya
Bookshop.

Centre for Arab Unity Studies, 2001.
"Nadwat Nahw Mashrou' Hadari Nahdawi 'Arabi" ["Seminar on
Towards An Arab Renaissance Project "]. Beirut.
-----------------------------------, 1985.
"Nadwat Al-Torath wa Tahadyat Al-'Asr fi-l-Watan Al-'Arabi"
["Seminar on Heritage and the Challenges of Today in the Arab
World"]. Beirut.

Donors' Co-ordination Committee, 2002.
"Taqyeem Al-Adrar Al-Maddya w-al Mo'ssassya- Mohafazat Al-
Daffa Al-Gharbya" ["Evaluation of physical and institutional dam-
ages- West Bank"]. March-May 2002.

Fergany, Nader, 2002.
"Khitat Daman At-Ta'leem Lil-Jami' (2003-2015), Saltanate Oman:
as-Siyaq AL-'Aam, Tahleel Al-Qita' fi Bidayat Al-Khittah, Tahdid Al-
Ghayat wa-t-Tawajohat al-'Amah" [The Plan of Education for All
(2003-1015), Sultanate of Oman: General Policy, Sector Analysis at
the Beginning of the Plan, Specification of the Goals and General
Orientations." Almishkat, Cairo, October 2002.
-----------------, 2000.
"Al-Arab fi Muwajahat Israel, Al-Qudrat Al-Bashariya wa-t-
Tiqaniya."["The Arabs versus Israel: Human and Technological
Capabilities."] Al-Mustaqbal Al-Arabi, no.252, Markaz Dirasat Al-
Wihda Al-Arabiya, Beirut.
-----------------, 1998a.
"Athar E'adatt Al-Haikala a'ala Al-Bashar fi-l-Beldan Al-'Arabia"
["The Impact of Restructuring on people in Arab Countries"].
Megallat Al-Tanmya w-wl Seyasat Al-Ektesadya, Part One, No. 1,
Arab Planning Institute, Kuwait, December 1998.
-----------------, 1998b.
"Ro'iah Mustaqbaliyah lil Ta'leem fi-l-Wattan Al-'Arabi: Al-
Watheeqa Ar-Rai'eesiyah." ["A Future Vision for Education in the
Arab World: The Main Document."] Almishkat, Cairo, June 1998.
-----------------, 1998c.
"Musahamat At-Ta'leem Al-'Ali fi Tanmiyat Al-Bildan Al-
Arabiya"["The Contribution of Higher Education to Development
in the Arab Countries."] Almishkat, Cairo, May 1998.
-------------------, 1994.
"Dirasat Al-Iltihaq bi-Ta'leem al-Ibtida'i wa-Iktisab Al-Mahrat Al-
Assassiyah fi Al-Qira'ah wa-l-Kitabah wa-r-Riyadiyat, Mas-h Maydani
bi Misr."["A Study on Enrolment in Elementary Education and the
Acquisition of the Basic Skills of Reading, Writing and Mathematics:
A Field Survey in three Governorates in Egypt."] Almishkat, Cairo,
October 1994

Ghalyoun, Borhan, 1990.
Eghteyal Al-'Akl [Assassination of the mind]. Third Edition,
Madbouli Bookshop, Cairo.

Hijazy, Ezzat 1994.
Mo'assasat wa aghezat al-bahs al-e'almy (wa-l-tadrib wa takdim al-
mashoura, wa ghayrahouma, fe al-magal al-egtema'i) fe Mesr
[Research, Consulting and Training Organisations in the social sci-
ences in Egypt]. National Centre for Social and Criminiological
Studies, Cairo, May 1994.

Hitti, Phillip, Edward Gergi and Gabrael Gobour, 1990.
Tareekh Al-'Arab [History of the Arabs]. Dar Ghandour l-el-Teba'a
w-al Nashr, Beirut.

Hourani, Albert, 1997.
Al-Fekr Al-'Arabi fi 'Asr Al-Nahda 1798-1939 [Arabic Thought in
the Liberal Age, 1798-1939]. Dar Nofal, Beirut.

Human Rights Watch, 2001
A Referendum on the National Charter in Bahrain:
A background paper by Human Rights Watch, Feb, 2001.

Ibn Al-Nadeem, 1348 (Hijri).
Al-Fehrest [The Index]. Al-Togarya Al-Kobra bookshop, Beirut.

Ibn Rushd, Abou-l-Walid Mohammad Ibn Ahmad Ibn Mohammad
Al-Andalusi Al-Malki, 1999.

Fasl Al-Makal fi Taqrir ma bain Al-Shari'a wa-l-Hekma men-al-Etesal, m'a Madkhal wa Mokademah Tahlilya l-el-Doctor Mohammad 'Abed Al-Jabri The final say on the link between wisdom and Sharia'a, with an Analytic Introduction for Dr. M. A. Al-Jabry]. Centre for Arab Unity Studies, Beirut, Second Edition, September 1999.

Ismail, Sayyed Ali, 1997.
Ar-Riqabah wa-l-Masrah Al-Marfood, 1923-1988 [Censorship and the Rejected Theatre: 1923-1988], General Book Authority, Cairo.

Jada'an, Fahmi, 1997.
Al-Madi fi-l-Hadir [The Past in the Present]. Arab for Studies and Publications, Beirut.

Jalal, Shawqi, 1999.
At-Tarjamah fi-l-'Alam Al-'Arabi, Al-Waqi' wa At-Tahadi [Translation in the Arab World: Reality and the Challenge]. The Supreme Council of Culture, Cairo.

League of Arab States, 2002.
"Arab Economic Report, 2002".

Ministry of Education, Bahrain and Almishkat Centre for Research, Cairo, 2001.
Taqyeem Etkan Al-Kefayat Al-Asasya fi Al-Logha Al-'Arabia wa-l-Riyadyat E'and Nehayat Al-Halaka Al-'Oula mena Al-Ta'aleem Al-Asasi [Evaluating the Outcomes of Primary Education at the End of the First Stage]. Centre for Educational and Development Research, Bahrain, May 2001.

Qassem, Subhi, 2002.
"Istratijyat Tatweer al-'Oloom wa-Thaqafa fi-l-Wattan Al-'Arabi (Al-Istratijiya Al-'Arabia):" [A Strategy for Developing the Sciences and Culture in the Arab Nation (Arab Strategy)]." A paper presented to the Arab Meeting on the Implementation of a Strategy for the Development of Sciences and Culture in the Arab World, Sharjah, 24-27 March 2002.
------------------, 1999.
"Nozom Al-Bahs w-al Tatweer fi Al-Beldan Al-'Arabia, Wake'ha w-al-Eltezamat Al-Gadida l-Taqwimeha" ["Research and Development Systems in Arab Countries: present state and requirements of reform."] Alecso and Unesco, Cairo.

Shihab Ad-Din, Adnan, 2002.
Al-Bo'd Al-'Ilmi wa-t-Taqani Lil-Mashroo' An-Nahdawi Al-'Arabi, An-Nahda wa Iktsab Al-Ma'rifa fi-l-Wattan Al-'Arabi [The Scientific and Technological Dimension of the Arab Renaissance Project: The Renaissance and Knowledge Acquisition in the Arab World.] Studies in memoriam of Osama Amin el-Kholy, Centre for Arab Unity Studies, Beirut.

Tarabishi, George, 1996
Naqd Al-'Aql Al-'Arabi [A Critique of the Arab Mind]. First edition, Dar Al-Saqi, Beirut.

The Association of Bahraini Physicians, Arab Gulf University, 1993.
Mu'tamar Ta'reeb Ta'leem At-Tib wa-l-'oloom At-Tibbiyah fi-l-Wattan Al-'Arabi, Khotowat Tatbiqiyah [Conference on the Arabisation of Medicine and Medical Sciences in the Arab World: Application Steps.] Bahrain, February 1993.

Annex 1: List of background papers

Annex 1: List of Background Papers

(Author name, paper title, number of pages)

IN ARABIC:

Al-Taher Labib, Scientific Production in the Humanities and Social Sciences, 14

Baqer Alnajjar, the Impact of the Contemporary Social and Economic Formation on Innovation, 7

Taoufik Jebali, Artistic Production and Innovation: Theatre, 6

Hayder Ibrahim Ali, The System of Incentives and Innovation in the Arab World, 5

Khalida Said, The Arabic Language and Knowledge Acquisition, 26

Dina El Khawaga, Governing and the Legal and Procedural Context for the Production and Acquisition of Knowledge, 39

Roshdi Rashed, The Arab World and the Internalization of Science, 23

Rukia El Mossadeq, Towards a Political Government in the Service of the Knowledge Society, 13

Sa'adallah Agha Al Kala'a, Artistic Production and Innovation, Music, 21

Sami Al Banna, The Conceptual Framework, 54

Siham A. Al-Sawaigh, the System of Upbringing (Education) and its Relationship with Knowledge Acquisition in Arab Societies, 26

Shawki Galal, Transfer of Knowledge and Translation in the Arab World, 29

Tarek Al-Bishry, Observations (Comments) on Religion and Knowledge, 8

Taher Hamdi Kanaan, Entrepreneurship and Arab Economic Development, 12, (translated)

Atif Kubursi, The Necessary Conditions for the Transition to a Knowledge Based Society, 14 (translated)

Abd El Hameed Hawwas, Popular Culture and Knowledge Acquisition, 15

Aziz Al-Azmeh, Arab Intellectual Heritage, 22
Aziz Al-Azmeh, The General Intellectual Pattern (Paradigm) in the Arab Countries, the Arab Mind, 6

Imad Moustapha, The Organizational Context for Acquiring Knowledge: Transfer, Administration and Internalization of Technology, 22

Amr Najeeb Armanazi, Scientific Production in Natural Sciences and Technological Development, 40

Fadle M. Naqib, Knowledge and Economic growth, 12

Fowziyah Abdullah Abu-Khalid, Poetry in the Arab World, 17

Clovis Maksoud, Introduction to the Arab Human Development Report 2003, 19

Laila Abdel Majid, Information Media in the Arab States and the Transfer of Knowledge, 57

Mari Rose Zalzal, Freedom and Knowledge between Ordinary and Condensed Time, 14

Mohamed Al-Mili, Cultural Diversity and Acculturation, 18

Mohammed Berrada, Literary Production and Innovation: The Short Story and Novel, 6

Muhammad Hassan Al-Amin, Religion and Knowledge Acquisition, 8

Mohamed Mahmoud El-Imam, Demand for Knowledge, 51

Mohammad Malas, Artistic Production and Innovation: Cinema, 12

Muna Al-Khalidi, Health and Environment in the Arab World, 7

Munir Bashshur, Contemporary Education Systems in the Arab Countries: Their Contribution to Knowledge Acquisition, 38

Nabil Ali, Arabic Language and the Knowledge Society, 16

Hichem Djait, Knowledge in the Arab World: The Problem of the Intellectual Heritage, 13

Atif Kubursi, The Necessary Conditions for the Transition to a Knowledge Based Society, 14

Atif Kubursi, The Socio-economic Context of Arab Society and Economy, 23

IN ENGLISH:

Inglehart R., Arab Development: the World Values Survey, 10

A. B. Zahlan, The Arab Brain Drain and the Promotion of a Knowledge Based Society, 53

Taher H. Kanaan, Entrepreneurship and Arab Economic Development, 8

Annex 2: Designing a questionnaire to sample the opinions of faculty members in higher education institutions.

A questionnaire was designed to explore the opinions of small samples of Arab intellectuals of different ages and both sexes about incentives and obstacles to innovation in the Arab countries and the extent to which knowledge production and societal institutions in the area in question contribute to the promotion of knowledge acquisition. The survey was conducted under the auspices of UNDP offices in the Arab countries which host them. The survey also sought to explore the opinions of 96 Arab intellectuals active in public life chosen, for convenience, from members of faculties at the universities in each country. (To ensure fair representation, it was stipulated that 48 cases would be surveyed from the biggest and oldest universities, and 48 from the small and recently established universities.) It was also decided that the sample would be distributed according to three criteria: sex, academic specialization and academic level as follows: half representing the humanities and social sciences, and the second half other sciences. Half men and half women. One quarter from each of the following four academic levels: Assistants - tutors - teachers- primary academic level, associate professors - the middle academic level and professors - the highest academic level. Hence, the intersection of the four criteria would be represented in 32 cells, for which it was suggested that the sample cover three items in each one.

Given that the survey addressed a sample of highly qualified academics, it was not expected that problems which other field surveys usually encounter in the Arab countries would arise since the respondents were well able to respond the questionnaire by themselves. As such it was assumed that the whole process would be limited to sample selection, sending the questionnaires to the chosen intellectuals and ensuring the retrieval of completed forms. However, the report team only succeeded in obtaining the results of the surveys from 15 out of 22 Arab countries. Only three Arab countries (Tunisia, Algeria, and Morocco) succeeded in completing the survey, while the results from the other four countries which responded to the questionnaire fell short of the survey goal: twenty responses from Bahrain, Lebanon, and Sudan, and 39 from Egypt only.

Elements of opinion survey of Arab intellectuals
Arab Human Development Report 2003
Building a Knowledge Society in Arab Countries

Country: ....
General guidelines----------------------

Please circle the right answer when there is more than one option. Please answer briefly, write clearly, and put the numbers in the defined boxes.

Name (optional).........................   **age:** .... year   **sex**: male female
Highest degree: Bachelor Master PhD **Scientific Branch:** .... Specialization:...............
Rank in the academic profession: faculty assistant (tutor, assistant teacher) First level for faculty (Teacher)
                            Intermediate Level (associate professor) Highest Level (Professor)

What is the extent of your satisfaction with the state of knowledge acquisition in your country (1%- 100%) ....%
What is your evaluation of the extent to which knowledge acquisition serves economic development in your country (1% - 100) ....%
What is in your opinion the most important obstacle to innovation in your country? ....
....
Other comments about knowledge acquisition in your country ....
....
Other comments about knowledge acquisition in the Arab countries ....
....

Please evaluate the fields which are embodied in the columns against the nine criteria given in the rows:

Field: (these were the knowledge acquisition/diffusion/production areas selected for the survey).

Criteria: (in each case, concrete criteria illustrative of the field in question were indicated to guide respondents.)

The extent of sufficiency of the right to knowledge in society (1%- 100%)..... ....
The extent of sufficiency of the incentive system for knowledge acquisition in society (1% - 100%) ... ...
The extent to which the field serves human development (1% - 100%) ....
The extent to which cultural diversity in the society is reflected in the field (1% - 100%) ....
The extent to which the field keeps pace with the global state of the art in knowledge (1%-100%) ....
The extent of improvement in the field over the last ten years (1% - 100%) ....

How do you compare the situation in the Arab countries in this field with that in India*?
                                          China?
                               East Asian Tigers?

* 1% to 100% or more than 100% if you think the situation in your country is better. You can put the sign
" - " to denote " don't know"

Statistical Tables on Knowledge in Arab Countries

Table A-1

NET ENROLMENT RATIOS (%) IN PRE-PRIMARY EDUCATION BY GENDER,
ARAB* AND COMPARATOR COUNTRIES, 1999/2000

Country	Males	Females	Total
Arab countries			
Algeria	2.78	2.76	2.77
Bahrain	36.89	35.52	36.22
Comoros	1.79	1.76	1.78
Djibouti	0.32	0.40	0.36
Egypt	10.54	10.00	10.28
Iraq	5.74	5.73	5.74
Jordan	29.21	26.83	28.05
Kuwait	66.03	35.48	65.75
Lebanon	64.92	63.62	64.28
Libya			
Mauritania			
Morocco	59.06	34.21	46.87
Oman	4.54	3.96	4.25
Palestine	34.52	32.45	33.51
Qatar	25.47	24.84	25.16
Saudi Arabia	5.31	4.80	5.06
Somalia			
Sudan			
Syria	8.90	8.03	8.47
Tunisia	11.88	15.71	13.73
UAE	60.77	60.82	60.79
Yemen	0.93	0.76	0.85
Comparator countries			
China			
India			
Israel	75.89	76.07	75.97
Republic of Korea	44.73	44.71	44.73

* Data in shaded cells refer to the year 1998/99.

Source: UNESCO 2003. UNESCO web site (www.unesco.org).

Table A-2

NET ENROLMENT RATIOS (%) IN PRIMARY EDUCATION BY GENDER,
ARAB* AND COMPARATOR COUNTRIES, 1999/2000

Country	Males	Females	Total
Arab countries			
Algeria	98.79	95.59	97.23
Bahrain	92.56	95.48	93.98
Comoros	59.58	49.87	54.78
Djibouti	34.85	26.29	30.59
Egypt	94.96	89.55	92.32
Iraq	100.00	85.66	93.06
Jordan	93.23	93.93	93.57
Kuwait	68.12	64.56	66.37
Lebanon	70.82	71.08	70.95
Libya			
Mauritania	63.04	59.37	61.21
Morocco	78.97	69.81	74.48
Oman	65.60	64.57	65.09
Palestine	98.91	99.38	99.14
Qatar	94.76	95.75	95.24
Saudi Arabia	60.02	55.78	57.95
Somalia			
Sudan	48.60	40.75	44.74
Syria	95.88	88.85	92.43
Tunisia	99.15	97.14	98.17
UAE	77.94	78.56	78.24
Yemen	75.84	44.82	60.71
Comparator countries			
China	91.80	94.67	93.16
India			
Israel	100.00	100.00	100.00
Republic of Korea	96.71	97.91	97.27

* Data in shaded cells refer to the year 1998/99.

Source: UNESCO 2003. UNESCO web site (www.unesco.org).

Table A-3

NET ENROLMENT RATIOS (%) IN SECONDARY EDUCATION BY GENDER, ARAB* AND COMPARATOR COUNTRIES, 1999/2000

Country	Males	Females	Total
Arab countries			
Algeria	57.26	59.83	58.52
Bahrain	76.93	86.63	81.64
Comoros			
Djibouti			
Egypt	81.29	76.65	79.03
Iraq	39.61	26.04	32.99
Jordan	73.40	78.46	75.87
Kuwait	49.23	50.23	49.72
Lebanon	67.21	73.34	70.24
Libya			
Mauritania			
Morocco	32.74	27.04	29.94
Oman	58.32	58.77	58.54
Palestine	74.65	79.27	76.90
Qatar	74.55	81.64	78.01
Saudi Arabia			
Somalia			
Sudan			
Syria	39.21	35.92	37.59
Tunisia	65.86	69.95	67.86
UAE	63.38	72.14	67.46
Yemen	52.08	21.07	36.98
Comparator countries			
China			
India			
Israel	87.35	88.86	88.08
Republic of Korea	94.46	94.24	94.35

* Data in shaded cells refer to the year 1998/99.

Source: UNESCO 2003. UNESCO web site (www.unesco.org).

Table A-4

GROSS ENROLMENT RATIOS (%) IN TERTIARY EDUCATION BY GENDER, ARAB* AND COMPARATOR COUNTRIES, 1999/2000

Country	Males	Females	Total
Arab countries			
Algeria			14.98
Bahrain	19.60	31.13	25.20
Comoros	1.26	0.92	1.09
Djibouti	0.39	0.33	0.36
Egypt			39.00
Iraq	17.46	9.49	13.57
Jordan	26.76	30.63	28.62
Kuwait	13.01	29.98	21.08
Lebanon	35.22	38.15	36.67
Libya	51.74	50.58	51.17
Mauritania			5.60
Morocco	10.59	8.04	9.34
Oman			
Palestine	26.96	24.89	25.95
Qatar	13.68	46.16	27.66
Saudi Arabia	19.59	25.35	22.44
Somalia			
Sudan	7.14	6.56	6.85
Syria			6.09
Tunisia	19.58	19.00	19.30
UAE			12.10
Yemen	16.65	4.58	10.77
Comparator countries			
China			7.45
India			
Israel	41.75	59.38	50.30
Republic of Korea	90.28	51.97	71.69

* Data in shaded cells refer to the year 1998/99.

Source: UNESCO 2003. UNESCO web site (www.unesco.org).

Table A-5

PUPILS PER TEACHER RATIO BY EDUCATION LEVEL,
ARAB* AND COMPARATOR COUNTRIES, 1999/2000

Country	Pre-primary education	Primary education	Secondary education
Arab countries			
Algeria	26.87	28.40	18.06
Bahrain	20.97	17.81	14.27
Comoros	25.93	34.77	10.97
Djibouti	35.67	31.97	21.41
Egypt	24.00	22.98	16.95
Iraq	14.82	21.39	19.74
Jordan	21.88		
Kuwait	15.70	13.78	11.01
Lebanon	14.38	18.69	11.81
Libya	8.36	8.44	7.08
Mauritania		44.99	26.79
Morocco	18.25	28.76	16.97
Oman	19.19	25.08	17.93
Palestine	22.02	31.07	31.61
Qatar	29.05	13.12	10.16
Saudi Arabia	10.48	11.99	12.73
Somalia			
Sudan	29.82	26.72	23.04
Syria	23.54	22.91	14.67
Tunisia	20.41	23.21	19.14
UAE	18.62	16.57	12.81
Yemen	16.55	29.84	14.11
Comparator countries			
China	26.66	19.78	17.11
India		43.00	
Israel		13.39	10.37
Republic of Korea	23.82	32.23	22.13

* Data in shaded cells refer to the year 1998/99.

Source: UNESCO 2003. UNESCO web site (www.unesco.org).

Table A-6

PUBLIC EXPENDITURE ON EDUCATION AS A PERCENTAGE OF GNI,
ARAB* AND COMPARATOR COUNTRIES, 1999/2000

Country	1999/2000
Arab countries	
Algeria	
Bahrain	3.66
Comoros	3.50
Djibouti	3.40
Egypt	4.05
Iraq	
Jordan	5.09
Kuwait	
Lebanon	1.92
Libya	
Mauritania	4.52
Morocco	5.19
Oman	
Palestine	
Qatar	
Saudi Arabia	9.27
Somalia	
Sudan	
Syria	3.53
Tunisia	7.82
UAE	
Yemen	
Comparator countries	
China	2.12
India	2.88
Israel	7.61
Republic of Korea	3.80

* Data in shaded cells refer to the year 1998/99.

Source: UNESCO 2003. UNESCO web site (www.unesco.org).

RELATIVE DISTRIBUTION OF TERTIARY EDUCATION STUDENTS (%) BY LEVELS OF
HIGHER EDUCATION, ARAB* AND COMPARATOR COUNTRIES, 1999/2000

Country	Lower than first university degree	First university degree	Higher degrees
Arab countries			
Algeria			
Bahrain	94.48	5.52	0.00
Comoros	64.29	35.71	0.00
Djibouti	31.05	68.95	0.00
Egypt	94.92	4.40	0.68
Iraq			
Jordan	78.83	20.89	0.28
Kuwait	98.34	0.00	1.66
Lebanon	88.83	10.47	0.70
Libya	64.94	32.56	2.50
Mauritania			
Morocco	92.76	2.06	5.19
Oman			
Palestine	92.76	7.24	0.00
Qatar			
Saudi Arabia	92.80	4.67	2.53
Somalia			
Sudan		.	
Syria			
Tunisia	83.42	10.84	5.74
UAE	100.00	0.00	0.00
Yemen	85.07	14.92	0.01
Comparator countries			
China	51.77	47.49	0.73
India			
Israel	77.75	19.65	2.60
Republic of Korea	58.69	40.29	1.02

* Data in shaded cells refer to the year 1998/99.

Source: UNESCO 2003. UNESCO web site (www.unesco.org).

PERCENTAGE OF FEMALES AMONG TERTIARY EDUCATION STUDENTS (%) BY LEVELS OF
HIGHER EDUCATION, ARAB* AND COMPARATOR COUNTRIES, 1999/2000

Country	Lower than first university degree	First university degree	Higher degrees	Percentage of females in higher education
Arab countries				
Algeria				60.01
Bahrain				41.88
Comoros	33.77	56.47		46.84
Djibouti	23.73	57.25		
Egypt				34.05
Iraq				51.41
Jordan	47.11	67.98	24.62	67.66
Kuwait	67.96		53.64	51.72
Lebanon	53.35	39.22	32.39	48.62
Libya	50.59	45.23	41.98	
Mauritania				42.30
Morocco	43.13	33.05	31.12	
Oman				46.52
Palestine	45.96	53.69	20.00	71.85
Qatar				55.93
Saudi Arabia	55.64	94.78	36.66	
Somalia				47.20
Sudan				
Syria				48.29
Tunisia	49.28	40.13	49.28	
UAE				20.75
Yemen	22.07	13.26	6.25	
Comparator countries				
China			22.10	
India				57.30
Israel	58.12	54.88	51.11	35.18
Republic of Korea	35.10	35.57	23.83	

* Data in shaded cells refer to the year 1998/99.

Source: UNESCO 2003. UNESCO web site (www.unesco.org).

STATISTICAL TABLES ON KNOWLEDGE IN ARAB COUNTRIES

RELATIVE DISTRIBUTION OF TERTIARY EDUCATION STUDENTS (%) BY LEVELS OF
HIGHER EDUCATION, ARAB* AND COMPARATOR COUNTRIES, 1999/2000

Gender	Country/Region	1960	1965	1970	1975	1980	1985	1990	1995	2000
MALES	Algeria	1.19	0.50	1.53	1.77	2.34	2.97	3.95	4.93	5.74
	Bahrain	1.73	1.86	2.37	3.20	3.52	4.12	5.05	5.75	6.27
	Egypt	0.00	0.30	1.16	2.02	3.12	4.22	4.91	5.58	6.32
	Iraq	0.35	0.64	1.19	2.03	2.70	3.38	4.45	5.15	5.41
	Jordan	2.11	2.58	3.36	4.11	4.13	5.33	6.72	7.31	8.34
	Kuwait	2.26	2.34	3.34	3.43	4.60	5.26	6.06	6.68	7.19
	Sudan	0.54	0.58	0.67	0.82	1.02	1.49	1.85	2.20	2.47
	Syria	1.62	2.13	2.66	3.37	4.26	5.06	5.92	6.75	7.12
	Tunisia	0.94	1.13	1.48	1.85	2.83	3.50	4.06	4.60	5.14
	Hong Kong	6.65	6.78	6.82	7.13	7.97	8.53	9.18	10.00	10.09
	Korea	4.58	5.81	6.23	7.22	8.26	9.36	10.47	11.23	11.54
	Taiwan	4.64	5.23	5.86	6.27	7.48	8.07	8.64	9.04	9.32
Average	Arab countries	0.56	0.67	1.35	1.95	2.72	3.57	4.34	5.01	5.61
	Hong Kong, Korea and Taiwan	4.80	5.72	6.16	6.92	7.98	8.88	9.78	10.45	10.73
FEMALES	Algeria	0.76	0.79	0.23	0.49	0.86	1.32	2.07	2.89	3.70
	Bahrain	0.89	0.94	1.08	1.43	2.36	3.16	4.56	5.26	5.81
	Egypt	0.00	0.00	0.01	0.63	1.33	1.67	2.24	2.89	3.76
	Iraq	0.08	0.16	0.33	0.62	0.96	1.29	1.93	2.83	3.25
	Jordan	0.65	0.79	1.19	1.66	1.70	2.52	4.00	5.48	6.35
	Kuwait	1.42	1.34	2.06	2.44	3.76	5.31	5.87	6.40	6.89
	Sudan	0.04	0.04	0.08	0.15	0.28	0.42	0.68	1.05	1.35
	Syria	0.35	0.55	0.67	0.96	1.44	2.03	2.79	3.68	4.38
	Tunisia	0.13	0.26	0.40	0.65	1.01	1.46	1.98	2.57	3.26
	Hong Kong	2.83	3.10	3.44	4.13	5.39	6.42	7.52	8.64	8.83
	Korea	2.04	3.16	3.38	4.38	5.42	6.76	8.08	8.99	9.42
	Taiwan	1.84	2.19	2.63	3.60	5.12	5.56	6.14	6.93	7.69
Average	Arab countries	0.19	0.22	0.20	0.59	1.06	1.46	2.05	2.75	3.46
	Hong Kong, Korea and Taiwan	2.06	2.90	3.18	4.15	5.33	6.39	7.48	8.38	8.88
TOTAL	Algeria	0.97	0.65	0.82	1.08	1.55	2.14	3.01	3.91	4.72
	Bahrain	1.37	1.42	1.82	2.44	3.12	3.78	4.87	5.57	6.09
	Egypt	0.00	0.00	0.57	1.32	2.21	2.93	3.57	4.24	5.05
	Iraq	0.21	0.40	0.76	1.33	1.83	2.34	3.20	4.00	4.34
	Jordan	1.40	1.70	2.29	2.91	2.93	3.94	5.39	6.42	7.37
	Kuwait	2.59	2.41	2.88	3.03	4.29	5.28	5.99	6.54	7.05
	Sudan	0.29	0.31	0.37	0.48	0.64	0.95	1.26	1.62	1.91
	Syria	0.99	1.34	1.67	2.17	2.86	3.54	4.35	5.21	5.74
	Tunisia	0.54	0.71	0.91	1.25	1.92	2.48	3.02	3.58	4.20
	Hong Kong	4.74	4.90	5.11	5.66	6.73	7.51	8.37	9.33	9.47
	Korea	3.23	4.43	4.76	5.77	6.81	8.03	9.25	10.09	10.46
	Taiwan	3.32	3.80	4.39	5.04	6.37	6.87	7.44	8.03	8.53
Average	Arab countries	0.38	0.39	0.76	1.26	1.88	2.51	3.20	3.88	4.54
	Hong Kong, Korea and Taiwan	3.40	4.30	4.68	5.55	6.67	7.64	8.63	9.41	9.80

Source: Barro, R. J. and Jong-Wha Lee (2000)."International Data on Educational Attainment: Updates and Implications". Harvard University, April 2000 (http://www.cid.harvard.edu/ciddata/ciddata.htm, visited on 24 October 2002).

Country	Group	Quality Adjusted MYS 15+, 2000*	Daily news-papers (per 1000 people), 1996**	Radios (per 1000 people), 1997**	Television sets (per 1000 people), 1998**	Scientists and engineers in R&D (per million people), 1990-2000***	Patent applica-tions filed (per million people) 1997**	Number of book titles (per million people), 1990s****	Number of tele-phones mainline, (per 1000 people), 2000***	Cellular mobile sub-scribers (per 1000 people), 2000***	Internet hosts (per 1000 people), 2000***+
Algeria	Arab	2.3	38	241	105		7.9	4.4	57.0	3.0	0.3
Argentina	Other	4.9	123	681	289	711	158.4	324.1	213.0	163.0	7.4
Armenia	Other		23	224	218	1308	6611.1	135.8	152.0	5.0	0.8
Australia	Other	5.7	293	1376	639	3320	2524.1		525.0	447.0	85.7
Austria	Other	4.4	296	753	516	1605	13731.4	994.57a	467.0	762.0	59.0
Azerbaijan	Other		27	23	254	2735	3038.5	55.5	104.0	56.0	0.2
Bangladesh	Other	0.7	9	50	6	51	1.6		4.0	1.0	0.3
Belarus	Other		174	296	314	2296	2552.5	595.4	269.0	5.0	0.2
Belgium	Other	5.0	160	793	510	2307	8494.6		498.0	525.0	29.4
Benin	Other	0.7	2	108	10	174		1.4	8.0	9.0	0.0
Bolivia	Other	2.4	55	675	116	171	14.8		60.0	70.0	0.2
Botswana	Other	3.2	27	156	20		62.0		93.0	123.0	1.5
Brazil	Other	2.1	40	444	316	168	187.7	127.3	182.0	136.0	5.2
Bulgaria	Other		257	543	398	1289	3544.3	629.2	350.0	90.0	2.2
Burkina Faso	Other		1	33	9	17		0.4	4.0	2.0	0.3
Burundi	Other		3	71	4	21	0.8		3.0	2.0	0.0
Cameroon	Other	1.5	7	163	32			3.5	6.0g	10.0	0.3
Canada	Other	6.0	159	1077	715	3009	1767.7	744.8	677.0	285.0	77.4
Central African Rep.	Other	0.7	2	83	5	47			3.0	1.0	0.3
Chile	Other	4.0	98	354	232	370	129.0	94.9	221.0	222.0	4.9
China	Comparator	4.7		333	272	459	48.1		112.0	66.0	0.1
Colombia	Other	2.0	46	581	217		29.9	125.9	169.0	53.0	1.1
Congo	Other	2.2	8	124	12	34			7.0	24.0	0.3
Congo, Dem. Rep.	Other	1.3	3	375	135		0.6	2.2	0.3	0.3	0.3
Costa Rica	Other	3.1	94	271	387	533		366.0	249.0	52.0	1.9
Croatia	Other		115	336	272	1494	151.5	694.7	365.0g	231.0	3.7
Czech Rep..	Other		254	803	447	1317	2968.6	1218.5	378.0	424.0	15.4
Denmark	Other	4.6	309	1141	585	3240	20577.6	2727.4	720.0	631.0	62.9
Dominican Republic	Other	2.1	52	178	95			120.6b	105.0	82.0	0.9
Ecuador	Other	3.3	70	419	293	140	24.6	83.3	100.0	38.0	0.3
Egypt	Arab	2.3	40	324	122	493	17.8	20.8	86.0	21.0	0.3
El Salvador	Other	2.2	48	464	675	19	10.6	105.2	100.0	118.0	0.1
Estonia	Other		174	693	480	2164	19031.4	2332.1	363.0	387.0	28.4
Ethiopia	Other		1	195	5			0.1	7.1	4.0	0.3	0.3
Finland	Other	5.2	455	1496	640		21045.6	2533.3	550.0	720.0	102.3

VALUES OF INDICATORS ON KNOWLEDGE CAPITAL IN 109 COUNTRIES, AROUND THE YEAR 2000

Country	Group	Quality Adjusted MYS 15+, 2000*	Daily news-papers (per 1000 people), 1996**	Radios (per 1000 people), 1997**	Television sets (per 1000 peo-ple), 1998**	Scientists and engineers in R&D (per million people), 1990-2000***	Patent applica-tions filed (per million people) 1997**	Number of book titles (per million people), 1990s****	Number of tele-phones mainline, (per 1000 people), 2000***	Cellular mobile sub-scribers (per 1000 people), 2000***	Internet hosts (per 1000 people), 2000***+
France	Other	3.9	218	937	601	2686	1902.6	660.2	579.0	493.0	19.1
Germany	Other	5.2	311	948	580	2873	2141.4	951.7	611.0	586.0	24.8
Ghana	Other	1.6	14	238	99		1767.0	0.4	12.0	6.0	0.3
Greece	Other	4.1	153	477	466	1045	7777.6	383.7	532.0	557.0	10.5
Guatemala	Other	1.5	33	79	126	103	11.8		57.0	61.0	0.5
Haiti	Other	0.8	3	55	5		1.1	42.0	9.0	3.0g	0.3
Honduras	Other	2.0	55	386	90		21.3	4.1	46.0	24.0	0.3
Hong Kong	Comparator	5.1	792	684	431	93	345.7		583.0	809.0	34.3
Hungary	Other	4.8	186	689	437	1249	3010.5	1035.2	372.0	302.0	10.4
India	Comparator	2.1		121	69	158	10.1	14.0	32.0	4.0	0.3
Indonesia	Other	2.1	24	156	136		21.3	0.6	31.0	17.0	0.1
Iran	Other	2.3	28	265	157	590	6.0	210.3	149.0	15.0	0.3
Ireland	Other	4.8	150	699	403	2132	21955.3		420.0	658.0	29.7
Israel	Comparator	5.7	290	520	318	1570	5057.3	328.2	482.0	702.0	29.5
Italy	Other	4.8	104	878	486	1322	1589.7	562.9	474.0	737.0	17.8
Japan	Other	5.4	578	955	707	4960	3288.5	442.3cd	586.0	526.0	36.5
Jordan	Arab	3.4	58	287	52			5.1	92.0	58.0	0.1
Kenya	Other	1.8	9	104	21		1627.4		10.0	4.0	0.1
Korea, Rep. Of	Comparator	6.2	393	1033	346	2139	2783.3	652.8cd	464.0	567.0	8.5
Kuwait	Arab	2.9	374	660	491	214		115.3	244.0	249.0	1.8
Kyrgystan	Other		15	112	45	574	5123.1	85.7	77.0	2.0	0.4
Latvia	Other		247	710	492	1090	11259.6	907.5	303.0	166.0	10.7
Lesotho	Other	1.8	8	49	25		24741.5		10.0	10.0	0.3
Lithuania	Other		93	513	459	2031	7242.7	1107.3	321.0	142.0	4.8
Macedonia	Other		21	200	250	387	13076.5		255.0	57.0	0.8
Madagascar	Other		5	192	21	12	1635.9	6.8	3.0	4.0	0.3
Malawi	Other	1.4	3	249	2		4418.9		4.0	5.0	0.3
Malaysia	Other	3.5	158	420	166	154	290.6	229.0	199.0	213.0	3.1
Mali	Other	0.3	1	54	12			2.9	3.0	1.0	0.3
Mexico	Other	3.8	97	325	261	213	363.3	70.3	125.0	142.0	5.7
Moldova	Other		60	740	297	334	5889.5	271.2	133.0	32.0	0.4
Mongolia	Other		27	151	63	468	10553.2		56.0	45.0	0.1
Morocco	Arab		26	241	160		10.9	13.0	50.0	83.0	0.1
Myanmar	Other	0.8	10	95	7			4.8	6.0	0.3	0.3
Netherlands	Other	5.0	306	978	543	2490	5699.9		618.0	670.0	101.9
New Zealand	Other	5.8	216	990	508	2197	9246.6	1422.4	500.0	563.0	90.6

Country	Group	Quality Adjusted MYS 15+, 2000*	Daily news-papers (per 1000 people), 1996**	Radios (per 1000 people), 1997**	Television sets (per 1000 people), 1998**	Scientists and engineers in R&D (per million people), 1990-2000***	Patent applications filed (per million people) 1997**	Number of book titles (per million people), 1990s****"	Number of tele-phones mainline, (per 1000 people), 2000***	Cellular mobile sub-scribers (per 1000 people), 2000***	Internet hosts (per 1000 people), 2000***+
Nicaragua	Other	1.9	30	285	190	203			31.0	18.0	0.3
Nigeria	Other		24	223	66	15		11.5	4.0	0.3	0.3
Norway	Other	5.9	588	915	579	4095	7112.7	1107.8	532.0	751.0	101.1
Pakistan	Other	1.6	23	98	88	78	5.7		22.0	2.0	0.3
Panama	Other	4.7	62	299	187		59.7		151.0	145.0	5.4
Peru	Other	4.0	0	273	144	229	31.3	75.6	67.0	50.0	0.4
Philippines	Other	4.6	79	159	108	156	47.1	18.2	40.0	84.0	0.3
Poland	Other	5.2	113	523	413	1460	843.0	497.2	282.0	174.0	8.8
Portugal	Other	2.6	75	304	542	1583	10668.7	218.6	430.0	665.0	6.2
Romania	Other		300	319	233	1393	1297.1	351.5	175.0	112.0	1.9
Russian Federation	Other		105	418	420	3397	331.4	249.1	218.0	22.0	2.2
Saudi Arabia	Arab		57	321	262		52.1	186.2	137.0	64.0	0.2
Senegal	Other	0.7	5	142	41	2			22.0	26.0	0.2
Sierra Leone	Other	0.7	4	253	13		2160.5		4.0	2.0	0.3
Singapore	Other	4.2	360	822	348	2182	9413.8		484.0	684.0	45.2
Slovakia	Other		185	580	402	1706	5223.5	583.9	314.0	205.0	7.0
Slovenia	Other		199	406	356	2161	13723.5	1725.0	386.0	612.0	11.0
South Africa	Other	2.1	32	317	125	992		125.1	114.0	190.0	4.4
Spain	Other	3.5	100	333	506	1562	2851.3	1483.1	421.0	609.0	11.3
Sri Lanka	Other	3.6	29	209	92	188	1397.0	246.3	40.0	23.0	0.1
Sweden	Other	5.8	445	932	531	4507	13068.2	1425.8	682.0	717.0	67.3
Switzerland	Other	5.4	337	1000	535	3058	15673.9	2537.9	727.0	644.0	36.7
Syria	Arab	2.4	20	278	70	29			103.0	2.0	0.3
Tajikistan	Other		20	142	285	660	4059.8	1.5	36.0	0.3	0.3
Thailand	Other	3.3	63	232	236	102	86.7	129.7	92.0	50.0	1.1
Togo	Other	1.4	4	218	18	102		1.1	9.0	11.0	0.3
Tunisia	Arab	2.1	31	223	198	124	18.3	132.6	90.0g	6.0g	0.3
Turkey	Other	2.2	111	180	286	303	423.1	43.8	280.0	246.0	1.1
Uganda	Other	1.5	2	128	27	25	2135.6	12.4	3.0	8.0	0.3
Ukraine	Other		54	884	490	2121	659.8	126.7	206.0	16.0	0.7
United Kingdom	Other	4.8	329	1436	645	2678	2495.1	1868.1	589.0	727.0	28.2
United States	Other	6.1	215	2146	847	4103	835.8	240.7def	700.0	398.0	295.2
Uruguay	Other	4.0	293	607	241		121.8	204.2	278.0	132.0	16.3
Uzbekistan	Other		3	465	275	1754	1096.7	40.3	67.0	2.0	0.3
Venezuela	Other	3.4	206	468	185	194	104.3	159.1c	108.0	217.0	0.7
Vietnam	Other		4	107	47	274	351.3		32.0	10.0	0.3
Zambia	Other	2.3	12	121	137		9.2		8.0	9.0	0.1
Zimbabwe	Other	2.3	19	93	30		1743.6		18.0	23.0	0.3

Notes:

- Quality adjusted MYS15+: Calculated by multiplying the mean years of schooling and the average test scores.

The average test scores is the average of the test scores data available from both sources (Barro & Lee, 1997 and TIMSS).

Test scores used from Barro & Lee, 1997 refer to the years 1990-91 & 1993-98.

Countries were categorised by level of mean years of schooling and missing data of average test scores was filled by the average test scores available for

other countries in the same category.

- Source of Population (in millions), 2000 used to compute Patents applications filed per million people and Number of book titles per million people was the HDR 2002,

- Book titles data for Qatar and Malawi were considered missing because the figures refer to School textbooks, Children's books or government publications only.

- Missing data for Cellular mobile subscribers and Internet hosts from HDR 2002, and referred to as "less than half the unit shown" by the symbol (.), was replaced by 0.25.

+ Data refer to the most recent year available during the period specified for all countries except Malta, Nicaragua, Guatemala, Nigeria, Benin and Burundi.

Their data refer to a year before 1990.

^ Patent applications filed figures are for residents and non-residents of the the country. Missing figures for residents are considered zero.

(a) Not including school textbooks or yearbooks.
(b) Partial data
(c) First editions only.
(d) Not including pamphlets.
(e) Not including government publications and university theses but including juvenile titles for which a class breakdown is not available .
(f) Not including school textbooks.
(g) Data refer to 1999.

Sources:

*   MYS: Barro and Lee, 2000. "International Data on educational Attainment: Updates and Implications, CID Working Paper no. 42, April.

Test Scores: Barro and Lee, 1997. "Schooling Quality in a Cross-section of Countries", August.

Test Scores: International Association for the Evaluation of Educational Achievement (1996), Science (Mathematics)

Achievement in the Middle School Years: IEA's Third International Mathematics and Science Study (TIMSS),

TIMSS International Study Centre, Boston College, Chestnut Hill, MA, USA, November.

"

**   World Bank, 2000. "World Development Report 2000/2001: Attacking Poverty", Oxford University Press,

New York.

***   UNDP, 2002. "2002 Human Development Report", Oxford University Press, New York.

**** UNESCO, 2002. UNESCO Web site (www.unesco.org).

REPORT AND IMPUTED VALUES OF INDICATORS ON KNOWLEDGE CAPITAL IN 109 COUNTRIES, AROUND THE YEAR 2000

Country	Group	Quality Adjusted MYS 15+, 2000	Daily news-papers (per 1000 people), 1996	Radios (per 1000 people), 1997	Television sets (per 1000 people), 1998	Scientists and engineers in R&D (per million people), 1990-2000	Patent applica-tions filed (per million people) 1997	Number of book titles (per million people), 1990s	Number of tele-phones mainline, (per 1000 inhabi-tant), 2000	Cellular mobile sub-scribers (per 1000 people), 2000	Internet hosts (per 1000 people), 2000
Algeria	Arab	2.3	38.0	241.0	105.0	-59.7	7.9	4.4	57.0	3.0	0.3
Argentina	Other	4.9	123.0	681.0	289.0	711.0	158.4	324.1	213.0	163.0	7.4
Armenia	Other	2.6	23.0	224.0	218.0	1308.0	6611.1	135.8	152.0	5.0	0.8
Australia	Other	5.7	293.0	1376.0	639.0	3320.0	2524.1	1020.3	525.0	447.0	85.7
Austria	Other	4.4	296.0	753.0	516.0	1605.0	13731.4	994.6	467.0	762.0	59.0
Azerbaijan	Other	2.4	27.0	23.0	254.0	2735.0	3038.5	55.5	104.0	56.0	0.2
Bangladesh	Other	0.7	9.0	50.0	6.0	51.0	1.6	-204.0	4.0	1.0	0.3
Belarus	Other	3.6	174.0	296.0	314.0	2296.0	2552.5	595.4	269.0	5.0	0.2
Belgium	Other	5.0	160.0	793.0	510.0	2307.0	8494.6	1284.4	498.0	525.0	29.4
Benin	Other	0.7	2.0	108.0	10.0	174.0	1848.0	1.4	8.0	9.0	0.0
Bolivia	Other	2.4	55.0	675.0	116.0	171.0	14.8	482.4	60.0	70.0	0.2
Botswana	Other	3.2	27.0	156.0	20.0	-190.5	62.0	-51.7	93.0	123.0	1.5
Brazil	Other	2.1	40.0	444.0	316.0	168.0	187.7	127.3	182.0	136.0	5.2
Bulgaria	Other	4.2	257.0	543.0	398.0	1289.0	3544.3	629.2	350.0	90.0	2.2
Burkina Faso	Other	2.4	1.0	33.0	9.0	17.0	1921.9	0.4	4.0	2.0	0.3
Burundi	Other	2.4	3.0	71.0	4.0	21.0	0.8	-165.1	3.0	2.0	0.0
Cameroon	Other	1.5	7.0	163.0	32.0	-212.1	1159.5	3.5	6.0	10.0	0.3
Canada	Other	6.0	159.0	1077.0	715.0	3009.0	1767.7	744.8	677.0	285.0	77.4
Central Arican Rep.	Other	0.7	2.0	83.0	5.0	47.0	1858.8	-32.6	3.0	1.0	0.3
Chile	Other	4.0	98.0	354.0	232.0	370.0	129.0	94.9	221.0	222.0	4.9
China	Comparator	4.7	76.1	333.0	272.0	459.0	48.1	139.4	112.0	66.0	0.1
Colombia	Other	2.0	46.0	581.0	217.0	290.5	29.9	125.9	169.0	53.0	1.1
Congo	Other	2.2	8.0	124.0	12.0	34.0	1490.4	-51.2	7.0	24.0	0.3
Congo, Dem. Rep..	Other	1.3	3.0	375.0	135.0	-473.1	0.6	2.2	0.3	0.3	0.3
Costa Rica	Other	3.1	94.0	271.0	387.0	533.0	2478.9	366.0	249.0	52.0	1.9
Croatia	Other	4.1	115.0	336.0	272.0	1494.0	151.5	694.7	365.0	231.0	3.7
Czech Rep.	Other	4.6	254.0	803.0	447.0	1317.0	2968.6	1218.5	378.0	424.0	15.4
Denmark	Other	4.6	309.0	1141.0	585.0	3240.0	20577.6	2727.4	720.0	631.0	62.9
Dominican Republic	Other	2.1	52.0	178.0	95.0	277.6	2025.4	120.6	105.0	82.0	0.9
Ecuador	Other	3.3	70.0	419.0	293.0	140.0	24.6	83.3	100.0	38.0	0.3
Egypt	Arab	2.3	40.0	324.0	122.0	493.0	17.8	20.8	86.0	21.0	0.3
El Salvador	Other	2.2	48.0	464.0	675.0	19.0	10.6	105.2	100.0	118.0	0.1
Estonia	Other	3.3	174.0	693.0	480.0	2164.0	19031.4	2332.1	363.0	387.0	28.4
Ethiopia	Other	2.4	1.0	195.0	5.0	-243.8	0.1	7.1	4.0	0.3	0.3
Finland	Other	5.2	455.0	1496.0	640.0	3340.8	21045.6	2533.3	550.0	720.0	102.3
France	Other	3.9	218.0	937.0	601.0	2686.0	1902.6	660.2	579.0	493.0	19.1

Country	Group	Quality Adjusted MYS 15+, 2000	Daily news-papers (per 1000 people), 1996	Radios (per 1000 people), 1997	Television sets (per 1000 people), 1998	Scientists and engineers in R&D (per million people), 1990-2000	Patent applica-tions filed (per million people) 1997	Number of book titles (per million people), 1990s	Number of tele-phones mainline, (per 1000 inhabi-tant), 2000	Cellular mobile sub-scribers (per 1000 people), 2000	Internet hosts (per 1000 people), 2000
Germany	Other	5.2	311.0	948.0	580.0	2873.0	2141.4	951.7	611.0	586.0	24.8
Ghana	Other	1.6	14.0	238.0	99.0	-371.2	1767.0	0.4	12.0	6.0	0.3
Greece	Other	4.1	153.0	477.0	466.0	1045.0	7777.6	383.7	532.0	557.0	10.5
Guatemala	Other	1.5	33.0	79.0	126.0	103.0	11.8	-187.7	57.0	61.0	0.5
Haiti	Other	0.8	3.0	55.0	5.0	-392.3	1.1	42.0	9.0	3.0	0.3
Honduras	Other	2.0	55.0	386.0	90.0	-132.0	21.3	4.1	46.0	24.0	0.3
Hong Kong	Comparator	5.1	792.0	684.0	431.0	93.0	345.7	-166.1	583.0	809.0	34.3
Hungary	Other	4.8	186.0	689.0	437.0	1249.0	3010.5	1035.2	372.0	302.0	10.4
India	Comparator	2.1	45.1	121.0	69.0	158.0	10.1	14.0	32.0	4.0	0.3
Indonesia	Other	2.1	24.0	156.0	136.0	-175.4	21.3	0.6	31.0	17.0	0.1
Iran	Other	2.3	28.0	265.0	157.0	590.0	6.0	210.3	149.0	15.0	0.3
Ireland	Other	4.8	150.0	699.0	403.0	2132.0	21955.3	2331.4	420.0	658.0	29.7
Israel	Comparator	5.7	290.0	520.0	318.0	1570.0	5057.3	328.2	482.0	702.0	29.5
Italy	Other	4.8	104.0	878.0	486.0	1322.0	1589.7	562.9	474.0	737.0	17.8
Japan	Other	5.4	578.0	955.0	707.0	4960.0	3288.5	442.3	586.0	526.0	36.5
Jordan	Arab	3.4	58.0	287.0	52.0	197.8	-371.4	5.1	92.0	58.0	0.1
Kenya	Other	1.8	9.0	104.0	21.0	-307.6	1627.4	-18.4	10.0	4.0	0.1
Korea(Rep. of)	Comparator	6.2	393.0	1033.0	346.0	2139.0	2783.3	652.8	464.0	567.0	8.5
Kuwait	Arab	2.9	374.0	660.0	491.0	214.0	352.1	115.3	244.0	249.0	1.8
Kyrgystan	Other	2.8	15.0	112.0	45.0	574.0	5123.1	85.7	77.0	2.0	0.4
Latvia	Other	3.6	247.0	710.0	492.0	1090.0	11259.6	907.5	303.0	166.0	10.7
Lesotho	Other	1.8	8.0	49.0	25.0	973.6	24741.5	1954.0	10.0	10.0	0.3
Lithuania	Other	3.2	93.0	513.0	459.0	2031.0	7242.7	1107.3	321.0	142.0	4.8
Macedonia	Other	2.7	21.0	200.0	250.0	387.0	13076.5	1103.7	255.0	57.0	0.8
Madagascar	Other	2.9	5.0	192.0	21.0	12.0	1635.9	6.8	3.0	4.0	0.3
Malawi	Other	1.4	3.0	249.0	2.0	-161.8	4418.9	352.3	4.0	5.0	0.3
Malaysia	Other	3.5	158.0	420.0	166.0	154.0	290.6	229.0	199.0	213.0	3.1
Mali	Other	0.3	1.0	54.0	12.0	-170.1	2725.5	2.9	3.0	1.0	0.3
Mexico	Other	3.8	97.0	325.0	261.0	213.0	363.3	70.3	125.0	142.0	5.7
Moldova	Other	3.1	60.0	740.0	297.0	334.0	5889.5	271.2	133.0	32.0	0.4
Mongolia	Other	2.5	27.0	151.0	63.0	468.0	10553.2	727.6	56.0	45.0	0.1
Morocco	Arab	2.5	26.0	241.0	160.0	119.4	10.9	13.0	50.0	83.0	0.1
Myanmar	Other	0.8	10.0	95.0	7.0	-147.8	2139.6	4.8	6.0	0.3	0.3
Netherlands	Other	5.0	306.0	978.0	543.0	2490.0	5699.9	675.1	618.0	670.0	101.9
New Zealand	Other	5.8	216.0	990.0	508.0	2197.0	9246.6	1422.4	500.0	563.0	90.6
Nicaragua	Other	1.9	30.0	285.0	190.0	203.0	-615.5	-57.8	31.0	18.0	0.3
Nigeria	Other	2.6	24.0	223.0	66.0	15.0	878.7	11.5	4.0	0.3	0.3
Norway	Other	5.9	588.0	915.0	579.0	4095.0	7112.7	1107.8	532.0	751.0	101.1

REPORT AND IMPUTED VALUES OF INDICATORS ON KNOWLEDGE CAPITAL IN 109 COUNTRIES, AROUND THE YEAR 2000

Country	Group	Quality Adjusted MYS 15+, 2000	Daily news-papers (per 1000 people), 1996	Radios (per 1000 people), 1997	Television sets (per 1000 people), 1998	Scientists and engineers in R&D (per million people), 1990-2000	Patent applica-tions filed (per million people) 1997	Number of book titles (per million people), 1990s	Number of tele-phones mainline, (per 1000 inhabi-tant), 2000	Cellular mobile sub-scribers (per 1000 people), 2000	Internet hosts (per 1000 people), 2000
Pakistan	Other	1.6	23.0	98.0	88.0	78.0	5.7	-148.7	22.0	2.0	0.3
Panama	Other	4.7	62.0	299.0	187.0	428.9	59.7	106.6	151.0	145.0	5.4
Peru	Other	4.0	0.0	273.0	144.0	229.0	31.3	75.6	67.0	50.0	0.4
Philippines	Other	4.6	79.0	159.0	108.0	156.0	47.1	18.2	40.0	84.0	0.3
Poland	Other	5.2	113.0	523.0	413.0	1460.0	843.0	497.2	282.0	174.0	8.8
Portugal	Other	2.6	75.0	304.0	542.0	1583.0	10668.7	218.6	430.0	665.0	6.2
Romania	Other	4.1	300.0	319.0	233.0	1393.0	1297.1	351.5	175.0	112.0	1.9
Russian Federation	Other	3.1	105.0	418.0	420.0	3397.0	331.4	249.1	218.0	22.0	2.2
Saudi Arabia	Arab	2.8	57.0	321.0	262.0	730.4	52.1	186.2	137.0	64.0	0.2
Senegal	Other	0.7	5.0	142.0	41.0	2.0	1685.4	13.9	22.0	26.0	0.2
Sierra Leone	Other	0.7	4.0	253.0	13.0	-320.8	2160.5	136.8	4.0	2.0	0.3
Singapore	Other	4.2	360.0	822.0	348.0	2182.0	9413.8	1139.9	484.0	684.0	45.2
Slovakia	Other	3.7	185.0	580.0	402.0	1706.0	5223.5	583.9	314.0	205.0	7.0
Slovenia	Other	3.7	199.0	406.0	356.0	2161.0	13723.5	1725.0	386.0	612.0	11.0
South Africa	Other	2.1	32.0	317.0	125.0	992.0	1286.3	125.1	114.0	190.0	4.4
Spain	Other	3.5	100.0	333.0	506.0	1562.0	2851.3	1483.1	421.0	609.0	11.3
Sri Lanka	Other	3.6	29.0	209.0	92.0	188.0	1397.0	246.3	40.0	23.0	0.1
Sweden	Other	5.8	445.0	932.0	531.0	4507.0	13068.2	1425.8	682.0	717.0	67.3
Switzerland	Other	5.4	337.0	1000.0	535.0	3058.0	15673.9	2537.9	727.0	644.0	36.7
Syria	Arab	2.4	20.0	278.0	70.0	29.0	420.1	165.4	103.0	2.0	0.3
Tajikistan	Other	2.2	20.0	142.0	285.0	660.0	4059.8	1.5	36.0	0.3	0.3
Thailand	Other	3.3	63.0	232.0	236.0	102.0	86.7	129.7	92.0	50.0	1.1
Togo	Other	1.4	4.0	218.0	18.0	102.0	473.5	1.1	9.0	11.0	0.3
Tunisia	Arab	2.1	31.0	223.0	198.0	124.0	18.3	132.6	90.0	6.0	0.3
Turkey	Other	2.2	111.0	180.0	286.0	303.0	423.1	43.8	280.0	246.0	1.1
Uganda	Other	1.5	2.0	128.0	27.0	25.0	2135.6	12.4	3.0	8.0	0.3
Ukraine	Other	3.1	54.0	884.0	490.0	2121.0	659.8	126.7	206.0	16.0	0.7
United Kingdom	Other	4.8	329.0	1436.0	645.0	2678.0	2495.1	1868.1	589.0	727.0	28.2
United States	Other	6.1	215.0	2146.0	847.0	4103.0	835.8	240.7	700.0	398.0	295.2
Uruguay	Other	4.0	293.0	607.0	241.0	1908.0	121.8	204.2	278.0	132.0	16.3
Uzbekistan	Other	2.7	3.0	465.0	275.0	1754.0	1096.7	40.3	67.0	2.0	0.3
Venezuela	Other	3.4	206.0	468.0	185.0	194.0	104.3	159.1	108.0	217.0	0.7
Vietnam	Other	2.5	4.0	107.0	47.0	274.0	351.3	-96.0	32.0	10.0	0.3
Zambia	Other	2.3	12.0	121.0	137.0	-194.2	9.2	-144.4	8.0	9.0	0.1
Zimbabwe	Other	2.3	19.0	93.0	30.0	-248.1	1743.6	-8.3	18.0	23.0	0.3
Percentage imputed		25.7	1.8	0.0	0.0	22.9	15.6	25.7	0.0	0.0	0.0

RANKING OF 109 COUNTRIES ON KNOWLEDGE CAPITAL INDICATORS AROUND THE YEAR 2000
(SORTED BY TOTAL RANKS)

Country	Group	Quality Adjusted MYS 15+, 2000	Daily news-papers (per 1000 people), 1996	Radios (per 1000 people), 1997	Television sets (per 1000 people), 1998	Scientists and engineers in R&D (per million people), 1990-2000	Patent applica-tions filed (per million people) 1997	Number of book titles (per mil-lion peo-ple), 1990s	Number of tele-phones mainline (per 1000 people), 2000	Cellular mobile sub-scribers (per 1000 people), 2000	Internet hosts (per 1000 people), 2000	Total Rank
Finland	Other	11.0	4.0	2.0	6.0	6.0	3.0	3.0	12.0	6.0	2.0	55.0
Sweden	Other	6.0	5.0	14.0	15.0	2.0	10.0	10.0	4.0	7.0	8.0	81.0
Switzerland	Other	9.5	9.0	8.0	14.0	9.0	6.0	2.0	1.0	13.0	12.0	83.5
Denmark	Other	25.5	12.0	5.0	9.0	8.0	4.0	1.0	2.0	14.0	9.0	89.5
Norway	Other	4.0	2.0	15.0	11.0	4.0	19.0	15.0	13.5	3.0	4.0	90.5
United Kingdom	Other	21.0	10.0	3.0	5.0	14.0	38.0	7.0	8.0	5.0	19.0	130.0
Netherlands	Other	15.0	13.0	10.0	12.0	15.0	22.0	26.0	6.0	10.0	3.0	132.0
Japan	Other	9.5	3.0	11.0	3.0	1.0	29.0	35.0	9.0	21.0	13.0	134.5
New Zealand	Other	5.0	23.0	9.0	18.0	18.0	15.0	11.0	16.0	19.0	5.0	139.0
Australia	Other	8.0	16.5	4.0	7.0	7.0	37.0	19.0	15.0	24.0	6.0	143.5
Germany	Other	12.0	11.0	12.0	10.0	11.0	41.0	21.0	7.0	17.0	20.0	162.0
Canada	Other	3.0	32.0	6.0	2.0	10.0	49.0	23.0	5.0	29.0	7.0	166.0
Austria	Other	27.0	15.0	21.0	16.0	29.0	7.0	20.0	21.0	2.0	10.0	168.0
United States	Other	2.0	24.0	1.0	1.0	3.0	64.0	45.0	3.0	26.0	1.0	170.0
Singapore	Other	28.0	8.0	18.0	37.0	19.0	14.0	14.0	18.0	9.0	11.0	176.0
Belgium	Other	16.0	31.0	20.0	17.0	16.0	16.0	12.0	17.0	22.0	17.0	184.0
Ireland	Other	18.5	35.0	24.0	32.0	23.0	2.0	5.0	25.0	12.0	15.0	191.5
Korea (Rep. of)	Comparator	1.0	6.0	7.0	38.0	22.0	34.0	28.0	22.0	18.0	31.0	207.0
France	Other	36.0	22.0	13.0	8.0	13.0	46.0	27.0	11.0	23.0	21.0	220.0
Estonia	Other	49.0	29.5	25.0	24.0	20.0	5.0	4.0	30.0	27.0	18.0	231.5
Israel	Comparator	7.0	18.0	36.0	39.0	31.0	25.0	40.0	19.0	8.0	16.0	239.0
Czech Rep.	Other	24.0	20.0	19.0	27.0	37.0	32.0	13.0	27.0	25.0	24.0	248.0
Slovenia	Other	39.0	26.0	46.0	36.0	21.0	8.0	8.0	26.0	15.0	26.0	251.0
Italy	Other	20.0	41.0	17.0	23.0	36.0	55.0	32.0	20.0	4.0	22.0	270.0
Hungary	Other	18.5	27.0	26.0	28.0	40.0	31.0	18.0	28.0	28.0	29.0	273.5
Latvia	Other	41.0	21.0	23.0	20.0	41.0	11.0	22.0	34.0	39.0	27.0	279.0
Greece	Other	32.0	34.0	38.0	25.0	42.0	17.0	36.0	13.5	20.0	28.0	285.5
Spain	Other	43.5	42.0	51.5	19.0	32.0	33.0	9.0	24.0	16.0	25.0	295.0
Slovakia	Other	38.0	28.0	33.0	33.0	28.0	23.0	31.0	33.0	36.0	33.0	316.0
Lithuania	Other	51.0	46.0	37.0	26.0	25.0	18.0	16.0	32.0	42.5	39.0	332.5
Bulgaria	Other	29.0	19.0	34.0	34.0	39.0	28.0	29.0	31.0	49.0	43.5	335.5
Portugal	Other	62.0	49.0	58.0	13.0	30.0	12.0	47.0	23.0	11.0	34.0	339.0
Poland	Other	13.0	38.0	35.0	31.0	34.0	63.0	33.0	35.0	38.0	30.0	350.0
Hong Kong	Comparator	14.0	1.0	27.0	29.0	81.0	72.0	107.0	10.0	1.0	14.0	356.0

RANKING OF 109 COUNTRIES ON KNOWLEDGE CAPITAL INDICATORS AROUND THE YEAR 2000
(SORTED BY TOTAL RANKS)

Country	Group	Quality Adjuste d MYS 15+, 2000	Daily news- papers (per 1000 people), 1996	Radios (per 1000 people), 1997	Television sets (per 1000 people), 1998	Scientists and engineers in R&D (per million people), 1990-2000	Patent applica- tions filed (per million people) 1997	Number of book titles (per mil- lion peo- ple), 1990s	Number of tele- phones mainline (per 1000 people), 2000	Cellular mobile sub- scribers (per 1000 people), 2000	Internet hosts (per 1000 people), 2000	Total Rank
Uruguay	Other	34.0	16.5	31.0	54.0	26.0	79.0	49.0	37.0	45.0	23.0	394.5
Croatia	Other	31.0	37.0	50.0	48.5	33.0	77.0	25.0	29.0	32.0	41.0	403.5
Argentina	Other	17.0	36.0	28.0	44.0	46.0	76.0	41.0	44.0	40.0	32.0	404.0
Kuwait	Arab	56.0	7.0	30.0	21.0	63.0	70.0	63.0	41.0	30.0	47.0	428.0
Romania	Other	30.0	14.0	56.0	56.0	35.0	58.0	39.0	48.0	48.0	45.5	429.5
Russian Federation	Other	54.0	40.0	45.0	30.0	5.0	73.0	43.0	43.0	72.0	43.5	448.5
Costa Rica	Other	52.0	45.0	65.0	35.0	50.0	39.0	37.0	40.0	61.0	45.5	469.5
Moldavia	Other	55.0	53.0	22.0	42.0	57.0	21.0	42.0	54.0	66.0	59.0	471.0
Ukraine	Other	53.0	58.0	16.0	22.0	24.0	65.0	59.0	45.0	76.0	55.5	473.5
Belarus	Other	40.0	29.5	60.0	41.0	17.0	36.0	30.0	38.0	88.0	96.0	475.5
Chile	Other	35.0	43.0	49.0	57.0	56.0	78.0	66.0	42.0	33.0	38.0	497.0
Malaysia	Other	43.5	33.0	43.0	64.0	74.0	74.0	46.0	46.0	35.0	42.0	500.5
Macedonia	Other	60.0	80.0	78.0	53.0	55.0	9.0	17.0	39.0	58.0	53.5	502.5
Venezuela	Other	45.0	25.0	39.0	63.0	67.0	80.0	52.0	58.0	34.0	55.5	518.5
Mexico	Other	37.0	44.0	53.0	51.0	64.0	69.0	70.0	55.0	42.5	35.0	520.5
Panama	Other	22.0	52.0	59.0	62.0	54.0	83.0	64.0	51.0	41.0	36.0	524.0
Turkey	Other	79.0	39.0	81.0	45.0	58.0	67.0	72.0	36.0	31.0	50.0	558.0
Brazil	Other	87.5	63.5	42.0	40.0	71.0	75.0	58.0	47.0	44.0	37.0	565.0
China	Comparator	23.0	48.0	51.5	48.5	53.0	85.0	53.0	57.0	54.0	103.0	576.0
Armenia	Other	63.0	78.5	73.0	58.0	38.0	20.0	55.0	50.0	88.0	53.5	577.0
SouthAfrica	Other	87.5	67.0	57.0	72.0	43.0	59.0	61.0	56.0	37.0	40.0	579.5
Saudi Arabia	Arab	58.0	55.0	55.0	50.0	45.0	84.0	50.0	53.0	55.0	96.0	601.0
Colombia	Other	89.0	61.0	32.0	59.0	59.0	88.0	60.0	49.0	60.0	50.0	607.0
Thailand	Other	47.5	51.0	72.0	55.0	79.5	81.0	57.0	65.5	62.5	50.0	621.0
Ecuador	Other	47.5	50.0	44.0	43.0	75.0	89.0	68.0	62.5	65.0	78.5	622.5
Azerbaijan	Other	71.0	73.0	109.0	52.0	12.0	30.0	71.0	60.0	59.0	96.0	633.0
Dominican Republic	Other	86.0	59.0	82.0	78.0	60.0	44.0	62.0	59.0	52.0	52.0	634.0
Mongolia	Other	65.0	73.0	87.0	85.0	52.0	13.0	24.0	75.0	64.0	103.0	641.0
El Salvador	Other	81.0	60.0	41.0	4.0	89.0	97.0	65.0	62.5	47.0	103.0	649.5
Bolivia	Other	72.0	56.5	29.0	74.0	70.0	94.0	34.0	72.0	53.0	96.0	650.5
Philippines	Other	25.5	47.0	84.0	75.0	73.0	86.0	76.0	78.5	50.0	62.0	657.0
Uzbekistan	Other	61.0	100.0	40.0	47.0	27.0	61.0	74.0	70.5	98.0	78.5	657.0
Lesotho	Other	92.0	90.5	107.0	93.0	44.0	1.0	6.0	89.5	80.0	78.5	681.5
Peru	Other	33.0	109.0	64.0	67.0	62.0	87.0	69.0	70.5	62.5	59.0	683.0
Iran	Other	76.0	71.0	66.0	66.0	48.0	101.0	48.0	52.0	77.0	78.5	683.5
Sri Lanka	Other	42.0	70.0	77.0	79.0	68.0	57.0	44.0	78.5	70.5	103.0	689.0
Kyrgystan	Other	59.0	84.0	94.0	88.0	49.0	24.0	67.0	69.0	98.0	59.0	691.0

Country	Group	Quality Adjuste d MYS 15+, 2000	Daily news- papers (per 1000 people), 1996	Radios (per 1000 people), 1997"	Television sets (per 1000 people), 1998	Scientists and engineers in R&D (per million people), 1990- 2000	Patent applica- tions filed (per million people) 1997	Number of book titles (per mil- lion peo- ple), 1990s	Number of tele- phones mainline (per 1000 people), 2000	Cellular mobile sub- scribers (per 1000 people), 2000	Internet hosts (per 1000 people), 2000	Total Rank
Egypt	Arab	74.0	63.5	54.0	73.0	51.0	93.0	75.0	68.0	73.0	78.5	703.0
Tajikistan	Other	80.0	81.5	88.5	46.0	47.0	27.0	91.0	80.0	107.0	78.5	726.5
Jordan	Arab	46.0	54.0	61.0	86.0	66.0	108.0	84.0	65.5	57.0	103.0	730.5
Syria	Arab	68.0	81.5	63.0	82.0	86.0	68.0	51.0	61.0	98.0	78.5	737.0
Tunisia	Arab	84.0	68.0	74.5	60.0	76.0	92.0	56.0	67.0	85.5	78.5	741.5
Botswana	Other	50.0	73.0	85.5	96.0	100.0	82.0	101.0	64.0	46.0	48.0	745.5
Morocco	Arab	66.0	75.0	69.5	65.0	77.0	96.0	79.0	76.0	51.0	103.0	757.5
Honduras	Other	90.0	56.5	47.0	80.0	95.0	91.0	87.0	77.0	68.5	78.5	770.5
Nicaragua	Other	91.0	69.0	62.0	61.0	65.0	109.0	102.0	83.5	74.0	62.0	778.5
Guatemala	Other	98.0	66.0	102.0	71.0	78.0	95.0	108.0	73.5	56.0	57.0	804.5
Malawi	Other	100.0	100.0	68.0	109.0	97.0	26.0	38.0	100.5	88.0	78.5	805.0
Algeria	Arab	77.0	65.0	69.5	76.0	94.0	100.0	86.0	73.5	93.5	78.5	813.0
India	Comparator	83.0	62.0	92.5	83.0	72.0	98.0	77.0	81.5	91.0	78.5	818.5
Nigeria	Other	64.0	76.5	74.5	84.0	91.0	62.0	81.0	100.5	107.0	78.5	819.0
Vietnam	Other	67.0	96.0	96.0	87.0	61.0	71.0	103.0	81.5	80.0	78.5	821.0
Zimbabwe	Other	78.0	83.0	100.0	91.0	104.0	51.0	97.0	87.0	70.5	62.0	823.5
Madagascar	Other	57.0	93.5	80.0	94.5	92.0	53.0	83.0	106.0	91.0	78.5	828.5
Ghana	Other	94.0	85.0	71.0	77.0	107.0	50.0	96.0	88.0	85.5	78.5	832.0
Sierra Leone	Other	107.0	96.0	67.0	98.0	106.0	40.0	54.0	100.5	98.0	78.5	845.0
Congo	Other	82.0	90.5	91.0	99.5	85.0	56.0	100.0	95.0	68.5	78.5	846.0
Senegal	Other	105.5	93.5	88.5	89.0	93.0	52.0	78.0	85.5	67.0	96.0	848.0
Togo	Other	99.0	96.0	76.0	97.0	79.5	66.0	93.0	91.5	78.0	78.5	854.5
Indonesia	Other	85.0	76.5	85.5	69.0	99.0	90.0	94.0	83.5	75.0	103.0	860.5
Uganda	Other	97.0	104.0	90.0	92.0	87.0	43.0	80.0	106.0	84.0	78.5	861.5
Cameroon	Other	96.0	92.0	83.0	90.0	102.0	60.0	88.0	96.5	80.0	78.5	866.0
Burkina Faso	Other	73.0	107.0	108.0	102.0	90.0	45.0	95.0	100.5	98.0	78.5	897.0
Myanmar	Other	103.0	87.0	99.0	103.0	96.0	42.0	85.0	96.5	107.0	78.5	897.0
Benin	Other	108.0	104.0	95.0	101.0	69.0	48.0	92.0	93.5	82.5	108.5	901.5
Pakistan	Other	95.0	78.5	98.0	81.0	82.0	102.0	105.0	85.5	98.0	78.5	903.5
Zambia	Other	75.0	86.0	92.5	68.0	101.0	99.0	104.0	93.5	82.5	103.0	904.5
Kenya	Other	93.0	88.5	97.0	94.5	105.0	54.0	98.0	89.5	91.0	103.0	913.5
Congo, Dem. Rep.	Other	101.0	100.0	48.0	70.0	109.0	106.0	90.0	109.0	107.0	78.5	918.5
Mali	Other	109.0	107.0	105.0	99.5	98.0	35.0	89.0	106.0	103.0	78.5	930.0
Central African Rep.	Other	105.5	104.0	101.0	106.0	84.0	47.0	99.0	106.0	103.0	78.5	934.0
Ethiopia	Other	70.0	107.0	79.0	106.0	103.0	107.0	82.0	100.5	107.0	78.5	940.0
Haiti	Other	102.0	100.0	104.0	106.0	108.0	104.0	73.0	91.5	93.5	78.5	960.5
Bangladesh	Other	104.0	88.5	106.0	104.0	83.0	103.0	109.0	100.5	103.0	78.5	979.5
Burundi	Other	69.0	100.0	103.0	108.0	88.0	105.0	106.0	106.0	98.0	108.5	991.5

VALUES OF KNOWLEDGE OUTCOMES AND OTHER DEVELOPMENT INDICATORS IN 109 COUNTRIES, AROUND THE YEAR 2000

Country	Group	High-technology exports (% of total goods exports), 1999	Nuclear Facilities*_	Space programs*	TAI value, 1999	AHDI rank	HDI value, 2000	GDP per capita (PPP$), 2000
Algeria	Arab	0.3	1	0	0.221	97	0.697	5308
Argentina	Other	3.0	1	1	0.381	32	0.844	12377
Armenia	Other	4.0	1	0			0.754	2559
Australia	Other	5.0	1	1	0.587	8	0.939	25693
Austria	Other	12.0	1	0	0.544	9	0.926	26765
Azerbaijan	Other	1.0	0	0			0.741	2936
Bangladesh	Other	0.3	1	0		83	0.478	1602
Belarus	Other	5.0	0	0			0.788	7544
Belgium	Other	11.0	1	0	0.553	16	0.939	27178
Benin	Other		0	0		78	0.420	990
Bolivia	Other	21.0	0	0	0.277	60	0.653	2424
Botswana	Other		0	0		62	0.572	7184
Brazil	Other	9.0	1	1	0.311	53	0.757	7625
Bulgaria	Other	6.0	1	0	0.411	34	0.779	5710
Burkina Faso	Other		0	0		91	0.325	976
Burundi	Other		0	0		104	0.313	591
Cameroon	Other	1.0	0	0		95	0.512	1703
Canada	Other	11.0	1	1	0.589	3	0.940	27840
Central African Rep..	Other	0.3	0	0		96	0.375	1172
Chile	Other	1.0	1	1	0.357	31	0.831	9417
China	Comparator	21.0	1	1	0.299	72	0.726	3976
Colombia	Other	2.0	1	0	0.274	40	0.772	6248
Congo	Other		0	0		111	0.512	825
Congo, Dem. Rep..	Other		1	0			0.431	765
Costa Rica	Other	44.0	0	0	0.358	23	0.820	8650
Croatia	Other	8.0	0	0	0.391		0.809	8091
Czech Rep..	Other	12.0	1	0	0.465		0.849	13991
Denmark	Other	19.0	1	0		10	0.926	27627
Dominican Republic	Other	0.3	0	0	0.244	37	0.727	6033
Ecuador	Other	1.0	0	0	0.253	49	0.732	3203
Egypt	Arab	2.0	1	1	0.236	92	0.642	3635
El Salvador	Other	6.0	0	0	0.253	48	0.706	4497
Estonia	Other	17.0	0	0			0.826	10066

VALUES OF KNOWLEDGE OUTCOMES AND OTHER DEVELOPMENT INDICATORS IN 109 COUNTRIES, AROUND THE YEAR 2000

Country	Group	High-technology exports (% of total goods exports), 1999	Nuclear Facilities	Space programs	TAI value, 1999	AHDI rank	HDI value, 2000	GDP per capita (PPP$), 2000
Ethiopia	Other		0	0		101	0.327	668
Finland	Other	27.0	1	0	0.744	7	0.930	24996
France	Other	22.0	1	1	0.535	15	0.928	24223
Germany	Other	18.0	1	1	0.583		0.925	25103
Ghana	Other	2.0	1	0	0.139	71	0.548	1964
Greece	Other	5.0	1	0	0.437	29	0.885	16501
Guatemala	Other	4.0	0	0		64	0.631	3821
Haiti	Other	3.0	0	0		87	0.471	1467
Honduras	Other	1.0	0	0	0.208	56	0.638	2453
Hong Kong	Comparator	24.0	0	0	0.455		0.888	25153
Hungary	Other	24.0	1	0	0.464	24	0.835	12416
India	Comparator	5.0	1	1	0.201	80	0.577	2358
Indonesia	Other	7.0	1	0	0.211	69	0.684	3043
Iran	Other	0.3	1	0	0.260	101	0.721	5884
Ireland	Other	42.0	0	0		17	0.925	29866
Israel	Comparator	29.0	1	1	0.514		0.896	20131
Italy	Other	11.0	1	0	0.471	15	0.913	23626
Japan	Other	30.0	1	1	0.698	18	0.933	26755
Jordan	Arab		0	0		68	0.717	3966
Kenya	Other	2.0	0	0	0.129		0.513	1022
Korea(Rep. of)	Comparator	33.0	1	0	0.666	38	0.882	17380
Kuwait	Arab	0.3	0	0		70	0.813	15799
Kyrgystan	Other	4.0	0	0			0.712	2711
Latvia	Other	6.0	1	0			0.800	7045
Lesotho	Other		0	0			0.535	2031
Lithuania	Other	7.0	1	0			0.808	7106
Macedonia	Other	3.0	0	0			0.772	5086
Madagascar	Other	2.0	0	0			0.469	840
Malawi	Other		0	0		83	0.400	615
Malaysia	Other	52.0	1	0	0.396	59	0.782	9068
Mali	Other		0	0		86	0.386	797
Mexico	Other	28.0	1	0	0.389	45	0.796	9023
Moldova	Other	2.0	0	0			0.701	2109
Mongolia	Other	0.3	0	0			0.655	1783
Morocco	Arab	0.3	0	0		79	0.602	3546

VALUES OF KNOWLEDGE OUTCOMES AND OTHER DEVELOPMENT INDICATORS IN 109 COUNTRIES, AROUND THE YEAR 2000

Country	Group	High-technology exports (% of total goods exports), 1999	Nuclear Facilities	Space programs	TAI value, 1999	AHDI rank	HDI value, 2000	GDP per capita (PPP$), 2000
Myanmar	Other		0	0			0.552	1027
Netherlands	Other	26.0	1	0	0.630	4	0.935	25657
NewZealand	Other	5.0	0	0	0.548	6	0.917	20070
Nicaragua	Other	0.3	0	0	0.185	51	0.635	2366
Nigeria	Other	0.3	0	0		107	0.462	896
Norway	Other	5.0	1	0	0.579	5	0.942	29918
Pakistan	Other	1.0	1	0	0.167	90	0.499	1928
Panama	Other	2.0	0	0	0.321	35	0.787	6000
Peru	Other	1.0	0	0	0.271	54	0.747	4799
Philippines	Other	26.0	1	0	0.300	33	0.754	3971
Poland	Other	8.0	1	0	0.407	30	0.833	9051
Portugal	Other	7.0	1	0	0.419	19	0.880	17290
Romania	Other	4.0	1	0	0.371	44	0.775	6423
Russian Federation	Other	3.0	1	1			0.781	8377
Saudi Arabia	Arab	0.3	0	0			0.759	11367
Senegal	Other	7.0	0	0	0.158	89	0.431	1510
Sierra Leone	Other		0	0			0.275	490
Singapore	Other	58.0	0	0	0.585	43	0.885	23356
Slovakia	Other	7.0	1	0	0.447		0.835	11243
Slovenia	Other	12.0	1	0	0.458		0.879	17367
South Africa	Other	4.0	1	0	0.340		0.695	9401
Spain	Other	10.0	1	0	0.481	13	0.913	19472
Sri Lanka	Other	3.0	0	0	0.203	46	0.741	3530
Sweden	Other	26.0	1	0	0.703	1	0.941	24277
Switzerland	Other	26.0	1	0		2	0.928	28769
Syria	Arab	0.3	0	0	0.240	103	0.691	3556
Tajikistan	Other		0	0			0.667	1152
Thailand	Other	30.0	1	0	0.337	52	0.762	6402
Togo	Other	0.3	0	0		94	0.493	1442
Tunisia	Arab	3.0	0	0	0.255	93	0.722	6363
Turkey	Other	7.0	1	1		67	0.742	6974
Uganda	Other	0.3	0	0			0.444	1208
Ukraine	Other		0	0			0.748	3816
United Kingdom	Other	29.0	1	1	0.606	12	0.928	23509
United States	Other	32.0	1	1	0.733	11	0.939	34142

Table A-13

Country	Group	High-technology exports (% of total goods exports), 1999	Nuclear Facilities	Space programs	TAI value, 1999	AHDI rank	HDI value, 2000	GDP per capita (PPP$), 2000
Uruguay	Other	2.0	1	0	0.343	21	0.831	0.831
Uzbekistan	Other		0	0			0.727	0.727
Venezuela	Other	0.3	1	0		47	0.770	0.770
Vietnam	Other		1	0			0.688	0.688
Zambia	Other		0	0		84	0.433	0.433
Zimbabwe	Other	1.0	0	0	0.220	76	0.551	0.551

Notes

* "1" means "exist" and "0" means does not exist.

_ A country is identified to have a nuclear capability (taking the value "1") if it has either power reactor(s), constructed or under construction, or research reactor(s), constructed or under construction, or both.

Sources:

AHDI:	Arab Human Development Report, 2001.
HDI value & GDP per capita (PPP$)	UNDP, 2002. "2002 Human Development Report", Oxford University Press, New York.
TAI value & High-Technology exports	UNDP, 2001. "2001 Human Development Report", Oxford University Press, New York.
Nuclear facilities	Compiled by Ted Flaherty, 19 September 1996 (www.cdi.org\issues\proliferation\reactab.html) from: "Nuclear Non-Proliferation Treaty". Arms Control reporter (1996), pp.602.A.7-602.A.10. "World List of Nuclear Power Plants". Nuclear News, September 1993, pp. 43-62.
Space Programs	Indicator was identified through an internet search.